WOLFE'S HISTORY

WOLFE'S HISTORY

A Family Story

BRENDAN WOLFE

ILLUSTRATED

CHARLOTTESVILLE, VIRGINIA
2019

Copyright © 2019 by Brendan Wolfe

All rights reserved.

First Printing

ISBN 978-0-578-56401-2

Permissions:

"Mise Éire." Copyright © 1967 by Eavan Boland, from OUTSIDE HISTORY: SELECTED POEMS 1980–1990 by Eavan Boland. Used by permission of W. W. Norton & Company, Inc.

Photo credits:

Frontispiece: *standing left to right, Sarah McAndrews Wolfe, Ray Wolfe, and Phil Wolfe, ca. 1920; courtesy of the author. Cover photo includes, at far right, Melvin Wolfe.*

Pages 2, 48, 75, 77, 80, 241, 283, 325: *courtesy of the author;* **page 5:** *Davenport Democrat and Leader, June 12, 1922, 1;* **page 15:** *Marin History Museum, Images of America: Early San Rafael (Charleston, South Carolina: Arcadia Publishing, 2008), 63;* **page 18:** *Plat Book of Clinton County, Iowa (Philadelphia: North West Publishing Co., 1894), 50;* **page 24:** *William H. Stuart, Share the Profits! The Story of Richard W. Wolfe and His Conclusions (Chicago: M. A. Donohue and Company, 1939), ii;* **pages 28, 225:** *Seán de Bhulbh, Sloinnte na hÉireann: Irish Surnames (Limerick, 2007) iv, 385;* **page 32:** *Chicago Daily Tribune, February 8, 1931, 1;* **page 41:** *Map of Ireland, Compiled from the Surveys of the Board of Ordnance and other approved Documents (Liverpool: Edward Holt, 1838);* **page 43:** *public domain;* **pages 52, 55, 70:** *courtesy of Sadhbh Lyons and family;* **page 63:** *public domain;* **page 66:** *Military Service Pensions Collections, MA/MSPC/RO/119 West Limerick Brigade, Military Archives of Ireland;* **pages 125, 215, 338, 339:** *courtesy of Ann McClary;* **pages 173, 195, 271:** *courtesy of Tom Woulfe;* **page 177:** *public domain;* **page 190:** *Barry McLoughlin, Fighting for Republican Spain, 1936–38: Frank Ryan and the Volunteers from Limerick in the International Brigades (self-published, 2014), 84.*

Cover design: John Grant (JohnGrantStudios.com) with assistance from Daniella Chadwick for Dad

CONTENTS

Acknowledgments xi
Note to Readers xiii
The Book of Athea 1
Notes 85
Biographies 103
Appendices 343
Family Trees 423
Index 475

ACKNOWLEDGMENTS

MUCH OF WHAT FOLLOWS is built on the strong foundation laid by others, in particular Michael Woulfe, whose WoulfeFamily.com is indispensable, and Kathy Struck and Ann McClary, whose research has been equally so. Seán de Bhulbh dug into the family's past with characteristic energy, precision, and generosity, and although I never got to meet him, his daughter and son-in-law, Sadhbh and Tony Lyons, graciously hosted me for lunch and tea in Limerick city. They shared stories and pictures, and corrected some important facts. Making their acquaintance has been a highlight of this project. The same can be said of meeting Timothy and Nancy Woulfe, who welcomed me into their home for a few hours in Athea, County Limerick, and showed me the original letters written by Tim's granduncle Maurice H. Woulfe, who served in the U.S. Army from 1866 to 1874. The West Limerick scholar Gerard Curtin helped put me in touch with Tim, while Kerby Miller at the University of Missouri provided transcripts of the documents. Without the staff and friendly patrons of Dick White Lounge Bar, my trips to Athea would have been much duller, but I also would not have met Jimmy Dalton. The nephew of the legendary Paddy Dalton, Jimmy allowed me to buy him a whiskey when he made his regular Friday night visit to the pub. Helen Barry, of Batt Fitz's pub, also in Athea, kindly put me in touch with other Woulfes, including Dickie and Risteárd, while the Geoghegan family of nearby Glin, publicans since 1860, put me up with unswerving kindness and many a well-poured Guinness. Thanks, too, to Gemma Hensey, Philomena Buckley, and Séamus and Philomena Woulfe for having me to lunch in Beale Hill. And to Tom Woulfe for sharing his family album in Abbeyfeale. Closer to home, my late father and his first cousin Jack Wolfe, of Clinton, Iowa, were the first to inspire me to learn about Wolfe history. That was more than thirty years ago now, and countless of my cousins, aunts, and uncles have helped since then—some of these relatives close, some distant but kind and helpful—all sharing their memories and helping me to put this huge, complicated puzzle together.

Thank you all!

NOTE TO READERS

WOLFE'S HISTORY HAS BEEN divided into four parts.

First comes "The Book of Athea," which serves as an introductory essay on the subject at hand and a more thorough explanation of what this volume means and how it came to be. Don't assume that remembering names and relationships is the point of any of this (I have my own trouble keeping it all straight!), but if you want to learn more, notes on my sources appear at the essay's conclusion.

Next, you'll find a biographical dictionary. Think of it like a more traditional dictionary, but with life sketches instead of definitions. You can dip in and out or take a more methodical approach, following your own particular line through the generations. Whatever approach you take, you'll find some pretty amazing stories: Gold Rush pharmacists, Old West barkeeps, and even a corrupt politician or two; copper miners, horse breeders, and dairy farmers; suicides, homicides, and a whole family swept away by a hurricane; war heroes, rebel priests, and IRA martyrs; nuns, housewives, suffragists, missionaries, and school teachers; and many, many Irish speakers. You'll encounter both saints (one, almost literally) and scoundrels, and I've tried to be fair and honest in my depictions. Browse the index if you want to zero in on the most interesting characters, or just discover them by chance.

Part three is a small collection of primary documents—letters, newspaper articles, book chapters, obituaries, and essays. Most of these are mentioned in the essay and biographies, but they can be read with interest on their own. They're annotated for clarity and ordered chronologically.

Finally, I've included a family tree, several trees really, that will help readers better understand the relationships of the people who appear in this book.

A note on names: in Ireland, most members of the family spell their surname "Woulfe," while in the United States, most spell it "Wolfe." References are inconsistent on both sides of the Atlantic, however, and immigrants to the United States who were born Woulfes often inscribed their tombstones with Wolfe. It can be confusing, and I worried that any attempt at keeping it all straight might distract readers. As a result, the dictionary portion of the book and the index use the spelling "Wolfe" almost exclusively.

One last thing: as much as I have attempted to give it the polished veneer of a finished product, this book is forever in progress. There are mistakes, the result either of my carelessness or my ignorance. If you notice them, let me know and I'll promptly make a correction. There also are gaps, lines of the family about which I know little or nothing (Australian Woulfes, I'm sorry!), and stories of lives that I have not yet heard. I encourage you to fill me in. Send an email to brendanwolfe [at] yahoo.com. Share your memories, your oral history, your research, and your photographs. This won't be for me or for you but for our kids, our grandkids, and all the future generations of Wolfes who will be lucky to have this history preserved.

THE BOOK OF ATHEA

"I said that is the writing of a Woulfe." – *Dicky Ned Woulfe, 1910*

1.

THIS BOOK BEGAN WHEN I was a kid. Not even four, I found myself down in that cool, dank basement of ours where my dad would sit on the edge of a folding chair in front of his humming electric typewriter and pound out all manner of texts, from letters to speeches to manifestos. In this instance, late in the summer of 1975, with me listening to the rhythmic clack-clacking of his keyboard, it was a history of the Wolfe family: "Origin of the Species; or, Whatever Happened to Good Old What's-His-Name." Composed on the occasion of the family's biennial reunion, the essay charted out his paternal line in a voice that was self-consciously silly and heavily ironic while also somewhat apologetic. It was almost as if he had the humorist Richard Armour perched on one shoulder, egging him on to make the next dumb joke, while on the other stood my mom, puffing on a Marlboro and reminding him that he would do well to tread carefully. It's easy to forget, sitting way down there in the basement, slurping from your bottomless can of PBR, that not everyone will be in on the joke.

"If the writer digresses here or there and the reader should happen to learn something," my dad typed, "he should savor this knowledge like a fine wine, lobster, or, at today's prices, hamburger." And then, as if in response to a smoky exhale coming from his other shoulder, he also wrote, "Certainly, no attempt has been made to embarrass anyone. The intent has been merely to put some life into something that might otherwise be about as exciting as outlining a declarative sentence for an English grammar class."

But here, I think, the old man protested too much. There was nothing at all boring about the stories that poured forth when he got to talking, or for that matter typing, about the Wolfe family. For instance, there was his great grandfather, John Richard Wolfe, who fled the Irish potato famine and perhaps, too, the British authorities, travel-

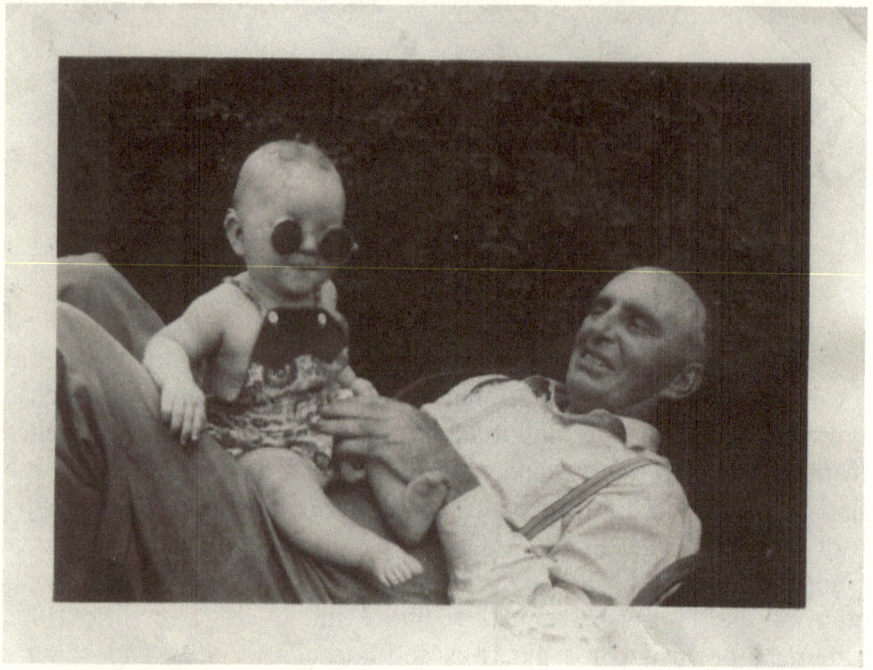

Tom Wolfe and his father, Ray, 1941

ing all the way to the farmland of Lost Nation, in Clinton County, Iowa. There was John Richard's son Maurice—pronounced "Morris"—who, my dad wrote, still spoke with the family's North Kerry brogue and carried more than a bit of the Wolfe lawlessness.

"The writer knows little about him," Dad admitted, "but it can be assumed he became a Catholic and a Democrat at approximately the same time. It is possible, however, that he inherited some of his father's Marxist revolutionary ideas although there is no record of political insurrection in Lost Nation or Toronto during his lifetime. It is well known in Lost Nation, though, that Grandfather Maurice attended his agrarian pursuits in spurts which he called 'five year plans.' His favorite tools were the hammer and sickle."

My dad's own father, Ray, shoveled horse manure for the Navy during World War I. "He caught no Germans," Dad wrote, "but he did catch the flu. In 1925 he caught Gladys McGinn of Petersville. (She was only twenty-two at the time, but that didn't stop her from continually telling her own children that no one with a grain of sense married under thirty. To gently remind her of her own age in 1925 only brought about a foot stomping and the response, 'That was different.')"

Gladys died before I was born, but I remain grateful for this brief but vivid portrait of her. Dad once told me that she taught him the birds and the bees by leaving a textbook of sorts on the dining room table, open to the appropriate pages. She never broached the subject again.

Ray died of cancer in 1941, leaving his nine-month-old son, his wife, and their three daughters to fend for themselves on a couple hundred acres of Iowa farmland. There, Dad lived inside his imagination. He became his hero, Jackie Robinson, by throwing balls against the barn and scooping up grounders. He found stacks of freshly mown hay to be occasions for an intense kind of dreaming. "What I remember most about farm life," he once wrote, "was an aching feeling of loneliness." That's how Dad described those years in his less guarded moments—lonely and even a little scary. I was raised on stories of hopscotching tornadoes, man-eating sows, and a downed power line that nearly killed him.

There were stories, too, of the Wolfes who had settled that land, John R. and the rest, who built their farms, their churches, their large families. Perhaps because I grew up in the city and preferred, whenever possible, to remain indoors, these tales occasioned my own sort of dreaming. They activated in me a longing for this place for which I was deeply unsuited to live—not so different maybe from the way the loss of a father had activated in my dad a need to know his own family, to map it across the hills of Clinton County and all the way back to Kerry and West Limerick.

Hence the clack-clack-clack of Dad's electric typewriter in the summer of '75. When his parents should have been celebrating their golden anniversary, they lived, precariously, only in stories. And when Dad himself died, in 2012, I felt called to collect and preserve and even proselytize those stories—if nothing else, as a gift to him.

This book, in other words, began then, too.

• • •

2.

IN 1911, MY GREAT-GREAT UNCLE, Judge Patrick B. Wolfe, published in two volumes *Wolfe's History of Clinton County*. In the tradition of this sort of local history, which had become popular during the centennial celebration of 1876, his book provides background on the politics, geography, education, and religion of Clinton County, Iowa, in addition to notes on the judiciary, medicine, and journalism. There are also several in-depth reminiscences that serve only to confirm my largely uncongenial impressions of life on the prairie. On page 412 of volume 1, for instance, a short account describes the "Storm of 1898," a dark green funnel cloud about a half-mile wide that killed children and their parents and whole droves of cattle in the field, while leaving in ruins the farms of my great grandfather Maurice Wolfe and his brother-in-law Pete McAndrews.

"Sheep are seen hanging in the trees," the *Clinton Herald* reported. "Not a drop of rain fell either before or after the wind storm, which is a singular thing."

It could have been my dad telling that story—else it was something straight out of the Book of Revelations. There is a fair amount of this in *Wolfe's History*, if you have the time and wherewithal to find it. The better part of the book's nearly twelve hundred pages, however, is devoted not to events but to people, to biographical sketches "of representative citizens of this county whose records deserve preservation because of their worth, effort and accomplishment." These include at least one woman and three members of the Wolfe family, including the Judge himself. His entry, which begins in volume 2 on page 912, is notable less for what it says about its subject than its remarkable thumbnail sketch of the Judge's father. For most of my life, this amounted to everything we knew about the man whom my dad half-jokingly referred to as the Kunta Kinte of the Iowa Wolfes:

JUDGE P. B. WOLFE.

John R. Wolfe was born in county Kerry, Ireland, in 1824, the son of Richard Wolfe, who was the agent having charge of the property of the Knight of Kerry. He received an excellent education. During his young manhood he helped to organize the "Young Ireland" party. He left Ireland in 1848, coming to America, first locating at Ottawa, Illinois. Here he remained on a farm until 1854, when he moved to Clinton county, Iowa, to land near Lost Nation, which he had entered the winter before, and lived there until his death in 1885, becoming one of the largest landholders and most successful farmers of his township. Mr. Wolfe did not take any great interest in politics. He was opposed to slavery. In religion he and his entire family were staunch Catholics, and active workers in the church.

From this snippet of biography we spun grand tales of revolution (Young Ireland rose up in 1848), of life on the run, and of redemption claimed from the black soil of far-off Iowa. But my dad was a history teacher; eventually, he smelled a rat. In the summers, he liked to pile my sisters and me into the old Pontiac station wagon and drive the forty-five minutes or so northwest to Clinton County for what us youngsters derisively referred to as the "Dead Man's Tour." This included a stop at St. James Cemetery, hidden behind the church in the tiny town of Toronto and where John R. Wolfe had been laid to rest. His gray marble stone, which for years stood taller than me, reads:

> JOHN R. WOLFE
> BORN
> AT LISTOWEL
> CO. KERRY IRELAND,
> NOV. 15, 1809,
> DIED
> AUG. 19, 1883
> AGED
> 73 YRS. 9 MOS. 4 DYS.
>
> REQUIESCAT IN PACE.

Dad looked at those dates, he drove home and double-checked our *Wolfe's History*, and then he wondered: why the difference? Why would a book edited by John R. Wolfe's own son, the Judge, give us birth and death dates different from his gravestone? And this was hardly the only discrepancy. Additional research indicated that John R. left Ireland in 1847, not 1848, complicating the idea that revolution had prompted his decision to emigrate. And what about the claim that he had "helped to organize" the Young Ireland party? The archives have remained silent on any role played by a Wolfe (or, as the Irish spell it, Woulfe) in that movement, let alone a prominent one. But even if the claim were true, how does it square with the idea that "Mr. Wolfe did not take any great interest in politics"? And how does *that* square with the very next sentence: "He was opposed to slavery"?

As I joined my dad in the genealogical project, this represented my first historical problem, and one that I wrote papers about in college. Unfortunately, it never yielded a satisfactory answer. I've never been able to find my great-great grandfather's birth, baptismal, or marriage records, or learn more about his father's relationship to the knight of Kerry or how the family fared during *an Gorta Mór*, the Great Hunger, or what sort of education (beyond "excellent") he received. There are no extant photographs of him and his name rarely appeared in the newspaper.

If John R. Wolfe remains something of a mystery, then what isn't mysterious is the motivation behind the writing of these sketches in *Wolfe's History*. Disguised as history, they are in fact a form of immigrant propaganda. Take the biography of John R.'s eldest son, Jimmy. "The Emerald Isle, far-famed in song and story, has furnished a large number of enterprising and high-minded citizens to the United States," it begins,

> and they have ever been most welcome, for we have no better class of citizens. They are, almost with no exception, industrious, and they are loyal to our institutions, and may always be relied upon to do their full duty as citizens in whatever community they may cast their lot. Among this large class the name of James B. Wolfe, whose long, strenuous and interesting career has resulted in much good to himself, his family and to his friends and neighbors, for his example has ever been exemplary and his influence salutary.

Even in 1911, such special pleading was necessary for the Irish, more than five million of whom had immigrated to the United States since 1845. Most of them, like the Wolfes, were Catholic, and their religion was perceived to be foreign, subversive, even dangerous. According to many Americans, then and even now, the pope represented a threat to democracy. He was a tempter of patriotic hearts, his adherents bound to him like slaves to their master. Protestantism, meanwhile, was so deeply embedded in the national ethos that freedom of religion, at least in the beginning, had meant simply the freedom to be a different *kind* of Protestant. So when a huge influx of "Romanists" arrived during the mid-nineteenth century it caused an upheaval in American politics. The Native American Party, or the Know Nothings as they sometimes called themselves, organized around violent anti-Catholic feeling, burning churches, tarring and feathering priests, and, in 1855, rioting in Louisville, Kentucky. The Irish found refuge in the Democratic Party, and after the American Party dissolved in 1860, the Know Nothings swelled the base of Abraham Lincoln's Republican Party, establishing what historians have noted to be a curious link between anti-Catholicism and anti-slavery sentiment.

All of which only complicates further the biography of John R. Wolfe. It follows that his son Maurice would become, as we've already heard, "a Catholic and a Democrat at approximately the same time," but it doesn't help explain the insistence on John R.'s antislavery bona fides. Or his public identity as a "staunch Catholic" or even as a Young Irelander. (Some in the United States had expressed skepticism of the Young Ireland movement on the unfounded suspicion that it sought to replace Parliament with the pope.) So while the Wolfes seemed intent on ingratiating themselves as good immigrants, my great-great grandfather stands out in many respects.

But so too did the Wolfes in general, at least compared with most other Irish immigrants. As "two-boat Irish," they arrived in New York and then immediately took off again, this time for the West. No big cities for them, no cops walking the beat. They opted instead for the open prairie, the attendant cyclones, the sheep hanging from trees. For all the ways in which the Wolfe family, by their mere presence, challenged the political and social order, they also participated in something profoundly American when they embarked on this second journey. It marked them as pioneers, as adventurers, as cowboys.

"Go west, young man," my dad liked to say when it was time for me to leave for school in the morning. "And write if you find work!"

That's what the Wolfes have always done, and you can see it expressed in the obituary of that same Jimmy Wolfe—John R.'s son and Maurice and the Judge's older brother—published on February 3, 1916. "Where there are now prosperous well tilled farms," it reads,

> there [once] was a vast unbroken prairie over which the deer roamed at will and through which surged the all devouring prairie fire sweeping everything before it. Here, the deceased experienced the struggles and privations of pioneer life. Through the sides of the rude hut of a home, the wind and the weather blew. Often did he tell of how he shook the snow from the bed covers on awakening and brushed it aside on the floor to make a bare place upon which to stand while dressing. He lived to see the great evolution and progress of the past almost three quarters of a century. He saw the railroad, the steam engine, and the automobile displace the rail and the ox drawn wagon of the pioneer and the transformation which has made an unbroken, unpeopled prairie the garden spot of the world.

While it's true that the Wolfes clung to the "Emerald Isle," to Holy Mother Church and revolution, in the end they also claimed their Americanness as thoroughly as did Billy the Kid or John Ford, both of whom spoke Irish. In fact, my dad liked to whisper stories of his grandfather Maurice's feats with a six-shooter, claiming he had once ridden with the Texas Rangers. Another Maurice Wolfe, this one a distant cousin who immigrated in the 1860s, fought Indians with the 4th Infantry. More than most he understood that the prairie had been far from "unpeopled." In fact, the romance of Rangers and outlaws only served to obscure an essential truth: that the Wolfes, like many others, played their part in stealing this land and killing or exiling its rightful occupants. "This is a wild reckless Country," he wrote to yet another Maurice Wolfe, this one back home in Ireland. "… A man will Shoot another man upon the Slightest provocations, every man here Carries his brace of Revolvers and Bowie Knife in his waist belt."

Sergeant Wolfe promised to find for his cousin a fabulous souvenir, but in 1870, from Wyoming Territory, he wrote with some bad news. "I had a fine 'Scalp' I was going to Send home," he said, "but the Captain asked it of me to give the Indian chief in order to have a Scalp Dance, which they gave us last night in all its glory." Wolfe went on to describe how the visiting Shoshone Indians, numbering three thousand or more warriors and women, had danced and prayed through the night. "You may be Sure it was a grand and Strange sight," he wrote, "to see all of them Indians by the glare of the Camp fires, in their War Paint ... and if the 'Great Spirit' did not hear all that drumming and yelling, he must be Somewhat deaf."

3.

JOHN RICHARD WOLFE—MY great-great grandfather, the pioneer, the adventurer—arrived in New York City on August 23, 1847. He sailed on the *Cornelia* with his wife, Honora Buckley Wolfe, and their four-year-old son, the aforementioned Jimmy, along with John R.'s first cousin Maurice—the fourth of that name we've encountered so far—and his wife and five children (including, yes, another Maurice).

Built by Brown and Bell of New York, the packet ship *Cornelia* weighed 1,040 tons and was part of the Black Star Line, which ran eighteen ships between Liverpool and New York that year, sailing every six days. Newspaper records provide a bare-bones account of the *Cornelia*'s journey—passed a ship bound for Liverpool on July 20, sighted what was perhaps the *John R. Skiddy* on August 1, encountered a fishing boat off Marblehead on the sixth—while mentioning that 5 out of 319 passengers had died en route.

The *Cornelia* landed on pier 30 or thereabouts, releasing the Wolfes into a city already overwhelmed with immigrants. Close to eighteen thousand had arrived in the month of April alone, and there existed no formal center to take them all in. Instead, they crowded near the water, in search of reliable maps, a boarding house, and something to eat, making them ripe for the abuses of gangs and confidence artists. Crooks might help them with their bags and speak reassuringly in their native tongues, only to take them for every coin they carried. The sick, meanwhile, usually suffering from typhus, were whisked off to the Quarantine Station on Staten Island.

Somehow John R. and his family navigated their way through this chaos, probably spending a night or two in New York before setting off for Chicago. It's not clear how they traveled—likely some combination of train and water—but once they arrived, they spent a fair bit of time in the city, to regroup and investigate their next steps. John R.'s son the Judge was born there in 1848. By 1850, though, the family had relocated to LaSalle County, a flat, open landscape where they bought land, built farms, and established a fledgling community of rural Irishmen. Over the next few years other Wolfes followed, including several brothers (among them, Maurice no. 6) and a cousin.

All of these families settled initially in LaSalle County before spreading out (some of them, anyway) across the continent—from Iowa and the Dakotas to Wyoming, Texas, and California. They were not, however, the first Wolfes to come to America. For that story, we must rewind several decades, to 1819, when James Harnett Wolfe, the son of Maurice James (no. 7?), left his home in West Limerick and established a school in Virginia. He had been educated in the classics, probably in preparation for the priesthood, but decided a life of adventure would be more to his liking. After a dozen years in the Old Dominion, he heeded my dad's advice and went west, all the way to Monticello, in Lewis County, Missouri. Once he found work, he wrote, informing his parents and brothers back home of his success on the land. On October 16, 1835, he made five purchases totaling more than 505 acres in nearby Marion County, and by 1836 his estate was worth an estimated nine thousand dollars. Brothers Richard and John Wolfe must have been impressed, likely showering James with congratulations and asking him about life on the mighty Mississippi River. But then the letters from America suddenly stopped.

Fearing the worst, Richard and John sailed across the Atlantic in an effort to find their brother. Once in Missouri they discovered the sad truth about their well-educated, almost-priest of a brother. In a letter home dated December 26, 1836, John wrote that "Brother James Wolfe died in the state of Mississippi the first [of the year] he went to Natchez. The fine learned man."

There were rumors of murder, perhaps a deal gone bad on a riverboat. One's imagination can run hot here—"this is a wild reckless Country"—but the historical record is thin. Whatever happened, it must have been a devastating experience for the Wolfes. "There is nothing grieves Richard [and me] more than to say that we cant see, hear or find our brother alive on his Estate," John wrote, "after the bold stroke we made in going to him five thousand miles from home." And what a journey it had been! The Wolfe brothers had sailed to New York and then boarded the steamboat *John Jay*, traveling the Erie Canal at twelve cents per mile. They withstood dangerous seas in Lake Michigan and then floated down the Mississippi to Missouri, all at a cost of more than one thousand dollars.

"Travelling is very expensive in America," they told their father, who was probably footing the bill.

What they found in Missouri, though, helped make those difficult few weeks well worth the trouble. The late James's estate contained "first rate land, timber oak and water and [a] trained limestone quarry"—enough to convince the brothers to stay and raise families.

A small colony of Wolfes was founded there in Missouri, and after a generation or two at least a few seem to have wandered up to Iowa. But it wasn't until An Gorta Mór that the family sailed in numbers. Whole chunks of the family tree were lopped off and sent packing. John R., several of his brothers, and a couple cousins all left Kerry and Limerick in the 1840s and subsequent decades. But so did sisters, nieces and nephews, and another cousin whose son Maurice would be, I think, Maurice no. 8.

What lured all of these industrious relations to LaSalle County, of all places? Had my great-great grandfather scouted the area, pronounced it good, and then sent for the others? Did any of them know about the Missouri Wolfes? I have no idea. As it happens, the only ones who eschewed the West were the children of one of John R.'s sisters. They found their way instead to Newport, Rhode Island, where Dennis Wolfe Sheehan went into business for himself, dealing in liquor, cigars, and groceries. He died at Eston's Beach on August 25, 1907, probably of a stroke. He had been playing at the time with his little daughter Margaret.

"They had just gone in at the west end of the beach, somewhat separated from the mass of bathers," the local paper reported, "when

Mr. Sheehan, while in shallow water, settled down to his knees and the little girl ran to her mother's house and told that her father had a cramp in his foot. Bathers went to his assistance as he fell face downward in the water ..."

4.

IT'S WORTH PAUSING HERE for a moment to take note of one curious aspect of genealogy: its preoccupation with death. Most folks don't show up in the newspaper until the end has arrived, and sometimes only if their last moments proved remarkable. As a result, collecting Wolfe family stories has been, at times, a gruesome business. Take, for instance, thirteen-year-old Arthur Collison, whose mother, Ann Wolfe, emigrated in 1849. He met his maker on a Sunday morning in Carroll, Iowa, when he was run over by a wagon. That was in 1903. Six years later, Maurice Wolfe (no. 9, and the grandson of John R.'s brother), along with his entire family, were killed when a hurricane struck the gulf coast of Texas and Louisiana. He had been in a boat when the tidal wave came crashing down, while Mrs. Wolfe and their six children had been at the house, presumably in a safer haven. Rescuers found their bodies days later, three miles away.

Then there's the death of Daniel F. Wolfe, the son of John R. Wolfe's first cousin Richard. It could have come straight out of a dime novel. Born in County Kerry, Wolfe worked as a distiller and liquor store owner in Illinois before striking out for the Dakota Territory. He ran a saloon in the town of Wessington where, on November 14, 1882, he was murdered by William McComber. According to one newspaper account, a few days earlier "a robust fellow" had entered the tavern "and, as he tossed his grip-sack on the bar, announced that he had come to buy a farm." This was Mr. McComber. The next day, when Wolfe mentioned he was going to pay some bills, "McComber asked permission to join his host in the buggy ride, explaining that he wished to get a glimpse of the country."

A newspaper in West Virginia, the *Wheeling Register*, picks the story up from there. While Wolfe was driving the buggy with McComber as his passenger, the two were observed to have separated, with one remaining in the buggy and the other going on foot. "A little while after," the paper reported, "some farmers in the vicinity, noticing that the prairie was on fire, went to put it out, and found Wolfe dead in the midst of the fire with a bullet through his head." Authorities speculated that McComber had set the fire to destroy evidence of the shooting. The report continued:

> From Wessington the murderer drove to St. Lawrence, and, with no apparent thought of the blood upon his hands, engaged in a game of cards. From there he went to Miller. The sheriff, ascertaining the facts in the case, went to arrest him. On entering the house where he was, the sheriff said: "Mr. McComber, I have come to arrest you on a very grave charge." "Are you an officer" said McComber, coolly. The sheriff handed him his commission. McComber took it in his left hand (his right hand in his pocket), read it slowly and carefully through, remarked that it appeared all right, and then, suddenly drawing his revolver, said, "I'm a gone coon," and shot himself through the head, dying in fifteen minutes.

If this bleeds a shade too red for you, then consider the more fortunate case of John R. Wolfe's nephew, John W. Maher, who grew up in LaSalle County. After studying law at the University of Michigan, he made the fateful decision to hang his shingle in North Dakota. In 1895, one of Maher's former clients disputed a bill of one hundred dollars for a land case that had failed in court. The feud escalated until the client tracked Maher down on the street and, according to the local paper, "emptied four chambers of a 44-caliber bull-dog revolver" into his six-foot-six frame. Amazingly, just one of those bullets found its mark, and Maher survived. He lived into his eighties, dying at sea in 1936, near the isthmus of Panama.

5.

OF COURSE, LIVES, TOO, could be eventful. Among their large brood the Wolfes counted copper miners, dairy farmers, distillers, gold-panners, teachers, nuns, suffragists, and realtors, in addition to

John C. Wolfe in his drugstore in San Rafael, California

the odd politician and more than a few lawyers. John C. Wolfe, the son of John R. Wolfe's first cousin Maurice, made his living as a Gold Rush pharmacist. Born in Kerry, he sailed on the *Cornelia* and was raised in both Illinois and Iowa. In 1858, he set out for California, eventually landing in Grass Valley, the heart of California gold country and the richest, most famous mining district in the state. He found employment at a local drug store before going into business for himself.

"From time to time he added to his stock," a state history explains, "distinct advantage being found in the fact that he manufactured many of his own medicines, which came to be known for their efficacy in the common disorders. Through the length and breadth of the county, and even beyond, Wolfe's liniment, pile cure, worm powder, catarah snuff, and corn cure were household treasures and found their way into thousands of individual medicine chests."

In 1872, he moved his business to tiny, still-unincorporated San Rafael, just north of San Francisco, finding success and, through his connected wife, a little taste of high society. A photographic portrait taken in his large, well-stocked drugstore shows Wolfe with a long white beard and eyes that, even from a distance, seem to burn a hole in the camera's lens. A small stretch of steep and winding road in San Rafael—Wolfe Grade and Wolfe Canyon Road—still bears the name of the old pharmacist.

As an aside, Wolfe's only son, Maurice (no. 10), followed him into the family business only to die on the way to work. According to a notice in the newspaper, "While going to his store a derrick used on a new building fell and struck him." Maurice's son, meanwhile, became the proud owner of Wolfe Paper Box Company, of San Carlos. Late one night in 1951 he fell asleep at the wheel while driving home and struck another vehicle head-on. He was gone before the police arrived.

6.

HERE'S ANOTHER CURIOUS ASPECT of genealogy: the way it flattens people into their relationships, privileging the one thing they cannot help: their DNA. It simplifies otherwise complex lives, reducing us to our deaths—swept away by a hurricane, set ablaze in the middle of the prairie—or to some peculiar scrap of trivia. John R. Wolfe helped to organize Young Ireland? I'm still not even sure what that means. It certainly hasn't helped illuminate his life, which I care about only because he was a Wolfe and because I was raised with this notion that something called family exists. That it's not a choice or something we can easily ignore.

One morning in college I sat at the table waiting for a seminar to begin when a classmate strode in and took the seat beside me. I'd never met her or spoken to her; in fact, I'd actively avoided her. She was older, brash, not crippled by insecurity like my friends and me. Her mere presence left us all feeling a bit exposed.

After settling herself she turned and looked me over, handing down what felt like an indictment: "You're a Wolfe, aren't you?"

She was married, it turned out, to a second cousin of mine, someone I myself couldn't have picked from a lineup. "I can see it in the forehead," she explained. "The cut of the jaw."

We carry our families around with us without always fully understanding what that means. At a funeral, another cousin, stricken with grief, graciously received me in line only to have his face suddenly bloom with laughter. "Jesus Christ," he said. "You look exactly like your dad!" And it's true. We have the same ruddy face and graying beard. It's as if, eerily, I reside inside his body—he has been dead for seven years now—and experience the world with his extra bit of heft, his nervous crack of the knuckles.

We can stop funerals, Dad and I. So I wonder: Did he carry his own father around in the same way? Do we both have some Maurice and John R. in us, too, or maybe our grandmothers?

Of course, DNA is only part of it. We also carry with us history, memory, place, language, and, in the Wolfe family, an insatiable love of stories. My great uncle Melvin was born in 1904. "The nurse ... reports that thirty minutes after his birth he said to the assembled doctor, nurses, midwives, family, and friends, 'Did you hear the one about ...'" Dad later wrote. "The story is reported to have lasted sixteen minutes and twelve seconds by actual timing, included three delightful sub-stories, and was told in a marvelous Irish accent which has, unfortunately, disappeared among third generation Wolfes."

Melvin spent his entire life in the tiny Iowa town of Lost Nation, which is another thing the Wolfes carry around with them. Or at least many of us do. Lost Nation is the terminus of an epic journey, a pilgrim's progress from Ireland to New York to Chicago to LaSalle, and then finally home to this Celestial City of sorts, with its odd, ironic name. *Wolfe's History* tells us that there is no definitive explanation for how that name came to be. "One version, not very widely credited, has it that a tribe of Indians starved and froze to death here in early times," the Judge writes. "Many people give credence to the story that a German named Balm was looking for some relatives here in the times when the prairie was unbroken and covered with grass high as a horse, and when asked where he was going, said that he was looking for the 'lost nation.'"

The Wolfes arrived about 1854 and made this place their own. Located 150 miles west of LaSalle County and across the Mississippi, Lost Nation and greater Clinton County boasted some of the most fertile land in the country, and it came relatively cheap. That's probably what motivated the move—the soil and its price—although the anti-Catholic Know Nothings were beginning to agitate at exactly this time. Perhaps the getting was good, and, if so, John R. got first. By

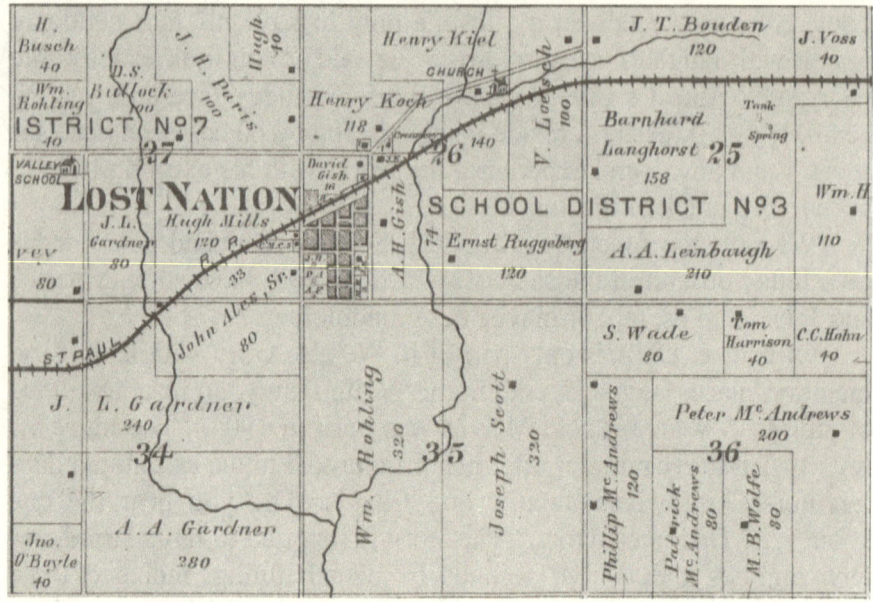

Detail from a map of Sharon Township, Clinton County, 1894

1856 he had purchased eighty acres of government land in Clinton County, eventually becoming the largest landholder in Liberty Township, with eleven hundred acres. By 1859, his cousin Maurice had joined him, and other Wolfes soon followed. They farmed through the Civil War and into the twentieth century, their holdings passed down from father to son to grandson.

When my dad came of age, the farm was his if he wanted it, but he'd always had more of a bookish bent. He attended college and became a teacher. Lost Nation, though, still called. Every summer we drove up from Davenport on our Dead Man's Tour, stalking gravestones and then barbecuing with Uncle Melvin and a host of cousins. We usually gathered at the farm of Melvin's son Dave. A big, shaggy bruin of a man, Dave possessed that high Wolfe forehead, blue eyes, and a surprisingly aggressive handshake. He was perpetually sunburnt and lightly crusted with dirt, as if one spring he himself had sprouted up in the fields, no different from the corn and beans. Earnest to a fault, Dave always seemed perplexed by my aversion to farm life, my fear of the sheep and the cows, the roosters and the smoking block of dry ice. I spent several summers laboring out there in an effort to prove to myself that he was wrong. But in the end he and his kids were of Lost Nation, while I stood just on the outside, dreaming in.

Somewhere between them and me—that's where to find the Lost Nation of Wolfe's history.

It's a place of stories. On our tours, Dad would point out the exact spot his best friend Pat fell from a grain silo and died. "The tornado came down this road here," he'd say, suddenly recalling a different memory, this one from his childhood. "We were just ahead of it in the Ford when we drove by Pat's house. I remember the front door was open and he was just standing there. Looking at us."

Another time a boyfriend of one of Dad's older sisters landed his plane in the pasture. And a Greyhound bus once pulled into the drive and went all the way up to the gate before turning around and leaving. Nothing much ever happened, he said, so you remembered what did.

"Towards dusk of a summer evening, I would ride my bike out to a hay field and climb onto a hay stack that had not yet been taken into the barn," he once wrote. "There, I would sniff the sweet aroma of freshly mown hay, then stare across the fields and into the sky, watching planes go by and imagining life far away. My imagination would soar, and I would yearn for exciting things and places totally unknown to me at that time. Dreams became my constant companion and friend, and still are these many years later. As long as I live, I'll associate freshly mown hay with those dreams and yearnings, and I won't know whether to be happy or sad."

This is where John R. Wolfe came in 1854 and where he stayed. This is what he left us.

7.

DURING THE CHRISTMAS HOLIDAY in 1997, Dad was running to catch a connecting flight in the St. Louis airport when he suffered a massive heart attack. Somehow he survived, and while lying in the hospital bed he vowed to visit Ireland the next chance he got. He'd never been much of a traveler, having ridden the train to Philadelphia a few times to visit his sister and the bus to Washington, D.C., to chaperone field trips with eighth-graders. He'd never gone to Ireland, though—*the ould sod*, as he liked to call it in a ridiculously bad accent.

Faith and Begorrah, he'd say and we'd all cringe.

Early the next summer the two of us landed in Dublin and spent a few days testing out the Guinness before we rented a car and motored north. Dad had met some Irish folk singer in Iowa who was now booked to perform in a tiny seaside town in northern Ulster. After scheduling our entire trip around the show, we arrived there to find no sign of the singer. No posters and only bored shrugs from the employees of the hotel where the singer was supposed to appear.

Standing out on the street, Dad pulled a piece of paper from his jeans pocket and carefully unfolded it, square by square, until it was a full, wrinkled, printed-out email. He'd been carrying it around for the whole trip, apparently.

"Oh crud," he said, scanning the page. "It's not until a *week* from today."

In that moment Dad's disappointment stretched across all of Ulster. We couldn't get out of there fast enough. Next morning we climbed back into the Fiat and drove six or seven hours south, arriving that afternoon in Listowel, County Kerry. Situated on the River Feale and surrounded by hills of limestone, Listowel was all brightly painted shops and confusing one-way streets when we arrived. In 1847, though, when John R. and his wife Honora left for America, the town was in the terrible grip of famine. On April 14, a month before they weighed anchor, the *Kerry Examiner* reported on the alarming spread of fever.

"The hospital [in Listowel] is crowded," the paper wrote, "and can no longer afford shelter or admittance to numbers who drag their sickly and fever-burnt bodies to its gates." With nowhere else to go, the poor ended up in the ditches and the bogs. A local priest found a woman named Daly "stretched in fever on a wisp of straw in a dyke," her twenty-four-year-old daughter "dead by her side in the same wretched place."

The Wolfes were far from starving. If the Judge's *History* is correct, then John R.'s father, dead now five years, had been "the agent having charge of the property of the Knight of Kerry." Said knight was Maurice FitzGerald, the eighteenth of his line, who kept a secondary residence near Listowel—"a mere cottage," one visitor described it, "but gentlemanlike and comfortable." An association with the knight likely provided a small bit of material comfort, and the Wolfes in general were already well endowed with land that they leased. It's unclear, though, what, if anything, John R.'s father had left behind, and John R. himself was not the first son or even the second. With nothing to inherit and a biblical pestilence overtaking the land, it made sense for him to leave and bring his family with him.

"If the Almighty God does not interfere," the *Kerry Examiner* wrote, "our unhappy country will be a grave, its people dead, and no priest left to intone a nation's requiem."

Dad and I pulled the car up onto a curb near the town center. "It's so much bigger than I expected," Dad whistled. "I thought it would be more like Lost Nation. Blink an eye and you miss it." The Celtic Tiger was purring nicely in those days and the streets bustled with tourists. We wandered into the first pub we saw, a dark and smoky place where we could order a sandwich.

"We're Americans," Dad informed the burly woman behind the bar.

"Sure you are," she replied politely, suggesting that perhaps we weren't the first. "Here to find your roots is it?"

She pointed us in the direction of the old cemetery, a few blocks away. We walked it row by row that afternoon, and as we poked through the weeds, passing Stacks and Sullivans and O'Sheas and Dannahers; Enrights and Lyonses and Aherns and Barretts; Carrolls and Caseys and Dineens and O'Flahertys and Lynches and Kennellys and Mahoneys and MacKenzies, we became increasingly anxious. Where were the Wolfes?

In the end we found one, a fellow named Liam who had passed away just a few years ago. The stone's inscription bore the omega shape of a horseshoe on it, next to the word "Pub." We headed back to the town center and sure enough there it was: Woulfe's Horseshoe Pub. Inside, Dad introduced himself to Mrs. Woulfe, Liam's widow. She poured us two pints and we all chatted rather awkwardly until her attention was required elsewhere. We hurriedly downed our beers and left. Across the street, the Catholic church had no birth records for anyone called John R. Wolfe. Dad snapped a couple pictures and then we squeezed back into the car and drove away.

8.

THAT SENSE OF LOSS, of having missed something important, has stayed with me all these years. What did it mean to be a Wolfe if we could travel all the way back to Kerry and find nothing of ourselves there?

A few years after my dad typed up his first family history, "Origin of the Species," an academic named Benedict Anderson published a study of what he called "imagined communities." A nation, he argued, is socially constructed. It's something we must forge with our imaginations, our stories, our "ribbons of myths," as another historian recently put it.

"It is *imagined* because the members of even the smallest nation will never know most of their fellow-members, meet them or even hear of them," Anderson writes, "yet in the minds of each lives the image of their communion."

Anderson quotes a scholar who puts it another way: "Nationalism is not the awakening of nations to self-consciousness: it *invents* nations where they do not exist." But according to Anderson this is not quite right. Nations are not invented *ex nihilo* or fabricated; rather, and more positively, they are imagined and created. "Communities are to be distinguished, not by their falsity/genuineness," he writes, "but by the style in which they are imagined."

In other words, we have always lived with these connections to people we don't see and haven't met. What distinguishes one nation from another is *how* we imagine these connections. *How* we express them.

And, of course, the same must be true for families.

To be a Wolfe is not something rooted in American soil only; we span the Atlantic. Or so my dad thought upon returning to Ireland. That was the image of his communion.

But did Ireland's Wolfes (or Woulfes) share in it? What does the family look like over there?

• • •

9.

IN 1931 ANOTHER WOLFE returned to Ireland from his home in America. Richard White Wolfe had emigrated in 1885, two years after John R.'s death. He had been nineteen at the time and in the company of at least a few of his dozen or so siblings, all of them native to the Glen, the family farm in the townland of Cratloe, just a few kilometers east of Listowel, in western County Limerick. His older brother Patrick ended up as a book agent in Philadelphia, where he married a girl from Listowel and eventually moved to the Bronx. The rest of the siblings took the train to Chicago.

There Dick Wolfe went to school and eventually found his true calling in politics. He sat on various boards, climbed his way up the social ladder, and in 1927 joined Big Bill Thompson's mayoral campaign, serving as the candidate's "orator and wordsmith," according to one historian. Thompson ran in part on an America First, anti-British platform, aided by Wolfe's sometimes inflammatory rhetoric. "Capitol hill is influenced by the king of England," Wolfe wrote in a campaign flyer, "while the plain people are guided by the teachings of Washington, Jefferson, and Lincoln." He vowed that Thompson would "uphold the Americanism of the fathers." And indeed the mayor later did. Once in office again (this was his third, nonconsecutive term), he threatened to burn any books in the Chicago Public Library that he perceived to be anti-American, not-100-percent-American, or pro-British.

Wolfe, meanwhile, was appointed commissioner of public works. His four-year tenure was marked by continued efforts to straighten the Chicago River, the establishment of a water-filtration system, and controversies over the conditions of city streets. Complicating these issues was the air of corruption that surrounded the mayor's office, which many assumed to be on the payroll of the mobster Al Capone. By 1931, the year he left office, Wolfe was a well-known figure and, back in Ireland, something of a celebrity.

Early that year the *Kerryman* newspaper announced him to be "Chicago's Greatest Commissioner" and ballyhooed his many achievements in office—all accomplished, one imagines, while brandishing his Limerick brogue the way that Capone's boys did their Tommy guns. Just the year before, the *New York Times* had reported how the Italians—silk-suited "union members"—had regularly sent

The Commissioner

their representatives to Wolfe's little corner of City Hall. "It has been noticeable to many employees of the office," the *Times* wrote, "that when these men call they brush the secretaries aside and rattle on Wolfe's door until they get in."

Dick Wolfe embodied the American dream. "When a lad of but [nineteen] years"—the *Kerryman* again—"he landed on American shores filled with ambition to become a leader of men." He worked his way through the University of Chicago and lectured on economics at a local arts college. He sold fire insurance, wrote for the *Stockyards Daily Sun*, and finally took up real estate, through which he made his name and his fortune. He also published a forty-three-page lecture titled, simply, *Culture*, which featured his own original poetry. And he helped author a bill in the Illinois Senate to make American—as opposed to English—the state's official language. This was in 1923, on the heels of Britain's recognition of the Irish Free State, and it was meant to serve as one last what-for to the Union Jack and, especially, its American supporters, "who have never become reconciled to our republican institutions and have ever clung to the tradition of King and Empire." The bill passed, although in 1969 the legislature substituted "English" for "American."

A few months before Wolfe arrived back in Limerick, the *Cork Examiner* printed an excerpt from one of his speeches, about how there are two kinds of Americans: "There is the real, upstanding, red-blooded American, the product of the comingling of the healthy, wholesome, vigorous, ambitious blood of Europe. He is broadminded, tolerant; his vision as wide as his prairies; his ideals as lofty as high mountain peaks."

The Wolfes fit this definition quite nicely, the Commissioner likely assumed. The problem is that you also have this *other* kind of American.

"He is the Tory American," Wolfe said. "... He loves kings, titles and class distinction ... He is responsible for most of the religious and racial hatreds which curse America. From historical causes he is in control of much of the money and wealth of America, and therefore controls the agencies of publicity and propaganda, as well as dominates our Governmental institutions and our educational life."

In a series of addresses on the subject—in Ireland and throughout his subsequent European tour—Wolfe rarely offered anything more specific than what appeared in the *Examiner*. So who *was* this so-called Tory American? He controlled the banks, the papers, the radio broadcasters, the schools, and the Congress, and he leveraged this vast power to stoke hatred against those whose blood, like Wolfe's, ran red and clean.

The Commissioner's wife, it should be noted, was German. She kept him on schedule, which during that visit home in August of 1931 involved motoring to several appointments from their base at the charming Dunraven Arms Hotel in Adare, County Limerick. In nearby Cappagh they visited Wolfe's cousin, Father Patrick Woulfe, and then dashed over to Bruff to see Father Pat's younger brother, Dr. Timothy Woulfe, and Tim's new wife, Malvena. Also in Bruff they met with another relation, Maurice Woulfe (no. 11), who worked, somewhat awkwardly perhaps, for the National Bank.

The historical record of these reunions, contained in an article published in the *Limerick Leader* on August 22, suggests that a reporter had come from Kilmallock to follow the Wolfes around and take notes, and that the Commissioner had fully seized the opportunity. He declared himself "happily impressed" by Ireland's progress, especially in the decades since his last visit, referring "particularly to the now bright and prosperous appearance of rural Ireland."

"I'm weary of the city life," began one of Wolfe's verses in his book *Culture*. "Its noise and dust and ceaseless strife."

The *Chicago Tribune*, a committed enemy of Wolfe and the Thompson administration more generally, had once mocked the Commissioner's love of language. "Critic of Streets Urges Wolfe to a Life of Poesy," read the headline of a story calling for his resignation. "Wasted as Official, Alderman Mose Says."

> O, let me live beside the sea,
> My soul is longing to be free,
> To hear the billows raging wild,
> Or wavelets cooing like a child.

Father Pat himself was the author of a slim but dense book on Irish names that had garnered both popular and academic praise. In Cappagh he introduced the Commissioner to Canon John Begley, who several years earlier had finished the second of a proposed three-book history of the Diocese of Limerick. Dick Wolfe soon commented to the waiting reporter on "the remarkable intellectual prowess of Canon

Begley and observed that his writings, as well as those of Father Woulfe, are very widely read in America"—a claim that was almost certainly untrue—"and added that their works are doing much to make known to the outside world the importance of Irish history civil and ecclesiastical."

For his part, Canon Begley counted himself blessed that his most recent book, *The Diocese of Limerick in the Sixteenth and Seventeenth Centuries*, existed at all. In September of 1926, while he was serving as the parish priest of nearby Dromcollogher, a roll of film had caught fire at a local cinema, blocking the only exit and killing dozens of his parishioners. "A holocaust of a grim and dreadful character, involving the incineration of close to fifty men, women and children, took place on Sunday night," a newspaper reported. For weeks Canon Begley struggled to sleep, let alone to write. Mercifully, the bishop transferred him to Kilmallock, where in relative peace he had finished volume 2 of his history—only for there to be another fire, this time at the publishing house. It destroyed the book's plates, leaving so few printed copies he wouldn't have been surprised to hear that not one of these oft-mentioned red-blooded Americans had cracked its spine.

In the book's preface, Canon Begley had gratefully acknowledged his good friend: "I beg to thank in a special manner the Rev. Patrick Woulfe, P.P., Cappagh, for giving me permission to use in this history some very rare and valuable papers in his possession. Father Woulfe also read all the proof sheets, and made valuable suggestions."

Father Pat was a big man, and broad, with the family's trademark blue eyes and high forehead. At fifty-nine he was six years his cousin's junior and still looked powerful, not the least bit stalked by death. And yet in less than two years he would be in the ground. His book and papers, like the ones he had so kindly lent to Canon Begley, were posthumously collected by a house in Cork and auctioned to the highest bidder. More than three hundred lots sold, "Comprising an Important Selection of Works on Ireland's History, Language, People, Literature, Archaeology, etc.," an advertisement bragged. Over the years, they became dispersed and eventually forgotten.

Canon Begley hung on for another decade, until he was eighty, but many of his contemporaries died young. Another of the Wolfe cousins, Richard Woulfe of Abbeyfeale, died in 1937 at just fifty-two,

an t-ač. pádraig de buló

Father Pat

and his obituary noted that "many people attributed his death indirectly to the heroic sacrifices which he made in the service of his country"—i.e., his membership in the Irish Republican Army and his life on the run during the War of Independence and the subsequent civil war.

Father Pat had seen his share of violence during those years, too. Born, like the Commissioner, in the townland of Cratloe and ordained in County Kildare, he was educated in the workhouse of Limerick city, where he served as chaplain. There the poor came to eat and the old came to die. Misery mixed with laughter, politics, and storytelling, much of it in the Irish language of Father Pat's youth. He joined the Gaelic League, an organization founded to foster the language, and began to understand how Irish Gaelic might represent something fundamental about the national identity. It was hardly a new insight—"The speech being Irish, the heart must needs be Irish," grumbled the English poet Edmund Spenser—but it thrust him into the maelstrom of resistance. In 1914, as the parish curate, he chaired the largest festival in the history of Kilmallock, one attended by armed Irish Volunteers. Two years later he gave a speech extolling Irish patriotism. Then, on May 28, 1920, the war against Britain arrived home when the IRA attacked and burned the barracks of the Royal Irish Constabulary, killing anywhere from one to eight policemen. Liam Scully, an Irish-speaking Kerryman, was the only republican to go down, and his mates managed to cart him off the street and into a nearby dressing station. Father Pat performed the Last Rites, possibly in Irish.

According to Woulfe's obituary, later that day he celebrated Mass at the workhouse and was forced to pass the barracks in order to get there, "an ordeal few would care to undertake having regard to the temper of the police." The newspaper reported that "from then to the Truce was a very anxious time" for the priest. In fact, earlier in the war, while in London on church business, his residence had been searched after six Irish republican prisoners had tied up their guard and escaped from a Manchester jail. Following the battle in Kilmallock he was again subjected to a search. This time the presbytery was quietly surrounded by soldiers who entered without warning.

No arrests resulted.

As it happens, Father Pat had been in London to advocate on behalf of seventeen Irish Catholic martyrs who in 1915 had been presented to Rome for possible beatification. Among them was Woulfe's own relative, Father James Woulfe. An outspoken Dominican preacher, Father James lived in Limerick city when Cromwell's brother-in-law Henry Ireton laid siege in 1650. At least one history recounts how Woulfe had only recently scotched a treaty with local Anglo-Irish royalists, causing them to abandon the city and abscond with its corn. It was a circumstance the inhabitants came to rue in the face of Ireton's guns. Within four months, plague and hunger had swept through Limerick's streets, but Woulfe counseled resistance and, according to one historian, "cautioned the trembling cravens as to what they were about."

Limerick surrendered anyway.

The standard account of Father Woulfe's subsequent death appears in *The Irish Dominicans of the Seventeenth Century* by John O'Heyne.

> At length [Woulfe] was captured in Limerick while celebrating mass and received sentence of death within a few hours; he was then brought to the market-place and having made a public profession of the Catholic faith, exhorted the faithful to constancy. When he reached the highest rung of the ladder from which he was to be thrown, he exclaimed with a joyful voice: "We are made a spectacle to God, to the angels, and to men: to God to his greater glory, to the angels to their joy, and to the men to their contempt." Soon after he expired on the gibbet.

Canon Begley is more laconic. The priest, he writes, "was taken and hanged, together with Father Francis Woulfe, guardian of St Francis." Was this a brother of Father James? The historians are unsure, although James did have two other brothers, Father Andrew and Captain George Woulfe, both of whom also found themselves trapped in Limerick during Ireton's siege. Legend claims that George alone managed to escape the city walls. After fleeing all the way to the north of England, he established an illustrious military family that included General James Wolfe, the hero of Quebec.

The Catholic historian Myles O'Reilly, writing in 1869, found the connection between Captain George and General James Wolfe to be lamentable, considering the fate of George's brother James. "It is a strange fact," he wrote, "and one that we must regret, that England should owe the final conquest of Canada to one [i.e., General James] who should have honored this martyr of his family [i.e., Father James], but who was really intensely English, and rivalled Ireton by his bloody march up the St. Lawrence, butchering priests at their own church doors with as little compunction as Ireton felt for Father James Wolf."

It's a complicated story, in other words, this Wolfe family story, especially, perhaps, on the Irish side of the Atlantic. And in the end, adding insult to the gibbet, Pope John Paul II passed over Father James for beatification.

Anyway, Commissioner Wolfe, on his visit home, preferred to focus on the positives of present-day Ireland: "The cessation of the British hold, he says, has benefited the Irish people in material things, but much more so because that grip has ceased to hamper our manly self-respect."

And it is at this point, one imagines, that Mrs. Wolfe gently urged her husband to wrap things up. To finish the last of their pints. After all, they had promised to meet Father Pat's brother, Dr. Timothy Woulfe, in Bruff.

10.

A VIOLENT CROSSROADS DURING the two wars, Bruff found room for only a few hundred people, all of them rock-jawed midwesterners. Dr. Tim ran the medical dispensary, which served the local poor, while another cousin, Maurice, managed the local branch of the National Bank.

The *Limerick Leader*'s reporter memorialized only bits of the subsequent conversation, for instance the Commissioner "explaining" to his cousin Dr. Tim "that in the matter of organised relief of the poor we are ahead of America, which has nothing to correspond exactly" with the Bruff Dispensary. In fact, said Dick Wolfe, his bile seeming to rise, this only laid bare "the utter falsehood of English propaganda," which insisted on portraying the Irish as a race of degenerate drunkards. Perhaps he already knew that Dr. Tim served as executive of the Catholic Total Abstinence Federation of Ireland. "Manly self-respect" was his byword. But then the Commissioner added that it was these same propagandists who falsely "attributed

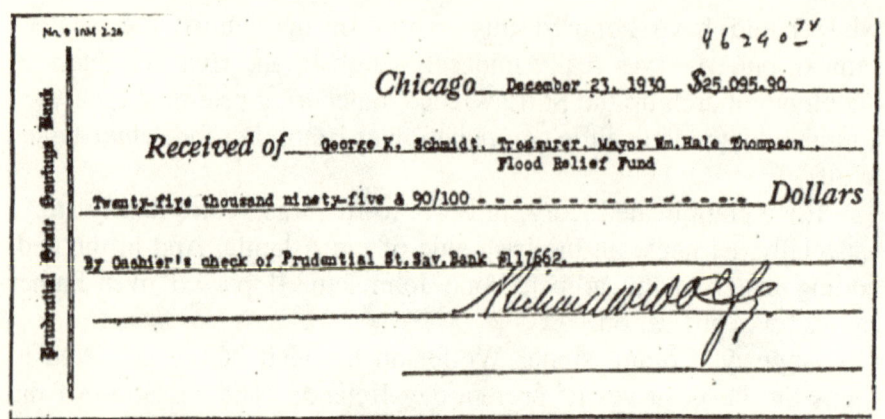

Receipt signed by Richard W. Wolfe, Chicago Daily Tribune, February 8, 1931

lawlessness to America, and particularly to Chicago," and so discrediting his adopted city and the country he loved so much.

The Bruff Woulfes might have been forgiven had they exchanged a quizzical glance at this moment. Was it the English who attributed lawlessness to America, or the drunks? And had they not read something in the paper about a man named Scarface Capone? Was there really no lawlessness in Chicago?

We all have our blind spots, of course, but the Commissioner's tended to be as wide as the prairies and as lofty as high mountain peaks. Only a few months previously, in February 1931, Commissioner Wolfe and Chicago's larger-than-life mayor, Big Bill Thompson, had come under investigation for diverting to their own coffers most of the $139,772 raised in a flood-relief campaign. Wolfe, in particular, was fingered as the one to whom the money was entrusted. On February 9, the hated *Tribune* published images of canceled checks and a bank statement, signed by the Commissioner, all suggesting that relief money had been used for political purposes. At the same time, the Illinois state's attorney opened a separate investigation into allegations of corruption in the finances of the river-straightening project. Not long after that, Wolfe was again accused of mishandling finances, with aldermen charging that he had neglected to collect thirty thousand dollars in rent owed by a transit company for space leased at Navy Pier.

In May, after Big Bill failed to win reelection, Wolfe appeared before a grand jury. He denied receiving payoffs from Capone but testified that he and seven others, some of whom were outside of government, all had attended a midnight meeting in which they each had contributed five thousand dollars toward a forty thousand dollar shortfall in the accounts of an unnamed city employee. The reason for the shortfall was not made clear, and favors paid to those who contributed were assumed.

One supposes that, over tea, the Commissioner neglected to mention his troubles with the state's attorney, although the Woulfes of Bruff may have noticed that, in spite of his relentless energy, their visitor looked a little tired.

> The lust of gold throughout the years
> Has drenched mankind in blood and tears,
> While sea and shore and land and sky
> Give all their wealth to man's frail eye.

Maurice Woulfe was tired, too. Seven years ago, or what still seemed like yesterday, he had been managing the bank in Baltinglass, County Wicklow, when a couple of men came in about two in the afternoon. One of them poked his head in the office door and asked to use the telephone, but Mr. Woulfe was in the middle of a meeting. "Send a telegram from the post office," he said, or something to that effect. A little bit later, the other one, the smaller of the two men, knocked at the door again, this time with a shiny black revolver that he soon pointed at the bank manager's head.

"Hands up," he barked. And then, confusingly, "Give me your keys."

Mr. Woulfe would later remember spying the taller of the two men standing guard outside the office door, looking tense and angry, and then he would remember slowly moving his right hand into his coat pocket, as if to retrieve his keys but feeling instead the cold barrel of his automatic. His hand slick with sweat, he released the safety and then, after taking a deep breath, drew the gun.

Back in Bruff, the cousins noisily slurped their tea and made small talk. Based on what later appeared in the *Limerick Leader*, they seemed to have chatted mostly about family. Dr. Tim, the authority on Woulfe history now that the Commissioner's father had died, delivered a lecture on the subject of Edmond Woulfe, the Commissioner's grandfather. "A well-known personality" is how the newspaper described Old Ned, with a load of historical context that likely only summarized what the doctor told his charges. None of this was new to the Commissioner, of course, who was not quite ten when his grandfather died. He had already heard these stories, and so, perhaps, his mind began to wander. It had been only about a year and a half since a man had been gunned down in Chicago under circumstances that seemed especially damning for Wolfe.

On March 5, 1930, the state's attorney had announced the resumption of a probe into City Hall payroll records. Looking for evidence of graft and payroll padding, he subpoenaed the appropriate records from the Commissioner's office and was promised cooperation. When he did not receive it, he informed a judge of his intention to confiscate the records from their storage place in a garage on West Harrison Street. Before he could do so, on March 9, gunmen entered the garage and threatened the sixty-two-year-old security guard, Thomas Coughlin.

"The two men, armed with pistols, walked into the garage and pushed their guns into Coughlin's ribs," the state's attorney told the *Tribune*. "They said, 'Stick 'em up.' But they immediately added that it was no ordinary stickup. 'We're not after money,' they said, 'we're after records.' Then one menaced Coughlin with his revolver while the other attacked a desk with a crowbar."

The state's attorney observed that the records were, and continued to be, somewhere else in the garage. "About the time they got the safe open there was a honking of automobile horns outside," he said. "Coughlin got up and tried to open the door. The hoodlums shot him and ran out."

Did the cousins compare stories? In Baltinglass, Mr. Woulfe had pulled his automatic and aimed it squarely at the taller man, the one standing by his office door. In doing so, he had startled the fellow, who hadn't taken the bank manager for a cowboy, but he had also startled himself. Because he wasn't one.

Had he witnessed something during the war? Or perhaps been the perpetrator himself? Whatever stopped him from firing his weapon, it did not stop the taller man from firing his.

According to the *Chicago Tribune*, the security guard Coughlin was taken to the nearest hospital, where he later died. The Harrison Street warehouse, meanwhile, was placed under police protection. "In the afternoon," the paper reported, "a city policeman, who did not give his name and has not been identified, entered the place and demanded the records in the name of Commissioner of Public Works Wolfe." When the guard refused, "the policeman telephoned to a person he said was Commissioner Wolfe and reported the failure of his mission."

In Baltinglass, the manager of the National Bank heard the shot but never actually saw the tall man pull the trigger. He was on the floor of his office before he could understand what had happened, a stream of his own blood pooling next to him. He called for help only to see the taller man, revolver in hand, now looming over him, threatening to blow out his brains. The shorter one yelled for the keys again and Mr. Woulfe emptied his pockets. He emptied them of keys and lint and a few coins. Everything, he thought, that was his in the world was now on the floor.

> But minds opprest seek balm of rest,
> And hearts in grief by friends are blest,
> And souls, O Lord, come nearer Thee
> In woods and fields beside the sea.

During the Black and Tan days, Dr. Tim had tended the wounds of IRA boys, some shot and spilling blood like his cousin, others just banged up and ill-treated by a life on the run. He had stories to tell, too, one presumed, but the case of the Woulfe family demanded something different.

According to the paper, "Dr. Woulfe explained the conditions which prevailed in Ireland 90 years ago …"

Powerful landlords, tenant agitation, rigged elections.

"However, in 1852 the grandfather of ex-Commissioner Woulfe went forward as a candidate in opposition to the estate agent, and all who have any idea of the conditions of the time will understand the magnitude of that venture and the task that he accomplished in being about the first farmer in Ireland to defeat, which he did, his landlord's nominee, for a seat on a public board."

The Woulfes certainly must have nodded at that. Of the myriad stories they had ready to go, this was the sort they best liked to tell. Ould rebels, every last one of them. It ran in their blood. The healthy, wholesome, vigorous blood of the Woulfe family. This, anyway, was the logic of that article in the *Limerick Leader*. This is what it meant to be a Woulfe.

11.

WHAT DOES THE FAMILY look like on the Irish side of the Atlantic? It looks like a confusing jumble of blue-eyed, fast-talking, writerly cousins, their histories interweaving in ways that are tangled and intricate and that move quickly between past and present—complete with periodic and sudden outbursts of violence.

It looks, in other words, a lot like it does on the American side.

And in many respects, the Commissioner serves as a bridge connecting these two identities, the American and Irish. He is the *über* Wolfe, a larger-than-life figure who was descended from the same (we'll meet his father shortly), an immigrant-made-good who dabbled in poetry, politics, and perhaps even murder. He also trafficked in the worst kind of bigotry.

On his 1931 visit to Ireland, Wolfe complained of the "powerful, ruthless hand and brain of big business" and how it was "practically in control of the money, business and natural resources of America." And after traveling on to Berlin, he noted how "the international banker and the international profiteer are raising hell with America." Then and now, of course, the phrase "international banker" was a euphemism for Jew.

In 1936, Wolfe was named national treasurer of the Union Party, a hastily organized third party that unsuccessfully ran North Dakota congressman William Lemke for president against Franklin D. Roosevelt. The party was organized in part by Father Charles Coughlin, a virulently anti-Semitic, anti–New Deal radio personality who, during the campaign, relentlessly attacked Jews and in one speech accused Roosevelt of being caught in "the tentacles of the Baruchs, the Morgans and the Rothschilds."

In 1939, the Chicago political reporter William H. Stuart authored a hagiographic biography of Wolfe, *Share the Profits! The Story of Richard W. Wolfe and His Conclusions.* In one chapter, "Manipulation of Money," Wolfe attacks Jews for their treatment of Jesus Christ, fabricates a Thomas Jefferson quotation on banking, and suggests that Jews conspired to assassinate Abraham Lincoln. Wolfe goes on to dismiss Adolf Hitler for his defense of capitalism but urges the United States to steer clear of the war that was imminent in Europe.

When I was growing up, my dad kept hundreds of books down in the basement with his typewriter, everything from Wodehouse to fat histories of Nazi Germany and World War II. But I remember in particular a single, trim, black-covered volume. Its translucent pages were neatly typed and the occasional mistake marked carefully in pen. This was Dad's master's thesis, earned in 1970 from Western Illinois University and titled *Anti-Semitism in the New Deal Era: The Case of Father Coughlin.*

I don't believe Dad had ever heard of Commissioner Wolfe, but he knew and abhorred Father Coughlin, considering him a stain on the church and a sober warning about the power of hatred and modern propaganda.

How might Dad have reacted, then, to knowing that a member of his own family appears to have been cut from the same cloth? The stories we tell are forever hiding the ones we don't.

12.

OLD NED—HE WAS the Commissioner's grandfather. When he wasn't agitating against the union of Britain and Ireland, he was farming a stead in the hills of West Limerick that he'd inherited from his father, Short Dick, who had inherited it from *his* father, Old Maurice. (Short Dick's brother was known as the Barrister on account of his general wisdom. He was John R. Wolfe's grandfather, which is to say my great-great-great-great grandfather.) About 1815, Ned built a sturdy, whitewashed house at the Glen for himself and his new wife, Nellie. Seven girls and two boys came screaming into the world at that house, including little Richard Edmond, born on April 7, 1825. He was the Commissioner's father. Everyone called him Dicky Ned.

After his father died, Dicky Ned took over at the Glen, and his farm was one of the largest in the parish. In his biography of the Commissioner, Stuart writes that the elder Mr. Woulfe "owned at one time fifteen cows, a herd of goats, sheep, pigs, two draft horses, geese, turkeys, chickens and two donkeys. On an extensive acreage he raised oats, rye, flax, and potatoes." He also raised children, a dozen of them, with a demeanor described as "strict and stern but of great humanity. He was loved by the countryside because of his good heart and his wise leadership, and when he rescued a little girl from drowning, his popularity grew." His wife, Kate, "spun the wool from her own sheep and made the children's caps, stockings, and sweaters." She also told her children stories—"about ghosts, devils, witches, banshees, fairy thorns, devil cats, elves, bewitched butter, horned women, blood-thirsty giants, and weird and startling enchantments."

One of the Glen's outbuildings housed a one-room school. These so-called hedge schools dated to the prohibition of Catholic schools in Ireland, which lasted from 1723 to 1782, although many survived well after that. A man named Michael Sheahan taught at the Glen, probably lived there too, and was responsible for an average of eighty to ninety pupils per year. "He spoke without affectation," one of those students later recalled, "and with an assured command of language, in a voice generally low." In the winter, the boys brought with them clumps of turf to burn, and when the fire eventually dimmed, classes were dismissed for the day. Discipline sometimes proved necessary, and Master Sheahan appeared to have worked out an arrangement with Mrs. Woulfe. He would dramatically raise his hand (or paddle or whatever the weapon of choice was that day), and his victim's "preparatory cry" would summon the lady of the house. She never failed to promptly accept the child's appeals for mercy.

A handful of girls also attended the school, including the one whom Dicky Ned apparently rescued from drowning. She had been hurrying home after classes one day—through patches of centuries-old trees that blanketed the hillsides, past old limekilns and the culm and coal pits, past the occasional fairy ring—when she attempted to cross one of the many streams that snaked through Cratloe and Keel. Flooded from recent rains, it carried her a hundred yards before Dicky Ned finally pulled her from the current.

The landscape teemed with narrative. According to his biographer, the future commissioner of public works slipped away from Master Sheahan's classes to roam the countryside, "always searching, exploring, thinking." The mountains "intrigued and coaxed him" and got him to wondering about America, about Irish lads who had made the voyage before him, including two from Limerick who had explored upper New York. He thought, of course, about the Hunger.

"The boy used the brain back of his eyes and sought the meaning of things," his biographer writes.

> The brook in which he waded so often had in it a horse-shoe curve in a corner of the pasture. Young Dick reflected. Why should there be that detour, lost motion, delay, in the flow to the sea? He brought a spade next day and laboriously dug out a channel making a straight line that eliminated and made unnecessary the laggard curve. Dick had straightened his first water course. He got more of a thrill in that than he did in his great achievement, straightening the Chicago River, years after.

You have to hand it to Wolfe's biographer. In just a few lines he manages to give us a landscape, illuminate character, and reveal the future. The place fairly shimmers with magical possibility, and one is tempted to keep it going. Perhaps Young Dick, after redirecting one of the local streams, now scrambles off to redirect some charity funds. Or perhaps steal some records.

Narrative is never neutral, and the Wolfes tend to be the heroes of our own stories—stories that shape the world around us every bit as much as the world shapes us. "We are made a spectacle to God," Father James had declared at Limerick, astride the gallows. He's a ghost now, but an important one.

Dicky Ned's granddaughter Dollie, the Commissioner's niece, eventually assumed management of the Cratloe farm and all of its various spirits. Like her grandmother Kate, she enjoyed a good scare. "There was Joan Grogan of Athea," she once wrote to a relative in America, "who, one night at the Glen, called on the dead of previous generations, naming each individually as they came in, one after another, out of the dark ... until my grandfather, then a young man, was driven into a fire-place corner by the press of the weird, if friendly, visitors."

In that same letter, written in 1956 from the Glen, Dollie accomplishes something similar, invoking past Woulfes, one after another, in tales she likely heard from Dicky Ned himself. Take Old Maurice, for instance. He was Dicky Ned's great grandfather, born in 1690, and only fourteen when his own father died. Maurice's "younger brother, Richard, died a young man," Dollie wrote. "The story is that he got chilled while on a visit eastward down the plain of Limerick and was buried in Monagay churchyard. It was winter and the snow lay so deep that the body could not be brought home."

Old Maurice did well enough on his farm that he could provide dowries for each of his six sisters, but he wasn't able to marry his own wife until he was forty. Thirty years later she died. "The churchyard, Templeathea, where she was buried was in plain sight of his house," Dollie wrote. "The tradition is that he could not bear to look at it." He left his farm and moved to nearby Cratloe, where he leased between two thousand and three thousand acres, amounting to the entire townland. "He lived ... here at the Glen and died [in his house] on Christmas night, 1792, being then, you will notice, 102 years of age. He had eaten his supper, possibly too good a one for his years, and was sitting in a corner of the kitchen beside the fire watching a dance of the young people that was in full swing, when he appeared to fall asleep. It was noticed that he had 31 of his own teeth in his mouth and the 32nd was in his waistcoat pocket when he died that night so that he was practically intact."

13.

FIND YOURSELF ON A MAP: in the southwest of Ireland, between the cities of Limerick and Tralee, and south of the River Shannon, three small towns crowd the border that divides northern County Kerry from western County Limerick. Listowel sits alone on the Kerry side, while tiny Athea—pronounced by the locals ah-TAY—can be found just about nine miles to the east, in Limerick.

Detail from a map of Ireland, 1838

The slightly larger Abbeyfeale is situated between the two but about seven miles south, completing a rough triangle. Templeathea and its cemetery are just east of Athea and the townland of Cratloe just south, on the road to Abbeyfeale.

The River Galey snakes through the high ground of Athea, and the town's name, which comes from the Irish *Áth an tSléibhe*, meaning "ford of the mountain," suggests there might have been a crossing there once. In his English translation of the Irish epic *The Táin*, Ciaran Carson notes how much of the action in these old stories occurs at fords like this one. They were "liminal zones," he writes, "between this world and the Otherworld," metaphysical spaces, portals, barriers. Cúchulainn might challenge his enemies at such crossings. Or Dicky Ned might pluck a girl from the rush of a river or stream. His son, the Commissioner, might even alter its course. The landscape teemed with narrative. In Scots Gaelic the Banshee is *Beannighe*, or the washerwoman at the ford, busily cleaning the clothes of those about to die.

It seems right, then, that Dollie and her grandmother managed to summon the ghosts in this place to come back across the water. A lost nation of ancestors.

14.

THE WOULFES DIDN'T OWN their land. Old Maurice had leased the entire townland of Cratloe, and in 1815 his son Old Ned had built his farmhouse. Then in 1817 an aristocratic Protestant named Thomas Goold purchased the estate from a Lord Courtenay for fifteen thousand pounds. Serjeant Goold, as he was known, was a Dublin lawyer, an accomplished orator—"Goold of the silver tongue," they called him—and a friend of Daniel O'Connell. Known as the Great Emancipator, O'Connell won legal rights for Irish Catholics in 1829 and after that fought to repeal the Act of Union, all with Serjeant Goold's fullest support.

The two periodically faced each other in court, and on one occasion Goold, acting as the Crown prosecutor, was getting the best of O'Connell. In the course of his argument, the serjeant happened to mention some estates connected to the defendants when O'Connell saw his opportunity and snapped back: "What about that property *you* purchased in West Limerick from Lord Courtenay, the one where you can turn out a two-year-old in May only for it to come back a yearling in November with the horns of a four-year-old?"

The serjeant, thunderstruck by the implication of dishonesty, could only huff and puff, and eventually he lost his case.

According to Dicky Ned's nephew Edmond Woulfe White, a lawyer himself, Serjeant Goold and his first son Wyndham acted as true and fair landlords. When tenants appealed to the serjeant that they could no longer afford their rents, he appointed an arbitrator and made sure that the farmers found representation. In this way the rents were fixed by mutual consent and hardly budged for the rest of the century. Dick Wolfe appears to have told a different story to his biographer, however. The book describes craven, absentee landlords, "most of them with royal titles," who employed spies and raised rents at the first sign of a farmer's prosperity. Of course, the Commission-

Athea, ca. 1900

er's hatred of Tory-ism burned with the heat of a thousand turf fires. Had the Woulfes accommodated their landlords, would they even have been Woulfes?

Young Dick might have found comfort in the story of his cousin, Thomas Woulfe, of Beale Hill, near Ballybunion and northwest of Listowel. The son of John R.'s eldest brother, Woulfe began renting a little more than 162 acres of land in 1870, probably about the same time he married. The couple farmed among the rocks of seaside North Kerry, producing nine children and each month paying their rent to the third earl of Listowel, a member of the House of Lords. Woulfe had signed his lease near the start of what historians call the Land War, a long period of social and political agitation between landlords and tenants. The latter were led by Charles Stewart Parnell, a member of Parliament whose outspokenness at one point landed him in Dublin's Kilmainham jail. In March 1882, the landlord Arthur Herbert, reviled by some for having leveled the house of an evicted family, was murdered in Kerry. Late in April, a farmhand was murdered in Limerick just for having volunteered to work on a farm where the family had been evicted. These "boycotted" properties were deemed off-limits.

The men responsible for this violence were called Moonlighters, and in April 1882 they were busy raiding the countryside around Tom Woulfe's farm. "A farmer named Patrick Quane, Kiloonly, Ballybunion, was taken out of his bed, put on his knee, and a double barrel gun presented at his head by one, and a revolver to his heart by another of the rulers of Ireland," the establishment *Kerry Evening Post* reported sarcastically, "threatening him with death if he paid his rent—he is a tenant of the Earl of Listowel—or dealt in any 'Boycotted house.'"

That same night the Moonlighters visited Beale Hill, and like the other farmers Woulfe "also gave up his gun without a word of refusal or an attempt to defend," according to the *Post*, "though his house is one from which a successful defence could have been made."

Whether out of fear, principle, or necessity, Woulfe refused to pay his rent for the next three years until, on April 6, 1885, he was evicted. According to the *Kerry Sentinel*, a sub-sheriff, three bailiffs, a sergeant, and three policemen all arrived at Beale Hill to execute the court order. He owed £528 1s 5d on a yearly rent of £187 0s 8d.

While the *Post* described Woulfe's acreage as "prime" and his rent "nominal," the *Sentinel* was more sympathetic, suggesting that the farm had been almost unworkable when Woulfe first occupied it, and "being situated just at the mouth of the Shannon, [it was] exposed to all the violence and severity of the Atlantic storms."

Woulfe himself claimed that despite all this he had made great strides in improving the farm, building a fine house with no help from the landlord and clearing a good road through the estate. He pointed to the gates he had built and the piles of stones he had retrieved from the fields, evidence of the toil and industry necessary "to bring even the [farm's usable] 80 acres ... into [their] present state of less than average quality." Adding to Woulfe's problems: the bog was worthless for turf and the market at Listowel was a full twelve miles away, causing him to "thereby [lose] a great deal of the profit of his produce." Worst of all, Woulfe had lost six hundred pounds worth of stock since 1877 "owing to the poisonous nature of the grazing." So often did he take his sick animals into the barn for care that his neighbors dubbed the building "Woulfe's Infirmary."

The eviction occurred without incident, and when the sheriff arrived he found two cows, a few sheep, two horses, a couple donkeys, and a number of small children. The family subsequently surrendered themselves to the local workhouse or perhaps moved in with one of Tom's brothers. Then, six weeks later, the landlord changed his mind and allowed the family back to Beale Hill. "When the fact became known in the neighbourhood," the *Kerry Weekly Reporter* wrote, "some three hundred persons including both sexes came on the farm with horses and carts, accompanied by about twenty musicians, and put down several acres of potatoes and oats. The greatest merriment prevailed during the day."

15.

SADLY, NOT ALL DISPUTES ended so peacefully. Tom Woulfe's brother Maurice (no. 13, I think) farmed at Kiltean, just west of Listowel. In August of 1892 two of his sons, Matthew and Richard, were accused of murder and eventually indicted in the death of the farmer Michael Dillane at Ballybunion. An early report on the case suggests that boycotted land may have been at the root of an argument on the street, an argument that led first to the exchange of blows and then to Dillane on the ground, dead. The Crown prosecutor later contended that it was unclear what had started the row. In the end, and despite their indictment, the Woulfe brothers were never tried. A letter to the editor of the *Irish Times* a year later complained of this fact, providing an eerie epitaph to the story. The writer notes that it was "well known in the county, and evidence would have been produced at trial to show, that the case was an agrarian murder"—or violence related to the ongoing Land War. In other words, the Woulfe brothers were murderers but no one possessed either the courage or the inclination to say it.

16.

TOM WOULFE'S EVICTION OCCURRED a year before John R. Wolfe died in Lost Nation, and three years before Dick Wolfe set sail for Chicago, with the Ballybunion murder happening several years after that. And while it's fair to say that the Commissioner and his biographer were true to the general state of landlord-tenant relations in Ireland during that period, the circumstances on the Goold estate were far kinder than they may have been willing to admit. The serjeant and his eldest son, Wyndham, were both well-liked and respected, although things did change somewhat upon Wyndham's death in 1854. The estate passed on to Wyndham's brother, the Very Reverend Frederic-Falkener Goold, archdeacon of Raphoe, near Derry. While he maintained the family tradition of fair rents, the archdeacon proved noticeably less flexible when it came to religion.

Shortly after inheriting his land, he constructed in the village of Athea a manor house and, a few hundred yards from that, a church—a Protestant church. Years later, Dicky Ned's nephew Edmond Woulfe White wrote that introducing such a house of worship in the midst of an all-Catholic population, distributing Protestant Bibles, and even planting a few Protestant families on the estate would have been fine.

But the archdeacon did more than that. He "inaugurated a system, I won't say of proselytism, but akin to it," White wrote, "which led to feuds and demoralisation over the estate." Local men were paid to distribute Protestant religious tracts and then record the names of whomever agreed to read them. Once "educated," these readers collected a few quid at the Protestant church in Listowel before heading off to the nearest pub to spend it.

At the same time, the archdeacon began to fixate on what he imagined to be the local priest's spiritual shortcomings. He accused Father Martin Ryan of, among other offenses, callously disregarding his flock. When the charges were made public the church convened an ecclesiastical court. It met in January 1867, with the Very Reverend Denn O'Brien presiding. His subsequent report acknowledged the charges against Father Ryan to be "truly grave," but then described the conduct of the archdeacon as "very singular."

"The very rev. gentleman made all the accusations just laid down," O'Brien wrote.

> He made them publicly in the newspapers, and to your lordship by private letter. He called very loudly for inquiry, and complained vehemently when inquiry was necessarily delayed. He pledged himself to prove "every one of the charges" before an ecclesiastical tribunal, and to "vindicate his poor tenantry," who, he said, "had been victims of Mr. Ryan's abuse." He "thanked God" that he did not belong to a church where such things were permitted to disgrace the ministry, and he appealed to the public, over and over again, for sympathy. And after all this, when the inquiry, instituted

at his instance, opened the doors and invited him to prove the accusations he had made, Very Rev. Mr. Goold is not there—nor anyone to represent him, or to explain his absence.

Instead, on the following Sunday, Archdeacon Goold strode into the local Catholic church, interrupted Mass, and delivered a speech defending several of the parish's women from the insults of anonymous maligners.

Had the archdeacon gone mad?

That spring the Fenians staged a scattershot rebellion against British rule, which included an attack on a police barracks up the road in Ardagh. When the uprising was quashed the archdeacon hosted a banquet for the Athea station of the Royal Irish Constabulary. He congratulated the policemen on their pluck and dismissed the rebels as "the scum and offscouring of society." But according to Edmond Woulfe White, during the worst of the fighting a group of pike-wielding rebels had surreptitiously pitched their camp just outside Goold's home, "within thirty yards of where the archdeacon slept, and within 200 yards of the nearest police station."

17.

UNLIKE IN KERRY, THE next several decades passed in relative peace among the Limerick Woulfes. Early in the twentieth century, with the Goold estate now in the surer hands of the archdeacon's grandson, Parliament came to recognize the advantage of ending the Land War and so passed several laws aimed at facilitating the transfer of property from landlord to tenant. The renters in the parish of Athea soon began discussing how they might accomplish this, and in 1906, with legal assistance from Edmond Woulfe White, they negotiated the estate's purchase. It was land the Woulfe family had faithfully sowed for more than two centuries, since the days of old, intact Maurice, with thirty-one of his thirty-two teeth.

It's a poignant and pivotal moment in Woulfe's history—to finally possess the land. I'm reminded of the character Bull McCabe from the play *The Field*, written by John B. Keane, a native, like my own

The author, Lost Nation, 1975

ancestor, of Listowel, County Kerry. In particular, there is the Bull's ode to the patch of ground he'd so lovingly cared for but never himself owned. "I watched this field for forty years," he says, "and my father before me watched it for forty more. I know every rib of grass and every thistle and every whitethorn bush that bounds it."

When the Bull's son turns his back on that field, and even sabotages his father's chance at owning it, the Bull's rage and sorrow sweep over the country like one of those Lost Nation tornadoes. Which makes me think of my own father. Like the Bull's son, he also said no—not just to a field but to a life on the land. Maybe with Dad it didn't matter quite so much; after all, when the Wolfes arrived in Iowa, property came cheap and ownership was a matter of paperwork. And yet my dad's father had farmed and so had his grandfather Maurice, and his great grandfather John R., the immigrant from Listowel. John R.'s father had farmed, as had his grandfather, the wise old Barrister, and his great grandfather Old Maurice. And Old Maurice's father and grandfather had too. That's as far back as we can trace the Woulfes. That's how far back they farmed.

What was it like to abandon the land after centuries of working it? Maybe such an act is meaningful only if you make land central to the story you tell, to what it means to be a Wolfe. And anyway, according to an old Iowa friend of mine, "It's all bullshit, this idea that you can have a connection with the land. You can't. It's not real." My friend is elvish and fierce, with long flames of red hair, and for years I assumed he was just being peevish, playing the devil's advocate. Over time, however, I came to understand how deeply his point of view had been informed by his own family of Hungarian Jews and their experience—their near annihilation—during the Holocaust. Their ideas of community, family, and home, forged by the twin fires of religion and history, created a different, infinitely more complicated relationship to blood and soil. (It's one the Commissioner would have done well to reflect on later in life.) For an exiled people, an identity that depends on the land is impossible and, over time, perhaps even absurd. For Bull McCabe, the land was a living, beautiful thing, every rib of grass, every thistle. And for the Woulfes/Wolfes who worked their plows on either side of the Atlantic it was something to be handed down from generation to generation—a heritage of sorts, although to be sure a blood-soaked one. That's something *The Field* well captures, that turn to violence in defense of the land. (The play was based on a real murder in North Kerry.) The killing at Ballybunion, in which two Woulfe brothers struck a man down over a boycott, is evidence of that. "This is a wild reckless Country," Sergeant Maurice Wolfe wrote from land that since time immemorial had belonged to Shoshone, Arapaho, Cheyenne, and Pawnee.

My own experience of the land is nothing by comparison; it matters only because it's mine: the sheep and the cows and the dry ice of Lost Nation. My dad's constant dreaming. "As long as I live, I'll associate freshly mown hay with those dreams and yearnings, and I won't know whether to be happy or sad."

Of course, it's worth remembering that the fields are not only for cultivation. They're not only a living thing but also something richly symbolic: a *here* and a *there*. The mud, the rocks, the loping green hills and the ribbony roads that cross them: they are from whence we came and where we ended up, anchors that situate our family and lend us meaning. Athea and Lost Nation. Without these anchors, where on Earth are we?

In Jim Sheridan's 1990 film adaptation of *The Field*, the Bull picks a dandelion and blows its seeds into the wind. "This is what we'd be without the land, boy," he tells his son.

The Palestinian-Lebanese writer Anton Shammas—who studied at the University of Iowa, as it happens—coined a word for this strange, dislocating process of finding yourself on a map: "autocartography." There is a difference, he once wrote, between going back and going home: "The difference being as simple as this: you go back to someplace where you have lived in the past, but you go home to a place that even though you may have never seen it in your life, still it is as if you had; it is a place that is the other, deep end of that pool of your created, acquired, and invented memories."

This is how Dad and I had expected to feel on our trip to Listowel, but as it happens we were just a few kilometers short of that deep end, a place that sadly Dad never got to visit.

For some of us Wolfes, the autocartography of our family involves both the real and the imagined. We've seen it, we've felt it—the green and yellow hills of Lost Nation, the sense of dread and subterranean excitement as we set out on our annual Dead Man's Tours—but we've never truly owned it. And yet we always go wandering back, my sisters and me.

On the outside dreaming in.

18.

THEN THERE IS ATHEA, a place that until recently I had never visited. The surrounding countryside had always been true and well cared for. "It's my child," the Bull tells his son, referring to his own land. "I nursed it. I nourished it. I saw to its every want. I dug the rocks out of it with my bare hands and I made a living thing of it!" The black dirt, the fields of lovely green grass—now, finally, in the year 1906, they were officially owned by the same men and women who actually worked them. The tenants at this historic moment included Paddy Woulfe, the father of Father Pat and Dr. Tim; a farmer called Brown Dick Woulfe; and, of course, the Commissioner's father, Dicky Ned, whose time on earth was quickly running out.

19.

DICKY NED WAS EIGHTY-SIX when he died at the Glen on May 24, 1910. His obituary in the *Limerick Leader* honored him as the "'Grand Old Man' of the Limerick Woulfes" and called attention to a letter he had dictated to Edmond Woulfe White a few days before his death. The note was addressed to Sister Teresa Woulfe, of the Ursuline Convent in New Orleans, on the occasion of her eighty-sixth birthday, and Dicky Ned praised her devotion to the church. He said it "makes me proud of our race and of our name," before continuing:

> Generations ago it was prophesied that there would be Woulfes in Limerick and in Kerry while the Shannon rolled into the Atlantic, and that more than an average number of them would devote their lives to the service of God. When I saw the inscription on your letter (for my vision, thank God, is still clear) I said that is the writing of a Woulfe, and when I read the letter it revived in my mind the memory of the prophecy mentioned, which was related to me in this house nearly eighty years ago by my poor father who survived my present age by three years and to the end retained his faculties undimmed and unclouded.

I've always pictured Dicky Ned as being a bit like Bull McCabe, a round, rough oak tree of a man, big enough to plunge his arm into the rush of a flooded stream and grab a drowning schoolgirl by the scruff of her neck. The one image I've seen, an etching of Dicky Ned and his wife, Kate, in front of the Glen, gives him a long beard and a fierce visage. They called him the "Book of Athea" for his voluminous knowledge of local lore—a learned Bull who spoke Irish fluently, recited long poems verbatim, and remembered the histories of all the West Limerick and North Kerry families.

Little is known of his life. There was the farm and the hedge school, a marriage and all the children, many of whom, of course, emigrated. But his obituary is typical of other sources in its general

The Glen, with Dicky Ned and Kate Woulfe in foreground

disinterest in mere vital statistics. What mattered most to the old Book, and what we must accept from him, are the stories. And in these the obituary overflows. His letter alone speaks of a prophecy that defines the Woulfe family by where it resides and what god it serves. You can identify members by nothing more than the scratch of their hand: "I said that is the writing of a Woulfe."

According to a manuscript preserved by the Irish Folklore Commission, Dicky Ned was one of just three *seanchaí* in West Limerick at the turn of the century. The word is defined on the page in terms that are less than inspiring: "In 1903 these three old people could read and write Irish." But it has always meant much more than that—a wise man, a keeper of histories and lore, a storyteller. When Father Pat Woulfe, who years later would have tea with the old Book's son the Commissioner, required information for a scholarly article about a prominent North Kerry family, he consulted Dicky Ned. In the resulting publication, which appeared in 1906, he even transcribed their interview word for word.

The Book had plenty to say about the Woulfes, as well. In his letter to Sister Teresa, he wrote that "I am the man, I think, now living that can from personal knowledge trace them back to the days of Cromwell." Dicky Ned's niece Dollie—who, it bears repeating, probably owes much if not all of her family history to the Book himself—goes back even further, dating the family to the Anglo-Norman invasion. The Woulfes weren't even Irish then but French- and Saxon-speaking former Vikings who, a century earlier, had sailed across the channel from Normandy and conquered England. In the years since then, many families had congregated in Wales, where they had become powerful and restless enough to worry the king. When a deposed Irish chief whose wife had been kidnapped sought their help, the English king gave his blessing. Better these families raise havoc in Ireland than England.

The Woulfes, then, probably arrived with these Normans invaders in 1169 and may have been taken their surname from Hugh d'Avranches, a gluttonous, warlike, and long-dead Anglo-Norman earl who was known, variously, as Hugh the Fat and Hugh the Wolf. By the time they landed in Ireland, however, the Woulfes seem to have associated themselves with the elderly lord Maurice FitzGerald, whose name literally meant "Maurice, son of Gerald," and who had a number of sons, among them Gerald FitzMaurice and Maurice Fitz-Maurice. These names, especially Maurice, show up again and again in the Woulfe family tree, while the FitzMaurice landholdings eventually became the earldom of Desmond in the province of Munster, an area that includes what is now Limerick and Kerry. The Woulfes, however, settled first a bit to the north, on a patch of land called Corbally, just east of Limerick city on the River Shannon. In Irish the place was called *An Corrbhaile*—the odd (or round or pointed or distinctive, depending on whom you ask) hill town. It was "a lovely place," Dollie wrote the Commissioner in 1947. "How they got it is explained, I should think, by the simple explanation that they took it."

Three centuries later, in 1476, a Thomas Woulfe was elevated to sheriff of Limerick, a rather prominent position. And a century after that, in 1582, another Woulfe appeared in the records, a Gerald Woulfe who died in fighting that came toward the end of the Desmond Rebellion, a series of armed uprisings against English rule in Munster that were led by Gerald FitzGerald. Almost two decades of violence finally ended with Gerald's death in 1583, and it appears to have cost the family of that other Gerald, Gerald Woulfe, their land.

"She blasted us clean out of Corbally," Dollie wrote, referring to Queen Elizabeth, "and scattered us here and there over the plain of Limerick—a few of us without heads."

This marks just one of the many crossings, fords, translations, and exiles that have come to dominate the telling of Woulfe—and for that matter Irish and certainly Irish American—history. Hundreds of years later, when those dead ancestors waded the Galey at *Áth an tSléibhe* and paid night visits to the Glen, some of them likely had been born on the Continent, others in Britain, still others on the Odd Hill. They wore the clothes of soldiers, farmers, and merchants and spoke the tongues of Welshmen and Irishmen.

They were forever trailing west. From Corbally they trekked the fifteen or sixteen miles to Croagh and Rathkeale, which is where they seem to have been when Dicky Ned picks up the story, in 1641. That's when a confederation of Irish Catholic gentry unsuccessfully attempted to overthrow English rule, leading to a bloodbath in which "numbers of the Woulfes were obliged to leave the rich plains of Limerick, and became scattered and separated never to meet again." As the old Book wrote to Sister Teresa, some fled to nearby County Clare, while others wandered farther south and west to Kerry.

Then, in 1649, Oliver Cromwell's army showed up. The scourge that followed has been elegized by the Irish for more than three hundred and fifty years and included the leveling of Drogheda and the siege of Limerick, where—this is Dicky Ned again—"some were hanged, others shot in cold blood, for no greater crime than defending their country, and probably the ample possessions then held in Limerick and Tipperary." We've already met Father James Woulfe, who exclaimed on the scaffold, "We are made a spectacle to God!"

That was in 1651, and the Woulfes were being pushed west yet again. Call it karma, but where the family had once taken Irish land, now the English took theirs. It's indicative of almost five centuries of assimilation that they now even considered themselves Irish, or at least Old English (*Sean-Ghaill*), having fully adopted the language, manners, and sense of grievance characterized by the people they

Dollie Woulfe, 1905

themselves had once terrorized. The so-called New English (*Nua-Ghaill*) had been imported by Elizabeth to plant the fields she had brutally conquered, and they brought with them the Reformation and a typically violent mistrust of priests. That the Woulfes kept the old faith was an important factor in their gradual Gaelicization. One David Wolfe stands out in this respect. Born in Limerick, he studied under Ignatius Loyola and Francis Borgia before being dispatched, in 1560, as the official papal legate in Ireland. He traveled the country organizing Catholics and provoking an exasperated letter from Elizabeth to Pius IV that complained Father Wolfe existed only "to excite disaffection against her crown." According to historians, the priest ended his days with his head still attached but his body and soul wrecked by a life on the run. According to Dicky Ned, whose very definition of a Woulfe included service to God, his only crime, and the only crime of those later Woulfes displaced by the hated Cromwell, "was their refusal to renounce the Faith as transmitted to mankind through the inspired Channels of Almighty God."

Back to Cromwell. Like Elizabeth, he moved the Irish and Old English off their land in favor of the New, and subsequent, even newer, English, and he kept thorough records of the entire process. Many of these manuscripts were lost when the Record Office in the Four Courts, Dublin, burned during the Easter Rising of 1916. A few scraps survived, however, and one found its way into the *Kerryman* newspaper a dozen years later: an excerpt from Cromwell's *Book of Transplanters' Certificates* that documents the removal of a number of Woulfes, including another David:

> We, the said Commissioners, do hereby certify that David Woulfe, of Limerick, hath, upon the 19th day of December, 1653, delivered unto us, in writing, the names of himself, and such other persons as are to remove with him, with the quantities, and qualities, of their stocks, the contents whereof are as followeth:—The said David Woulfe, aged 48, middle stature, black sanguine complexion; Ellen Woulfe, wife of aforesaid David, aged 46 years, middle stature, flaxen hair, full face; having five children, viz.: Stephen Woulfe, aged 13 years, flaxen hair, low stature; Nicholas, aged 9 years, flaxen hair, slender body; Ellen Woulfe, aged 7 years, flaxen hair, slender body.

Two servants came along, too, in addition to three cows and a pair of thin horses. Others followed: Thomas Woulfe, Richard Woulfe, and Anthony Woulfe on January 6 and another Thomas Woulfe a few weeks later. So the once-proud Norman family found itself exiled to the hills, woods, and streams of West Limerick and North Kerry—that deep end of the pool bounded by Listowel in the west, Athea in the east, and Abbeyfeale in the south.

It is here, wrote Dollie Woulfe, that "the curtain rises again on two brothers bearing the now recognised family names of Maurice and James who were living at a place called Inchreagh on the bank of the river Galey west of the village of Athea." Their father, you almost could guess, was James Maurice, and as a young man he and his own brother had been busy ploughing under a hot day's sun when they spied a man bounding across the field toward them. The runner disappeared over a fence, however, and only later did the brothers find him passed out in a dyke. Once revived, he identified himself as a messenger from Limerick to the lords of Kerry, the FitzMaurices. Limerick, he was shocked to report, had fallen to William of Orange.

This remarkable bit of Woulfe family oral history, handed down from generation to generation, puts the elder set of brothers near Athea in the year 1690, the same year that James Maurice's son Maurice—Dicky Ned's great grandfather—was born. Old Maurice is how he came to be known, and he eventually moved to the townland of Cratloe, just south of Athea, where he built a house for himself at the Glen. When he died, you'll recall, he retained all but one of his thirty-two teeth.

20.

THE BOOK OF ATHEA was every bit the seanchaí people claimed him to be. In fact, his obituary bragged that Father Pat Woulfe was "indebted" to him "for much of the information" in the scholar-priest's famous work, *Sloinnte Gaedheal is Gall* (*Irish Names and Surnames*). I admit to having wondered, perhaps a bit cynically, whether this was actually true, but in his scholarly article—the one in which he transcribed his conversation with Dicky Ned—the priest vouches for his octogenarian cousin as "a good authority on local history and traditions, and knows all about every family in Limerick and Kerry." Father Pat, meanwhile, was an impressive authority in his own right. His slim but celebrated volume, published in 1923, lectures on naming practices throughout Irish history, noting, for instance, that Norman names tended toward the Frankish, and listing, in order of frequency, the most common. *Maurice* comes in at twenty-first, or about halfway down the list and just behind *Baldwin*, *Herbert*, and *Martin*. The book also collects surnames from across Ireland and provides their English and Irish Gaelic equivalents. For example, from page 54:

> *de Bhul*, *de Bhulbh*, Woulfe, Wolfe, etc.

Father Pat often signed himself in Irish, *Pádraig de Bhulbh*, as too did Dicky Ned: *Risteárd Éamonn de Bhulbh*. (This last part is pronounced, roughly, "Wuluv.") It's a practice that took off with the new nationalism of the mid- to late nineteenth century, the idea being that only in their family's native language could these men find their truest (and most patriotic) selves.

"The speech being Irish," you'll recall the Elizabethan poet Edmund Spenser having grumbled, "the heart must needs be Irish." Thomas Davis, one of the legendary founders of the Young Ireland movement that my great-great grandfather John R. Wolfe may, or may not, have "helped to organize," put it somewhat differently. "A people without a language of its own," Davis wrote, "is only half a nation." And elsewhere: "To lose your native tongue and learn that of an alien, is the worst badge of conquest—it is the chain on the soul."

Of course, it's worth asking an obvious question here: what constitutes one's native tongue? As the son of a Welshman, Davis did not grow up speaking Irish himself and in his short life picked up only a little bit of it. The Woulfes likely spoke something akin to French when they first arrived, and seven centuries later John R. or Dicky Ned may or may not have been raised speaking Irish, although current scholarship suggests that Limerick and Kerry, at least until the Hunger, were bilingual. Father Pat learned his Irish in Rome. "I suppose you have heard I am very learned now in that grand old tongue," he wrote his sister Johanna (Sister Bonaventure) from the Irish College in 1893. "I was going to write a letter in it to Aunt Ellie some time ago but I thought she was not book-learned enough in it to read it."

Language and religion are fundamental to Woulfe history and identity. A fellow priest once wrote of Father Pat: "He believes in the Holy Ghost, the Holy Catholic Church and the Irish language. He uses Irish for thinking, talking, praying, dreaming. He speaks English to you as a concession—because you are a foreigner; but if you can distinguish the difference between *slán leat* and *táim go maith*, he carries you along in Irish."

It's interesting, then, that only the church, and not the tongue, survived the transatlantic journey. Perhaps this had the effect of heightening the American family's attachment to Catholicism over the generations. We are not simply Irish or Irish-American; we are Irish-Catholics. My grandfather's first cousin, Father Thomas Wolfe, was the sort who would have made Dicky Ned proud. One of a great many priests and nuns in the family, he entered the seminary as a young man and during the Second World War served as chaplain of the XX Corps, in George C. Patton's Third Army. In August 1944, he and his sergeant were among the first Americans to liberate Chartres cathedral. According to a newspaper report, Wolfe and his driver came under sniper fire on their approach to the church. "I could see no damage [to the cathedral] except [for] a few bullet marks," Wolfe said. The story continued: "During the successful battle to drive out snipers, he related, two middle-aged French women remained alone at devotions before the altar of the Virgin Mary."

"Love God and your fellow man, and *serve* both," my dad scribbled in my baby book, back in 1972. "Remember the Sermon on the Mount."

And yet somewhere along the line, during my childhood, Dad fell out with Holy Mother Church and, more immediately, with Father Martin, for whom I (*Brendan Maaaaartin*, as he liked to call me, rolling his *r*'s in a fake Irish accent) was named. We stopped attending Mass and I was never confirmed. When Dad died, he wanted his funeral to be stripped of all things religious. "I don't care what you do in this regard," he wrote in a letter to my sisters and me, "but try to make those attending show some degree of remorse over my passing, even if you need to pistol whip them. Also, try to make it a festive occasion, although those gathered will probably think that anyway! If I have any money lying around to finance it, make it a party."

So we did. But it was no small thing that he had abandoned the Church just as he had the land: twice an exile. And he recoiled just as much from the Irish language.

"Do they speak much Irish over there?" he asked me when we were preparing for our visit to Ireland. "Is that all they speak? Will I be able to understand *anything*?" I reassured him that there were more native speakers of Navajo than Irish. I told him with some enthusiasm, though, about how the water-pipe caps on Dublin sidewalks are marked *Uisce*, for water, as in *uisce beatha*, or water of life, which is Irish for whiskey. After I pointed out the phonetic origins of "whiskey," he snorted impatiently. So I explained that Irish was gasping and almost dead.

Only then did he relax.

Although the Iowa Wolfes rehearse a kind of determined monolingualism—our English is like a lot of Midwesterners': flat, suggestive, a little indignant—I think we are haunted by the ghost of this long gone language. The Irish poet Eavan Boland writes:

> a new language
> is a kind of scar
> and heals after a while
> into a passable imitation
> of what went before

When John R. Wolfe immigrated to Iowa, his fellow Irishmen were abandoning the Irish language wholesale. While a few radicals like Thomas Davis clung to those old consonants (or, more accurately, learned them anew), mothers were only speaking English to their sons and daughters. They were ashamed but convinced it was necessary. And maybe it was.

Now, only a few generations removed, Dad actually seemed afraid of the language. He was hostile toward it. Could it be a scab was being picked at that he didn't even know was there?

The title of Boland's poem is "Mise Éire," and it means "My name is Ireland," or, more literally, "I am Ireland." It's a simple enough concept. To say *Mise Brendan* is to say, in a manner of speaking, that I am my name, that it was no accident my parents named me for both a Dublin playwright who drank himself to death and a Catholic priest. Perhaps the hope, or at least the hedge, was that I'd split the difference. But to say *Mise Éire* is to go a step further and argue that Ireland is her language. "We exist in the element of language," the Kiowa poet N. Scott Momaday has written. And in "Mise Éire" Ireland exists by virtue of a language that is vanishing.

So what is hiding under all that scar tissue? What does my family no longer know about itself because at some point we stopped speaking Irish?

While in graduate school I drove several hours to a town in Wisconsin with a wonderfully dense Indian name—Oconomowoc—in order to study Irish for a weekend. Ghosts of missing languages were everywhere, as were elderly priests and fussy nuns who were gracious enough to host the event. They taught us call and response, a little elementary grammar, and even some *sean nós*, or old style, singing. The rest of the time we loitered around kegs donated by the Miller Brewing Company.

Driving home, new words popped and buzzed between my ears. I made all sorts of resolutions about how I was going to keep up with it on my own, only to promptly abandon them. My guilt was vague and sinking. Then I read this line in a magazine: "But there is a sharp difference between ethnic identity as something you claim and something that makes claims on you."

You cannot wear you language like your drunk cousin wears a "Screw me, I'm Irish" pin on St. Patrick's Day. You must wear it like your name—you must be it. Around that same time a friend sent me an essay titled, "Just Speak Your Language." I've heard its story expressed several times before, the importance of knowing your ancestors' language. How else will you be able to communicate with them in the afterlife?

"I know that Cheyenne is the only language they know, the only language they ever needed to know," writes Richard Littlebear, a community college instructor in Montana. "And I hope when I meet them on the other side that they will understand me and accept me."

It's a beautiful story, one that suggests language is more than *uisce beatha*. It is the water of life and afterlife.

In aninm an Athar, in the name of the Father, *agus a Mhic, agus an spioraid Naoimh* …

21.

IN HIS PLAY *TRANSLATIONS* (1980), Brian Friel also wonders what goes missing when a language changes. In 1833, a young Irish-speaking man named Owen returns to his village in the company of two British engineers who are part of the Ordnance Survey project charged with mapping the country. They must collect all of the place names and, if possible, translate them into English. These foreigners have no knowledge of the native tongue, however; they even misunderstand Owen's name as Roland.

"Owen—Roland—what the hell?" Owen shrugs, not wanting to make a big deal of the situation. "It's only a name. It's the same me, isn't it?"

That's the question, of course. Some names contain within them whole narratives. Owen tells one of the engineers about a crossroads called Tobair Vree, a corruption of the Irish meaning "Brian's Well." You see, there once was an old man named Brian who, afflicted with a disfigured face, came to the well everyday to wash himself. Hoping the water might cure him, he found that instead it killed him. One morning Brian was found drowned in the well.

"And ever since that crossroads is known as Tobair Vree," Owen explains, "even though that well has long since dried up. I know the story because my grandfather told it to me."

The engineers decide to keep this particular name, but in other instances their changes and translations result in such stories disappearing. Bun na hAbhann, or mouth of the river, becomes Burnfoot, while Áth an tSléibhe, or ford of the mountain, became Athea.

What's contained in a name?

Lost Nation … Brendan Martin … Dicky Ned … or Dicky Ned's great grandson John Maurice Woulfe, who adopted the Irish version of his name, Seán Muiris de Bhulbh. An engineer himself, as it happens, de Bhulbh was a fluent Irish speaker and spent much of his life promoting the language. In the 1970s he served as *cathaoirleach*, or

North Main Street, Lost Nation, Iowa, 1916

presiding officer, of the Limerick branch of Conradh na Gaelige (formerly the Gaelic League)—the same position Father Pat had held earlier in the century. The league's work had been successful enough that by the 1960s and 1970s the Irish language was taught in national schools and passing the course was required to graduate. Nevertheless, skepticism of the language remained widespread. On March 17, 1962—St. Patrick's Day—the playwright John B. Keane (*The Field*) published a column in the *Kerryman* newspaper suggesting that other school subjects were more important than Irish. He even wondered whether the language wasn't being coopted for social and political advancement. "People whose names are written in English on Baptismal and Birth Certificates have found it politic and profitable to sign themselves in Irish," he wrote, an accusation that prompted a swift response from de Bhulbh:

> Finally, I fear I must offend against Mr. Keane's dictum by signing my name in Irish, even though it is in English on my birth certificate. I have been doing this for many years ever since I became convinced, after giving the matter some thought, that Irish was of the utmost im-

portance in our national life. I must confess that so far this procedure has not yielded any profit!

Seán de Bhulbh was particularly interested in names. In 1997, after ten years of work, he updated Father Pat's book with his own, *Sloinnte na hÉireann: Irish Surnames*. Both books, and a new edition that de Bhulbh published in 2002, examined the origins of Irish names and provided a reference for names as they appeared in Irish and English.

Both projects, in a sense, sought to undo the Ordnance Survey. To remove the scab. Where the English had mapped onto Ireland a new language and cultural sensibility—a new history even—the Woulfes have clamored for a return. It's complicated, of course. "Seán" is nothing more than Irish for the much older "John." "De Bhulbh," in its very construction, suggests its Franco-Norman origins. In this case, though, the Irish language, in all its guttural mystery, plunges us deep into that pool of invented memories. It is a means of asserting our Woulfe-ness and, just as crucially, our Irish-ness.

22.

HERE'S A STORY. ONCE upon a time a man called Dick Woulfe, but known locally as the Chemist, ran a pharmacy on New Street in Abbeyfeale. When the wind of rebellion whipped up early in 1916, he put his face to it. For instance, a few days before the Easter Rising, a German U-boat quietly surfaced and deposited three men at windswept Banna Strand, in County Kerry. Roger Casement was a mustachioed former British diplomat from Dublin who was running guns, wooing the Germans on behalf of Irish independence, and, as it happens, battling malaria. He was soon captured and executed. In Abbeyfeale, the Chemist got word that one of Casement's comrades had somehow evaded the authorities and was holed up in Ballymacelligott, just east of Tralee. Woulfe dispatched one of his apprentices to borrow a local priest's Model T, which was then cranked into action to rescue the fugitive. The man eventually made it safely back to Berlin.

Born in Cratloe, not far from the Glen, Dick Woulfe had studied pharmacy in Dublin, which is where he met Catherine Colbert. Katty, as she was called, was the fourth of thirteen Colbert children and had been raised on a farm just outside of Athea. After the deaths of her parents, she moved to the capital, working as a dressmaker and acting the mother to her six younger siblings. She and the Chemist married in 1913 but soon returned to County Limerick, apparently at the urging of his father. The other Colberts stayed behind, including child number ten, Cornelius "Con," who attended a Christian Brothers school, joined the Irish Republican Brotherhood, and eventually hired on at St. Enda's school, a nursery of revolution founded by the poet Patrick Pearse. Con served as a drill instructor and, in 1916, took up arms with Pearse.

On April 30, after a week of bitter fighting, the boy—now calling himself Concobar O'Colbaird—finally waved the white flag. He and fourteen others were soon condemned to the firing squad. Late on May 7, just hours before his death, he scrawled a note to his sister from his lonely, candlelit cell in Kilmainham jail:

> My dear Katty,
> Goodbye and God bless you,
> Forgive me the little I owe you—I would I could ere I died, but 'twas not to be.
> Pray for me when I am gone and I hope we'll all meet in Heaven—Give my love to Dick and the children and remember me.
> Ever your fond brother,
> Conn.

The Woulfes' children by then included Johanna and Hanora. The next year Cornelius Colbert Woulfe was born, followed by two more sons: Richard and Michael. All five grew up to take orders, as either priests or nuns.

The Chemist, meanwhile, remained on New Street, taking on apprentices and raising his deeply religious family above the shop. At first the Irish public had demonstrated no appetite for yet another failed rebellion. The Desmonds and the Geraldines, the United Irishmen, Young Ireland, and the Fenians had all been quite enough, thank you, and the fact that a world war raged in Europe only made the sen-

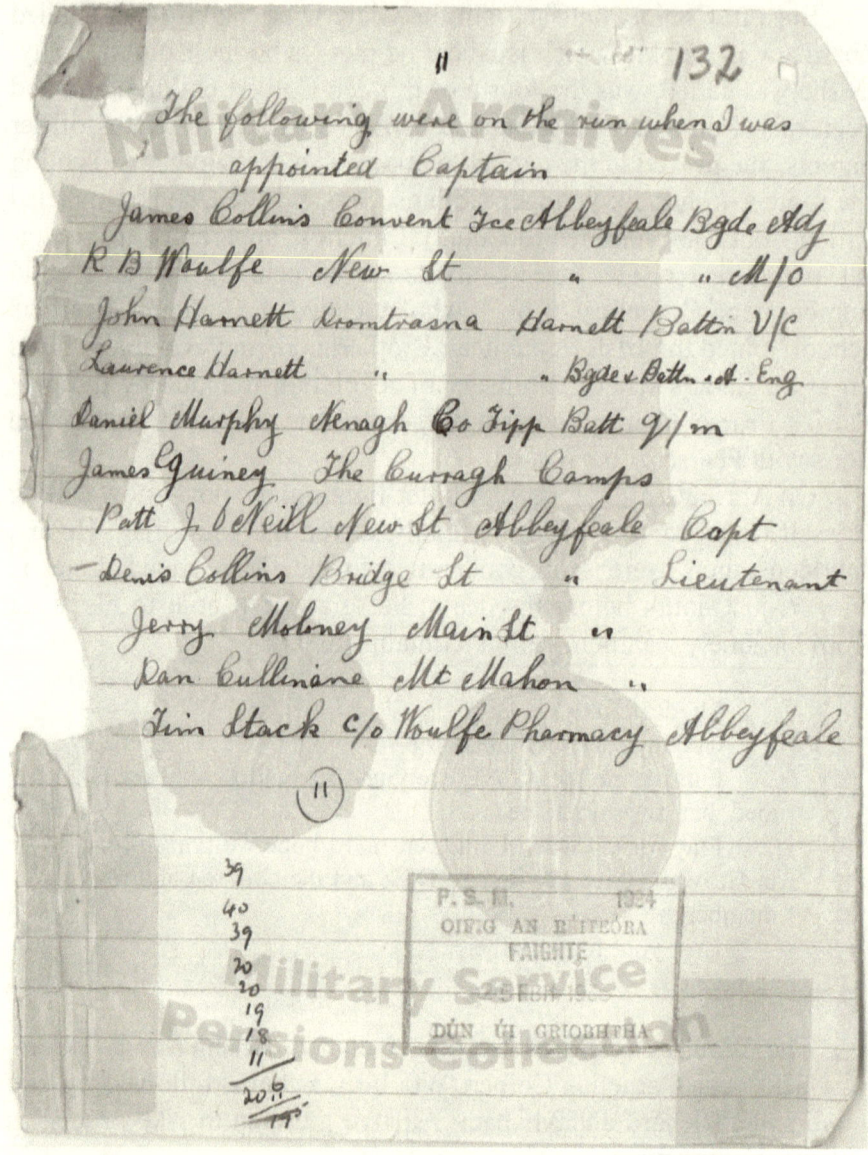

IRA records showing the Chemist, his former apprentice Jimmy Collins, and his assistant Tim Stack all on the run

timent stronger. But after the bloodletting in Kilmainham's back yard, opinions began to change. In 1919, a guerrilla war erupted in Kerry and soon spread to other parts of the country. The Irish Republican

Brotherhood morphed into the Irish Republican Army, and the Chemist joined the West Limerick Brigade as medical officer. His pharmacy once again hosted the type of men who spent a lot of time looking over their shoulders.

One of the Chemist's apprentices, Jimmy Collins, later recalled how one such man, calling himself Peadar Clancy and claiming to be from the IRA's General Headquarters in Dublin, had raised suspicions within the West Limerick Brigade. He was "a stranger to us"—that's how one of his comrades put it. And so he was brought to the pharmacy on New Street. "I was working in the shop at the time," Collins said. "Mrs. Woulfe called me and told me that she knew the Clancy family of Dublin and that this man was not one of them." Collins explained that "as a result of Mrs. Woulfe's suspicions," the man was arrested, tried, and executed as a British spy.

In *Victory and Woe*, his memoir of the West Limerick Brigade, Mossie Harnett doesn't mention the Woulfes or their role in exposing Peadar Clancy. He notes only that "our intelligence received information that led" to his arrest. Harnett then relates how Clancy was found with hidden money and papers that, once decoded, exposed his guilt. His execution took place in the spring of 1920: "Fully realising now his terrible predicament, and visibly trembling, he clutched his Rosary beads in his hands. Near the place of execution, a priest heard his confession; then he shook hands with his executioners and admitted his crime." The man was eventually identified as Denis Crowley, a former British soldier.

The IRA waged its brutal war against the police in fits and starts. Armed units might attack a barracks here and ambush a patrol there, only to melt back into the countryside. The Chemist appeared not to have been one of the gunmen. Instead, he worked intelligence, gathered munitions, and helped to treat the wounded, all the while maintaining a respectable business. For all we know, he may have been asleep on the night of September 18, 1920, when a group of forty to fifty of those gunmen, including Jimmy Collins and Mossie Harnett, surprised a handful of policemen on patrol just outside of Abbeyfeale. Hiding in a ditch, inside a church wall, and behind some fences, the IRA opened fire at a crossroads. One of the attackers accidentally snapped a branch, giving away his position. When John Mahony, a twenty-six-year-old constable from County Cork, peered through a hedge to investigate, he was shot dead. Two other policemen were wounded in the firefight.

The next morning a large number of men in uniform arrived, members of both the Royal Irish Constabulary and the RIC Special Reserve, or so-called Black and Tans—temporary constables recruited from England and notoriously violent. "The Tans remained for a couple of hours while they fired some thousands of rounds of ammunition all round and bombed several houses," Collins recalled. According to a newspaper report, "The local Temperance Hall was subsequently burned, [and] Mr. Woulfe's pharmacy was considerably damaged."

The British blamed the Chemist for the fire, claiming that he had been fashioning bombs in his shop when one of them popped off by mistake. However, one of his daughters remembered that night rather differently. In her ninety-ninth year, Sister Íde (Hanora) recalled how the Black and Tans had barged in and attempted to arrest her father. She was just four at the time. "They were going to shoot him," she said, "and I understand my mother screamed. She was upstairs. They'd locked my mother and one of the babies in [...] They were trying to burn the house and my mother in it." Dick Woulfe was able to rescue his daughter and then escape out the back.

"Now, at the back of our house," Sister Íde said, "our garden opened into the river, and it seems he got out to the river and walked the river that night." Her father eventually made it to a nearby convent. "And the nuns took him in and hid him behind the altar." The soldiers came looking but the reverend mother denied them access. "I think she must have told them they couldn't go into the chapel, and they respected that.

Little Hanora, her mother, and her siblings all went to stay at the nearby home of the Chemist's sister, Kate White, while he remained on the run. He sometimes visited, though, calling himself Uncle Jack. He had shaved his mustache, which altered his appearance just enough that even his own daughter didn't recognize him.

"They told me he was Uncle Jack because there were girls in the school whose people were on the other side," the elderly nun recalled, "and they would ask you, 'Who was at your house last night?'" In other words, in order to protect her father, little Hanora's family had found it necessary to lie to her. When the fighting stopped, her mother told her the truth, but it only caused her to cry. "I went under the table and said, 'No, no, no, it was Uncle Jack.' And I was crazy about Uncle Jack because, naturally, when he would come to the house he was everything to me. But he was *definitely* Uncle Jack. And it took them quite awhile to get it into my mind that this was my father."

The Anglo-Irish War ended in 1921 with an 1,800-word treaty that partitioned off part of Ulster, granted Ireland its own parliament, and required that the new parliament's members swear an oath to the Crown. By the middle of 1922, the IRA had split and a civil war begun. The Chemist opposed the Treaty, and according to his daughter their neighbors boycotted the pharmacy as a result. He went on the lam again. Meanwhile, the mothers, wives, and sisters of anti-Treaty fighters, including Katty Woulfe, congregated each night in the Square at Abbeyfeale to say the rosary. One night a group of pro-Treaty locals attacked them with rotten eggs.

23.

HERE'S ANOTHER STORY, ONE that rhymes but at a slant. It's about a man named Maurice Woulfe who was known locally as the Solicitor. He was born in 1884, the same year as the Chemist but a bit farther afield, in Yorkshire, England. He was Dollie's younger brother and a grandson of Dicky Ned. His father, yet another Maurice, had been raised at the Glen before joining the British civil service as a gauger. For forty years the elder Maurice's job was to test the alcoholic content of whiskey, which in those days was barreled by distilleries and sold to independent bottlers in concentrated form. The Gauger Woulfe checked that *an uisce beatha* had not been too watered down and, in the process, is said to have become too fond of the drink.

Maurice the younger attended school in Aberdeen and worked briefly in London before reading law in Dublin. In 1915 he hung a shingle out in Abbeyfeale, just a few blocks from the Chemist's pharmacy. There he plied his trade until March 1916, when he volunteered for the 10th Battalion of the Royal Dublin Fusiliers, an infantry regiment in the British army. What might have motivated him to enter a recruiting station and sign on the dotted line isn't clear, although Irish boys had long fought in British uniform. In 1914, a full 10 per-

The Solicitor

ent of the army hailed from Ireland, and many of these boys marched off to war to the sound of crowds singing "Rule Britannia." These new soldiers recoiled at gruesome tales of German atrocities and hoped, perhaps naively, that cooperation with the war effort might result in Home Rule. The Solicitor, meanwhile, was tied to Britain through birth and education. His mother was a Presbyterian from Glasgow. Who could blame him if he sympathized with the Union Jack more readily than did his cousin the Chemist?

Whatever his reasoning, Maurice joined his unit at the Royal Barracks, a stately stone building in the center of Dublin that in 1798 had served as the site of Theobald Wolfe Tone's trial and pre-execution suicide. Among the ghosts of revolutions come and gone—this is where the Solicitor was on April 24, 1916, preparing to ship out to France, when that poet Patrick Pearse, his young drill instructor Con Colbert, and the others commenced their attack. British authorities immediately called on the 10th to cross the River Liffey and engage rebel forces at Dublin Castle and the South Dublin Union, the country's largest poorhouse, where Colbert himself helped direct the action.

As you might imagine, Katty Woulfe's brother was flush with patriotic vigor, so much so he had written a poem for the occasion, which begins:

> Hail! Ye the dawning, hail!
> The dawn of blood and steel.

One expects that the Solicitor felt less sanguine about the occasion, although his thoughts about, or indeed any of his actions during, that fateful day have been lost to history. He may have been angry, similar to one Irish soldier on the Western Front who wrote to his mother, "I am glad the rebels are getting squashed. The Irish regiments out here would like nothing better than to have a go at them with a bayonet."

Or maybe he felt more akin to Willie Dunne, the protagonist of Sebastian Barry's wonderful novel *A Long Long Way* (2005), who, like the Solicitor, found himself wearing a British uniform in Dublin on Easter Monday. The battle shocked Willie's fragile idealism, as did the violent death of a young rebel right beside him. Blood flowed, and so too did the questions. How had Irishmen come to fight Irishmen? Who was the real enemy?

And no matter how hard he tried, Willie couldn't rid himself of that encounter's awful stain: "He tried again in the morning but in the main he carried the young man's blood to Belgium on his uniform."

24.

THE SOLICITOR HAD ONLY begun to see the dawn of blood and steel. Like Willie he sailed to Europe—but only after officer's training and a transfer to the Royal Munster Fusiliers—and like Willie he was gassed at the Somme. "The gas boiled in like a familiar ogre," Barry writes in his novel. "With the same stately gracelessness it rolled to the edge of the parapet and then like the heads of a many-headed creature it toppled gently forward and sank down to join the waiting men."

Unlike Willie, however, the Solicitor got to come home, honorably discharged with a Silver War Badge. He resumed his practice in Abbeyfeale while making himself at home back at the Glen—which is where the IRA man Mossie Harnett found him in 1919. The boys of the West Limerick Brigade were going house to house collecting weapons, much as the Moonlighters had done during the Land War. It was a tried-and-true tactic, allowing them to disarm the countryside while sorting friend from foe based on who dared resist. After taking a Colt revolver and shotgun from the home of a British officer without any fuss, the party arrived at the Glen. "There we got some shotguns and cartridges after being strongly obstructed in our search," Harnett recalled with a certain sense of understatement. "Ned Ryan took strong objection to this behavior, and pointing his gun around, threatened to blow the brains out of anyone not staying quiet. In the confusion created we missed a fine revolver owned by Maurice."

It was, as it happens, his black Webley service revolver.

A year or so later, on September 18, those same IRA men ambushed the police patrol outside of town, killing Constable Mahony. Then the Black and Tans arrived, burning the pharmacy and sending the Chemist into the wind. The violence didn't end there, though.

Just two days later, at about six or seven o'clock in the evening, a rural postman named Patrick Harnett ambled out of town on the way to his uncle's house in Kilconlea. At some point he ran into Jerry Healy, a blacksmith's apprentice headed in the same direction. They were on the Castleisland road when witnesses spied a Black and Tan named Thomas Huckerby leave the barracks. Huckerby followed them out of town, after which witnesses heard two shots. The young men were both found dead in a field.

So egregious were the killings that on September 22 the authorities took the unusual step of opening an inquiry, during which the Solicitor represented the Harnett and Healy families. On the stand, a police sergeant testified that Huckerby had confessed to killing the boys, claiming that he had followed them and, when they ran, shot them. Huckerby even led the sergeant to the bodies. "They were about a yard apart and the younger of the two had a soft hat clutched in his left hand as though he had taken it off to enable him to run faster," according to an account of the trial. "They had climbed through the hedge before they had been shot. There was no sign of a struggle."

In reply to a question from the Solicitor, the sergeant admitted that the young men had been unarmed. He said, one imagines reluctantly, "that the shooting struck him as being drastic under the circumstances."

Huckerby, meanwhile, was an eighteen-year-old West Indian who only recently had been transferred to Abbeyfeale after being accused of killing a sixty-year-old man in nearby Shanagolden. In fact, Jimmy Collins, the Chemist's apprentice, later claimed that the IRA ambush that killed Constable Mahony actually had been an attempt to assassinate Huckerby. "He was a thorough blackguard from his first day in the town," Collins remembered, and "a crack-shot with a revolver."

At the inquiry, a few additional witnesses testified before the court adjourned. Appearances had been maintained, and in the end Huckerby was not disciplined.

Then, on the morning of October 7, just after arriving at his office in Abbeyfeale, the police arrested the Solicitor. They charged him with the unlawful possession of a weapon—that same black Webley service revolver that Mossie Harnett later regretted not having confiscated for the IRA. The authorities transferred Woulfe to Limerick city, and according to one account Huckerby even helped accompany him there. Maurice Woulfe was released a couple weeks later and fined ten shillings.

25.

THESE TWO STORIES, OF the Chemist Woulfe and his cousin the Solicitor, have interested me for years, probably because they represent two contrasting ideas of Ireland, of patriotism, and of what it means to be a Woulfe. Of course, without their own words to inspect, we should be careful not to parse their differences with too fine a comb. Still, I think it would be fair to say that the Chemist subscribed to a more romantic view than his cousin. That his nationalism was the nationalism of the Desmonds and the Fenians, of blood gloriously spilt—"Hail! Ye the dawning, hail!" as Con Colbert wrote—while the Solicitor likely learned very different lessons in the trenches.

Then there is religion. Remember Dicky Ned's prophecy, "that there would be Woulfes in Limerick and Kerry while the Shannon rolled into the Atlantic, and that more than an average number of them would devote their lives to the service of God"? In the Woulfe family, that God had always been a Catholic God, the Pope's God, and yet the Solicitor's own mother was a Presbyterian. When it came time to bury her in the ancient graveyard at Templeathea, old Bessie Cockburn was not allowed in. So Maurice, perhaps with the help of his son Seán de Bhulbh, built her a stone mausoleum just on the outside of the cemetery walls. A fluent Irish speaker, the Solicitor attached a sign above the door that reads, "Muintir de Bhulbh," or Woulfe Family.

On the outside dreaming in, you might say.

And yet, even after years of relative peace, the violence continued. A newspaper report from the summer of 1934—more than a decade after the end of the war—notes that the Solicitor's home, just outside of Abbeyfeale, "was attacked at night. Mr. Woulfe's bedroom was fired into and the window shattered by gunshot pellets. Several rifle bullets were also fired through the roof of the house." The article didn't say whether anyone was hurt or what might have provoked the

The Woulfe mausoleum at Templeathea

attack. For that you have to consult the archived police reports, twenty-nine pages in all.

Unsurprisingly, the "outrage," as the police called it, was related to an ongoing lawsuit. It involved a foreclosed-upon pub, a massive debt to the bank, and a group of sureties: several local men who were on the hook should the debtor not agree to terms. As a representative for the local deep pockets, the Solicitor found himself in the gunsights of the debtor's brother and his gang. By intimidating Woulfe, they hoped that the sureties would not sign off on a deal that forfeited the debtor's house and land.

This, the police understood, served as the immediate provocation for the middle-of-the-night attack. But their reports acknowledge that it also carried with it a "political tinge." After all, Woulfe was president of the local Fine Gael, a political party formed out of the remnants of the pro-Treaty forces, while the debtor was Fianna Fáil, the party whose core members had fought the Treaty. In fact, the local

Fianna Fáil club—whose vice president just happened to be the Chemist—had posted a letter to the bank's directors warning them not to take any "drastic action" against the debtor.

The civil war's violence threatened to boil over once again. When the police executed search warrants they discovered a hiding spot for weapons in a ceiling crawl space as well as an empty, shotgun-sized strap under a kitchen table. Fears were widespread that the IRA might go to war again, and Fine Gael responded with the creation of a quasi-Fascist group known as the Blueshirts. Just five days before the attack, the Solicitor had published a letter to the editor complaining that the police had not properly responded to a violent attack on Fine Gael dancegoers in Abbeyfeale just a few months earlier.

The papers didn't report on the police investigation into the starlit shotgun blast through the Solicitor's bedroom window. His own granddaughter knew nothing about it, only remembered that her father—Seán de Bhulbh—had mentioned the family finding need of a bodyguard when he was a boy. Were these two Woulfes, the Chemist and the Solicitor, whose offices were just yards apart in tiny Abbeyfeale, friendly with each other? For that matter, did they even consider themselves to be related?

No one seems to know, and of course the answers would only further complicate our idea of Muintir de Bhulbh.

Remember: the stories we tell are forever hiding the ones we don't.

26.

MY SISTERS AND I grew up surrounded by the totems of American Irish-ness: Clancy Brothers records, family history, Dad's silly Irish accent. And, of course, more than a fair amount of alcohol.

"Brendan Maaaaartin," Dad liked to call out, and when I was a kid a cheap paperback copy of my namesake Brendan Behan's *Confessions of an Irish Rebel* sat on one of the blue-painted bookshelves in the basement, serving as the quintessential expression of a certain kind of loud, mischievous, language-obsessed Irishman. Meanwhile,

Brother and sister, ca. 1975

my sisters and I learned—in this instance from the Clancys—to yell at the top of our lungs bits of rhyme like

> Up the long ladder and down the short rope
> To hell with King Billy and God bless the pope
> If that doesn't do, we'll tear them in two
> And send them to hell with their red, white, and blue!

    We had no idea what any of that meant, of course, and were barely old enough to read in the papers about IRA bombs and hunger strikes. I watched my dad fill up the fridge with his PBR and noticed the way his body slumped at night in his favorite chair. I didn't know yet that Behan, too ill to type, had been forced to dictate his *Confessions*, or that he'd died at forty-one. All that mattered to me was the Irish-ness of my name, the literary energy of it, how its gravity helped draw me into the safety of my family's orbit. This is who we are: the Wolfes of Davenport, Iowa. *Brendan Maaaaartin.* It took me years to notice that I had never met Father Martin or to wonder why.

And what does that even mean, the Wolfes of Davenport, Iowa? Bridget and Sara had never cottoned to their Irish-ness in the way I had. That may have been why, in addition to still-raw feelings stemming from our parents' divorce, they chose not to accompany Dad on his trip back to Kerry in 1998. To be a Wolfe meant something slightly different to them. For starters, they both had been adopted, although Bridget's story is the more typically Irish American. I know because, one afternoon in the summer of 2007, a woman emailed me claiming to be her half-sister. She explained that her mother, an Irish Catholic teenager living in Davenport in the 1960s, had become unexpectedly pregnant. Rather than acknowledge the situation, her parents had hidden her away in an out-of-town hospital for months, forcing her to wear a wedding ring and lie about a husband in Vietnam. The man who had arranged this peculiarly Irish Catholic form of exile was none other than Father Martin, who, when the baby was born, handed her over to Mom and Dad.

Unplanned pregnancies can undo some families while creating new ones. "Father Martin set the whole thing up," Dad told me on a visit shortly before he died. He considered us to be good Catholics—we *were* good Catholics—and it helped that I was Irish. Or at least of Irish ancestry."

He paused for effect.

"It was my only redeeming quality."

"Bridget Colleen!" he liked to call when my sister walked into a room, always keeping her close within the orbit.

I showed him pictures on Facebook of Bridget's birth mother. The physical resemblance between the two was striking, and it turned out that both were nurses. And yet it's also true that people comment about how much Bridget and I look alike—*How can you not be related?*—as if the prerogatives of family don't exert their own kind of control.

A few weeks later, Dad was back home in Iowa and out listening to Irish music when he texted me that he was "looking right at Bridget Colleen's birth mother!!"

"Life is way way too weird," he added.

Though tempted, and probably full of beer, Dad decided not to introduce himself. It's not always clear which relationships we should acknowledge and celebrate and which we should keep to ourselves. But that's the thing about DNA: it simplifies otherwise complex lives, reducing us to the moment of our birth, a fake wedding ring, an expectant couple waiting nervously just outside the hospital room.

Bridget has always been a Wolfe in ways that may have defied DNA yet conformed in other ways, in ways that we could instinctively understand. Sara didn't have even that. She was married that summer of the flood in a Lutheran church, and I remember her telling me how odd it was that she and her husband were the only black people at their own wedding.

27.

IN THE SPRING OF 2019, Bridget and I flew to Ireland. She had never been there, despite having traveled the globe, while I had been working on this book for years and wanted to explore some of the places I'd written about. The day we landed we met Gemma Hensey and her first cousin Philomena Buckley in West Limerick for lunch. Their great-great grandfather and mine (the immigrant John R. Wolfe) had been brothers, and when we arrived, never before having seen each other, we nevertheless recognized the Wolfe face.

"It's round, a little fat," Gemma said, and then gestured at my sister: "Now she's something different altogether, isn't she?"

Gemma is a generous and outspoken seventy-something, and she invited us both to lunch the next day at the family homestead at Beale Hill, near Ballybunion, in North Kerry. Bridget was to be in Dublin that day but Gemma sent me directions and in the morning I set off. When I pulled in, a few minutes past twelve, a white-haired old man stood in the driveway with his hands clasped behind his back. I rolled down the window and asked whether he was Séamus Woulfe.

The old house at Dromlought

"I am indeed and you're very welcome," he said, shaking my hand through the window.

He showed me the name of the house, Dúinín, after the nearby Cliffs of Dooneen, made famous by a folk ballad of the same name. The lyrics were written by Séamus's wife's grand-uncle Jack McAuliffe, who had visited this area for a week back in the 1930s, after which he disappeared. This last part is according to Gemma's father, Tom Woulfe, in an oral history conducted when he was in his late nineties. People thought McAuliffe had gone to America, Woulfe said, but in fact he'd gone to London and died in the Coventry Blitz.

> You may travel far far from your own native home
> Far away o'er the mountains, far away o'er the foam
> But of all the fine places that I've ever seen
> There is none to compare with the Cliffs of Dooneen

McAuliffe was from Lixnaw, only about fifteen kilometers away, but such were the effects of the cliffs, I suppose! Séamus told a story of some old lady who, upon leaving her house, put her hand to her brow and declared, "Sure I hate to leave dear old Beale."

"She was only going seven miles to the store!" he laughed.

The landscape has its claws in people out here. You can see the Atlantic from the house, and smell it. The salt has settled into the rocky soil, making farming difficult. Séamus raised dairy cows for a living here, while his great grandfather, Thomas Woulfe, leased a farm, Beale Hill, just a few hundred yards away. This is the same Tom Woulfe who began plowing his land in 1870, promptly fathered nine children, and after armed Moonlighters harassed him, stopped paying rent for three years. He was evicted in 1885.

This same lovely, wind-blistered countryside where I was treated to a lunch of ham, pork short ribs, green cabbage, and baked potatoes is where three hundred friends and neighbors, including twenty musicians, showed up to help Tom and his family put in the crops after the landlord had suddenly allowed them to return.

There's word in Irish for this kind of cooperative labor: *meitheal*. "Everybody needed help back then," Séamus's wife, Mina, told me. "There weren't enough horses and draft animals so we all had to share."

The music is an especially memorable detail, but this happy ending can obscure how difficult and violent life was out here. Tom's brother Maurice farmed at Kiltean, near Beale. Two of his sons, you'll recall, were indicted for murder but never tried. Séamus took me on a tour of the area, pointing out what he called the old, worthless bogs. He's an aggressive driver, my cousin Séamus is, and I'll admit I was worried some about another death occurring in these parts.

The fields lay flat and open, the clouds hang low. This is where John R. Wolfe grew up. When his father left Athea for North Kerry, this is where they came. And when John R. journeyed to Lost Nation, this is what he left behind. His farm bordered Kiltean in an area called Dromlought.

"There's still an old house there," Séamus said, so we sped off in that direction.

An old whitewashed cottage sat adjacent to a more modern abode, its thatched roof caved in. The place had an Ozymandias feel to it, and as I walked around Séamus hummed a bar of "The Cliffs of Dooneen."

> *You may travel far far from your own native home ...*

I remembered Dollie Woulfe's letter, about how she and her grandparents could summon the dead of previous generations, calling each by name.

Dicky Ned, I thought to myself as a bit of rain began to squirt down. *The Book of Athea.*

John R. and his son, the Judge.

Father Pat.

Ray, Gladys, and Maurice.

Not to mention all the other Maurices: Maurice the Indian fighter and Maurice the Solicitor.

Old Maurice.

Young Maurice.

The Chemist.

The Commissioner.

The Barrister and the Gauger.

Short Dick and Brown Dick.

Uncle Melvin of Lost Nation.

Dollie herself and her grandmother Kate.

Sister Íde, Seán de Bhulbh, and old Bessie Cockburn.

Thomas Woulfe of Beale Hill.

And of course my dad, Tom Wolfe, of Davenport, Iowa.

We're always coming back, aren't we? As we left the caved-in house at Dromlought, another car pulled in and Séamus stopped to chat with the driver. She rented the newer house and he wanted to explain our presence. "We have a Woulfe from America in the car with us," he told the woman behind the wheel. "Ah sure, more Woulfes," she laughed. "Don't you know a whole van of them showed up another time."

Séamus motored back in the direction of Beale, maneuvering quickly down impossibly narrow roads and through a landscape that reminded me a lot of Lost Nation.

"Now. You've seen where you came from, Brendan," he said. "Where, then, are you going?"

In the backseat his wife cackled. "Isn't that a question for a priest?"

NOTES

1.

page 1, "Origin of the Species": Tom Wolfe, "Origin of the Species; or, Whatever Happened to Good Old What's-His-Name," unpublished, August 10, 1975.

page 1, the humorist Richard Armour: Armour (1906–1989) was a poet and historical satirist who authored, among many others, *It All Started with Columbus* (New York: Bantam, [1953] 1963), which sat on Dad's bookshelf for my entire childhood and which influenced the brand of humor in "Origin of the Species."

page 3, "What I remember most": Tom Wolfe, "Memories," unpublished, 2004.

2.

page 4, *Wolfe's History*: P. B. Wolfe, editor-in-chief, *Wolfe's History of Clinton County, Iowa* (Indianapolis, Indiana: B. F. Bowen & Company, 1911).

page 4, referred to as the Kunta Kinte: Kunta Kinte was the enslaved protagonist of Alex Haley's *Roots: The Saga of an American Family*, published in 1976 and the next year adapted into a popular television miniseries. Brought from Africa in chains, Kunta Kinte was not an immigrant, and my dad likely meant to compare John R. Wolfe with him only in the sense that they both were the progenitors of American families.

page 7, left Ireland in 1847: *New York, Passenger Lists, 1820–1957*, online database at Ancestry.com. Year: 1847; Arrival: New York, New York; Microfilm Serial: M237; Microfilm Roll: 68; Line: 6; List Number: 621.

page 7, "The Emerald Isle": P. B. Wolfe, *Wolfe's History*, 1:628.

page 8, their religion was perceived: David M. Emmons, *Beyond the American Pale: The Irish in the West, 1845–1910* (Norman: University of Oklahoma Press, 2010), 44ff.

page 8, "staunch Catholic": The biography actually describes John R. Wolfe as a "stanch Catholic," which I assume to be a typographical error.

page 8, two-boat Irish: Emmons, *Beyond the American Pale*, 1, 3, 9–10.

page 9, "Where there are now": "Obituary of John B. Wolfe, Pioneer," *Oxford Mirror* (Oxford Junction, Iowa), February 3, 1916, 5. The obituary was mistitled, although James Wolfe did have a younger brother John.

page 9, "This is a wild reckless Country": Maurice H. Wolfe to Maurice Woulfe, April 12, 1868. Irish National Archives. Transcription courtesy of Kerby Miller. The original letters are held by Timothy Woulfe, Athea, County Limerick.

page 10, "I had a fine 'Scalp'": Maurice H. Wolfe to Maurice Woulfe, September 11, 1870.

3.

page 10, first cousin Maurice: Accompanying John R. Wolfe and his family were Maurice Wolfe (ca. 1800–1879), his wife, Ellen Catherine Carey Wolfe, and their children James Carey, Ellen, Maurice Carey, Mary, and Johanna.

page 10, Black Star Line: Carl C. Cutler, *Queens of the Western Ocean: The Story of America's Mail and Passenger Sailing Lines* (Annapolis, Maryland: U.S. Naval Institute, 1961), 381–382, 384–385.

page 10, bare-bones account: "Arrived," *New York Daily Tribune*, August 23, 1847, 3.

page 10, landed on pier 30: Cutler, *Queens of the Western Ocean*, map inside front cover.

page 11, usually suffering from typhus: See Arthur L. Gelston and Thomas C. Jones, "Typhus Fever: Report of an Epidemic in New York City in 1847," *The Journal of Infectious Diseases* 136, no. 6 (December 1977): 813–821.

page 11, other Wolfes followed: John R. Wolfe's brother Thomas Richard Wolfe (1811–1876) immigrated in 1848 and his brothers Maurice Richard (1802–1870) and Richard (1815–1906) in 1849. His cousin Maurice Wolfe's brother Richard (1795–1871) came from Ireland in 1848.

page 11, son of Maurice James: This was Maurice James "Young Maurice" Woulfe (ca. 1763–before 1838).

page 11, five purchases: U.S. General Land Office, Certificates 5902, 5919, 5920, 5939, and 5950, dated October 14, 1835, at Marion County, Missouri. Accessed via Ancestry.com.

page 11, Brothers Richard and John: They were Richard Wolfe (1802–btw. 1850 and 1860) and John Harnett Wolfe (1807–before May 25, 1856).

page 11, In a letter home: J. D. H., "Written Over a Century Ago; Interesting Letter from West Limerick Exile," *Limerick Leader*, May 13, 1939, 10.

page 12, nieces and nephews: Several children of John R. Wolfe's sister Margaret Ellen Wolfe Sheehan (b. 1818) immigrated to Newport, Rhode Island, including Patrick W. Sheehan (1843–1894), Dennis Wolfe Sheehan (1852–1907), Bridget Ellen Sheehan Nixon (1853–1910), and Thomas Sheehan (b. 1860).

page 12, another cousin: This is John E. Wolfe (1837–1918), whose son Maurice Vincent Wolfe was born in 1874.

page 12, "They had just gone": "Death of Dennis W. Sheehan," *The News* (Newport, Rhode Island), August 26, 1907, 7.

4.

page 13, thirteen-year-old Arthur Collison: "Arthur Collison Instantly Killed; Thrown from a Wagon and Run Over; His Chest Being Crushed," *Carroll Sentinel* (Iowa), November 3, 1903, 1. His mother was Ann Wolfe Collison (1845–1912), who emigrated with her parents and siblings in 1849.

page 13, killed when a hurricane struck: "Maurice Wolfe, His Wife and Six Children Drown At Angelton, Texas," *Laredo Times*, July 25, 1909, 12; "Dead Body Found," *Galveston Daily News*, August 17, 1909, 1; "Man and Six Children Are Drowned Near Angleton," *Denton Record Chronicle*, July 24, 1909, 2. Maurice Patrick Wolfe (1873–1909) was the son of Richard Downey Wolfe (1829–1885), who emigrated in 1849. His wife was Mary Ellen Morrow Wolfe, of Lafayette, Indiana, and their children Mildred, Richard, Julia, Margaret, Mary, and an unnamed infant.

page 13, the death of Daniel F. Wolfe: Untitled, *Indiana Weekly Messenger* (Pennsylvania), November 22, 1882, 2.

page 14, "From Wessington the murderer drove": "Murder and Suicide," *Wheeling Register* (West Virginia), November 16, 1832, 1.

page 14, John W. Maher: "John Maher Shot," *Grand Forks Daily Herald*, July 23, 1895, 1. See also a belated obituary: "Stayed on the Land; An Irish Colony in U.S.A.," *Limerick Leader*, November 26, 1938, 13.

5.

page 15, "From time to time": James Miller Guinn, *History of the State of California and Biographical Record of Coast Counties* (Chicago: Chapman Publishing Company, 1904), 563.

page 15, photographic portrait: Marin History Museum, *Images of America: Early San Rafael* (Charleston, South Carolina: Arcadia Publishing, 2008), 63.

page 16, "While going to his store": Untitled, *Upper Des Moines Republican* (Algona, Iowa), July 17, 1918, 4.

page 16, Maurice's son: "Pioneer Family Scion: John M. Wolfe Killed in Bayshore Accident," *Daily Independent Journal* (San Rafael, California), July 13, 1951, 6.

6.

page 17, great uncle Melvin: This is Melvin Maurice Wolfe (1904–1990).

page 17, "The nurse ... reports": Tom Wolfe, "Origin of the Species."

page 17, "One version, not very widely credited": P. B. Wolfe, *Wolfe's History*, 1:274.

page 18, with eleven hundred acres: *The History of Clinton County, Iowa* (Chicago: Western Historical Company, 1879), 645.

page 19, "Towards dusk of a summer evening": Tom Wolfe, "Memories," unpublished, 2004.

7.

page 20, "The hospital [in Listowel] is crowded": *Kerry Evening Post* (Tralee, County Kerry), April 14, 1847 (reprinted from the *Kerry Examiner*). Quoted in Bryan MacMahon, *The Great Famine in Tralee and North Kerry* (Cork, Ireland: Mercier Press, 2017), 129. See also John D. Pierse, *Teampall Bán: Aspects of the Famine in North Kerry, 1845–1852* (Listowel, Ireland: Tidy Towns Committee, 2014).

page 20, "the agent having charge": P. B. Wolfe, *Wolfe's History*, 2:912.

page 20, "a mere cottage": Lord John Russell, ed., *Memoirs, Journal, and Correspondence of Thomas Moore* (New York: D. Appleton and Company, 1857), 467.

8.

page 22, "ribbons of myths": Jill Lepore, *These Truths: A History of the United States* (New York: W. W. Norton & Company, 2018), 9.

page 22, "It is *imagined* because": Benedict Anderson, *Imagined Communities: Reflections on the Origin and Spread of Nationalism*, revised edition (London: Verso Books, [1983] 2006), 6. Anderson, as it happens, was an Irishman.

page 22, Anderson quotes: Anderson, *Imagined Communities*, 6.

9.

page 23, emigrated in 1885: U.S. Passport Application, Chicago, May 11, 1899. Accessed via Ancestry.com. It indicates that Richard W. Wolfe came to the United States in 1885. Although it lists his birth as August 1870, civil records from the union of Newcastle, County Limerick, Ireland, give his birthdate as August 25, 1866.

page 23, older brother Patrick: This is Patrick Richard Wolfe (1861–1939).

page 23, "orator and wordsmith": Gerald Leinwand, *Mackerels in the Moonlight: Four Corrupt American Mayors* (Jefferson, North Carolina: McFarland & Company, Inc. Publishers, 2004), 52.

page 23, "Capitol hill is influenced": "Admirer Writes Thompson Guards U.S. from British King," *Chicago Daily Tribune*, March 20, 1927, 5.

page 23, *Kerryman* newspaper announced: "Chicago's Greatest Commissioner: Visit of Mr. Richard W. Woulfe of Chicago to Ireland," *Kerryman* (Tralee), May 16, 1931, 15.

page 23, silk-suited "union members": "'Political Racket' Is Laid to Capone: Gangster Is Becoming a Power in the Chicago City Hall, According to Rumors," *New York Times*, April 19, 1930, 9.

page 25, "a lad of but [nineteen] years": The newspaper has Wolfe coming to America at the age of sixteen, which would fit with the date of birth on his passport but not with Irish birth records (see above).

page 25, forty-three-page lecture: Richard W. Wolfe, *Culture: A Lecture* (Chicago: A. Kroch, 1928).

page 25, helped author a bill: William H. Stuart, *Share the Profits! The Story of Richard W. Wolfe and His Conclusions* (Chicago: M. A. Donohue & Company, 1939), 59–60.

page 25, in 1969 the legislature: Raymond Tatalovich, *Nativism Reborn? The Official English Language Movement and the American States* (Lexington: University Press of Kentucky, 1995), 69.

page 25, "There is the real, upstanding": "Chicago Commissioner: West Limerick Man's Views on the U.S.A.," *Cork Examiner*, March 2, 1931, 4.

page 26, The Commissioner's wife: This is Helen Lenz (1873–1961), a native of Illinois whose parents were German immigrants.

page 26, historical record of these reunions: "The New Ireland: Impressions of Changes, Views of Ex-Commissioner Wolfe," *Limerick Leader*, August 22, 1931, 7. The article begins, "Our Killmallock correspondent writes ..."

page 26, "I'm weary of the city life": Richard W. Wolfe, *Culture*, 22. The poem is titled "Beside the Sea."

page 26, once mocked the Commissioner's love: "Critic of Streets Urges Wolfe to a Life of Poesy: Wasted as Official, Ald. Mose Says," *Chicago Daily Tribune*, July 28, 1928, 3.

page 26, "O, let me live": Richard W. Wolfe, *Culture*, 22.

page 26, slim but dense book: Patrick Woulfe, *Sloinnte Gaedheal is Gall: Irish Names and Surnames* (Dublin: M. H. Gill & Son, 1922).

page 26, "the remarkable intellectual prowess": "The New Ireland: Impressions of Changes, Views of Ex-Commissioner Wolfe," *Limerick Leader*, August 22, 1931, 7.

page 27, "holocaust of a grim": "Irish Cinema Tragedy; Shocking Holocaust in Co. Limerick," *The Liberator* (Tralee), September 7, 1926, 4.

page 27, "I beg to thank": John Begley, *The Diocese of Limerick in the Sixteenth and Seventeenth Centuries* (Dublin: Browne and Nolan, 1927), viii.

page 27, posthumously collected ... and auctioned: "Irish Library, Being the Collection of Rev. Patrick Woulfe, P.P.," advertisement, *Cork Examiner*,

June 17, 1933, 4; "Auction of Library," *Irish Press* (Dublin), June 27, 1933, 7.

page 27, Richard Woulfe of Abbeyfeale: "Funeral of Mr. R. B. Woulfe, Brother-in-law of 1916 Leader," *Irish Press* (Dublin), April 23, 1937, 2.

page 29, "speech being Irish": Quoted in Aidan Doyle, *A History of the Irish Language from the Norman Invasion to Independence* (Oxford, United Kingdom: Oxford University Press, 2015), 43.

page 29, largest festival: Mainchín Seoighe, *The Story of Kilmallock* (Kilmallock, Ireland: Kilmallock Historical Society, 1987), 258.

page 29, Last Rights ... According to Woulfe's obituary: "Late Rev. P. Wolfe: Regret in Kilmallock at Cappa P.P.'s Death," *Kerryman* (Tralee), May 13, 1933, 1.

page 29, his residence: "Escaped Prisoners: Irish Priest's Residence Searched in London," *Cork Examiner*, November 22, 1919, 8.

page 29, again subjected to a search: "Kilmallock Presbytery Searched," *Cork Examiner*, September 25, 1920, 8.

page 30, standard account: John O'Heyne, *The Irish Dominicans of the Seventeenth Century* (Dundalk, Ireland: William Tempest, [1706] 1902), 85–87.

page 30, "was taken and hanged": John Begley, *The Diocese of Limerick in the Sixteenth and Seventeenth Centuries*, 338.

page 30, "It is a strange fact": Myles O'Reilly, "Ireland's Martyrs," *Catholic World: A Monthly Magazine of General Literature and Science* 8 (March 1869): 849–850.

10.

page 31, memorialized only bits: "The New Ireland: Impressions of Changes, Views of Ex-Commissioner Wolfe," *Limerick Leader*, August 22, 1931, 7.

page 31, executive of the Catholic: "Pithy Provincial News," *Irish Independent* (Dublin), May 18, 1927, 8.

page 32, come under investigation ... checks: "Sue Mayor for Flood Funds: Charge Misuse of Money Given for Sufferers," *Chicago Daily Tribune*, February 8, 1931, 1.

page 32, opened a separate investigation: "Swanson Opens Secret Quiz on City Contracts," *Chicago Daily Tribune*, February 20, 1931, 6.

page 32, neglected to collect: "Wolfe Charged with Neglect in $30,000 Deal," *Chicago Daily Tribune*, March 19, 1931, 10.

page 33, appeared before a grand jury: "Jury Quiz on City Treasury: Ex-Officials Will Be Asked about Charges," *Chicago Daily Tribune*, May 7, 1931, 1; "Accuses Wolfe of Favoritism in Civil Service," *Chicago Daily Tribune*, June 3, 1931, 12.

page 33, "The lust of gold": Richard W. Wolfe, *Culture*, 22.

page 33, a couple of men came in: "A Life Saved; Wicklow Bank Manager and Raider; Murder Charge," *Freeman's Journal*, March 5, 1924, 1, 3.

page 33–34, delivered a lecture: "The New Ireland: Impressions of Changes, Views of Ex-Commissioner Wolfe," *Limerick Leader*, August 22, 1931, 7. Edmond Richard "Old Ned" Woulfe lived from 1788 to 1876. Dr. Timothy Woulfe (1885–1969) was the son of James P. "Paddy" Woulfe (1842–1922) and Honora "Nanno" Maher (1844–1927) and the brother of Father Patrick Woulfe (1872–1933).

page 34, probe into City Hall payroll records: "Swanson Begins Move to Probe City Hall Books; Overloaded Pay Rolls His Target in Inquiry," *Chicago Daily Tribune*, March 5, 1930, 3.

page 34, gunmen entered the garage: "Slaying Linked to Pay Roll Quiz: Gunmen Kill in Raid to Get City Records; Books Also Sought by Prosecutor," *Chicago Daily Tribune*, March 10, 1930, 1.

page 35: "But minds opprest": Richard W. Wolfe, *Culture*, 22.

11.

page 36: "powerful, ruthless hand and brain": "Commissioner Woulfe's Views on Ireland and America; Corrective Ideas of Chicago," *Liberator* (Tralee), June 20, 1931, 4.

page 36, "the international banker": "How America Is Hit by the International Banker; Some Staggering Figures," *Limerick Leader*, October 10, 1931, 3.

page 36, "tentacles of the Baruchs": Oswald Garrison Villard, "Coughlin Attacks Jews," *Decatur Herald* (Illinois), August 31, 1936, 4.

page 37, in one chapter: Stuart, *Share the Profits!*, 115–130.

12.

page 37, agitating against the union: Old Ned is mentioned in "Repeal in Newcastle—Grand Entertainment to Ten Catholic Clergymen," *Freeman's Journal* (Dublin), December 19, 1842, 4 (abridged from the *Cork Examiner*); "Repeal Meeting at the Trades' Hall," *Cork Examiner*, December 30, 1842, 1.

page 37, Short Dick: Richard Maurice "Short Dick" Woulfe died in 1824. His brother was James Maurice "The Barrister" Woulfe (1732–1817). Their father was Maurice James "Old Maurice" Woulfe (1690–1792).

page 38, "owned at one time ... spun the wool": Stuart, *Share the Profits!*, 6.

page 38, taught at the Glen: This is Michael Sheahan (ca. 1832–1902).

page 38, "He spoke without affectation": J. D. H., "Last of the Limerick Hedge Schools," *Limerick Leader*, April 27, 1935, 12. J. D. H. was the journalist J. D. Harnett.

page 38, rescued from drowning: J. D. H., "Last of the Limerick Hedge Schools"; Stuart, *Share the Profits!*, 6.

page 39, "always searching": Stuart, *Share the Profits!*, 8.

page 39, "The boy used the brain": Stuart, *Share the Profits!*, 9.

page 39, "There was Joan Grogan": Jane C. "Dollie" Woulfe to Sister M. Caelan Wolfe, August 1956.

13.

page 41, *Áth an tSléibhe*: Gerard Curtin, *Every Field Had a Name: The Place-Names of West Limerick* (Sliabh Luachra Books, 2012).

page 41, "liminal zones": Ciaran Carson, *The Táin: A New Translation of the Táin Bó Cúailnge* (New York: Viking, 2008), xviii.

14.

page 42, "Goold of the silver tongue ... estates": "Veraschoyle Goold Estate, West Limerick," letter to the editor by E. W. White, *Kerry People* (Tralee), September 29, 1906, 3. A longer version of the cow anecdote also appears in Kevin Danaher, ed., *Folktales from the Irish Countryside* (New York: MJF Books, 1998), 45–46. It is told by Richard "Old Dick"

Denihan, of the parish of Athea. Kevin Danaher (Caoimhín Ó Danachair) was himself a native of Athea and responsible for copying the Sergeant Maurice H. Wolfe letters for the Irish National Archives.

page 42, Dicky Ned's nephew: Edmond Woulfe White (bap. 1854–1922) was the son of Dicky Ned's sister Bridget Woulfe White (ca. 1829–1911) and her husband, Michael White (d. after 1903). He practiced law in Belfast.

page 42, true and fair landlords: E. W. White, "Veraschoyle Goold Estate, West Limerick."

page 42, "most of them with royal titles": Stuart, *Share the Profits!*, 12.

page 43, story of his cousin: Thomas Woulfe (1841–1915), of Beale Hill, was the son of James Richard Woulfe (1800–1875).

page 43, murdered in Kerry: "The Horrible Tragedy in Kerry: A Landlord Murdered," *Cork Examiner*, April 1, 1882, 2; "Terrible Agrarian Murder in Kerry: A Magistrate Shot Dead," *Kerry Evening Post* (Tralee), April 1, 1882, 3.

page 43, farmhand was murdered: "A Noteworthy Funeral," *Nenagh Guardian*, April 26, 1882, 4.

page 43: "A farmer named Patrick Quane": "The Release of Mr. Parnell—Further Raids," *Kerry Evening Post* (Tralee), April 15, 1882, 3.

page 44: a sub-sheriff, three bailiffs: "An Eviction on the Property of Lord Listowel," *Kerry Sentinel* (Tralee), April 10, 1885, 4.

page 44, acreage as "prime": "Evictions in North Kerry," *Kerry Evening Post* (Tralee), April 11, 1885, 3.

page 45, "some three hundred persons": "Past and Present," *Kerry Weekly Reporter and Commercial Advertiser* (Tralee), May 23, 1885, 2.

15.

page 45: Tom Woulfe's brother: Maurice Woulfe (ca. 1823–1909) farmed in Kiltean, County Kerry, and had nine children with his wife, Mary Cronin Woulfe.

page 45: accused of murder: "The Ballybunion Homicide," *Cork Examiner*, September 8, 1892, 3.

page 45: early report: "The Ballybunion Homicide," *Cork Examiner*, September 15, 1892, 6.

page 45: prosecutor later contended: "Kerry Cases at the Winter Azzises," *Kerry Sentinel* (Tralee), December 10, 1892, 3.

page 45: letter to the editor: A. M. Bowan (Rowan?), "Answer to Mr Morley—Murders in Kerry," letter to the editor of the *Irish Times*, *Kerry Evening Post* (Tralee), March 8, 1893, 4.

16.

page 46, "inaugurated a system": E. W. White, "Veraschoyle Goold Estate, West Limerick."

page 46, "truly grave": "The Rev. Ryan and Archdeacon Goold," *Cork Examiner*, January 29, 1867, 4; "Archdeacon Goold and the Administrator of Athea," *Freeman's Journal and Daily Commercial Advertiser* (Dublin), January 31, 1867, 3 (reprinted from the *Munster News*).

page 47, hosted a banquet: "Banquet at Athea to the Royal Irish Constabulary," *Cork Examiner*, September 23, 1867, 3 (reprinted from the *Limerick Chronicle*).

page 47, during the worst of the fighting: E. W. White, "Veraschoyle Goold Estate, West Limerick."

17.

page 47, began discussing: "The Goold Estate, Co. Limerick," *Kerry Weekly Reporter* (Tralee), October 24, 1903, 3; "The Goold Estate," *Cork Examiner*, May 22, 1905, 5.

page 48, "I watched this field": John B. Keane, *The Field*, new revised text, edited by Ben Barnes (Dublin: Mercier Press, 1991), 26.

page 50, "This is what we'd be": *The Field*, directed by Jim Sheridan, 1990.

page 50, "The difference being as simple": Anton Shammas, "Autocartography: The Case of Palestine, Michigan," in *The Geography of Identity*, edited by Patricia Yeager (Ann Arbor: University of Michigan Press, 1996), 466.

18.

page 50, "It's my child": *The Field*, directed by Jim Sheridan, 1990.

page 50–51, tenants at this historic moment: Richard James "Brown Dick" Woulfe (1853–1915) was the son of John Maurice Woulfe (1830–1876) and Honora Barry Woulfe (b. 1831) and the husband of Ellen Maher Woulfe (ca. 1849–1943), whose sister Honora "Nanno" Maher Woulfe (1844–1927) married James Patrick "Paddy" Woulfe (1842–1922) and became the mother of Father Pat and Dr. Tim.

19.

page 51, His obituary: "Obituary: Death and Funeral of Mr. R. E. Woulfe, Cratloe, Athea; an Appreciation," *Limerick Leader*, June 1, 1910, 4.

page 52, "In 1903 these three old people": National Folklore Collection, The Schools' Collection, Volume 0485, Page 321. Accessed via dúchas.ie.

page 52, scholarly article: Patrick Woulfe, ed., "Elegy on Capt. O'Sullivan," *Irisleabar na Gaedhilge: The Gaelic Journal* 16, no. 6 (February 1906): 82–87.

page 53, sailed across the channel: See Richard Roche, *The Norman Invasion of Ireland* (Blackrock, Ireland: Anvil Books, 1970).

page 53, elderly lord: Born about 1105, FitzGerald was in his sixties by the time he arrived in Ireland.

page 53, *An Corrbhaile*: P. W. Joyce, *Irish Local Names Explained* (Dublin: Roberts Books, 1923), 34.

page 53, "a lovely place": Jane C. "Dollie" Woulfe to Richard W. Woulfe, January 5, 1947. Transcription courtesy of Sadhbh Lyons.

page 54, "She blasted us clean": Stuart, *Share the Profits!*, 5.

page 54, "numbers of the Woulfes": "Obituary: Death and Funeral of Mr. R. E. Woulfe, Cratloe, Athea; an Appreciation," *Limerick Leader*, June 1, 1910, 4.

page 54, Old English (*Sean-Ghaill*): Doyle, *A History of the Irish Language*, 40.

page 56, David Wolfe: See Thomas J. Morrissey, S.J., "The Career and Problem of David Wolfe, 1528–1579? Jesuit, and Papal Commissary to Ireland," *North Munster Antiquarian Journal* 49 (2007): 21–37; and

Begley, *The Diocese of Limerick in the Sixteenth and Seventeenth Centuries*, which contains a Latin summary of Wolfe's *Description of Ireland* (494–515).

page 56, "We the said Commissioners": "Limerick Confiscations: West Limerick and Kerry Family," *Kerryman* (Tralee), June 9, 1928, 4; Begley, *The Diocese of Limerick in the Sixteenth and Seventeenth Centuries*, 234.

page 57, "the curtain rises again": Jane C. "Dollie" Woulfe to Sister M. Caelan Wolfe, August 1956.

page 57, Their father: This was James Maurice Woulfe (ca. 1651–1704).

20.

page 57, his obituary bragged: "Obituary: Death and Funeral of Mr. R. E. Woulfe, Cratloe, Athea; an Appreciation," *Limerick Leader*, June 1, 1910, 4.

page 57, "a good authority": Patrick Woulfe, ed., "Elegy on Capt. O'Sullivan," *Irisleabar na Gaedhilge: The Gaelic Journal* 16, no. 6 (February 1906): 86.

page 58, tended toward the Frankish ... Maurice: Patrick Woulfe, *Sloinnte Gaedheal is Gall: Irish Names and Surnames*, 10–11.

page 58, "A people without a language" ... "To lose": Quoted in F. S. L. Lyons, *Culture & Anarchy in Ireland, 1890–1939: From the Fall of Parnell to the Death of W. B. Yeats* (Oxford, United Kingdom: Oxford University Press, 1939), 32.

page 58, Davis did not grow up: T. W. Moody, "Thomas Davis and the Irish Nation," *Hermathena* 103 (autumn 1966): 22.

page 58, "I suppose you have heard": Patrick Woulfe to Sister Bonaventure (1871–1929), May 8, 1893. Courtesy of Tom Woulfe. Aunt Ellie likely was Ellen Maher Woulfe (ca. 1849–1943), their mother's sister, who also married a Woulfe, Richard James "Brown Dick" Woulfe (1853–1915).

page 59, "He believes in the Holy Ghost": P. J. Carroll, "How a 'Miracle' Was Worked," *Limerick Leader*, November 5, 1932, 11.

page 59, "I could see no damage," Associated Press, "Iowa Chaplain First to Enter Cathedral," *Waterloo Daily Courier* (Iowa), August 18, 1944, 1. Thomas Lyons Wolfe (1894–1974) was the son of John Buckley Wolfe (1851–1923) and Mary Ann Lyons Wolfe (1861–1946).

page 60, "a new language": Eavan Boland, *Outside History: Selected Poems, 1980–1990* (New York: W. W. Norton, 1990), 79.

page 61, "We exist in the element of language": N. Scott Momaday, *The Man Made of Words: Essays, Stories, Passages* (New York: St. Martin's Press, 1997), 87.

page 61, "I know that Cheyenne": Richard Littlebear, "Just Speak Your Language," *Whole Earth* (spring 2000).

21.

page 62, "Owen—Roland—what the hell?": Brian Friel, *Translations* (New York: Farrar, Strauss and Giroux, 1981), 37.

page 62, "And ever since": Friel, *Translations*, 53.

page 63, "People whose names": John B. Keane, "Compulsory Irish is achieving nothing by way of advancement of the Language," *Kerryman* (Tralee), March 17, 1962, 5.

page 63, "Finally, I fear": Seán de Bhulbh, "Mr. Keane has no time for Irish," *Kerryman* (Tralee), March 31, 1962, 18. Seán Muiris de Bhulbh (1922–2009) was the son of Maurice James Woulfe (1884–1973) and Sarah McCarthy Woulfe.

22.

page 64, the Chemist got word: James J. Collins, Statement W.S. 1,272, File S.2564, Bureau of Military History, October 5, 1955, 2–3.

page 65, the Chemist's father: This is Richard Maurice Woulfe (ca. 1843–1913).

page 65, Cornelius "Con": see John O'Callaghan, *16 Lives: Con Colbert* (Dublin: The O'Brien Press, 2015). The book mistakenly identifies the Chemist's father as Maurice Woulfe, a national school teacher in Athea.

page 65, "My dear Katty": O'Callaghan, *16 Lives: Con Colbert*, 207.

page 67, joined the West Limerick Brigade: Military Service Pensions Collection, MA/MSPC/RO/119, West Limerick Brigade 2nd Battalion, Military Archives Ireland.

page 67, "a stranger to us": Mossie Harnett, *Victory and Woe: The West Limerick Brigade in the War of Independence* (Dublin: University College Dublin Press, 2002), 31.

page 67, "I was working in the shop": Collins statement, 4.

page 67, "our intelligence received": Harnett, *Victory and Woe*, 48.

page 67, "Fully realising now": Harnett, *Victory and Woe*, 50.

page 67, eventually identified: "The West Limerick Mystery; Unknown Man's Identity," *Limerick Leader*, April 30, 1920, 3. In *Victory and Woe*, Harnett refers to the spy only as "A."

page 67, treat the wounded: Daniel Doody, Statement W.S. 796, File S.2084, Bureau of Military History, February 3, 1953, 3.

page 67, surprised: Collins statement, 16–17; Harnett, *Victory and Woe*, 65–66; "Police Patrol Ambushed Near Abbeyfeale," *Kerryman* (Tralee), September 25, 1920, 7. The numbers of IRA men (forty to fifty) and policemen (six to ten) vary from source to source, as does the number of men wounded in the attack (two to five).

page 67, Hiding: Collins statement, 16.

page 67–68, peered through a hedge: Harnett, *Victory and Woe*, 66.

page 68, "The Tans remained": Collins statement, 17.

page 68, "The local Temperance Hall": "Police Patrol Ambushed Near Abbeyfeale," *Kerryman* (Tralee), September 25, 1920, 7.

page 68, "They were going to shoot him": Sister Íde Woulfe (1915–2015), oral history conducted in Belfast, Northern Ireland, by Maurice O'Keefe, Irish Life and Lore, 2015.

page 68, "They told me": Sister Íde Woulfe, oral history.

page 69, an 1,800-word treaty: Liam Weeks and Mícheál Ó Fathartaigh, eds., *The Treaty: Debating and Establishing the Irish State* (Newbridge, County Kildare: Irish Academic Press, 2018), 6.

page 68, congregated each night: Sister Íde Woulfe, oral history.

23.

page 69, Dollie's younger brother: They had one additional sibling, whose name combined those of his father and grandfather: Richard Edmund Maurice Woulfe (1883–1963).

page 69, His father: This is Maurice Richard Woulfe (1853–1928).

page 69, he volunteered: Short Service Attestation form for Maurice James Woulfe, The National Archives of the United Kingdom: Public Record Office. Accessed via Ancestry.com. See also notice in the *Irish Independent* (Dublin), April 5, 1916, 4.

page 69–70, a full 10 percent: Paul Taylor, *Heroes or Traitors? Experiences of Southern Irish Soldiers Returning from the Great War 1919–1939* (Liverpool: Liverpool University Press, 2015), 7.

page 71, crowds sang: Taylor, *Heroes or Traitors?*, 10.

page 71, Theobald Wolfe Tone's trial: Marianne Elliott, *Wolfe Tone: Prophet of Irish Independence* (New Haven, Connecticut: Yale University Press, 1989), 392. Tone (1763–1798), who was descended from French Protestants, led a revolt of the United Irishmen. Historians disagree over whether his father was a Wolfe; he likely was not related, or at least not closely related, to the Woulfes of Limerick and Kerry.

page 71, his cousin the Chemist: The exact nature of their relationship is (frustratingly) unknown.

page 71, engage rebel forces: See Pádraig Yeates, *A City in Wartime: Dublin 1914–1918* (Dublin: Gill & Macmillan, 2011).

page 71, where Colbert: O'Callaghan, *16 Lives: Con Colbert*, 150.

page 71, "Hail!": O'Callaghan, *16 Lives: Con Colbert*, 149.

page 71, "I am glad": Taylor, *Heroes or Traitors?*, 11.

page 72, "He tried again": Sebastian Barry, *A Long Long Way* (New York: Viking Penguin, 2005), 97.

24.

page 72, officer's training and a transfer: Statement of the Services of No. 10/26538, Maurice J. Woulfe. The National Archives of the United Kingdom: Public Record Office. Accessed via Ancestry.com. Woulfe transferred to the 7th Officer Cadet Battalion on April 29; on December 19 he was commissioned a 2nd lieutenant in the Royal Munster Fusiliers.

page 72, "The gas boiled": Barry, *A Long Long Way*, 111.

page 72, "There we got some shotguns": Harnett, *Victory and Woe*, 32.

page 73, Just two days later: J. D. H., "Black and Tans in West Limerick," in *Limerick's Fighting Story 1916–21*, edited by Brian Ó Conchubhair (Cork, Ireland: Mercier Press, 2009), 293–298. J. D. H. was the pseudonym of the Abbeyfeale journalist and auctioneer J. D. Harnett. In his account, first published by the *Kerryman* newspaper in 1948, he incorrectly identifies Huckerby as Huckerbery, without any first name.

page 73, "They were about a yard apart": J. D. H., "Black and Tans in West Limerick," 296–297.

page 73, accused of killing: "Shanagolden Tragedy; What Lord Monteagle Found," *Kilkenny People*, September 11, 1920, 7.

page 73, "He was a thorough blackguard": Collins statement, 15.

page 73, the police arrested the Solicitor: "Co. Limerick Solicitor Arrested Yesterday," *Cork Examiner*, October 8, 1920, 5; "Abbeyfeale Arrests," *Cork Examiner*, October 9, 1920, 7.

page 74, helped accompany him: J. D. H., "Black and Tans in West Limerick," 298.

page 74, released: "Abbeyfeale Solicitor Fined," *The Liberator* (Tralee), October 19, 1920, 1.

25.

page 74, old Bessie Cockburn: This is Elizabeth Malcolm "Bessie" Cockburn Woulfe (1856–1943).

page 74, A newspaper report: "Shots into Limerick House," *Irish Independent* (Dublin), July 18, 1934, 10.

page 75, archived police reports: Armed assault on the residence of Maurice Woulfe, Abbeyfeale, County Limerick 15 July 1934, 2011/25/917, Jul 1934–Jul 1935, Department of Justice, National Archives of Ireland.

page 75, "political tinge": Gárda Síochána report, Newcastlewest, July 16, 1934.

page 76, executed search warrants: Gárda Síochána report, Newcastlewest, July 18, 1934.

page 76, known as the Blueshirts: See Maurice Manning, *The Blueshirts* (Toronto, Canada: University of Toronto Press, 1971); Mike Cronin, "The Blueshirt Movement, 1932–5: Ireland's Fascists?" *Journal of Contemporary History* 30, no. 2 (April 1995): 311–332.

page 76, published a letter: M. J. Woulfe, "Attack on Limerick Blueshirts," *Cork Examiner*, July 10, 1934, 4.

26.

page 76, cheap paperback copy: Brendan Behan, *Confessions of an Irish Rebel* (New York: Lancer Books, [1965] 1967). I have it now on my shelf. The cover price is seventy-five cents.

page 77, "Up the long ladder": From the Clancy Brothers and Tommy Makem, "Children's Medley," *In Person at Carnegie Hall*, Columbia Records, 1963.

27.

page 79, their great-great grandfather: This is James Richard Woulfe (1800–1875).

page 80, according to Gemma's father: Thomas Woulfe (1915–2015), oral history conducted by Maurice O'Keefe, Irish Life and Lore, 2015.

BIOGRAPHIES

ANN WOLFE COLLISON
(1845–1912)

ANN WOLFE was born in May 1845 in Listowel, County Kerry. She was the daughter of John Wolfe and his second wife, Bridget Foley Wolfe. She had six full siblings: Katherine Marie (b. 1832), Maurice (b. 1837), Daniel, Johanna (b. ca. 1841), Bridget (b. ca. 1846), and Julia (b. ca. 1848). She also had four half siblings by her father's first wife, Julia Stack Wolfe: Margaret (b. ca. 1821), Eleanor (b. ca. 1821), Mary (b. 1826), and Ellen (b. 1827).

In 1849, Wolfe, her parents, and her siblings, immigrated to the United States, sailing aboard the *Mary Ann Henry* and arriving in New York on July 9. Numerous members of the Wolfe family immigrated around the same time, nearly all of them settling in LaSalle County, Illinois. A few moved on from there to Clinton County, Iowa.

Ann Wolfe and her parents were living in Deer Park Township, LaSalle County, by 1850. In February 1874 she married Joseph Collison, a native of Leeds, England, in Ottawa, Illinois. He farmed in Ottawa with his father. The couple had nine children: William (b. 1875); John R. (b. 1877); Joseph B. (b. 1878); Daniel A. (b. 1880); Frederick Paul (b. 1882); Mary (b. 1885); twins, Maurice L. "Mort" and Frank L. (b. 1887); and Arthur (b 1890).

The next year, the family moved west to Iowa. Many Wolfes settled in Clinton County, but Carroll is 220 miles to the west. Joseph Collison's obituary described the journey he took with his wife and infant son William as being "a long and tedious one made by oxen." They had about $1,000 in savings, having heard "there was a good opportunity in Carroll County for an ambitious man with a small amount of money."

Joseph and Ann Collison farmed the rest of their lives on land four miles west of Carroll. At the time of his death, Joseph Collison owned 720 acres.

Ann Collison died on February 10, 1912, at Saint Anthony Hospital in Carroll. Her husband died on April 23, 1928, and they are buried together at Saint Joseph's Cemetery in Carroll.

ARTHUR COLLISON
(1890–1903)

ARTHUR COLLISON was born in April 1890, in Carroll County, Iowa. He was the son of Joseph Collison, a Catholic farmer and native of Leeds, England, and Ann Wolfe Collison, a native of County Kerry. His siblings included William (b. 1875), John R. (b. 1877), Joseph B. (b. 1878), Daniel A. (b. 1880), Frederick Paul (b. 1882), Mary (b. 1885), twins Maurice L. "Mort" and Frank L. (b. 1887), and Arthur (b 1890).

Collison died on November 1, 1903, in Carroll. His obituary, published in the *Carroll Sentinel* on November 3, explained that he was killed on a Sunday morning "by a loaded wagon passing over him."

> The parents were attending early mass in Carroll and Arthur, in company with an elder brother, was hauling a load of fodder from the field. In going over a ditch in the road the boy was thrown to the ground, the wagon passing over his breast, crushing him and killing him instantly. Arthur's death is a terrible blow to the family as he was the youngest child and an exemplary manly boy.

He is buried at Saint Joseph's Cemetery in Carroll, Iowa.

MAURICE L. COLLISON
(1887–1981)

MAURICE L. COLLISON was born on October 19, 1887, in Carroll County, Iowa. He was the son of Joseph Collison, a Catholic farmer and native of Leeds, England, and Ann Wolfe Collison, a native of County Kerry. His siblings included William (b. 1875); John R. (b. 1877); Joseph B. (b. 1878); Daniel A. (b. 1880); Frederick Paul (b. 1882); Mary (b. 1885); his twin, Frank L.; and Arthur (b 1890).

Mort Collison was educated in the public schools. On June 12, 1923, he married Florence Ryant of Carroll, in Carroll. They had five children: Margaret Mary, Marilyn, Carol, Art, and Pheanis. Before their marriage, Ryant had taught school, worked in the U.S. Department of the Treasury, and, from 1917 to 1918, served as the deputy county treasurer.

Collison farmed until 1928, when, according to his obituary, he opened a hog-buying station, which he operated until his retirement in 1957. His business was both domestic and foreign. In 1938 and 1939 he served as a member of the Carroll city council, representing the second ward. His wife sat on the board of the Carroll Public Schools for three years, serving as president for at least part of that time.

Collison died at Baptist Hospital in Phoenix, Arizona, on February 5, 1981, while wintering in the state. His wife, Florence, died on December 24, 1986, also in Phoenix. They are buried together at Mount Olivet Cemetery in Carroll, Iowa.

PATRICK DALTON
(1896–1921)

PATRICK DALTON was born on February 23, 1896, in Coole, County Limerick, the son of Michael Dalton and Honorah White Dalton. His siblings included James (b. 1882), Thomas (b. 1890), Johanna (b. 1893), Bridget (b. 1894), Richard (b. 1897), and Mary "Mollie" (b. 1901).

Little is known of Dalton's early life and education. At the time of his death, during the War of Independence (1919–1921), he was working as a hardware assistant in Listowel, County Kerry. For reasons both political and familial, it is possible he was employed at J. McKenna's in that town. On October 7, 1920, for instance, the *Irish Independent* reported that Tim Stack, an apprentice at Richard B. Wolfe's pharmacy in nearby Abbeyfeale, County Limerick, and Michael Wolfe, an employee of McKenna's, both were arrested on suspicion of republican activity.

Patrick Dalton was himself a Wolfe and a member of the North Kerry Brigade of the Irish Republican Army (IRA). His maternal grandmother, Bridget Wolfe White, was a sister of Richard E. "Dicky Ned" Wolfe, of the Glen, Cratloe, County Limerick. Another Wolfe relative, the pharmacist Dick Wolfe, was an active member of the West Limerick Brigade of the IRA. Wolfe's brother-in-law, Con Colbert, was one of sixteen men executed by the British after the Easter Rising of 1916.

The months of April and May 1921 were particularly violent in the seven-mile stretch between Listowel on the west and Athea, County Limerick, on the east. Sir Arthur Vicars, fired for negligence as Ulster King of Arms after the theft of the Irish crown jewels in 1907, lived at nearby Kilmorna House. The IRA believed that he was informing on their activities to the British army, and on April 7 they ambushed a group of soldiers returning to Listowel after a visit to Kilmorna. An IRA man was killed. On April 14, about thirty IRA men raided Kilmorna House. According to a report in the *Irish Independent* the next day, the republicans escorted Vicars from his bedroom while he was still wearing his dressing gown and shot him outside the house in the garden. Around his neck was a note: "Spies and informers beware; the I.R.A. never forgets." The IRA then burned the house.

A month later, three IRA men, including Patrick Dalton, were shot dead near Kilmorna, at Gortaglanna, Knockanure, County Kerry. The official British account of the incident, published on May 14 in the *Irish Examiner* newspaper, stated that three police vehicles had been ambushed by 100 armed men, slightly wounding two policemen. "The police returned the fire," according to the report, "and the dead bodies of three unknown men were later found at the scene of the ambush, and it is believed that the assailants suffered heavy casualties. The Crown forces also captured a number of shot guns, revolvers, and ammunition."

On May 17, the three men were publicly identified as Patrick Dalton, of Athea; Jeremiah Lyons, of Duagh; and Patrick Walsh, of Coolard.

The next month, Cornelius "Con" Dee, an IRA man who had survived the shooting, testified before Thomas R. Hill, a justice of the peace in Tarbert, County Kerry, about what had happened. Dee, Dalton, and Walsh had been in Athea to warn of a possible police ambush and had stayed for several days. They attended religious devotions and spent their nights in the Dalton home, about a mile from the town. On the morning of May 12, they left for Listowel and met Lyons on the road.

> He dismounted [from his bicycle] and began talking about various happenings. After a few minutes Paddy Walsh suggested that we should go into a field as it would be safer than the road-side. We moved and were just inside the fence when we heard the noise of a lorry. "Take cover, lads," I advised, and we tried to conceal ourselves as best we could. Jerry Lyons, Paddy Dalton and I took cover immediately. Paddy Walsh ran to the end of a field and lay down. Very soon we were surrounded by men in the uniforms of the Royal Irish Constabulary. "We are done, Connie," said Paddy Dalton. "Come out, lads," I said, "with our hands up."

The policemen, correctly believing that they had captured IRA men, called them murderers, searched them for weapons, and severely beat them. They were then driven down the road about a mile, and then back in the other direction, before being beaten again and forced into a field by the side of the road. "We asked for a trial," Dee said, "but the Black and Tans laughed and jeered and called us murderers."

> We were put standing in line facing a fence about forty yards from the road. I was placed first on the right, Jerry Lyons was next, Paddy Dalton next, and Paddy Walsh on the left. Then a Black and Tan with a rifle resting on the fence was put in front of each of us, about five yards distant. There were about ten more Black and Tans standing behind them. I looked straight into the face of the man in front of me. He delayed about twenty seconds as if he would like one of his companions to fire first. The second Black and Tan fired. Jerry Lyons flung up his arms, moaned and fell backwards. I glanced at him and noticed blood coming on his waistcoat; I turned round and ran. I was gone about twelve yards when I got wounded in the right thigh. My leg bent under me, but I held on running although I had to limp. I felt that I was being chased and I heard the bullets whizzing past me.

Dee eventually escaped.

According to newspaper reports, the bodies of Dalton, Lyons, and Walsh were brought first to the Listowel police barracks and then to Tralee. On May 18, the *Irish Examiner* wrote that they were then returned to Listowel by train. Many people along the route shut their window and door blinds in sympathy, "but the police immediately after compelled them to raise their blinds and re-open the doors on penalty of having them burst in forcibly."

Dalton is buried with his family at the Temple Athea graveyard. His stone reads, "Murdered At Gurtaglanna By British Forces."

Several ballads were subsequently composed about the deaths of Dalton, Lyons, and Walsh. The most popular and oft-recorded is "The Valley of Knockanure," written in 1946 by the Listowel school teacher Bryan MacMahon with material provided by Pádraig Ó Ceallacháin. It ends:

Oh, Walsh and Lyons and Dalton brave, although your hearts are clay,
Yet in your stead we have true men yet to guard the gap to-day,
While grass is found on Ireland's ground your memory will endure
So God guard and keep the place you sleep and the Valley of Knockanure.

CATHERINE WOLFE FITZGERALD
(1860–1947)

CATHERINE WOLFE was born in March 1860, in Liberty Township, Clinton County, Iowa. Sources differ as to the spelling of her first name. In *Wolfe's History of Clinton County* (1911), her brother Patrick B. Wolfe spells it with a *k*. The 1860 federal census spells it with a *c*.

Kate Wolfe's parents were John Richard Wolfe, an Irish Catholic farmer, and Honora Buckley Wolfe. She had seven siblings who survived to maturity: James Buckley (b. 1843), Patrick Bernard (b. 1848), Johanna (b. 1849), John Buckley (b. 1851), Maurice Buckley (b. 1855), Margaret I. (b. 1857), and Richard Boyle (b. 1862). Two sisters, Margaret and Catherine, died in infancy.

In 1847, Wolfe's parents and brother James immigrated to the United States from Listowel, County Kerry, along with John R. Wolfe's first cousin Maurice Wolfe and his family. (John and Maurice Wolfe shared a grandfather, James M. "The Barrister" Wolfe.) The families arrived in New York on August 23, 1847, and from there made their way to Chicago and then to LaSalle County, Illinois, where a number of John R. Wolfe's brothers and cousins settled. John R. Wolfe and his cousin Maurice, with their families, both moved on to Clinton County, Iowa, arriving about 1855.

Little is known of Wolfe's early years. She may have studied at the Iowa State Normal School in Cedar Falls, Iowa, and worked as a teacher. At some point, she moved to Deer Lodge County, Montana, the home of her sister Margaret, also a teacher. In 1888, she began teaching in the public schools there. A cousin, Edmund D. Wolfe, lived in Anaconda, Deer Lodge County, beginning in 1893.

On November 28, 1894, Wolfe and her sister were both married at Saint Patrick's Church in Butte, Montana, Margaret Wolfe to Dr. Daniel Langan, of Clinton, Iowa, and Kate Wolfe to Thomas D. Fitzgerald, of Anaconda. The Wolfe sisters' brother Richard B. Wolfe served as groomsman at the private ceremony. The couple lived on

Cherry Street in Anaconda. They had one child, Margaret M., who was born on November 11, 1897.

Thomas D. Fitzgerald, widely known as Judge T. D. Fitzgerald, was born in October 1850 in County Waterford, and came to New York as a boy with his family. He worked as a bookkeeper for the Vulcan Iron Works Company in Saint Louis, then lived in Leadville, Colorado. In 1884, he moved to Anaconda, where he worked as a real estate agent and notary public. He served two terms as a justice of the peace (1886–1890) and as the newly incorporated city's first police magistrate. From 1901 until 1903 he was the county's public administrator. Fitzgerald also served in the Montana House of Representatives from 1893 until 1895, representing Deer Lodge County. (He was not, as claimed by Kate Wolfe's brother Patrick, the president of the Montana Senate.)

Kate Fitzgerald continued to teach after her marriage and served on the county school board. A newspaper report in 1895 indicates that she was an incumbent seeking another term. She also was a member of the Woman's Literary Club in Anaconda. In November 1900 she presented a paper on the "Church and Nation under Edward VI and Mary"; in March 1901, she gave a paper titled "The Influence of the French Revolution on English Literature"; and in October 1901 she lectured on the German poet Heinrich Heine (1797–1856).

On April 8, 1903, Judge Fitzgerald died suddenly in Anaconda of what the *Anaconda Standard* newspaper described as "an attack of apoplexy, following a severe cold and congested lungs." He had been visiting nearby mining claims he owned, and "even Mrs. Fitzgerald was not aware that he was afflicted with anything worse than a bad cold."

Kate Fitzgerald served as executor of her late husband's estate in Montana before returning to Clinton County, Iowa. By 1910 she lived there with her daughter. By 1920 she was living with her sister, Margaret Langan, whose husband died in 1914. By 1930, Fitzgerald was living in San Diego, California, with her daughter, who was working as a hospital nurse. She was still there a decade later.

Fitzgerald died in 1947, although the exact date and place are unclear. She is buried with her husband and daughter at Saint James Cemetery in Toronto, Clinton County, Iowa.

CATHERINE WOLFE HEPLER
(1842–1922)

CATHERINE WOLFE was baptized on December 7, 1842, in the parish of Listowel, County Kerry. She was the daughter of Maurice Richard Wolfe, who bred horses and came from a Catholic farming family, and Johanna Downey Wolfe. Her siblings included Margaret (b. 1827), Richard Downey (b. 1829), Stephen (b. 1833), James Downey (b. 1839), Johanna E. (b. 1840), Maurice (b. 1848), John Francis (b. 1850), and Edmund Dean (b. 1853). Her baptismal sponsors were Michael Downey and Margaret Nolan.

Little is known of Kate Wolfe's early life. She, her parents, and her siblings immigrated to the United States in 1849. They sailed from Liverpool to New York aboard the *Senator*, a 777-ton ship of the Black Star Line, owned by Samuel Thompson; they arrived on September 22, 1849. Maurice R. Wolfe's brother John R. Wolfe immigrated to the United States in 1847, his brother Thomas R. Wolfe in 1848, and his brother Richard Wolfe in 1849. They all settled, at least initially, in LaSalle County, Illinois. Catherine Wolfe's family bought land there, as well, and stayed.

On January 16, 1890, Wolfe married Joseph G. Hepler, a farmer and carpenter from Pennsylvania, at Saint Mary's Church in Eagle Township, LaSalle County. It was Hepler's second marriage; his first wife, Theresa Bell Alberts, died about 1881 after having two sons, William (b. 1876) and Clarence Burgess (b. 1878). Kate Wolfe Hepler had no children.

Hepler and her husband lived in LaSalle County for the rest of their lives. Kate Hepler died on November 6, 1922, from injuries sustained in a fall two months prior. She is buried at Saint Columba Cemetery in Ottawa, Illinois. Joseph Hepler died on June 13, 1923, and is buried at Saint Mary's Cemetery in Streator, Illinois.

MARGARET M. McCORMICK KUHN
(1877–1910)

MARGARET MARY MCCORMICK was born on July 18, 1877, in Grand Rapids Township, LaSalle County, Illinois. She was the youngest child of Richard McCormack and Elizabeth Maher McCormick, both Irish Catholic immigrants. Her siblings included Elizabeth "Lyda" (b. 1860), John Patrick (b. 1862), Andrew J. (b. 1864), Richard "Dick" (b. 1866), and Mary Ellen (b. 1867).

On February 19, 1901, she married John Kuhn, a farmer from DeKalb County, Illinois, in the village of Ransom, LaSalle County. The couple had three children: Margaret Elizabeth "Bessie" (b. 1902), Mary K. (b. 1905), and Arthur (b. 1909).

The couple farmed in Brookfield Township, LaSalle County. On March 15, 1910, at the age of twenty-seven, Margaret Kuhn died of pleurisy, an inflammation of the lung. Her husband, John, died on August 24, 1970, at Ryburn Hospital in Ottawa, Illinois. He was 103 years old and believed to have been the county's oldest resident at the time of his death.

His obituary in the *Ottawa Daily Republican Times* recalled a story about John Kuhn from the same paper a decade earlier:

> At that time, he still walked downtown to eat some of his meals and he came to the *Times* office so that his picture could be taken because "he didn't want to inconvenience the photographer." Comparing farming of 10 years ago with farming when he was a child, he said, "It's as much different as day and night." The new way "beats the old way," he said, but "it costs too much money." Mr. Kuhn recalled how a kerosene lamp was a luxury and homemade candles were the normal method of lighting. There were no overshoes, gloves were homemade and cobs helped provide fuel for the wintertime. A family did his marketing once a week, he said.

MARGARET I. WOLFE LANGAN
(1857–btw. 1930 and 1940)

MARGARET I. WOLFE was born in 1857 in Liberty Township, Clinton County, Iowa. Her parents were John Richard Wolfe, an Irish Catholic farmer, and Honora Buckley Wolfe. She had seven siblings who survived to maturity: James Buckley (b. 1843), Patrick Bernard (b. 1848), Johanna (b. 1849), John Buckley (b. 1851), Maurice Buckley (b. 1855), Catherine "Kate" (b. 1860), and Richard Boyle (b. 1862). Two sisters, Margaret and Catherine, died in infancy.

In 1847, Wolfe's parents and brother James immigrated to the United States from Listowel, County Kerry, along with John R. Wolfe's first cousin Maurice Wolfe and his family. (John and Maurice Wolfe shared a grandfather, James M. "The Barrister" Wolfe.) The families arrived in New York on August 23, 1847, and from there made their way to Chicago and then to LaSalle County, Illinois, where a number of John R. Wolfe's brothers and cousins settled. John R. Wolfe and his cousin Maurice, with their families, both moved on to Clinton County, Iowa, arriving independently, about 1855.

Little is known of Margaret Wolfe's early years. She may have studied at the Iowa State Normal School in Cedar Falls, Iowa, and worked as a teacher. About 1884, she moved to Deer Lodge County, Montana, where she served three terms as superintendent of the county schools (ca. 1886–1892). The elected position paid $1,250 per year. Wolfe also served as principal of the public school in Granite, Deer Lodge County. Wolfe's sister Kate, also a teacher, joined her in Anaconda in 1888. A cousin, Edmund D. Wolfe, lived there beginning in 1893.

As superintendent of the county schools Margaret Wolfe presided over a yearly Teachers' Institute. On November 4, 1893, the *Anaconda Standard* reported her views on recess:

> One of the very best papers of the day was presented by Miss Margaret Wolfe on the all-important theme of 'School Government,' in which, among other wise and good suggestions, she strongly condemned the recess, denouncing it as demoralizing to discipline and habits of study, and produc-

tive of many evils not balanced by the doubtful benefits that might come from the sort of exercise a band of school children usually take.

On November 28, 1894, Wolfe and her sister were both married at Saint Patrick's Church in Butte, Montana, Margaret Wolfe to Dr. Daniel Langan, of Clinton, Iowa, and Kate Wolfe to Thomas D. Fitzgerald, of Anaconda. The Wolfe sisters' brother Richard B. Wolfe served as groomsman at the private ceremony. Dr. Langan was born in County Donegal, on February 18, 1836. On September 5, 1865, he married Ellen Purcell, of Clinton County, and the couple had seven children before her death in 1892. Langan and Wolfe had no children of their own. After an extended trip, they settled in Clinton, Iowa.

In January 1898, the Langan home on Fifth Avenue in Clinton was destroyed by fire. The *Anaconda Standard* reprinted an account from the *Clinton Herald*, describing the event:

> The daughter, Miss Blanche [Blanche Irene Langan, b. 1878], was the first to notice smoke. She at once aroused the rest of the family and a general alarm was turned in over the telephone. This was at 15 minutes after 6 [a.m.]. By this time the hallways were so full of smoke that the family could not regain their apartments, and had to flee for their lives out into the cold, and make the best of their way through the snow to the nearest neighbors. On account of the heavy snowstorm of Saturday the roads were bad and the horses of the fire department had a long, hard pull through the packed and drifted snow.

Langan carried four fire insurance policies, each for $5,000. When an arbitration board ruled his home a total loss and the insurance companies disagreed, Langan sued. The companies then offered to rebuild the home, and when Langan refused, the suits moved forward. In *Langan* v. *Ætna Insurance Company*, *Langan* v. *Spring Garden Insurance Company*, *Langan* v. *German Alliance Insurance Company*, and *Langan* v. *Palatine Insurance Company*, a United States federal court ruled for Langan and awarded him the full amount of his policies.

Dr. Langan died on June 13, 1914. The federal census of 1920 indicates that Margaret Wolfe Langan lived in Clinton with her sister Kate, whose husband had died in Montana in 1903. She was still in Clinton in 1930 and is not listed in the census of 1940. She and her husband are possibly buried with other Langan family members at Saint Mary's Cemetery in Clinton.

ELLEN WOLFE MAHER
(ca. 1810–1886)

ELLEN WOLFE was born about 1810 in Listowel, County Kerry. She was the daughter of Richard James Wolfe, a Catholic farmer, and Johanna Relihan Wolfe. Her siblings included James Richard (b. 1800), Maurice Richard (b. 1802), John Richard (b. 1809), Thomas Richard (b. 1811), Johanna (b. 1812), Richard (b. 1815), Margaret Ellen (b. 1818), Edmond (b. 1821), and Patrick (b. 1822).

Virtually nothing is known of Wolfe's life. About 1828 she married Patrick Maher (sometimes spelled Meagher), and the couple had at least nine children: Margaret (b. 1829), Patrick (b. ca. 1831), Elizabeth (b. 1836), Johanna (b. 1838), Honora "Nanno" (b. 1844), Bartholomew (b. 1846), Mary (b. 1848), Ellen (b. ca. 1849), and Catherine (b. 1853).

Ellen Wolfe Maher's brothers James and Edward took over their father's land while her other brothers immigrated to the United States. These included her brother John R. Wolfe and their first cousin Maurice Wolfe, who sailed together on the *Cornelia* in 1847; her brother Thomas R. Wolfe, who sailed the *James H. Shepherd* in 1848; her cousin Richard Wolfe, who took the *Thomas H. Perkins* in 1848; and her brother Richard Wolfe, who sailed the *Liverpool* in 1849. Her cousin John E. Wolfe and his sisters also immigrated. Her daughter Honora married back into the Wolfe family, wedding James Patrick "Paddy" Wolfe.

In 1849, Ellen Maher's brother Maurice Wolfe took her daughter Margaret with him when he immigrated aboard the *Senator* in 1849. He and the other Wolfes settled in LaSalle County, Illinois; some later moved to Clinton County, Iowa.

Nothing else is known of Maher's life. She died in 1886 in the town of Duagh, about nine kilometers southeast of Listowel. Her husband, Patrick, died there in 1894.

JOHN W. MAHER
(1856–1936)

JOHN WALLACE MAHER was born on December 18, 1856, in Streator, Illinois, the son of Bartholomew "Batt" Maher and Margaret Wolfe Maher, both Irish immigrants. His siblings included Catherine "Kate" (b. 1852), Johanna (b. 1857), Jerry (b. 1860), Jeremiah Leonard (b. 1867), Bartholomew "Bartie" (b. 1868), Maurice Edward (b. 1869), and James Francis (b. 1870). Jerry died in 1862 and Bartie in 1880.

Maher attended Streator High School and studied law at the University of Michigan, earning a JD in 1880. He established a practice in Grand Forks, North Dakota, in partnership with George Walsh, and in 1883 moved to Devils Lake in Ramsey County. He practiced law there until 1905. He served as district attorney of Towner County and treasurer of Ramsey County, both in North Dakota. He established a farm loan business in Devils Lake, from 1890 to 1894 owned and managed the newspaper *Devils Lake News*, and founded the Devils Lake Nursery. He was an organizer of the Twin City Life Insurance Company and of the Farmers Railway.

Maher, who was six feet, six inches tall, married Sarah Cecelia "Sadie" Coleman, of Michigan, in Ann Arbor, Michigan, on May 29, 1884. The couple had six children: Mary (b. 1885), Josephine (b. 1886), Kathleen S. (b. 1889), Charles Howard (b. 1891), John Wallace Jr. (b. 1893), and Evangeline G. (b. 1897).

On July 22, 1895, one of Maher's former clients, who disputed a bill of $100 for services in a land case, shot the lawyer in Devils Lake. Maher survived. Patrick McNamara had lost his land case and blamed his lawyer, refusing to pay. In response, Maher put a lien on McNamara's property. The *Grand Forks Daily Herald* published a dramatic front-page account of the shooting on July 23:

> Patrick McNamara emptied four chambers of a .44-caliber bull-dog revolver at John W. Maher this afternoon [July 22]. The first bullet struck Maher in the back striking the spinal process of one of the lumbar vertebrae. Maher,

[who] was standing by a fence near a restaurant started to run yelling loudly—McNamara followed flourishing the revolver, overtook him on the porch of Sidney Thompson's residence endeavoring to gain admittance. McNamara fired again—the bullet missed, entering the woodwork of the residence. Maher turned and tried to catch McNamara, but fell off the sidewalk on the street. McNamara, standing over him, commenced shooting again, the bullets again going wide of the mark ... After being arrested, McNamara said he was sorry he hadn't killed him.

Maher was released from the hospital about a week later. McNamara was charged with assault with a deadly weapon with intent to kill; he pleaded innocent by reason of insanity. A jury convicted him on December 16, 1895, after seven hours of deliberation. A judge sentenced him to four years, nine months in prison. "The feeling against him [McNamara] was bitter," the *Grand Forks Daily Herald* reported on December 25, "and the sentence is regarded as a very light one."

In 1896, Maher, a Republican, served as a delegate to his party's state convention and as chair of the McKinley Club, a 100-member group in Devils Lake organized in support of William McKinley's presidential candidacy. Maher represented North Dakota's new state bar association at the annual meeting of the American Bar Association, at Saratoga, New York, August 29–31, 1900. He also was an officer of the North Dakota Chautauqua.

Sarah Coleman Maher died in 1923. John Maher died at sea on July 30, 1936, near the isthmus of Panama, en route from Balboa to San Francisco. He and his wife are buried at Saint Joseph's Catholic Cemetery in Devils Lake, Ramsey County, North Dakota. A belated obituary in the *Limerick Leader*, dated November 26, 1938, noted that "once or twice the late Mr. Maher came to Ireland, the native land of his parents. Often he preferred that his death should occur at sea."

MARGARET WOLFE MAHER
(1827–1906)

MARGARET WOLFE was born in August 1827 in Listowel, County Kerry. She was the daughter of Maurice Richard Wolfe, who bred horses and came from a Catholic farming family, and Johanna Downey Wolfe. Her siblings included Richard Downey (b. 1829), Stephen (b. 1833), James Downey (b. 1839), Johanna E. (b. 1840), Catherine "Kate" (b. 1842), Maurice (b. 1848), John Francis (b. 1850), and Edmund Dean (b. 1853).

Little is known of her early life. She, her parents, and her siblings immigrated to the United States in 1849. They sailed from Liverpool to New York aboard the *Senator*, a 777-ton ship of the Black Star Line, owned by Samuel Thompson; they arrived on September 22, 1849. Maurice R. Wolfe's brother John R. Wolfe immigrated to the United States in 1847, his brother Thomas R. Wolfe in 1848, and his brother Richard Wolfe in 1849. They all settled, at least initially, in LaSalle County, Illinois. Margaret Wolfe's family bought land there, as well, and stayed.

On May 2, 1852, Wolfe married Bartholomew "Batt" Maher at Saint Patrick's Church in LaSalle County. Maher had arrived in the United States from Ireland in 1848. The couple lived in Eagle Township, LaSalle County, for the rest of their lives. They had at least eight children: Catherine "Kate" (b. 1852), John Wallace (b. 1856), Johanna (b. 1857), Jerry (b. 1860), Jeremiah Leonard (b. 1867), Bartholomew "Bartie" (b. 1868), Maurice Edward (b. 1869), and James Francis (b. 1870). Jerry died in 1862 and Bartie in 1880.

Margaret Wolfe Maher's eldest child, Kate, married a cousin, Richard James Wolfe. (Kate Maher Wolfe's maternal grandfather, Maurice R. Wolfe, and Richard J. Wolfe's father, Richard Wolfe, were first cousins.) Margaret Maher's son John became a lawyer in North Dakota.

Batt Maher died on July 12, 1904, in Streator, Illinois. Margaret Maher died of pneumonia after a brief illness on October 12, 1906, in

Eagle Township, LaSalle County. They both are buried at Lost Land Cemetery in LaSalle County.

MAURICE E. MAHER
(1869–1964)

MAURICE EDWARD MAHER was born on April 24, 1869, in Eagle Township, LaSalle County, Illinois, the son of Bartholomew "Batt" Maher and Margaret Wolfe Maher, both Irish immigrants. His siblings included Catherine "Kate" (b. 1852), John Wallace (b. 1856), Johanna (b. 1857), Jerry (b. 1860), Jeremiah Leonard (b. 1867), Bartholomew "Bartie" (b. 1868), and James Francis (b. 1870). Jerry died in 1862 and Bartie in 1880.

Little is known of Ed Maher's early years. He married Julia L. Casey, a native of Streator, Illinois, on May 10, 1892, in LaSalle County. The couple had three children: Edward N. (b. ca. 1893), Jeremiah Leonard (b. ca. 1896), and Julia (b. ca. 1899).

By 1892, Maher and his wife were living in Superior, Wisconsin, where he operated Wolfe & Maher Grocers with his uncle Edmund D. Wolfe, his mother's brother. When Wolfe set out for Montana, Maher returned to Streator. By 1910, he had relocated again, this time to Chicago, where he worked as a real estate broker. In 1930, he was living in Bruce, LaSalle County.

Maher's wife, Julia, died on July 7, 1936, in Chicago. Ed Maher died on November 20, 1964. He and his wife are buried together at Saint Mary's Cemetery in Streator, Illinois.

Maurice E. Maher

AILEEN G. WOLFE McCALL
(1884–1956)

AILEEN GREGORY WOLFE was born on February 20, 1884, in Lebanon, Laclede County, Missouri. She was the daughter of Richard Downey Wolfe and his second wife, Margaret Shine Lyons Wolfe, both Irish immigrants. Aileen Wolfe had a half-sister, Katherine Collins (b. 1863), whose mother, Margaret O'Kane Wolfe, died in 1865. In addition, she had seven full siblings, all of them older than she: Johanna (b. 1867), Daniel Maurice (b. 1869), Honoria Euphrasia "Honor" (b. 1871), Maurice Patrick (b. 1873), Margaret Theresa (b. 1875), Richard (b. 1878), and Marie Louise (b. 1881).

Richard D. Wolfe had immigrated to the United States in 1849 from County Kerry. He farmed first in LaSalle County, Illinois, and then, beginning early in the 1870s, in Missouri. The son of a breeder, Wolfe loved horses and died from a kick in the head on April 12, 1885, a little more than a year after Aileen Wolfe was born.

By 1900, the family had moved to Angleton, Texas, a small town just south of Houston and near the Gulf Coast. The federal census describes Margaret Wolfe as a milliner and her son Daniel as a farmer. It is unclear what education Aileen Wolfe received.

On February 21, 1914, she married Hawley Sweet McCall in Waco. The couple had three children: Richard Hawley (b. 1917), Maurice Woulfe (b. 1920), and Margaret Frances "Peggy" (b. 1925). In 1921, they built a two-story, 2,320-square-foot house at 3028 Colcord Avenue, in Waco, which still stands.

H. S. McCall, a native of Sabine, Texas, and a graduate of Texas A & M University, began his career as a railroad engineer before founding the McCall-Moore Engineering Company, in Waco, with Bart Moore Jr. At some point, the two were joined by P. J. MacNaughton, and the resulting partnership legally dissolved on November 29, 1921. Soon after, McCall established the McCall Engineering Company and, at the time of his sudden death on February 18, 1939, he was president of the Texas Highway Branch of the Associated General Contractors.

Aileen McCall was active politically and socially. On May 19, 1917, the *Waco Morning News* reported that she had hosted a well-attended "Suffrage tea" at her home, complete with the Baylor Hawaiian Orchestra for entertainment and "refreshments in the equal suffrage colors, purple and yellow." She served as the McLennan County chairman of the library extension, and advocated for the county to build its own library. She was a longtime member, and at least twice president, of Waco's Shakespere Club. In 1926 she played the role of Nick Bottom in a club production of *A Midsummer Night's Dream*. She also belonged to a needlework guild and the Waco Federation of Women's Clubs.

Aileen McCall died on March 17, 1956, at a hospital in Austin, and is buried with her husband at Oakwood Cemetery in Waco.

ELIZABETH MAHER McCORMICK
(1836–1900)

ELIZABETH MAHER was baptized on May 26, 1836, in Duagh, County Kerry. Her parents were Patrick Maher and Ellen Wolfe Maher. Her siblings included Margaret (b. 1829), Patrick (b. ca. 1831), Johanna (b. 1838), Honora (b. ca. 1844), Bartholomew (b. 1846), Mary (b. 1848), Ellen (b. ca. 1849), and Catherine (b. 1853).

In 1849, Eliza Maher's sister Margaret immigrated to the United States with her mother's brother Maurice R. Wolfe. During the 1840s, many Wolfes left Ireland, including Elizabeth Maher's uncle John R. Wolfe and his cousin Maurice, who sailed together in 1847; her uncle Thomas R. Wolfe, who sailed in 1848; her mother's cousin Richard Wolfe, who also sailed in 1848; and her uncle Richard Wolfe, who sailed separately from her in 1849. A cousin, John E. Wolfe, also came to the United States, and all of these Wolfes, including Margaret Maher, settled first in LaSalle County, Illinois. Some went on to Clinton County, Iowa.

Elizabeth Maher is likely the same Eliza Maher who sailed aboard the *Isaac Webb* from Liverpool to New York, arriving on August 24, 1857. Like her sister and Wolfe relatives, she ended up in LaSalle County, where she married Richard McCormick, a native of County Longford, in February 1860. They had six children: Elizabeth "Lyda" (b. 1860), John Patrick (b. 1862), Andrew J. (b. 1864), Richard "Dick" (b. 1866), Mary Ellen (b. 1867), and Margaret Mary (b. 1877).

The couple farmed in Grand Rapids Township, LaSalle County, for the rest of their lives. According to his obituary, Richard McCormick was "one of the wealthiest farmers of the county."

Eliza McCormick died at her home on March 5, 1900, in Grand Rapids Township, after an illness lasting several months. Her husband died on November 26, 1911. They are buried together at Saint Columba Cemetery in Ottawa, Illinois.

ELLEN WOLFE MULVIHILL
(1833–1908)

ELLEN WOLFE was born on November 17, 1833, in Listowel, County Kerry. This date comes from her Iowa death record but is contradicted by another record that indicates she was baptized in the parish of Listowel on November 14, 1832. Her parents were Maurice Wolfe, a Catholic farmer, and Ellen Catherine Carey. Her baptismal sponsors were J. Carey and M. Carey.

Ellen Wolfe had ten siblings who lived to maturity: James Carey (b. 1831), Maurice Carey (b. ca. 1835), Mary (b. 1838), John Carey (b. 1840), Thomas Carey (b. 1843), Margaret (b. ca. 1845), Johanna (b. 1847), Richard Carey (b. 1848), Catherine "Kate" (b. 1851), and Bridget Veronica (b. 1854).

In 1847, Wolfe, her parents, and several siblings immigrated to the United States, along with Maurice Wolfe's first cousin John R. Wolfe and his family. (Maurice Wolfe and John R. Wolfe shared a grandfather, James M. "The Barrister" Wolfe.) The families arrived in New York on August 23, and from there made their way to LaSalle County, Illinois.

Many members of the extended Wolfe family made the same journey. Ellen Wolfe's uncle John Wolfe immigrated in 1849. John R. Wolfe's brother Thomas R. Wolfe came from Ireland in 1848 and his brothers Maurice R. Wolfe and Richard Wolfe separately in 1849. Other cousins came, as well, including Margaret and Elizabeth Maher, daughters of John R. Wolfe's sister Ellen, and Patrick, Dennis, Bridget, and Thomas Sheehan, the children of John R. Wolfe's sister Margaret. Another cousin, John E. Wolfe, and his sisters Ellen J. and Mary Agatha, also immigrated. All of these Wolfes, except for the Sheehans, settled in LaSalle County, Illinois. A few moved on to Clinton County, Iowa, including Ellen Wolfe's father, Maurice Wolfe, and Maurice's cousin John R. Wolfe

On September 28, 1854, Ellen Wolfe married Edmund George Mulvihill, a native of Newtown, County Kerry, in Ottawa, Illinois. The couple had ten children: Jeremiah (b. 1858), Mary Agnes "Minnie" (b. ca. 1860), Maurice (b. 1860), Ellen "Nellie" (b. 1862),

Edward (b. 1864), John Ambrose (b. 1866), Catherine "Katie" (b. 1867), James (b. 1870), Thomas S. (b. 1872), and William Henry (b. 1875). James died when he was seven months old. Thomas died of consumption at twenty-seven.

According to *Wolfe's History of Clinton County* (1911), written by John R. Wolfe's son Patrick B. Wolfe, Edmund Mulvihill had "farmed a while [in Illinois], then in 1852, crossed the plains of the West to the gold fields of California, where he remained two years, returning to Illinois in 1854."

In 1857, Edmund and Ellen Mulvihill moved to Toronto, Liberty Township, Clinton County, Iowa, where they joined her father and his relatives. There they purchased 400 acres from the U.S. government, which they farmed until 1865, when they moved to Sharon Township. They initially purchased 120 acres and, soon after, another 280 acres.

In 1895, the Mulvihills retired from farming and purchased a home in Oxford Junction, Jones County.

Edmund Mulvihill died on July 24, 1903, in Oxford Junction, of stomach cancer. Ellen Mulvihill died on April 20, 1908, and they are buried together at Saint James Cemetery in Toronto, Iowa.

MARGARET WOLFE MULVIHILL
(ca. 1845–1888)

MARGARET WOLFE was born about 1845, probably in Listowel, County Kerry. Her parents were Maurice Wolfe, a Catholic farmer, and Ellen Catherine Carey. Her baptismal sponsors were J. Carey and M. Carey.

Margaret Wolfe had ten siblings who lived to maturity: James Carey (b. 1831), Ellen (b. 1833), Maurice Carey (b. ca. 1835), Mary (b. 1838), John Carey (b. 1840), Thomas Carey (b. 1843), Johanna (b. 1847), Richard Carey (b. 1848), Catherine "Kate" (b. 1851), and Bridget Veronica (b. 1854).

In 1847, Wolfe, her parents, and several siblings immigrated to the United States, along with Maurice Wolfe's first cousin John R. Wolfe and his family. (Maurice Wolfe and John R. Wolfe shared a grandfather, James M. "The Barrister" Wolfe.) The families arrived in New York on August 23, and after a stop in Chicago made their way to LaSalle County, Illinois.

Many members of the extended Wolfe family made the same journey. Margaret Wolfe's uncle John Wolfe immigrated in 1849. John R. Wolfe's brother Thomas R. Wolfe came from Ireland in 1848 and his brothers Maurice R. Wolfe and Richard Wolfe sailed separately in 1849. Other cousins came, as well, including Margaret and Elizabeth Maher, daughters of John R. Wolfe's sister Ellen, and Patrick, Dennis, Bridget, and Thomas Sheehan, the children of John R. Wolfe's sister Margaret. Another cousin, John E. Wolfe, and his sisters Ellen J. and Mary Agatha, also immigrated. All of these Wolfes, except for the Sheehans, settled in LaSalle County, Illinois. A few moved on to Clinton County, Iowa, including Margaret Wolfe's father Maurice and Maurice's cousin John R. Wolfe.

In 1871, Wolfe married Cornelius Mulvihill, of County Kerry, in Clinton County, Iowa. Wolfe's sister Ellen also married a Mulvihill. Although both men hailed from the same county in Ireland, it's not clear whether they were related.

This was Cornelius Mulvihill's second marriage. On January 12, 1853, he married Ellen Nolan in Saint Andrew Parish, Dublin. The couple had seven children: William (b. 1853), Katherine (b. 1856), Cornelius (b. 1857), Jeremiah Nolan (b. ca. 1859), Margaret (b. ca. 1861), Patrick Nolan (b. 1861), and Mary (b. 1863). (Katherine Mulvihill later married Thomas L. Wolfe.) The couple appears to have immigrated to Clinton County, Iowa, after the birth of their last child, and Ellen Mulvihill died there on September 23, 1865. She is buried at Saint James Cemetery in Toronto, Clinton County.

Cornelius Mulvihill and his second wife, Margaret Wolfe Mulvihill, had four children: Honoria (b. ca. 1874), Elizabeth "Bessie" (b. 1876), Thomas Edward (b. 1878), and Cornelius (b. 1880).

The Mulvihills farmed for the rest of their lives in Clinton County. Margaret Mulvihill died on January 5, 1888, and her husband sometime before 1900. They are buried together in Saint James Cemetery.

BRIDGET E. SHEEHAN NIXON
(1853–1910)

BRIDGET ELLEN SHEEHAN was born on June 28, 1853, in the parish of Athea, County Limerick. Her parents were Dennis Sheehan, a Catholic farmer, and Margaret Ellen Wolfe Sheehan. Her siblings included Mary (b. 1841), Patrick W. (b. 1843), Margaret Ellen (b. 1847), Dennis Wolfe (b. 1852), and Thomas (b. 1860).

Sheehan's brothers Patrick and Dennis immigrated to the United States in 1872, eventually settling in Newport, Rhode Island. At some point, together or separately, Bridget Sheehan and her brother Thomas joined them in Newport.

On November 27, 1900, she married John Nixon, also an Irish immigrant, at Saint Mary's Church in Newport. They had one child: James Joseph (b. 1889).

Sheehan died on October 28, 1910, in Newport. Her husband died on February 10, 1912.

ELLEN J. WOLFE REDMOND
(1832–1902)

ELLEN J. WOLFE was born in April 1832, in Listowel, County Kerry. This is based on her obituary and gravestone; however, a record notes the baptism of "Ellen Wolf" of Garryantanvally on October 5, 1829, in the parish of Listowel. She was the daughter of an unknown father and a mother with the maiden name O'Sullivan. Her paternal grandparents were James Maurice "The Barrister" Wolfe and Johanna McCoy and her siblings included Mary Agatha (b. 1834), John Edmond (b. 1837), and Patrick (b. ca. 1844), the latter's relationship remaining unconfirmed.

Wolfe and all of her known siblings immigrated to the United States, but the circumstances of their travel is unclear. They probably were accompanied by other relatives, and during the 1840s many Wolfes left Ireland and settled first in LaSalle County, Illinois, and then in Clinton County, Iowa. These included Ellen Wolfe's uncle John R. Wolfe and cousin Maurice Wolfe, who sailed together on the *Cornelia* in 1847; Thomas R. Wolfe, who sailed the *James H. Shepherd* in 1848; Richard Wolfe, who took the *Thomas H. Perkins* in 1848; Maurice R. Wolfe, who took the *Senator* in 1849; and Richard Wolfe, who sailed the *Liverpool* in 1849. All these men shared a descent from Maurice J. Wolfe.

Census records and Wolfe's obituary state she came to the United States in 1848 or 1849. By 1850, she was living a hotel in Ottawa, LaSalle County, Illinois, with her sister Margaret. They possibly worked as teachers.

On April 23, 1854, she married Eugene P. Redmond, like her an Irish immigrant, in LaSalle County, and the couple had five children: Jane (b. ca. 1855), Arthur (b. ca. 1859), Margaret (b. ca. 1859), Edward J. (b. 1861), and Richard (b. 1868). Eugene Redmond died sometime between 1870 and 1880.

Ellen J. Redmond died at her home in Ottawa, Illinois, and is buried in Saint Columba Cemetery in that city.

DENNIS W. SHEEHAN
(1852–1907)

DENNIS WOLFE SHEEHAN (sometimes spelled Denis) was born on June 15, 1852, in the parish of Robertstown, County Limerick. He was the son of Dennis Sheehan, a Catholic farmer, and Margaret Ellen Wolfe Sheehan. He was baptized on Foynes Island, on the River Shannon, near the village of Foynes. His siblings included Mary (b. 1841), Patrick W. (b. 1843), Margaret Ellen (b. 1847), Bridget Ellen (b. 1853), and Thomas (b. 1860).

Sheehan immigrated to the United States with his brother Patrick Sheehan, arriving in New York City on May 22, 1872. They settled in Newport, Rhode Island, where their siblings Bridget and Thomas Sheehan later joined them. According to an article written at the time of his death, Sheehan "went to work, soon after his arrival, for the late Thomas J. Lynch, by whom he was employed for a number of years. He was active and obliging, and made friends among all with whom he came in contact ..."

About 1880 Sheehan went into business for himself on Kinsley's Wharf in Newport, dealing in liquor, cigars, "choice family groceries, and table delicacies." In 1894 he moved to what the *Newport Mercury* described as a multistory "business block" on Thames Street. The building still stands.

On September 12, 1882, Sheehan married Julia Ann Halpin, of Newport, at Saint Mary's Church in Newport. The couple had seven daughters: Pauline Ellen Genevieve (b. 1884), Theresa Clarissa (b. 1886), May A. (b. 1889), Dorothy E. (b. 1892), Natalie D. (b. 1892), an infant who was born in 1894 and who died two days later, and Marguerite M. (b. 1896).

Sheehan died probably of a stroke on August 25, 1907, while in the water at Easton's Beach in Newport. The *Newport News* reported what happened:

> Mr. Sheehan, together with his wife and some of the children, had taken a brief bath and Mrs. Sheehan had retired in her bath house. Little Margaret wanted to go in the water

again, and her father took her in. They had just gone in at the west end of the beach, somewhat separated from the mass of bathers, when Mr. Sheehan, while in shallow water, settled down to his knees and the little girl ran to her mother's house and told that her father had a cramp in his foot. Bathers went to his assistance as he fell face downward in the water, and brought him out on the sand, while the life savers who had been farther up the beach began their work of resuscitation, supposing that he had swallowed a quantity of water.

Sheehan was buried on August 28 at Saint Columba's Cemetery in Newport. His wife, Julia, died in New York in 1946.

MARGARET E. WOLFE SHEEHAN
(b. 1818)

MARGARET ELLEN WOLFE was born on September 27, 1818, in Listowel, County Kerry. Her parents were Richard James Wolfe, a Catholic farmer, and Johanna Relihan Wolfe. Wolfe's siblings included James Richard (b. 1800), Maurice Richard (b. 1802), John Richard (b. 1809), Ellen (b. ca. 1810), Thomas Richard (b. 1811), Johanna (b. 1812), Richard (b. 1815), Edmond (b. 1821), and Patrick (b. 1822).

According to *Wolfe's History of Clinton County* (1911), edited by Judge Patrick B. Wolfe, Richard J. Wolfe was "the agent having charge of the property of the Knight of Kerry." The eighteenth knight of Kerry was Maurice FitzGerald, and his property, near Listowel, was Ballinruddery.

Margaret Wolfe's brothers Maurice, John R., Thomas R., and Richard Wolfe, along with a first cousin, Maurice Wolfe, all immigrated to the United States between 1847 and 1849, settling first in LaSalle County, Illinois. Some later moved on to Clinton County, Iowa.

Little is known of Margaret Wolfe's life. She married Dennis Sheehan, and they may have lived in the village of Foynes, County Limerick, near the coast on the River Shannon, between Limerick city and Listowel. The couple had at least six children: Mary (b. 1841), Patrick W. (b. 1843), Margaret Ellen (b. 1847), Dennis Wolfe (b. 1852), Bridget Ellen (b. 1853), and Thomas (b. 1860).

Patrick and Dennis Sheehan immigrated to the United States in 1872, and settled in Newport, Rhode Island. Bridget and Thomas Sheehan later joined them there.

Nothing else is known of Margaret Wolfe Sheehan's life, although it is assumed that she and her husband remained in Foynes until their deaths.

PATRICK W. SHEEHAN
(1843–1894)

PATRICK W. SHEEHAN was born on November 13, 1843, in the parish of Athea, County Limerick. He was the son of Dennis Sheehan, a Catholic farmer, and Margaret Ellen Wolfe Sheehan. His siblings included Mary (b. 1841), Margaret Ellen (b. 1847), Dennis Wolfe (b. 1852), Bridget Ellen (b. 1853), and Thomas (b. 1860).

Sheehan immigrated to the United States with his brother Dennis Sheehan, arriving in New York City on May 22, 1872. They settled in Newport, Rhode Island, where their siblings Bridget and Thomas Sheehan later joined them.

Sheehan did not marry or have children. He died on October 19, 1894, in Newport. He left behind the following will, recorded by the Newport Probate Court:

> I, Patrick W. Sheehan, of the city of Newport and the state of RI, do hereby publish, declare and make this my last will and testament, that is to say as follows:
>
> First, I nominate and appoint Dennis W. Sheehan the executor of this my last will and testament without being required to give bond for the proper performance thereof.
>
> Second: I give, bequeath and devise to Dennis W. Sheehan and his heirs all the real estate of which I shall be seized at the time of my death.
>
> Third: I give to Julia A Sheehan, the sum of one hundred dollars
>
> Fourth: to Ellen Pauline Sheehan—one hundred dollars
>
> Fifth: to my niece Theresa Sheehan—one hundred dollars
>
> Sixth: to Mary Agnes Sheehan—one hundred dollars
>
> Seventh: to Natalie Sheehan—one hundred dollars
>
> Eighth: To my sister Bridget Sheehan—fifty dollars
>
> Ninth: to my sister Mary Harnett—fifty dollars
>
> Tenth: to my sister Margaret Harrington the sum of fifty dollars if she is alive and can be found within six years,

said sum of fifty dollars and if not found to my brother Dennis W. Sheehan

Eleventh: To my brother Thomas Sheehan—one hundred dollars

And lastly: The residue of my estate whether real or personal property I give and bequeath to my brother Dennis W. Sheehan

The eighteenth day of October 1894.

Patrick W. (his mark) Sheehan

Peter F. Curley

Grace D. Seeley

MARGARET MAHER TWOHEY
(1829–1872)

MARGARET MAHER was baptized on February 26, 1829, in Duagh, County Kerry. Her parents were Patrick Maher and Ellen Wolfe Maher. Her siblings included Patrick (b. ca. 1831), Elizabeth (b. 1836), Johanna (b. 1838), Honora (b. ca. 1844), Bartholomew (b. 1846), Mary (b. 1848), Ellen (b. ca. 1849), and Catherine (b. 1853).

In 1849, Margaret Maher joined her mother's brother Maurice R. Wolfe and his family when they immigrated to the United States. They sailed from Liverpool to New York aboard the *Senator*, a 777-ton ship of the Black Star Line, owned by Samuel Thompson, arriving on September 22. Wolfe appears to have treated Maher as his own daughter, and after his death in 1870, she was named as an heir to his estate.

During the 1840s, many Wolfes left Ireland, including Margaret Maher's uncle John R. Wolfe and his cousin Maurice Wolfe, who sailed together in 1847; her uncle Thomas R. Wolfe, who sailed in 1848; her mother's cousin Richard Wolfe, who also sailed in 1848; and her uncle Richard Wolfe, who sailed separately from her in 1849. A cousin, John E. Wolfe, also came to the United States, and all of these Wolfes, including Margaret Maher, settled first in LaSalle County, Illinois. Some went on to Clinton County, Iowa. Maher's sister Elizabeth also immigrated, sailing to New York, probably in 1857, before settling in LaSalle County.

On June 26, 1854, Maher married James Twohey, a native of County Cork, in LaSalle County. The couple had nine children: Jeremiah (b. 1855), Mary A. "Mollie" (b. 1857), Ellen Honora (b. 1858), John Joseph (b. 1860), Jeremiah Lawrence (b. 1861), James William "Will" (b. 1864), Thomas Francis "Frank" (b. 1867), Clara Elizabeth (b. 1869), and Margaret I. (b. 1872).

The family lived and farmed in Rutland Township, LaSalle County, Illinois. On October 30, 1872, Margaret Twohey died while giving birth to her daughter Margaret. Her husband, James, died on

October 23, 1890, of asthma, in Rutland Township. They are buried together at Saint Columba's Cemetery in Ottawa, Illinois.

MARY K. WOLFE WELSH
(1929–2004)

MARY KATHRYN WOLFE was born on November 26, 1929, in Delmar, Iowa, the daughter of Raymond Bernard Wolfe and Gladys Elizabeth McGinn Wolfe. Her siblings were Sara Terese (b. 1926), Margery, and Thomas Anthony (b. 1940). Ray Wolfe was the grandson of Irish immigrants and farmed not quite 200 acres in Clinton County. He died in 1941.

Mary K., as she was known, graduated from the Saint Ambrose College Division of Nursing, in Davenport, Iowa, and went on to work first at the Veterans Administration in Iowa City and then as a registered nurse at Mercy Hospital in Davenport.

She loved to play tricks. In an essay, her brother Tom Wolfe recalled a summer's night in 1948, when he, his mother, and his sister Marge returned home from a night out in the nearby town of Maquoketa. The front door of their farmhouse was open, the living room in disarray, and some ghost-like apparition making noise. They ran for help but soon realized what had happened.

> As I continued my puzzled approach to our porch, this specter lost its fright, and the mystery began to slowly become clear. It was my big sister Mary Kay, dressed in some weird, witchlike garb, shrieking and laughing at us. It seems that she, a nursing student in Davenport, had come home to find the house unlocked as usual and wanted to teach our mother a lesson: always lock the door. She therefore faked the unwanted entry and pored ketchup on the counter to simulate blood. The fact that she frightened us all half to death did not particularly dampen her joy at having played such a ghoulish joke on us.

Wolfe married John Paul Welsh, of Davenport, on November 26, 1955, at Saint Mary's Catholic Church, in Davenport. The ceremony was conducted by the groom's brother, the Reverend Richard J. Welsh. The couple had four children: Michael Joseph, Anne Marie, Thomas James, and Mary Kathryn.

They lived in west Davenport until Mary K. Welsh's death on December 16, 2004. John Welsh, who had been the Midwest distributor for Swingline, died in 2017. They were interred together at Mount Calvary Cemetery, in Davenport.

SARA T. WOLFE WISSING
(1926–1998)

SARA TERESE WOLFE was born on August 2, 1926, in Delmar, Iowa, the daughter of Raymond Bernard Wolfe and Gladys Elizabeth McGinn Wolfe. Her siblings were Mary Kathryn (b. 1929), Margery, and Thomas Anthony (b. 1940). Ray Wolfe was the grandson of Irish immigrants and farmed not quite 200 acres in Clinton County. He died in 1941.

Sara Wolfe attended Mount Saint Clair Academy, in Clinton, then Rosary College, in River Forest, Illinois, before receiving a BA from Marycrest College in Davenport. She earned a masters degree in counseling from Western Illinois University, in Macomb, Illinois.

She married George Richard "Dick" Wissing, a lawyer originally of Sioux City, Iowa, on October 26, 1957, at Sacred Heart Cathedral, in Davenport. The couple had four children: Matthew Richard, Mary Elizabeth "Beth," Catherine Constance "Kate," and John Martin.

Sara Wissing worked as a social worker. She served as director of the Davenport office of Information Referral and Assistance Services and on the boards of the Vera French Mental Health Center, the Vera French Housing Center, the Center for Aging Services Inc., and the Independent Living Center, and as chair of the Iowa State Health Facilities. Late in her life she worked as the facilitator of the Single Parent–Displaced Homemaker program at Scott Community College, Eastern Iowa Community College District.

Sara Wolfe Wissing died on October 3, 1998, at Genesis Medical Center–West Campus, in Davenport. Her body was donated to the University of Iowa College of Medicine, in Iowa City, and then interred with her husband, who died on September 11, 2011, at Saint Patrick's Cemetery, in Delmar, Iowa.

CATHERINE WOLFE
(1890–1989)

CATHERINE WOLFE, also known as Caitlín de Bhulbh, was born on November 27, 1890, in the townland of Knocknasna, near Abbeyfeale, County Limerick. She was the eldest child of Thomas Wolfe and Johanna O'Connell Wolfe, both of Ballybehy. Her siblings included Hanora (b. 1892), Maurice (b. 1894), Patrick (b. 1896), Bridget (b. 1901), and Ellen (b. 1903).

Wolfe attended Springmount National School, in Abbeyfeale, and the Dominican boarding school at 19 Eccles Street, Dublin. In 1909 she matriculated at University College, Dublin, where she joined the Conradh na Gaeilge, or the Gaelic League, and studied Irish history and language under its founder, Douglas Hyde, who later served as the first president of Ireland (1938–1945). It may have been at this time that Wolfe adopted the Irish-language form of her name, Caitlín de Bhulbh. She graduated in 1912 with a bachelor of arts degree and a higher degree in education. She went on to teach at the Loreto Sisters secondary school at 77 Saint Stephen's Green, in Dublin, Ursuline College secondary school, in Sligo, and Passion school in Kilcullen, County Kildare.

NA HAISTEOIRI

In 1913, the playwright Piaras Béaslaí, with help from Dublin's Keating Branch of the Gaelic League, founded Na hAisteoiri (The Players), a theater troupe that produced and performed its plays in Irish. De Bhulbh was one of the group's approximately ten original members, which included the future republican and Sinn Féin politician Con Collins, also of West Limerick, and the republican sisters Bríd and Máire Dixon. In 1914 and 1915 Na hAisteoiri staged its works in Dublin, while also touring for a week in counties Cork and Kerry during the summer of 1914.

In a newspaper piece published in 1954, Béaslaí recalled the troupe's performance in Inchigeelagh, County Cork, in July 1914.

A feis or aeriocht had been recently held in a field adjoining the village, and the improvised platform, made of planks stretched across empty barrels, was still standing. We transferred planks and barrels to the village hall and made our stage. We had brought curtains and a "set" (of scenery) with us, and we borrowed furniture from the hotel where we were staying. In those days there were no buses and very few motors, and the people in country villages seldom got a chance of seeing a stage performance, I think practically everybody in the village and neighbourhood came to the performance. The schoolmaster, Mr. Tadhg Herlihy, very kindly stood at the door and collected the entrance money; and the curate, Father Fitzgerald ... sat in a front seat and, at the conclusion, made a speech warmly commending our work.

On October 24, 1914, de Bhulbh published "Hata Sheáin Mhic Eoin" in *An Claidheamh Soluis*, the Gaelic League newspaper. It was an Irish translation of "Het Jac Jones," a Welsh short story published in *Straeon y pentan* (1895), a collection by Daniel Owen (1836–1895). It's not clear where or when de Bhulbh learned to read Welsh, but her fellow member of Na hAisteoiri, Fionán Lynch, later recalled his experience of teaching in Swansea, Wales, and forming a branch of the Gaelic League there. Perhaps de Bhulbh learned the language through him.

In addition to Irish, she spoke Latin and French, and according to a former student, Kat Ahern, regularly traveled to a small town near Lourdes to maintain her accent. "The year she did not go to France," Ahern wrote, "she would be found in Ballinskelligs [in County Kerry], teaching and polishing her Irish."

Coláiste Mhuire

In 1937 de Bhulbh established Coláiste Mhuire (Saint Mary's College), a secondary school for girls in Abbeyfeale. Located on New Street in a two-story house rented from Tim Scannell, the school had room for two downstairs classrooms heated in the winter by turf-burning stoves. De Bhulbh's living quarters were upstairs. She later purchased the property and, as enrollment increased, leased space across the street from the Geany family (her brother Maurice was married to Ellen Geany). Tuition totaled £9 per year and never changed in the school's twenty-nine years. Four competitive scholarships were offered each year based on examination results.

De Bhulbh had a reputation as a strict disciplinarian but never used corporal punishment. "She was very impatient with those who were inclined to be 'upstarts' or insincere," Ahern wrote. "Her heart, however, was in the right place." Writing in the Abbeyfeale history magazine *Macalla na Mainistreach* in 2001, Jim O'Malley wrote, "Her stern appearance and her commanding voice, which had a certain nasal tone, demanded immediate attention."

"What Miss Woulfe said was law," a student recalled.

Classes were conducted in Irish. Ahern credited de Bhulbh for prioritizing drama and music in her curriculum and for emphasizing physical exercise. According to Ahern, de Bhulbh "was somewhat a loner or very individualistic type of person. She was also 'elegant' to a degree and was, justifiably, very proud of the Woulfe family who were banished from Limerick city to Cratloe in the West Limerick hills."

Coláiste Mhuire closed in 1966. De Bhulbh, who never married, died in January 1989 and is buried in Abbeyfeale. In 1991 former students placed a commemorative plaque on the New Street building that once housed the school.

CORNELIUS C. WOLFE
(1917–2006)

CORNELIUS COLBERT WOLFE was born on June 11, 1917, on New Street, Abbeyfeale, County Limerick. He was the son of Richard Barrett Wolfe, a pharmacist who lived with his family above the shop, and Catherine Elizabeth Colbert Wolfe. His siblings were Johanna Frances (b. 1914), Hanora Josephine (b. 1915), Richard Michael (b. 1919), and Michael Joseph Colbert (b. 1922). All of them became priests or nuns.

Wolfe's parents were active nationalists before and during the War of Independence (1919–1921). Catherine Wolfe's younger brother, Con Colbert, participated in the Easter Rising of 1916 and was executed at Kilmainham jail, in Dublin. Dick Wolfe's pharmacy became a hub of nationalist activity, and in 1920 it was damaged by the Black and Tans after the Irish Republican Army killed a local constable.

In September 1935, Con Wolfe joined the Spiritan Congregation, in Kilshane, County Tipperary, as a novitiate, professing his vows on September 5, 1936. He studied theology in Kimmage, south of Dublin, and was ordained a priest on July 16, 1944. Founded in 1703, the Spiritans, also known as the Holy Ghost Fathers, began working with former slaves in Haiti in the 1840s and in Africa in the 1860s, opening schools and hospitals.

After being ordained, Father Wolfe immediately joined the Spiritan mission in Nigeria, remaining there for twenty-five years. His sister Johanna, or Sister Mary Agatha of the Missionary Sisters of the Holy Rosary, lived in Nigeria during the same period, from 1938 until 1965.

Francis Cardinal Arinze was a student of Father Wolfe in Nigeria. In *God's Invisible Hand: The Life and Work of Francis Cardinal Arinze*, published in 2006 in the form of a long interview, Cardinal Arinze said that "we cannot speak of the Catholic school system in Eastern Nigeria without saying the names of Father John Jordan and Father Cornelius Wolfe." He continued:

> When I gave a conference in Steubenville, the Franciscan University in Ohio, in 1998, [Father Wolfe] was in the U.S.A. at a priests' conference. And when I was speaking to the priests, there he was in the audience. I greeted him, and I told the priests, "This is the priest missionary who was assistant education secretary for the diocese when I was in primary school, and he gave me the certificate of a good pass in religion in 1946." He was eighty years old on that day. I asked him to speak, but he was rather hesitant to speak. A very good man!

Father Wolfe moved to the United States in 1970. In 1976 he served as the hospital chaplain in Kingston, New York, and the next year became pastor at Saint Mary's Church in the same city. On June 17, 2002, his eighty-third birthday, Father Wolfe left Kingston for Ireland. "To those outside the church and Kingston Hospital," the *Daily Freeman News* reported, "the diminutive priest is perhaps best known for his work with the local chapter of the Hibernians. In fact, it is named after Father Woulfe, a familiar figure in his bright green beret, marching at the head of the Hibernian contingent. He was co-grand marshal of the 1990 Kingston St. Patrick's Day Parade."

On August 16, 2002, Father Wolfe entered the Marian House nursing home in Kimmage. He died there on November 1, 2008, and is buried at Shanganagh Cemetery, in Shankill, County Dublin.

DANIEL F. WOLFE
(ca. 1832–1882)

DANIEL F. WOLFE was born about 1832 in County Kerry, the son of Richard Wolfe, a Catholic farmer, and Mary Foley Wolfe. His siblings included Margaret (b. ca. 1826), Mary (b. 1826), Maurice (b. 1828), Mary Ellen (b. 1829), Patrick (b. 1830), Richard (b. 1836), John Maurice (b. 1838), Bridget (b. 1839), Edmund (b. 1840), and Richard J. (b. 1843). The first Richard died before 1848, and Bridget before 1847.

Wolfe immigrated to the United States in the company of his parents and siblings, traveling in steerage class aboard the *Thomas H. Perkins*. They arrived in New York from Liverpool on September 29, 1848. The family settled in LaSalle County, Illinois, joining relatives there.

In 1870, Wolfe was living in Ottawa, LaSalle County, Illinois, active in Democratic Party politics, and working as a distiller and the proprietor of a liquor store. At some point he joined with his cousin, Richard Wolfe, in running R. Wolfe and Company, a wholesale and retail liquor store in Ottawa. The partnership dissolved in January 1871. Wolfe lived with his sister, Margaret Wolfe Fanning, and sometime after 1877 moved west to the Dakota Territory, where he ran a saloon in the town of Wessington. On November 14, 1882, he was murdered by William McComber.

According to a report published in the *Wheeling* (West Virginia) *Register* on November 16, Wolfe was driving in a buggy with McComber near Wessington, Dakota Territory, when the two were observed to have separated, with one remaining in the buggy and the other going on foot. "A little while after," the paper reported, "some farmers in the vicinity, noticing that the prairie was on fire, went to put it out, and found Wolfe dead in the midst of the fire with a bullet through his head." Authorities speculated that McComber had set the fire to destroy evidence of the shooting. The report continued:

> From Wessington the murderer drove to St. Lawrence, and, with no apparent thought of the blood upon his hands,

engaged in a game of cards. From there he went to Miller. The sheriff, ascertaining the facts in the case, went to arrest him. On entering the house where he was, the sheriff said: "Mr. McComber, I have come to arrest you on a very grave charge." "Are you an officer" said McComber, coolly. The sheriff handed him his commission. McComber took it in his left hand (his right hand in his pocket), read it slowly and carefully through, remarked that it appeared all right, and then, suddenly drawing his revolver, said, "I'm a gone coon," and shot himself through the head, dying in fifteen minutes."

According to the paper, Wolfe had a large sum of money and was killed for it. McComber and Wolfe were described as "intimate friends." Another report, appearing in the *Indiana Weekly Messenger* on November 22, portrays Wolfe and McComber as strangers:

On the 10th instant a robust fellow entered the tavern kept by Daniel Wolfe in Wessington and, as he tossed his grip-sack on the bar, announced that he had come to buy a farm. He gave his name as William McComber, but he did not mention the place whence he had departed. The next day Wolfe happened to let it be known that he was going to Huron to pay some bills. McComber asked permission to join his host in the buggy ride, explaining that he wished to get a glimpse of the country.

Wolfe was buried with his parents at Saint Columba Cemetery in Ottawa, Illinois.

DAVID WOLFE
(1528–after July 23, 1579)

DAVID WOLFE was born in 1528 in Limerick city, County Limerick. Nothing is known of his immediate relations, although he appears to have hailed from a well-to-do Anglo-Norman family that was one of a few dozen families that ruled the island-city as a merchant-class oligarchy. Wolfes regularly appeared on the city council and served as mayor and sheriff. Wolfe later described Limerick as "the mightiest and most beautiful of all the cities of Ireland." He noted that it was fortified and "only accessibly by two stone bridges, one of fourteen arches, the other of eight." The houses within were cut from "black marble and built in the style of towers or fortresses." Ships of up to 400 tons docked at the walls, making the city, with Galway and Dublin, a center of trading and culture.

Wolfe became a priest, and sometime before 1555 the pope appointed him dean of the diocesan chapter, an administrative position that reports to the bishop. In addition to Irish and likely some English, he spoke Italian, Spanish, and Portuguese, suggesting a European education. In 1551, he first visited Ignatius of Loyola in Rome. The Spaniard had founded the Society of Jesus (Jesuits) ten years earlier and become its first Superior General. In 1554, Wolfe became the group's first Irish member, and on June 21, 1555, resigned his deanery as a consequence. His relative, Thomas Fanning, succeeded him.

In November 1555, Wolfe traveled to Loreto, Italy, to study. After the death of Loyola in 1556, Diego Laínez became Superior General and in April 1558 sent Wolfe to Modena, where he served as vice rector and then rector of the college. Wolfe was a strict, even unforgiving member of the church. In a letter to Laínez, dated July 12, 1559, he complained that the Irish bishops passing through Modena were unworthy and included among them public sinners and even a murderer.

Papal Commissary

Elizabeth ascended to the throne late in 1558 and two years later officially established the Protestant Church in Ireland. On August 2, 1560, Pope Pius IV appointed Wolfe papal commissary to Ireland, with Dermot Geraldine serving as his diplomatic companion. Ambassadors of the pope generally took the title nuncio and were appointed bishops; however, the Jesuits preferred that Wolfe not indulge in the office's worldly trappings, even as he accepted its many responsibilities. He served with the lesser title of commissary and had instructions to establish poor relief funds and schools, and to reform monasteries, among other activities. He was to take no payment or rewards for his labors.

Wolfe arrived in Ireland early the next year, setting up base in his home city of Limerick. He celebrated a public Mass attended by 2,000 people and gave church blessing to more than a thousand marriages. He also sent to Rome three new candidates for Jesuit membership: Maurice Halley, David Dymus, and his own relative Edmund Daniel. Over the next few years Wolfe traveled throughout Ireland, with the exception of the area around Dublin known as the Pale, where English authority was strongest. In Munster, Connacht, and Ulster he found the church to be low on resources and corrupt, writing that the bishops were "hirelings and dumb dogs." He even accused his own relative, Thomas Fanning, of simony, or the selling of church favors.

About 1563 he established a quasi-religious order of "fallen" women in Limerick known as Menabochta (from the Irish *mná bochta*, or poor women). They were to follow the order's rule, written by Wolfe, while still living in their own homes. That some members reverted to their old ways may have provided an opening for Wolfe's enemies and occasioned various rumors about him. Many in the church already resented the Jesuit for his anti-corruption efforts and for his unwillingness to accept recompense, while the Irish chieftains preferred to control the bishoprics, which came with land and money. They also strenuously opposed the queen. Wolfe and other church officials, at least for now, treated the monarch more diplomatically, swearing allegiance to the Crown while continuing to proclaim the pope as true head of the church. The tension between these two views sometimes led to violence, with at least one priest hanged and a bishop run out of Ireland.

Wolfe's energy began to flag. On July 29, 1563, he wrote his fellow Jesuit Francis Borgia that he felt "exiled in Ireland, far away from the fathers and brothers of the Society." On May 28, 1564, another Jesuit elder, Everard Mercurian, wrote to Laínez that Wolfe was "in danger of losing soul and body; he desires to be recalled because he cannot achieve that for which he was sent." The pope had other plans, however. Just three days later he issued a bull that ordered Wolfe and the new archbishop of Armagh, Richard Creagh, to establish Catholic schools in Ireland, including at least one university. The Jesuits felt that they were now helpless to recall Wolfe and instead urged him to move to Ulster, to be close to Creagh, his fellow Limerick native. They also promised that Jesuits would be sent to help him.

In January 1565 English authorities captured Creagh shortly after he arrived in Ireland and sent him to the Tower of London. A month later the English-speaking Jesuit William Good, who had traveled separately from Creagh, arrived in Limerick. With Edmund Daniel, a new Jesuit and one of Wolfe's relatives, he established a school in Limerick. It lasted about eight months before the English lost their patience with the pope's men in Ireland. A court issued a warrant that denounced Wolfe a traitor and authorized his arrest. With a bounty of £100 on his head, Wolfe fled across the Shannon in a skiff. At about the same time, after three months of periodic torture, Creagh managed to escape from the Tower, making his way first to Antwerp and then to Ulster.

The pope died on December 9, 1565, effectively ending Wolfe's ambassadorship.

REBELLION

The new Jesuit Superior General, Francis Borgia, tried to recall Wolfe from Ireland and its attendant dangers, but his efforts were complicated by debt. Wolfe owed local merchants 200 ducats, or £66, for support of the Limerick school and had promised them he would not leave the country without making good. In November 1566, Wolfe traveled north to meet Creagh and there became embroiled in a dispute with Cornelius MacArdle, the bishop of Colgher. MacArdle had published a libelous pamphlet against Wolfe, who responded in kind. MacArdle was denounced by Creagh, who ordered him to pay the Jesuit a fine of two hundred cows. But the episode suggests that

Wolfe's numerous enemies felt empowered now that he no longer reported directly to the pope. Indeed, when Creagh was captured again during the summer of 1568, rumors circulated that Wolfe had betrayed him. When MacArdle made the charge before a large crowd, Wolfe barely escaped alive.

Through the chieftain Hugh O'Donnell, Wolfe arranged a meeting with the English viceroy, Sir Henry Sidney, who promised him a written pardon in Dublin. Once in the capital, however, Sidney demanded that any pardon must be accompanied by the swearing of allegiance to the queen as true head of the church. Wolfe refused and was imprisoned at Dublin Castle, where he was interrogated and periodically tortured. His hair and beard were torn out and he was stripped naked and whipped with rods.

Never blessed with a diplomatic temperament, Wolfe seemed to turn irrevocably against the English during his captivity, which lasted from 1568 to 1572. Even earlier he had raised eyebrows by becoming close to the chieftains O'Donnell and Shane O'Neill. Then, in June 1569, one of his friends and allies, James FitzMaurice FitzGerald, launched the first of the Desmond Rebellions against the English in Munster. It was crushed in less than a year, although Wolfe and others surely welcomed a new papal bull, issued in February 1570, excommunicating Queen Elizabeth.

As Wolfe languished in Dublin Castle, both the pope and the Jesuits sent money as ransom but it never arrived. Wolfe's relative, the Jesuit Edmund Daniel, traveled to Portugal to collect money but was captured and found with a copy of the pope's bull intended for FitzMaurice. He was hanged, drawn, and quartered in 1572.

In September 1572 Wolfe managed to pay his jailor ransom with money from a local merchant, whom Wolfe promised to reimburse with money obtained from Portuguese Jesuits. He spent the next year on the run in Ireland attempting to gain passage to Portugal while also collecting material for what became *Description of the Realm of Ireland*. On September 17, 1573, he left for the Continent in the company of the merchant and a seven-year-old boy, FitzMaurice's eldest son.

In Portugal, Wolfe received a cold welcome, with many Jesuits resenting the debt he had thrust upon them. Rumors began to fly that the boy with him was actually the product of a relationship between

Wolfe and his niece. Others claimed he planned to use any money he raised not for ransom but to purchase munitions for a planned invasion of Ireland. In fact, Wolfe supported such an invasion and presented King Philip II with his *Description*, written in part to aid such a venture. In 1575 the Spanish king approved an invasion but pledged only money.

After a Jesuit investigations into rumors surrounding the child, Wolfe was cleared and the ransom reimbursed. By this time, however, his health was largely destroyed and there was little trust remaining between him and his fellow Jesuits. By 1577, when he met FitzMaurice in Rome, he was no longer a member of the Society, and two years later, when FitzMaurice sailed for Ireland and launched his second, ill-fated rebellion, Wolfe likely did not accompany him. He last appears in Jesuit records on July 23, 1579, and may have died soon after.

EDMOND WOLFE
(b. 1821)

EDMOND WOLFE, also referred to in some places as Edward, was baptized on February 2, 1821, at Garryantanvalla, parish of Listowel, County Kerry. He was the son of Richard James Wolfe, a Catholic farmer, and Johanna Relihan Wolfe. His baptismal sponsors were Jeremiah Maher and Honora McCoy. Wolfe's siblings included James Richard (b. 1800), Maurice Richard (b. 1802), John Richard (b. 1809), Ellen (b. ca. 1810), Thomas Richard (b. 1811), Johanna (b. 1812), Richard (b. 1815), Margaret Ellen (b. 1818), and Patrick (b. 1822).

Virtually nothing is known of Ned Wolfe's life. In *Wolfe's History of Clinton County* (1911), Judge Patrick B. Wolfe describes his grandfather Richard J. Wolfe as "the agent having charge of the property of the Knight of Kerry." The eighteenth knight of Kerry was Maurice FitzGerald and one of his properties, located near Listowel, was Ballinruddery. Richard Wolfe likely leased his own land, as well, and in 1844, his eldest son James and James's son Edmond took responsibility for that property.

In the meantime, many of Edmond Wolfe's siblings and cousins immigrated to the United States. These included his brother John R. Wolfe and their first cousin Maurice Wolfe, who sailed together on the *Cornelia* in 1847; brother Thomas R. Wolfe, who sailed the *James H. Shepherd* in 1848; cousin Richard Wolfe, who took the *Thomas H. Perkins* in 1848; brother Maurice R. Wolfe, who took the *Senator* in 1849; and brother Richard Wolfe, who sailed the *Liverpool* in 1849. Their cousin John E. Wolfe and his sisters also immigrated. The Wolfes settled first in LaSalle County, Illinois; some moved on to Clinton County, Iowa.

About 1841 Wolfe married Mary Liston, and the couple had at least three, but likely as many as six, children: Edmond E. (b. ca. 1842), James (b. 1848), and Margaret (b. 1849).

In 1851, the couple moved with their children to Ashgrove, directly south of the city of Limerick. Nothing more is known of their lives. He is buried at the Temple Athea graveyard, County Limerick.

EDMOND E. WOLFE
(ca. 1842–1889)

EDMOND E. WOLFE was born about 1842, in County Kerry. He was the son of Edmond Wolfe, a Catholic farmer, and Mary Liston Wolfe. He had at least two siblings: James (b. 1848), and Margaret (b. 1849).

Little is known about Wolfe's early years except that he appears to have joined many others in the extended Wolfe family in immigrating to the United States.

These included his uncle John R. Wolfe and Wolfe's first cousin Maurice Wolfe, who sailed together on the *Cornelia* in 1847; his uncle Thomas R. Wolfe, who sailed the *James H. Shepherd* in 1848; his uncle Richard Wolfe, who took the *Thomas H. Perkins* in 1848; his uncle Maurice R. Wolfe and cousin Margaret Maher, who took the *Senator* in 1849; and his uncle Richard Wolfe, who sailed the *Liverpool* in 1849. A cousin John E. Wolfe and his sisters also immigrated. These Wolfes settled in LaSalle County, Illinois, with some moving on to Clinton County, Illinois.

Edmond Wolfe immigrated to the United States and settled in LaSalle County sometime before 1867. On June 29 of that year he married Nancy Hartnet, a native of County Limerick, in LaSalle County. The couple had four children: Maurice M. (b. 1869), Catherine (b. 1872), Mary (b. ca. 1874), and Richard J. (b. 1876). The family farmed in Grand Rapids Township.

This was Nancy Hartnet Wolfe's second marriage. She had been in LaSalle County at least since 1860, when she worked as a servant in the household of John Nattinger. On April 26, 1862, she married John Brosnahan, of County Kerry, and had two children: Julia (b. 1864) and Daniel (b. 1865). John Brosnahan died on May 3, 1866, and his children went on to be raised by Edmond Wolfe and his new wife.

Wolfe died on March 25, 1889, after a month-long illness. The cause of death, according to his death certificate, was "lung fever," or pneumonia. His wife, Nancy, moved to Chicago with her son Daniel and died there on January 19, 1905.

EDMOND R. WOLFE
(1788–1876)

EDMOND RICHARD WOLFE was born on June 15, 1788, in the townland of Cratloe, parish of Athea, County Limerick. His parents were Richard Maurice Wolfe and Ellen O'Sullivan. The family estate at Cratloe had been purchased in March 1760 by Wolfe's grandfather, Maurice J. Wolfe. Prior to that, the Wolfe family had lived in Templeathea.

"Old Ned" Wolfe, as he was known, had at least three siblings: Maurice Richard (b. 1778), Margaret "Peggy James" (d. 1874), and Patrick "Old Paddy." Little is known of Wolfe's life.

He married Ellen "Nellie" Brosnan, of Islandanny, County Kerry, on June 15, 1812. They had two sons and seven daughters, including Edmond, Richard Edmond "Dicky Ned" (b. 1825), Ellen "Nell," Johanna "Joan," Bridget (b. ca. 1829), and Julia (b. ca. 1838).

Family oral history—contained in a letter written by Wolfe's great-granddaughter Jane C. "Dollie" Wolfe and dated August 1956 from Cratloe, also known as the "Aunt Dollie" letter—suggests that Wolfe "was rather a prominent man in the district in his day. Amongst other things he was what was called a 'warden' in Daniel O'Connell's Repeal organisation in the thirties and forties of the last century." The Repeal Association sought an end to the Act of Union, which had joined Great Britain and Ireland. Wolfe's efforts on behalf of Repeal are corroborated by newspapers of the time, such as the *Cork Examiner*, which on December 30, 1842, reported that he had raised more than a pound for the movement. The *Freeman's Journal* of December 19 of that year describes a dinner in which a movement leader "begged to introduce Mr. Woulfe, a gentleman who had come in with 10 [pounds?], which he had collected in the mountainous parish of Athea. The gentleman was received with three enthusiastic cheers, and took his seat at the festive board."

Almost a century later, in 1931, the *Limerick Leader* reported on Wolfe's contributions to the Repeal movement. According to Timothy Wolfe, in 1842 Edmond Wolfe ran for the Board of Guardians to represent Monegay in the Newcastle West district of County Limerick in opposition to the candidate put forward by his landlord, William Courtenay, tenth earl of Devon. "And all who have any idea of the conditions of the time," the *Leader* wrote, "will understand the magnitude of that venture and task that he accomplished in being about the first farmer in Ireland to defeat, which he did, his landlord's nominee, for a seat on a public board."

Wolfe built a family home at the Glen, Cratloe, in 1815. Nellie Brosnan Wolfe died in 1869 and Edmond Wolfe on May 13, 1876. They are buried together at the Temple Athea graveyard.

EDMUND D. WOLFE
(1853–1921)

EDMUND DEAN WOLFE was baptized on October 19, 1853, in Vermillion Township, LaSalle County, Illinois. He was the son of Maurice Richard Wolfe, who bred horses and came from a Catholic farming family, and Johanna Downey Wolfe. His godparents were Bart Hepler and Anna Kearney. His siblings included Margaret (b. 1827), Richard Downey (b. 1829), Stephen (b. 1833), James Downey (b. 1839), Johanna E. (b. 1840), Catherine "Kate" (b. 1842), Maurice (b. 1848), and John Francis (b. 1850).

Wolfe's parents and all but one of his siblings had immigrated to the United States in 1849, settling with other Wolfes in LaSalle County.

Census data suggests that in 1880 Wolfe may have been living in District 87, Kanabec, Minnesota, working as a laborer in the household of T. P. McKussick.

On December 29, 1886, Wolfe married Margaret Estella Mooney, a native of Medina, Peoria County, Illinois, at Saint Joseph's Church in the city of Peoria. The couple had five children: Johanna Irene "Gerena" (b. 1887), William Anthony (b. 1889), Edward "Don" (b. 1891), Richard (b. 1896), and Maurice Eugene (b. 1897). Richard Wolfe died within days of his birth.

In 1887, Wolfe owned a hardware and general store in Peoria. Then, about 1891, he moved to Superior, Wisconsin, working initially in real estate. In 1892 he operated Wolfe & Maher Grocers with his nephew Maurice E. Maher, son of his sister Margaret.

On June 14, 1893, he signed a mortgage worth $3,000 to purchase Lot 18, Block 26, in Anaconda, Montana, a debt he discharged in July 1894. Located in southwestern Montana, Anaconda, Deer Lodge County, was mining country. Marcus Daly, an immigrant from County Cavan, founded the town in 1883 and attempted to name it Copperopolis, but the name was already taken. In 1893, the Amalgamated Copper Mining Company (later Anaconda Copper Mining Company) formed, with Daly as vice president. In 1895, Daly opened a smelter near the town, and city directories from 1896 and 1898 indicate that Wolfe worked there. Wolfe's cousin, Catherine "Kate" Wolfe Fitzgerald, also lived in Anaconda at the time.

On July 1, 1903, Wolfe paid a $22 filing fee toward a homestead application for 160 acres near the smelter (Section 14, Township 4 North, Range 11 West). He attested to having built an eight-room framed house on the property on May 10, 1898, and having lived there since with only a four-month absence. That absence, according to Wolfe, was provoked "by damage and sickness from smelter smoke of the smelters adjoining the homestead. We were compelled to leave." From November 22, 1902, until April 1, 1903, the family lived in Butte. His witness corroborated his story, describing "poisonous smelter fumes," and describing the property as "mountainous ... A small portion of it is agricultural and the balance of it is rocks ... He couldn't sell it for 25 cents."

By 1910 Wolfe and his family had moved to Deer Lodge City, Montana, and on or about September 5, 1911, he and his son William purchased about 200 acres there from C. M. and Lottie Hansen with the intention of starting a dairy farm. They soon organized a business they called Big Four Dairy. In 1913, the two bought 1,100 acres of land in Idaho. According to a Montana newspaper report, "Mr. Wolfe and a younger son will operate the stock ranch which is in the Lemhi valley, while W. A. Wolfe will keep up the interest here." On November 5, 1918, Wolfe purchased another 434 acres that were once part of the Lemhi Indian Reservation, abandoned in 1907.

Wolfe died on July 14, 1921, at his home in Lemhi, Idaho, about a week after being struck by lightning. According to an account in the *Idaho Recorder*, "Mrs. Wolfe had left him only a few minutes before when he was talking as usual. On her return to the room her husband had ceased to breathe. Apparently he passed on without a struggle." His wife, Margaret, died on July 22, 1946. They are buried together at Mountain View Cemetery in Dillon, Montana.

EDWARD A. WOLFE JR.
(1929–2009)

EDWARD ANTHONY WOLFE JR. was born on January 2, 1929, in Los Angeles, California, the son of Edward Anthony Wolfe and Anna Luetta Murphy Wolfe. His siblings included James Edward (b. 1921), Julianna A. "Julie" (b. 1923), Margaret Sue (b. 1925), and Jack Frankhobart (b. 1931).

The senior Wolfe was the son of Richard Carey Wolfe, whose parents had immigrated from County Kerry to LaSalle County, Illinois, and then to Clinton County, Iowa, where they farmed. He served in the U.S. Army Corps of Engineers from 1917 to 1919 and then worked on highway engineering projects in Jerome, Arizona, and Los Angeles, before settling in Escondido, San Diego County.

Ed Wolfe Jr. graduated from Escondido Union High School in 1946 and then served two years as a paratrooper in the U.S. Army, spending a year in occupied Japan. After his discharge, he attended Fullerton Junior College in Fullerton, Orange County, California. In 1949, he signed a contract to pitch for a minor league affiliate of the Pittsburgh Pirates, and spent eight years in baseball, playing in California, Oklahoma, South Carolina, and Louisiana.

In 1952, he was called up to pitch for the Pirates, making his Major League debut on April 19 against the Cincinnati Reds, a game the Pirates lost 9 to 3. In two-thirds of an inning Wolfe gave up two hits and two earned runs, an inauspicious start for the six-foot-three, hard-throwing right-hander and member of what a local paper dubbed general manager Branch Rickey's "Pirate kindergarten."

The Pirates were already showing signs of what would become a historically bad season. The team ended with a record of 42–112, putting them 54.5 games behind the first-place Brooklyn Dodgers. The team's .273 winning percentage is the seventh worst in baseball's modern era.

Wolfe pitched again on April 21 and April 25 before being sent back to the minor leagues. He never pitched in the Majors again, having thrown just three and two-thirds innings and given up seven hits, three earned runs, one home run, and five bases on balls. He struck out one and hit one batter. Wolfe's brother Jack played three seasons of minor league baseball but never made it to the Major Leagues.

Wolfe married Sally K. Grunning about 1950; the couple divorced in January 1977. He married Diane Marie Doer on May 11, 1980, in Contra Costa, California. Ed Wolfe died on March 8, 2009, and is interred at Oak Hill Memorial Park, in Escondido.

ELLEN MAHER WOLFE
(ca. 1849–1943)

ELLEN MAHER was born about 1849, probably near Listowel, County Kerry, the daughter of Patrick Maher and Ellen Wolfe Maher. Her siblings included Margaret (b. 1829), Patrick (b. ca. 1831), Elizabeth (b. 1836), Johanna (b. 1838), Honora (b. 1844), Bartholomew (b. 1846), Mary (b. 1848), and Catherine (b. 1853).

In 1849, Maher's sister Margaret immigrated to the United States with her mother's brother Maurice R. Wolfe. Her sister Elizabeth immigrated in 1857. During the 1840s, many Wolfes left Ireland, including Ellen Maher's uncle John R. Wolfe and his cousin Maurice, who sailed together in 1847; her uncle Thomas R. Wolfe, who sailed in 1848; her mother's cousin Richard Wolfe, who also sailed in 1848; and her uncle Richard Wolfe, who sailed separately from her in 1849. A cousin, John E. Wolfe, also came to the United States, and all of these Wolfes, including Margaret and Elizabeth Maher, settled first in LaSalle County, Illinois. Some went on to Clinton County, Iowa.

On February 26, 1881, Maher married Richard J. "Brown Dick" Wolfe in Listowel, and the couple had at least six children: Honora "Nora" (b. 1882), John R. J. (b. 1883), Ellen "Ellie" (b. 1885), Patrick (b. 1887), Kathleen (b. ca. 1889), and Maurice J. (b. 1891). Ellie Wolfe died of meningitis on October 11, 1894.

Ellen Maher Wolfe's sister Honora also married back into the Wolfe family, wedding James P. "Paddy" Wolfe.

For forty years Richard Wolfe sat on the Newcastle West Rural District Council and Board of Guardians, one of several such bodies in Limerick empowered by Parliament to aid the poor and help defray the costs of emigration. He died at the Limerick County Infirmary, after an operation, on June 7, 1915. Ellen Wolfe died in the townland of Cratloe on September 29, 1943. They are buried at the Temple Athea graveyard.

GEORGE WOLFE
(fl. 1643–1651)

GEORGE WOLFE was born in Limerick city, County Limerick, the son of James Wolfe and a mother whose identity is unknown. He had four, possibly five brothers: Patrick (the eldest), James, Andrew, Stephen, and Francis, the latter's relationship remaining unconfirmed.

Wolfe's father was a Catholic merchant who owned about 1,500 acres of land. At one point, George Wolfe was set to inherit the estate, but his father rewrote his will several times before finally awarding the land to his son Patrick.

In 1643, George Wolfe appears in the historical record as a magistrate. Three years later he is described as a merchant in support of the Irish Catholic Confederation making peace with its Anglo-Irish, royalist foes, led by James Butler, marquess of Ormonde. Wolfe's brother James, a Dominican friar, was one of the loudest voices against such a treaty, negotiated first in 1646 and then again in 1649. The purpose of the alliance was to oppose Oliver Cromwell's New Model Army, which invaded Ireland in 1649.

In October 1650, Cromwell's son-in-law, Henry Ireton, mounted a siege of Limerick only to abandon it by winter. In June 1651, however, he returned with 8,000 men, twenty-eight siege artillery pieces, and four mortars. By this time, Wolfe had joined the city's defense with the rank of captain.

Soon after the city surrendered to Ireton on October 27, 1561, the English commander arrested and hanged Fathers James and Francis Wolfe. The same fate was ordered for George Wolfe, and some histories claim he was, indeed, hanged. Others tell a different story. John Ferrar, in *The History of Limerick: Ecclesiastical, Civil and Military*, published in 1787, writes that, under the threat of death, Wolfe

> fled to the North of England, where he settled, and his grandson general Edward Woulfe, was appointed colonel of the 8th regiment of foot, in the year 1745. He transmitted his virtues with additional lustre, to his son major general

> James Woulfe, whose memory will be ever dear to his country, and whose name will be immortalized in history.

James Wolfe captured Quebec for the English in 1759 during the Seven Years' War (1756–1763).

The military historian E. M. Lloyd concurs in volume 62 of the *Dictionary of National Biography*, published in 1900, as does the historian Beckles Wilson, in a biography of James Wolfe published in 1909. Wilson suggests that Captain George Wolfe's family had originally been English, and that "before they emigrated to Ireland, were of respectable stock." Referring to the siege of Limerick, he accuses Wolfe and his brothers of having "urged the populace to protracted resistance." After being sentenced to death, Wolfe escaped to Yorkshire, "married, and adopted the Reformed faith. Thereafter the superfluous 'u' [of Woulfe] is erased from his name."

The Catholic historian Myles O'Reilly, writing in 1869, finds the connection between Captain George and General James Wolfe lamentable, particularly considering the fate of George's brother James.

> It is a strange fact, and one that we must regret, that England should owe the final conquest of Canada to one who should have honored this martyr of his family, but who was really intensely English, and rivalled Ireton by his bloody march up the St. Lawrence, butchering priests at their own church doors with as little compunction as Ireton felt for Father James Wolf.

There is no definitive evidence in favor of or against this theory regarding a family connection between George and James Wolfe.

HANORA J. WOLFE
(1915–2015)

HANORA JOSEPHINE WOLFE, later Sister Íde, was born on December 3, 1915, in Abbeyfeale, County Limerick, to Richard Barrett Wolfe and Catherine Colbert Wolfe. She had four siblings: Johanna Frances (b. 1914), Cornelius Colbert "Con" (b. 1917), Richard Michael (b. 1919), and Michael Joseph Colbert (b. 1922). All of the Wolfe children were priests or nuns.

Wolfe's parents were active nationalists before and during the War of Independence (1919–1921). Catherine Wolfe's younger brother, Con Colbert, participated in the Easter Rising of 1916 and was one of fifteen men executed at Kilmainham jail, in Dublin. Dick Wolfe ran a pharmacy on New Street in Abbeyfeale that became a hub of nationalist activity, and in 1920 it was damaged by the Black and Tans after the Irish Republican Army killed a local constable.

In an oral history conducted when she was in her nineties, Hanora Wolfe, then Sister Íde, recalled how the Black and Tans had attempted to arrest her father. "They were going to shoot him," she said, "and I understand my mother screamed. She was upstairs. They'd locked my mother and one of the babies in [...] They were trying to burn the house and my mother in it." Dick Wolfe, however, was able to free her and escape out the back.

> Now, at the back of our house, our garden opened into the river [Feale], and it seems he got out to the river and walked the river that night. And he walked, the story is told, in such a way that he got to the convent. And the nuns took him in and hid him behind the altar. And the soldiers came to the convent, and the reverend mother met them, but I think she must have told them they couldn't go into the chapel, and they respected that. And he escaped, and so he was on the run from then on until the Truce.

Dick Wolfe sometimes hid at the nearby home of his sister Catherine Wolfe White. Sister Íde recalled that he had shaved his mustache and pretended to be "Uncle Jack," so that even his young daughter, then about five years old, did not recognize him.

> They told me he was Uncle Jack because there were girls in the school whose people were on the other side, and they would ask you, "Who was at your house last night?" And I was, I suppose, so innocent [...] And when the Truce came, and I do remember this, they told me this was my daddy, and I went under the table and said, "No, no, no, it was Uncle Jack." And I was crazy about Uncle Jack because, naturally, when he would come to the house he was everything to me. But he was *definitely* Uncle Jack. And it took them quite awhile to get it into my mind that this was my father.

Hanora Wolfe attended primary school in Abbeyfeale and then, in October 1934, matriculated at the Saint Louis Secondary School in Tirkeenan, County Monaghan, run by the Sisters of Saint Louis. Classes were conducted in Irish, and Wolfe recalled that she attended this particular school largely because her father was "very keen" on the language. After she died, the nun who delivered her eulogy recalled that Wolfe was "by her own account, a bit of a tomboy, often disregarding the rules and getting herself into trouble. Such unseemly behavior was evidently no obstacle to pursuing a vocation in religious life." In August 1935 she began her novitiate, taking the name Sister Íde, after Saint Íte, of Killeedy, in West Limerick, who lived in the fifth century. Two years later, in August 1937, Sister Íde took her vows.

She taught in Aylesbury, Buckinghamshire County, England, and then in Balla, County Mayo. In 1946, she was appointed assistant mistress of novices at the convent in Monaghan. He eulogist recalled that Sister Íde "gained a reputation for being tough, strict, forthright, a straight talker who shot from the hip but at the same time she was always fair and just."

After four times being refused foreign missionary assignments, Sister Íde trained as a nurse in England and then as a midwife in Drogheda. She eventually was sent to Ghana, in West Africa, where she ran a hospital. She later worked as a nurse in Nigeria and trained for a year as a hospital chaplain in San Francisco, where her brother, Father Michael Wolfe, was then living.

She then became the Catholic chaplain at the City Hospital in Belfast, Northern Ireland, tending to the sick and dying until she herself died on July 4, 2015, at Musgrave Park Hospital, Stockman's Lane, Belfast. She is buried in that city's Hannaystown Cemetery.

HONORA MAHER WOLFE
(1844–1927)

HONORA MAHER, known as Nanno, was born in 1844, probably near Listowel, County Kerry, the daughter of Patrick Maher and Ellen Wolfe Maher. Her siblings included Margaret (b. 1829), Patrick (b. ca. 1831), Elizabeth (b. 1836), Johanna (b. 1838), Bartholomew (b. 1846), Mary (b. 1848), Ellen (b. ca. 1849), and Catherine (b. 1853).

In 1849, Maher's sister Margaret immigrated to the United States with her mother's brother Maurice R. Wolfe. Her sister Elizabeth immigrated in 1857. During the 1840s, many Wolfes left Ireland, including Honora Maher's uncle John R. Wolfe and his cousin Maurice, who sailed together in 1847; her uncle Thomas R. Wolfe, who sailed in 1848; her mother's cousin Richard Wolfe, who also sailed in 1848; and her uncle Richard Wolfe, who sailed separately from her in 1849. A cousin, John E. Wolfe, also came to the United States, and all of these Wolfes, including Margaret and Elizabeth Maher, settled first in LaSalle County, Illinois. Some went on to Clinton County, Iowa.

Virtually nothing is known of Wolfe's life except that on February 26, 1870, she married James P. "Paddy" Wolfe. Maher's sister Ellen also married a Wolfe, Richard J. "Brown Dick" Wolfe.

Paddy and Nanno Wolfe had at least eight children: Johanna (b. 1871), Patrick (b. 1872), Richard (b. 1873), Ellen (b. 1876), Maurice James (b. 1877), John J. (b. 1880), James (b. 1882), and Timothy (b. 1885). Johanna became Sister Bonaventure, Patrick a respected priest, nationalist, and scholar of the Irish language, and Timothy a medical doctor.

Paddy Wolfe died on April 26, 1922, and Honora Wolfe on April 22, 1927.

Honora "Nanno" Wolfe

HONORIA E. WOLFE
(1871–1951)

HONORIA EUPHRASIA WOLFE, known as Honor, was born on April 3, 1871, in Streator, Illinois. She was the daughter of Richard Downey Wolfe, a farmer and Irish Catholic immigrant, and his second wife, Margaret Shine Lyons, also an Irish immigrant. She had seven full siblings: Johanna (b. 1867), Daniel Maurice (b. 1869), Maurice Patrick (b. 1873), Margaret Theresa (b. 1875), Richard (b. 1878), Marie Louise (b. 1881), and Aileen Gregory (b. 1884). She also had a half sibling, Katherine Collins (b. 1863), whose mother was Richard Wolfe's first wife, Margaret O'Kane Wolfe.

Honor Wolfe's father farmed first in LaSalle County, Illinois, and then, beginning early in the 1870s, in Missouri. The son of a breeder, he loved horses and died from a kick in the head in 1885. Several years later his widow moved the family to Texas, eventually settling in Waco. There Daniel Wolfe opened Woulfe & Co., a bookstore and gift shop at 618 Austin Avenue. At some point his sisters took over its management until 1909, when they sold the business. This seems to have coincided with the tragic death of another brother, Maurice Wolfe, and his entire family in a hurricane west of Galveston. On December 1, 1913, Honor Wolfe and her sisters reopened the bookstore, which featured a tearoom and shared space with the Waco Talking Machine Co.

A notice in the *Waco Morning News*, ahead of the opening, described the store: "The interior and fixtures are done in which enamel. A reproduction of [Bertel] Thorwaldsen's frieze, the Triumphal Entrance of Alexander into Babylon, a masterpiece of modern sculpture seldom seen outside of museums, covers the walls, which are done in green."

It's unclear what education Wolfe received, but in 1897 she was advertised as an elocutionist and she traveled in literary circles. On March 24, 1912, the *New York Times* noted that a meeting of the American Playgoers would meet at Wolfe's home at 867 Riverside Drive, in New York. The next year she copyrighted a one-act play titled "What Is Love?" In 1907, while traveling in Ireland and Europe, she first met the Irish writer George Moore, who in 1899 helped W. B. Yeats establish what became the Abbey Theatre in Dublin. The two maintained a lifelong friendship that Wolfe described in an unpublished essay after the writer's death in 1933. She wrote of long walks through Saint Stephen's Green, talking literature, and even helping him write drafts of plays.

"Our chats or talks ranged over a variety of subjects in those early Dublin days," she wrote. "Coming from Texas he took it for granted that I should be an authority on the art and artifice of cowpunching, cattle branding, and the amazing intricacies of the lariat as exhibited by Will Rogers. In this, of course, he found me uninformed and vastly ignorant."

Wolfe noted that she preserved a number of his letters, which have been preserved at the University of Texas. One, dated June 2, 1917, suggests that their relationship had been intimate. "The letter before me is the letter of a woman to a man whom she knows to be a man," Moore wrote to Wolfe, "and this letter is the letter of a man to a woman whom he knew to be a woman. A sexual memory is a wonderful memory, it transcends all other memories, and I am sorry for those who have not tasted the poetry of sex."

Rumors of a relationship between the two dated at least to the publication, in 1914, of Moore's short story, "Euphorion in Texas." (It was later republished in 1921 as part of his *Memoirs of My Dead Life*.) In it, a Texas woman named Honor calls on Moore at his home in Dublin, showering him with compliments and, after the conversation takes a flirtatious turn, suggesting that she was in the market for a man who might father a child.

> "I have never thought of anybody definitely, only that I would like to give Texas a literature; and when I read your books—"
>
> "You thought of me?"
>
> She had paid me the compliment of thinking of me as a possible father for her son, as a man who was likely to beget a son who would give a literature to Teas; and my curiosity [was] now enkindled as it had never been before, and as it will never be again ...

In her own memoir of Moore, Wolfe explained that the story was about other people and "embroidered to fit into the Texas environment." She wrote that she "was not greatly impressed" by the story but that over the years it became a source of ribbing from her friends and annoyance for Moore, who continually and in vain asked her to help him expand upon it.

In 1915, Wolfe was serving as president of the Waco Business Woman's League and delivered a speech titled "The Users of Natural Gas." In the mid-1920s she owned and operated the Main Hotel in Corsicana, Texas, an oil-boom town north of Waco. During the next decade she appears to have worked as a writer in Hollywood. She later went to live with her sister Marie in Chicago, where she died on November 7, 1951. She was buried in Graceland Cemetery there.

Honor Wolfe, painting by Charles Courtney Curran, 1912

JAMES WOLFE
(d. before 1638)

JAMES WOLFE, also known as James Wolfe of Corbally, was born perhaps in the 1570s in Limerick city, County Limerick. He was the son of Richard Wolfe, who was sheriff of Limerick in 1591; the grandson of John Wolfe, bailiff of the city in 1567 and mayor in 1578; great grandson of Thomas Wolfe, city sheriff in 1520; and great-great grandson of Thomas Wolfe, also known as Thomas Wolfe of Ballyphilip, who was sheriff in 1476.

Wolfe was a Catholic merchant of Limerick and Corbally (present-day Longstone, parish of Geran). His wife is believed to have the surname Harold, and the couple had five, possibly six sons: Patrick, George, James, Andrew, Stephen, and Francis, the latter's relationship remaining unconfirmed. Patrick likely became a merchant or farmer, while George joined the military and James, Andrew, and Francis the priesthood.

Records indicate that, in 1611, Wolfe advanced £108 and twelve three-year-old milch cows to Edmund Burke of Garranekishy toward the purchase of land that had once been in the Wolfe family. He established title to the land three years later. His estate totaled about 1,500 acres.

Wolfe wrote his first will in 1620, awarding the property to his eldest son, Patrick. He twice revoked the will, however, each time leaving his estate to different sons. When he died, sometime before 1638, his will had been amended again, this time in favor of Patrick. Patrick Wolfe died soon after his father, and the estate's ultimate inheritor was his eldest son, James Wolfe.

JAMES WOLFE
(d. 1651)

JAMES WOLFE was born in Limerick city, County Limerick, Ireland, the son of James Wolfe and a mother whose identity is unknown. He had four, possibly five, brothers: Patrick (the eldest), George, Andrew, Stephen, and Francis, the latter's relationship remaining unconfirmed.

Wolfe's father was a Catholic merchant who owned about 1,500 acres of land. At one point, James Wolfe was set to inherit the estate, but his father rewrote his will several times before finally awarding the land to his son Patrick.

Little is known of Wolfe's early years. At some point, he joined the mendicant Order of Preachers (also known as the Dominicans) and was ordained a priest. The order, which emphasized academic study, was organized into three levels of schooling: prior, provincial, and general. Wolfe served as prior-provincial for several priories, responsible for the general oversight of teaching and curriculum. At the time of his death, he was preacher-general, an appointed position reserved for those who had studied theology at least three years. The preacher-general's main task was to preach, but he was limited to the area served by the priory.

Wolfe was preacher-general of the Limerick priory during the second of the Irish Confederate Wars (1649–1653), in which Oliver Cromwell led his New Model Army against a coalition of Irish Catholics and royalists. In October 1650, Cromwell's son-in-law, Henry Ireton, mounted a siege of Limerick, which he abandoned by winter. In June 1651, however, he returned with 8,000 men, twenty-eight siege artillery pieces, and four mortars.

Wolfe's brothers, Captain George Wolfe and Father Andrew Wolfe, also lived in the city at the time, as did Father Francis Wolfe.

According to Maurice Lenihan, who wrote an account of the siege in volume 2 of *Limerick; Its History and Antiquities, Ecclesiastical Civil and Military* (1866), Wolfe was an outspoken character. He had opposed both peace treaties (in 1646 and 1649) that allied members of the Irish Catholic Confederation, which had ruled Ireland from

1642 until 1649, with Anglo-Irish opponents of Cromwell, some of whom were Protestant and who had previously waged war on the Confederation. These royalists were led by James Butler, marquess of Ormonde.

Limerick was the seat of the Confederation, but when, in 1646, the city's mayor and Ormonde's representatives announced the treaty, Wolfe rose before a crowd of 500 armed citizens and "fulminated excommunication" against the treaty's supporters. On cue, the "people fell suddenly on the herald, flung stones at him, at Bourke the mayor, and all the aldermen who were about him, and all those of the 'better sort' who had countenanced the action."

When, on June 11, 1651, Ormonde proposed garrisoning some of his troops in Limerick, Wolfe "raised a tumult in the city to oppose his entrance," causing the royalist general to commandeer corn from the city and retire to the River Shannon, about four miles away. Soon after, Cromwell's men arrived and began their second siege.

The inhabitants of Limerick were led during the siege by Hugh Dubh O'Neill, the governor and military commander, and Terence Albert O'Brien, bishop of Emly. According to Lenihan, "they were nobly seconded by ... the zealous Father Wolfe," among others. Over four months, however, the siege caused food shortages and deadly outbreaks of disease. "Councils became divided within the walls," Lenihan wrote "Death stalked through the streets, grim and ghastly, whilst the plague-victims lay on the foot-paths, spectacles for men to weep over."

As the siege neared an end and Ireton's victory seemed certain, the English commander made clear his intentions to execute Bishop O'Brien, Governor O'Neill, and others who had refused to surrender. According to Lenihan, Wolfe still counseled resistance and "cautioned the trembling cravens as to what they were about." Limerick surrendered on October 27, 1651.

Ireton spared O'Neill but not O'Brien and Wolfe. One historian, writing in 1854, argues that Wolfe was not in Limerick during the siege, but "solicitous of the salvation of souls and of consoling the Catholics, privately reached the city, and after eight days was betrayed and delivered over to the heretics." Whatever the case, he was sentenced to death.

The standard account of Wolfe's death appears in *The Irish Dominicans of the Seventeenth Century*, written in Latin by John O'Heyne and published in 1706; an English translation appeared in 1902. It is written in the style of hagiography:

> At length he [Wolfe] was captured in Limerick while celebrating mass and received sentence of death within a few hours; he was then brought to the market-place and having made a public profession of the Catholic faith, exhorted the faithful to constancy. When he reached the highest rung of the ladder from which he was to be thrown, he exclaimed with a joyful voice: "We are made a spectacle to God, to the angels, and to men: to God to his greater glory, to the angels to their joy, and to the men to their contempt." Soon after he expired on the gibbet.

Wolfe, considered a martyr by the Irish church, was presented for beatification in 1915 but, unlike Bishop O'Brien, was not among the seventeen Irish martyrs so honored by Pope John Paul II on September 27, 1992.

JAMES B. WOLFE
(1844–1916)

JAMES BUCKLEY WOLFE was born on April 13, 1844, probably in Listowel, County Kerry. He was the eldest child of John Richard Wolfe, an Irish Catholic farmer, and Honora Buckley Wolfe. He had seven siblings who survived to maturity: Patrick Bernard (b. 1848), Johanna (b. 1849), John Buckley (b. 1851), Maurice Buckley (b. 1855), Margaret I. (b. 1857), Catherine "Kate" (b. 1860), and Richard Boyle (b. 1862). Two sisters, Margaret and Catherine, died in infancy.

In 1847, he accompanied his parents and other Wolfe family members to Liverpool and then to New York City. From there the family traveled to Chicago and then to Ottawa, in LaSalle County, Illinois. By 1856 they had arrived in Clinton County, Iowa.

In *Wolfe's History of Clinton County*, published in 1911, Wolfe's brother Patrick wrote that James Wolfe "was reared on a farm and educated in the common schools. He was put to work in the fields when old enough, and early in life became acquainted with general farm work."

Many years later, Wolfe's obituary described the Clinton County of his youth:

> At that time, where there are now prosperous well tilled farms, there was a vast unbroken prairie over which the deer roamed at will and through which surged the all devouring prairie fire sweeping everything before it. Here, [Wolfe] experienced the struggles and privations of pioneer life. Through the sides of the rude hut of a home, the wind and the weather blew. Often did he tell of how he shook the snow from the bed covers on awakening and brushed it aside on the floor to make a bare place upon which to stand while dressing.

In 1886, Wolfe owned 360 acres of farmland in section 12 of Liberty Township. In 1911, he owned 280 acres, having transferred 160 acres to one of his sons. He owned Wolfe and Company, a hardware business in Lost Nation, from 1880 until 1884, when the firm was purchased by William Meves of Wheatland. John Wolfe (possibly James Wolfe's brother) bought a minority interest and the store became Wolfe and Meves.

According to his brother Patrick, James Wolfe bred shorthorn cattle and raised both cattle and hogs. "Politically, Mr. Wolfe is a Democrat," P. B. Wolfe wrote, "and while he has never taken a very prominent part in public affairs, he has been more or less active in local matters, and has been school director for twenty years."

In 1870, Wolfe and his father were among the first members of the Saint James Catholic Parish, founded by Father James Scallon. A church was erected in 1883 and the first Mass celebrated in December 1885.

On February 8, 1872, Wolfe married Anne (also Anna) Ignatius O'Connor, the daughter of an Irish immigrant and a native of Jackson County, Iowa. They had seven children: John O. C. (b. 1873), Jeremiah "Jerry" (b. 1876), May R. (b. 1878), Honora L. "Nora" (b. 1880), James Leonard (b. 1881), Walter Ignatius (b. 1886), and Anna (b. 1887).

Wolfe signed his will on August 2, 1915, and died on January 27, 1916. At the time of his death, he was president of the Peoples Trust and Savings Bank in Lost Nation, to which he bequeathed one-sixth of his estate. He is buried at Saint James Cemetery in Toronto, Iowa.

JAMES D. WOLFE
(1839–1923)

JAMES DOWNEY WOLFE was born on March 1, 1839, in Listowel, County Kerry. He was the son of Maurice Richard Wolfe, who bred horses and came from a Catholic farming family, and Johanna Downey Wolfe. His siblings included Margaret (b. 1827), Richard Downey (b. 1829), Stephen (b. 1833), Johanna E. (b. 1840), Catherine "Kate" (b. 1842), Maurice (b. 1848), John Francis (b. 1850), and Edmund Dean (b. 1853).

Little is known of his early life. Wolfe, his parents, and his siblings immigrated to the United States in 1849. They sailed from Liverpool to New York aboard the *Senator*, a 777-ton ship of the Black Star Line, owned by Samuel Thompson; they arrived on September 22, 1849. Maurice Richard Wolfe's brother John immigrated to the United States in 1847, his brother Thomas R. Wolfe in 1848, and his brother Richard Wolfe in 1849. They all settled, at least initially, in LaSalle County, Illinois. James Wolfe's family bought land there, as well, and stayed.

On May 27, 1890, Wolfe married Mary Matilda Curtin in Ottawa, LaSalle County. Witnesses to the marriage were John Curtin and Maggie Curtin. The couple had two children: Margaret (b. 1893) and Johanna Josephine M. "Josie" (b. 1895).

Wolfe farmed in LaSalle County and by 1900 had retired and was living in Ottawa with his family. His wife, Mary, died unexpectedly at her Ottawa home on December 21, 1911. According to the obituary published in the *Ottawa Fair Dealer*, "Her daughter Josephine, who had been sleeping with her, when awaking in the morning noticed a peculiar look on her mother's face and putting her hands on her found her to be unconscious."

James Wolfe died on February 19, 1923, at the home of his daughter, Margaret Wolfe Finnerty, in Streator, Illinois. He and his wife are buried together at Saint Columba Cemetery in Ottawa.

JAMES E. WOLFE
(1909–1965)

JAMES EMMET WOLFE was born on September 11, 1909, near Lost Nation, Clinton County, Iowa. He was the son of Maurice Buckley Wolfe, a farmer in Lost Nation, and Sarah A. McAndrews Wolfe. Wolfe had four older brothers: Raymond Bernard (b. 1896), Philip James (b. 1898), John Joseph (b. 1901), and Melvin Maurice (b. 1904).

In an essay written in 1975, Jimmy Wolfe's nephew, Thomas A. Wolfe, wrote: "He was born in 1909 and promptly began enjoying himself. Life was seldom dull when he was around."

Wolfe inherited his parents' farm southeast of Lost Nation and farmed there his entire life. On July 27, 1937, he married Alice Marie Heath (b. 1911), of Waterloo, in Clinton. The couple had five children: Celine (b. 1938), James Patrick "Pat," Sarah, Alice Maureen, and Raymond.

One of Wolfe's barns apparently was struck by lightning on July 4, 1939, at two-thirty in the morning. According to a newspaper report, it burned to the ground, but the Lost Nation fire department was able to save nearby buildings. The damage was covered by insurance.

Wolfe died on April 28, 1965, his wife on February 1, 2000. They are buried together at Sacred Heart Cemetery in Lost Nation.

JAMES H. WOLFE
(btw. 1780 and 1800–ca. 1836)

JAMES HARNETT WOLFE was born between 1780 and 1800, probably at Templeathea, in western County Limerick. He was the son of Maurice James Wolfe and Hanora Harnett Wolfe. His middle name and his mother's maiden name are sometimes spelled Hartnett. Wolfe's siblings included Richard (b. 1802), John Harnett (b. 1807), Edmond, Timothy, Mary, Patrick Maurice, and Catherine.

Family oral history—contained in a letter between Wolfe relatives dated August 1956 from Cratloe, County Limerick, also known as the "Aunt Dollie" letter—suggests that James Wolfe "had intended to go into the Church and had acquired a good knowledge of the classics. He changed his mind, however, and left for the United States in 1824."

Other, more reliable sources relating to his brothers' attempt to claim his estate suggest that he immigrated in 1819, establishing a school, or working as a teacher, in Virginia. He remained there for about twelve years. According to the Aunt Dollie letter, he then moved west to Monticello, Iowa. Although many Wolfes later settled in Iowa, evidence conclusively indicates that James Wolfe actually moved to Monticello, Lewis County, in northeastern Missouri. The county, named for the Virginia explorer Meriwether Lewis, was established in 1833; a log courthouse was completed in Monticello, named for Thomas Jefferson's home, in June 1834.

On October 16, 1835, Wolfe made five purchases totaling more than 505 acres of land from the U.S. government in Palmyra, the seat of neighboring Marion County, in northeastern Missouri and bordering the Mississippi River. By 1836, the estate's estimated worth was $9,000.

According to the Aunt Dollie letter, Wolfe "had, throughout, kept in communication with his kinfolk in Cratloe and one, at least, of his letters is extant. Then the letters suddenly stopped."

Wolfe's brothers Richard and John Wolfe traveled to the United States to inquire after his whereabouts in 1836. In a letter home dated

December 26, 1836, John Wolfe writes that "Brother James Wolfe died in the state of Mississippi the first [of the] year he went to Natchez. The fine learned man. There is nothing grieves Richard [and me] more than to say that we cant see, hear or find our brother alive on his Estate after the bold stroke we made in going to him five thousand miles from home." A century later, on May 13, 1939, the letter was published in the *Limerick Leader* newspaper.

The Dollie letter speculates that Wolfe was murdered: "He had been drowned in the river and there had been a suspicion of foul play." Whatever the case, his brothers took title to James Wolfe's land and settled in Missouri. James Wolfe never married or had children.

JAMES J. WOLFE
(1899–1937)

JAMES JOSEPH WOLFE was born on June 9, 1899, in Athea, County Limerick. He was the son of John Patrick Wolfe, who farmed and ran a draper's shop, and Maryanne O'Connor Wolfe. His siblings were Margaret (b. 1895), Maryanne (b. 1896), Patrick (b. 1897), Bridget (b. 1902), Louise (b. 1904), and John (b. 1905).

Nothing is known of Jim Wolfe's early life or education. He joined the Irish Volunteers in 1916 and the Irish Republican Army (IRA) two years later, part of a movement that believed in forceful resistance to British rule in Ireland. Wolfe's relative Richard B. Wolfe, a pharmacist in Abbeyfeale, was a brother-in-law of Con Colbert, one of sixteen men executed by the British after the Easter Rising of 1916. During the War of Independence (1919–1921), Dick Wolfe served as an officer in the West Limerick Brigade of the IRA, and Jim Wolfe became a signaler in G Company of the brigade's 2nd Battalion.

After the signing of the Anglo-Irish Treaty on December 6, 1921, the IRA split between factions supporting and opposing the Treaty, which granted Ireland its own Parliament while keeping it a part of the United Kingdom. Jim Wolfe fought with anti-Treaty forces during the Civil War (1922–1923) and was captured in October 1922. He was released in December 1923, after the anti-Treaty IRA was defeated.

Wolfe immigrated to Canada in 1924, landing in Quebec on August 16 and eventually settling in Vancouver, British Columbia. A U.S. Department of Labor manifest card, dated November 24, puts him in the company of James O'Sullivan and Patrick J. O'Shaughnessy seeking permanent residence in Seattle, Washington. He soon returned to Vancouver, however, and worked as a logger from 1924 to 1929.

In 1932, Wolfe joined the Communist Party of Canada, at some point having been blacklisted from further employment, and was assigned to organize sailors. Early in 1937 he answered a call for volunteers to fight with anti-Fascist forces in the Spanish Civil War (1936–1939). He joined the XV International Brigade, arriving in Spain in March 1937 and the next month attending non-commissioned officer training at Pozo Rubio, southeast of Madrid. He likely earned the rank of sergeant.

Wolfe served in No. 1 Company of the mostly American Lincoln Battalion during the Battle of Brunete (July 6–25, 1937). Fought west of Madrid, it was a major defeat for Republican, or anti-Fascist, forces. A new offensive was then launched on August 24, in the north, and focused on the town of Belchite. Wolfe, then with the Canadian Mackenzie-Papineau Battalion, was fighting there on the steps of Saint Augustine Church when, on September 5, a hand-grenade injured him in the face and neck. "He collapsed in the church courtyard," according to Barry McLoughlin, in *Fighting for Republican Spain, 1936–38* (2014). "He could neither speak nor smoke, so he gave his cigarettes to his friend Peter Nielson"—a detail used later in recruiting materials. Wolfe died that evening in a hospital, probably in Hijar.

News of Wolfe's death reached Ireland in the form of a front-page story in *Irish Press* on November 28, 1937: "Five More Irishmen Killed In Spain." The curate in Athea, Father J. J. Hawke, requested a death certificate from Spain, which was provided in April 1938.

Wolfe's name is one of 1,546 volunteers listed on a memorial to the Canadian volunteers who fought for the Spanish Republic. It was unveiled in Ottawa, Ontario, on October 20, 2001. The destroyed town of Belchite, meanwhile, was not rebuilt and remains as a memorial to the battle's more than 11,000 casualties.

Commemorative poster for James J. Wolfe

JAMES M. WOLFE
(ca. 1651–1704)

JAMES MAURICE WOLFE, also known as James of Inchereagh, was born about 1651 at Inchereagh, near present-day Athea, on the River Galey, in western County Limerick. His father was Maurice James Wolfe, a Catholic farmer; the identity of his mother is unknown. He had at least one sibling, Maurice, and possibly another, Richard.

Virtually nothing is known of Wolfe's life except that he likely farmed in West Limerick and, with an unknown wife, had eight children: six daughters, three of whom are said to have immigrated to the United States; Maurice James (b. 1690); and Richard (b. ca. 1690). Family oral history—contained in a letter between Wolfe relatives dated August 1956 from Cratloe, County Limerick, also known as the "Aunt Dollie" letter—suggests that Richard died young.

"The story is that he got chilled while on a visit eastward down in the plain of Limerick and was buried in Monagay churchyard," the letter reads. "It was winter and the snow lay so deep that the body could not be brought home."

According to another letter by Dollie Woulfe, dated January 5, 1947, "This James Maurice was with a brother, named Richard, I think—ploughing one day near his house in Inchereagh when they saw a man running across the fields towards them. After crossing a fence, he disappeared. After a while James told his brother to go and see what had happened. He found the man lying senseless in a dyke. They brought him to and found out he was a messenger from Limerick to the Fizmaurices, Lords of Kerry, to tell them of the fall of Limerick to William of Orange." This would have been in 1690.

James Wolfe died in 1704 and is buried at the Temple Athea graveyard.

JAMES M. WOLFE
(1732–1817)

JAMES MAURICE WOLFE was born in 1732, probably at Templeathea in western County Limerick. He was the son of Maurice James Wolfe, a Catholic farmer, and Kathleen Rearden (also Riordan) Wolfe. His siblings included Richard Maurice "Short Dick" (b. ca. 1730), Edmond Maurice, Patrick, and Maurice James "Young Maurice" (b. ca. 1763).

Wolfe married Johanna McCoy of Coole, near Athea, County Limerick. The couple had three and possibly four sons: James, Maurice James (b. 1755), Richard James (b. 1763), and Edmund. The last son's relationship is unconfirmed. James Wolfe died at age twelve.

Virtually nothing is known about the elder James Wolfe. His nickname, the Barrister, suggested not a career in the law but that he was considered wise and the source of good advice. In *Wolfe's History of Clinton County* (1911), Judge Patrick B. Wolfe noted that "the Wolfe family were also prominent in the church and at the bar."

Wolfe's father was a wealthy farmer who, in March 1760, purchased or leased 2,000 acres of land, which constituted the entire townland of Cratloe, in County Limerick, a few kilometers from Templeathea. Wolfe's older brother, "Short Dick" Wolfe, inherited that property.

Records indicate that the Barrister Wolfe's eldest son, Richard, was born in the townland of Cratloe, suggesting that he followed his family there. Johanna Wolfe died in 1811, James Wolfe in 1817 at Garryantanvally, a townland near Listowel, County Kerry. They are buried together at the Temple Athea graveyard.

JAMES M. WOLFE
(1851–1921)

JAMES MAURICE WOLFE was born on July 26, 1851, in Monticello, Lewis County, Missouri. His parents were John Harnett Wolfe, an Irish Catholic farmer, and Louisa Durbin. Wolfe had four older sisters: Mary Ann (b. 1839), Lucretia Ann (b. 1843), Honora L. "Hannah" (b. ca. 1845), and Teresa Louisa (b. 1848).

Wolfe's father, a native of County Limerick, had traveled with his brother Richard Wolfe to the United States in 1836 in search of their brother, James H. Wolfe. In a letter home dated December 26, 1836, John Wolfe writes that "Brother James Wolfe died in the state of Mississippi the first [of the] year he went to Natchez. The fine learned man. There is nothing grieves Richard [and me] more than to say that we cant see, hear or find our brother alive on his Estate after the bold stroke we made in going to him five thousand miles from home." Family oral history—contained in a letter between Wolfe relatives dated August 1956 from Cratloe, County Limerick, also known as the "Aunt Dollie" letter—speculates that James Wolfe had been murdered. Whatever the case, John and Richard Wolfe remained in Missouri, settling next door to one another in Lewis County.

Nothing is known of James Wolfe's early life. At some point he moved from Lewis County, in northeastern Missouri, to Tarkio Township, Atchison County, in the northwestern part of the state. About 1885 he married Mary Jane "Jennie" Swan, of Peru, Nemaha County, Nebraska, and the couple had four children: Harvey Lewis (b. 1886), Ina W. (b. 1887), Lucretia Iona (b. 1889), and John (b. 1891).

The federal census of 1900 lists Wolfe as living in Tarkio and working as a brick manufacturer. By 1920, Wolfe had moved to Omaha, Nebraska, where he lived with his wife and son Harvey. The census also indicates that he served as caretaker for David Cole.

Wolfe died at the Swedish Mission Hospital in Omaha on November 4, 1921, of apoplexy complicated by arterio sclerosis. Jenny Wolfe died on May 6, 1943, in Maryville, Nodaway County, Missouri. She and her husband are buried together at Tarkio Home Cemetery.

JAMES P. WOLFE
(1842–1922)

JAMES PATRICK WOLFE was baptized on December 27, 1842, having been born in the townland of Cratloe, parish of Athea, County Limerick. He was the son of Patrick Maurice Wolfe and his second wife, Johanna Walsh Wolfe. Wolfe's grandfather was Maurice J. Wolfe, a farmer in the area. He had two half-siblings, Maurice and Honora (b. 1834) whose mother was Patrick Wolfe's first wife, Hanna McAuliffe Wolfe. His full siblings included Bridget (b. 1836), Ellen (b. 1840), John (b. 1844), and Mary (b. 1848).

Virtually nothing is known of Paddy Wolfe's life except that on February 26, 1870, he married Honora "Nanno" Maher, herself the daughter of a Wolfe: Ellen Wolfe Maher, of Listowel, County Kerry. Nanno Maher's sister Ellen also married a Wolfe, Richard J. "Brown Dick" Wolfe.

Paddy Wolfe and Nanno Maher Wolfe had at least eight children: Johanna (b. 1871), Patrick (b. 1872), Richard (b. 1873), Ellen (b. 1876), Maurice James (b. 1877), John J. (b. 1880), James (b. 1882), and Timothy (b. 1885). Johanna became Sister Bonaventure, Patrick a respected priest, nationalist, and scholar of the Irish language, and Timothy a medical doctor.

Wolfe died on April 26, 1922, and his wife on April 22, 1927. They are buried together at Saint Mary's Cemetery in Abbeyfeale.

James P. "Paddy" Wolfe

JAMES R. WOLFE
(1800–1875)

JAMES RICHARD WOLFE was born in 1800, possibly in the parish of Athea, County Limerick, the son of Richard James Wolfe and Johanna Relihan Wolfe. Wolfe's father was a prominent farmer whose family leased land in Athea and the townland of Cratloe. He also served as "the agent having charge of the property of the Knight of Kerry," according to *Wolfe's History of Clinton County* (1911), which likely involved care of Ballinruddery, the residence of Maurice FitzGerald, near Listowel, County Kerry.

James Wolfe was the eldest of at least nine children: Maurice Richard (b. 1802), John Richard (b. 1809), Ellen (b. ca. 1810), Thomas Richard (b. 1811), Johanna (b. 1812), Richard (b. 1815), Margaret Ellen (b. 1818), Edmond (b. 1821), and Patrick (b. 1822).

About 1837 Wolfe, as the eldest son, took over his father's land at Dromlought, in northern County Kerry. His brother Edmond joined him in 1844 and perhaps Patrick, too.

Many of Wolfe's siblings and cousins soon immigrated to the United States. These included his brother John R. Wolfe and their first cousin Maurice Wolfe, who sailed together on the *Cornelia* in 1847; brother Thomas R. Wolfe, who sailed the *James H. Shepherd* in 1848; cousin Richard Wolfe, who took the *Thomas H. Perkins* in 1848; brother Maurice R. Wolfe, who took the *Senator* in 1849; and brother Richard Wolfe, who sailed the *Liverpool* in 1849. Their cousin John E. Wolfe and his sisters also immigrated. The Wolfes settled first in LaSalle County, Illinois; some moved on to Clinton County, Iowa.

Little else is known of James Wolfe's life. He married and had at least three, but likely many more, children: Maurice (b. ca. 1823), Thomas (b. 1841), and Richard (b. 1842).

Wolfe died on May 26, 1875, and is buried at the Temple Athea graveyard, County Limerick.

JAMES R. WOLFE
(1863–1941)

JAMES RICHARD WOLFE was born on April 19, 1863, in LaSalle County, Illinois, the youngest child of Richard Wolfe, a distiller, and Mary Carney Wolfe. His siblings included Margaret (b. 1841), John (b. 1845), Michael (b. ca. 1848), Richard (b. 1847), Sarah Elizabeth (b. 1854), Ellen V. "Nellie" (b. ca. 1856), and James (b. ca. 1858). The other James Wolfe died sometime before 1862.

Wolfe's parents were Irish Catholic immigrants, having arrived on a wave of Wolfe relatives in LaSalle County, Illinois, in 1849.

On October 27, 1890, Wolfe married Johanna Josephine Wolfe, of Grand Rapids Township, LaSalle County. Wolfe's parents, Patrick and Catherine, were, like James Wolfe's parents, natives of County Kerry. The nature of the two Wolfe families' relationship is unknown. James and Johanna Wolfe had five children: Mary Josephine (b. 1891), Catherine (b. 1893), Edna (b. 1895), Richard (b. 1897), and Arthur (b. ca. 1900). Arthur died in 1903 and Mary Josephine in 1906.

Johanna Wolfe died on June 24, 1903, in Ottawa, Illinois, and is buried with her husband at Saint Columba Cemetery in Ottawa.

James Wolfe married his second wife, Mary Cull, in 1904. The couple had one child: Margaret Cull (b. ca. 1905). Mary Cull died of pneumonia on November 18, 1905. She is buried at Saint Columba Cemetery.

The federal census of 1900 describes James Wolfe as a "grocery man." He owned Wolfe's Groceries, a business that advertised in the *Republican Times* of Ottawa on January 26, 1906:

> WOLFE'S GROCERIES TASTE GOOD
>
> Because they are always fresh, first quality and all around dependable goods. Careful selections in buying, taking advantage of all discounts and low expenses make trading here economical and satisfactory. We know you can't all come in person, so we make a specialty of filling telephone orders with the same care and promptness that we

do orders that come over the counter. J.R. Wolfe, 921 LaSalle St. Phones: CU190 or Home 2338

The business appears not to have succeeded. The 1910 census describes Wolfe as doing odd jobs, and by 1920 he was working in a factory. At some point he and his family moved to Chicago, and in 1930 he worked as a package man in a dry goods store.

Wolfe died of bronchial pneumonia and a fractured femur on October 25, 1941, at Mercy Hospital in Chicago. He is buried at Saint Columba Cemetery in Ottawa.

JANE C. WOLFE
(1879–1964)

JANE COOPER WOLFE, better known as "Dollie," was born on December 25, 1879, in Glasgow, Scotland, the daughter of Maurice R. Wolfe and Elizabeth Malcolm "Bessie" Cockburn. Her siblings were Richard Edmund Maurice (b. 1883) and Maurice James (b. 1884). Her nickname referenced her unusually slight stature.

Wolfe's father had been born at the Glen, the large family farm in Cratloe, County Limerick, but his work with the Department of Inland Revenue took him to Scotland, where he met his wife and married. Little is known of Dollie Wolfe's early years, although her later writing suggests a sharp intelligence and a fair amount of education. In 1905, Dollie Wolfe's bachelor uncle Michael R. Wolfe, who ran the farm at the Glen, died at the age of thirty-two. At the time, Dollie and her family were living in Kilmainham, near Dublin, where her father continued to work for Inland Revenue, her brother Richard worked as a clerk, and her brother Maurice studied law. Management of the Glen fell to Dollie, and she soon moved to rural West Limerick, a circumstance that likely limited the possibilities of her life. She never married or had children, doting instead on her nieces and nephews.

The home at the Glen was built by Wolfe's great grandfather, Edmond R. "Old Ned" Wolfe, in 1815. Her grandfather, Richard E. "Dicky Ned" Wolfe, was born there in 1825 and his children after him. Dicky Ned Wolfe was a legendary storyteller, Irish speaker, and collector of folklore who gave a portion of his land for the operation of a hedge school. His wife, Catherine White Wolfe, according to one source, loved to tell "stories about ghosts, devils, witches, banshees, fairy thorns, devil cats, elves, bewitched butter, horned women, blood-thirsty giants, and weird and startling enchantments."

Dollie Wolfe inherited this tale-telling from her grandmother. In a letter to her uncle, Richard W. Wolfe, of Chicago, who himself was born at the Glen, she wrote of strange lights coming from the farm at night, and sightings of the ghost of Margaret O'Shanessy, hanged nearby in 1801 for the murder of her child. In a letter to another American relative, Sister Mary Caelan, dated August 1956 and later distributed widely throughout the family, she reveled in additional tales of ghosts and witches:

> There was Joan Grogan of Athea who, one night at the Glen, called on the dead of previous generations naming each individually as they came in, one after another, out of the dark in response to her call until my grandfather, then a young man, was driven into a fire-place corner by the press of the weird, if friendly, visitors. There was Biddy Airly, the Limerick witch and Moll Anthony, the Clare witch. Biddy Airly was seen on both sides of a fence at the same moment which, you will admit, demands a considerable degree of technical skill in her trade even for a boss-witch.

An enthusiastic painter, Wolfe also had a passion for history. On December 17, 1932, the *Irish Press* newspaper reported that she had discovered, at a nearby archaeological site, "an oval tracked-stone of a type used in mediaeval times in conjunction with a steel for striking fire." The site, Cnoc na bPoll, or hill of the bog-holes, was a largely uninhabited field located between Athea and Abbeyfeale in the townland of Cool West. Objects there, dating back to the Bronze Age, were first discovered while locals cut turf. Wolfe donated the tracked-stone to the National Museum. Two years later, on May 24, 1934, the *Liberator* newspaper reported that she had uncovered a coin dating to the Williamite War in Ireland (1688–1691) on the hill of Knocknaboul, not far from Cnoc na bPoll.

Wolfe also served as an authoritative and witty purveyor of family history. Her letter to Sister Mary Caelan traces the line from the Norman invasion of Ireland to the present day. About her great-great-great grandfather, Maurice J. "Old Maurice" Wolfe, she wrote that despite being only fourteen when his own father died, "he was strong and energetic, physically and mentally, and soon took charge of the family affairs. His younger brother, Richard, died a young man. The story is that he got chilled while on a visit eastward down the plain of Limerick and was buried in Monagay churchyard. It was winter and the snow lay so deep that the body could not be brought home."

She wrote that her ancestor moved from a farm at Inchereagh, on the River Galey, just west of Athea, to better land at Beenmore, closer to the village. "After many years, (thirty apparently), his wife, Kathleen, died. The churchyard, Templeathea, where she was buried was in plain sight of his house. The tradition is that he could not bear to look at it. He left Beenmore and took the entire Townland of Cratloe, some 2,000 acres, in March 1760." More than two centuries later the family continued to live in the same spot.

"He lived at the house ... below ours, here are the Glen," Wolfe wrote of Old Maurice, "and died there on Christmas night, 1792, being then, you will notice, 102 years of age. He had eaten his supper, possibly too good a one for his years, and was sitting on a corner of the kitchen beside the fire watching a dance of the young people that was in full swing, when he appeared to fall asleep. It was noticed that he had 31 of his own teeth in his mouth and the 32nd was in his waistcoat pocked we he died that night so that he was practically intact."

Dollie Wolfe died at the Glen on August 8, 1964, and is buried at the Temple Athea graveyard.

JOHANNA WOLFE
(1849–1926)

JOHANNA WOLFE, later Sister Mary Scholastica, was born in 1849 in LaSalle County, Illinois. Her parents were John Richard Wolfe, an Irish Catholic farmer, and Honora Buckley Wolfe. She had seven siblings who survived to maturity: James Buckley (b. 1843), Patrick Bernard (b. 1848), John Buckley (b. 1851), Maurice Buckley (b. 1855), Margaret I. (b. 1857), Catherine "Kate" (b. 1860), and Richard Boyle (b. 1862). Two sisters, Margaret and Catherine, died in infancy.

In 1847, Wolfe's parents and brother James immigrated to the United States from Listowel, County Kerry, along with John R. Wolfe's first cousin Maurice Wolfe and his family. (John and Maurice Wolfe shared a grandfather, James M. "The Barrister" Wolfe.) The families arrived in New York on August 23, 1847, and from there made their way to Chicago, where Patrick Wolfe was born. The Wolfes then traveled to LaSalle County, Illinois, where a number of John R. Wolfe's brothers and cousins settled. John R. Wolfe and his cousin Maurice both moved on to Clinton County, Iowa, arriving about 1855.

Virtually nothing is known of Johanna Wolfe's life. At some point she joined the Order of Sisters of Mercy, a Catholic order founded in 1831 in Dublin by Catherine A. McAuley (1778–1841). The Sisters of Mercy dedicated themselves, first in the British Isles and then in the United States, to caring for the poor and especially women and children. This led to the foundation of hospitals modeled after McAuley's House of Mercy, established in Dublin in 1827.

In *Wolfe's History of Clinton County*, edited by Patrick B. Wolfe and published in 1911, Johanna Wolfe is said to be "now Sister Scholastica of the Order of Sisters of Mercy at Sioux City, Iowa." The Sisters of Mercy had been in Sioux City since 1890, when the order established Saint Joseph Mercy Hospital there. In 1902, the Saint Joseph's School of Nursing opened, and by 1911 the hospital's capacity had grown from 20 to 200 patients. (Another source offers slightly different dates.)

A notice of Sister Scholastica's death appeared in the *Davenport Democrat and Leader* on July 11, 1926. It reported that Wolfe's brother Patrick Wolfe and others had "returned from Dubuque where they attended the funeral of Sister M. Scholastica ... Archbishop Daniel Mannix of Melbourne, Australia, cousin of the deceased, conducted the requiem high mass and the Rev. Thomas L. Wolfe gave the funeral sermon." The newspaper likely intended to attribute relationship to the Reverend Wolfe and not Archbishop Mannix. The former was the son of John Buckley Wolfe, or Sister Scholastica's nephew.

JOHANNA DOWNEY WOLFE
(ca. 1810–1886)

JOHANNA DOWNEY was born about 1810 in Listowel, County Kerry. Little is known about her early years. She married Maurice Richard Wolfe, who bred racehorses and came from a Catholic farming family, in Listowel in 1826. The two immigrated to the United States, sailing from Liverpool to New York aboard the *Senator*, a 777-ton ship of the Black Star Line, owned by Samuel Thompson; they arrived on September 22, 1849. With them were seven children: Margaret (b. 1827), Richard Downey (b. 1829), Stephen (b. 1833), James Downey (b. 1839), Johanna E. (b. 1840), Catherine "Kate" (b. 1842), and Maurice (b. 1848). Also accompanying the family was Margaret Maher (sometimes Magher or Meagher), daughter of Maurice Wolfe's sister Ellen. He and Johanna Wolfe appear to have treated her as their own daughter, and after Maurice Wolfe's death, she was considered an heir to his estate. After settling, with several of her husband's siblings, in LaSalle County, Illinois, Johanna Wolfe had two more children: John Francis (b. 1850) and Edmund Dean (b. 1853).

Maurice Wolfe died in 1870, leaving no will. His widow petitioned the court for his estate:

> Petition of Johanna Wolfe In the matter of the Estate of Maurice Wolfe deceased for Letters of Administration. Charles Gilman Judge of the County Court of LaSalle County, in the State of Illinois. The Petition of the undersigned, Johanna Wolfe respectfully represents that Maurice Wolfe late of the County of LaSalle aforesaid, departed this life at Osage in said County on or about the 12th day of October A.D. 1870, leaving no last will and testament as far as your petitioner knows or believes. And this Petition further shows that the said Maurice Wolfe died, seized and possessed of Personal Estate estimated to be worth about Twenty five hundred dollars. That said deceased left surviving him your petitioner his widow and Richard D. Wolfe, Margaret Meagher, James D. Wolfe, Catherine Wolfe, John

F. Wolfe and Edmund Wolfe his children, as heirs, That your petitioned (being the widow) believing that the said estate should be immediately administered as well for the proper management of said estate as for the prompt collection of the assets, by virtue of her right under the Statute she therefore prays that your honor will grant Letters of Administration to herself in the premises, upon her taking oath prescribed by the Statue and entering into bond in such sum and with securities as may be approved by your honor. Signed Johanna Woulfe 14th day of November 1870.

Johanna Downey Wolfe died on June 19, 1886, in Eagle Township, LaSalle County. She is buried with her husband in Lost Land Cemetery there.

JOHANNA F. WOLFE
(1914–1997)

JOHANNA FRANCES WOLFE, later Sister Mary Agatha, was born on January 17, 1914, on New Street, Abbeyfeale, County Limerick. She was the daughter of Richard Barrett Wolfe, a pharmacist who lived with his family above the shop, and Catherine Elizabeth Colbert Wolfe. Her siblings were Hanora Josephine (b. 1915), Cornelius Colbert "Con" (b. 1917), Richard Michael (b. 1919), and Michael Joseph Colbert (b. 1922). All of them became priests or nuns.

Wolfe's parents were active nationalists before and during the War of Independence (1919–1921). Catherine Wolfe's younger brother, Con Colbert, participated in the Easter Rising of 1916 and was one of fifteen men executed at Kilmainham jail, in Dublin. Dick Wolfe's pharmacy became a hub of nationalist activity, and in 1920 it was damaged by the Black and Tans after the Irish Republican Army killed a local constable.

On September 8, 1931, Johanna Wolfe entered the Missionary Sisters of the Holy Rosary (MSHR) at Killeshandra, County Cavan, becoming Sister Mary Agatha. The order was founded by Bishop Joseph Shanahan on March 7, 1924, to educate and work with the women of southern Nigeria. The convent in Killeshandra opened that year and the first ten members professed there on February 24, 1927. Half of them were sent to Nigeria the next year.

Sister Mary Agatha took her vows on October 9, 1934, and in March 1938 left Ireland to teach at the MSH missions in Ihiala, Nigeria. She later spent time in Enugu, Adazi, Port Harcourt, Ihitte, Onitsha, Adazi, Nsukka, and Okigwe, returning in 1965 to Killeshandra, where she continued to teach. In 1986, Sister Mary Agatha retired to the MSHR nursing home, and died at Saint Vincent's Hospital, in Dublin, on December 5, 1997. She is buried at Shanganagh Cemetery, in Shankill, County Dublin.

JOHN WOLFE
(ca. 1794–1863)

JOHN WOLFE was born about 1794 in County Kerry. He was the son of Maurice James Wolfe, a Catholic farmer, and Helen (sometimes Ellen) Dore Wolfe. His siblings included Richard (b. 1795), Edmund Maurice, Maurice (b. ca. 1800), Bartholomew (b. 1809), and Michael (b. 1813).

On March 6, 1821, he married Julia Stack, of Rathea, in the parish of Lixnaw, County Kerry. The couple had four children: Margaret (b. ca. 1821), Eleanor (b. ca. 1821), Mary (b. 1826), and Ellen (b. 1827). Julia Wolfe died sometime before 1830, possibly of complications from one of her births.

John Wolfe then married Bridget Ann Foley, probably about 1831. The couple had seven children: Katherine Marie (b. 1832), Maurice (b. 1837), Daniel, Johanna (b. ca. 1841), Ann (b. 1845), Bridget (b. ca. 1846), and Julia (b. ca. 1848).

Wolfe immigrated to the United States in the company of his wife and children in 1849, sailing aboard the *Mary Ann Henry* and arriving in New York on July 9. Wolfe's brothers Richard and Maurice Wolfe had already immigrated, the former in 1848, the latter, with their first cousin John R. Wolfe, in 1847. (Brothers John, Maurice, and Richard Wolfe shared a grandfather with John R. Wolfe: James M. "The Barrister" Wolfe.) In addition, John R. Wolfe's brother Thomas R. Wolfe came from Ireland in 1848 and his brothers Maurice R. and Richard Wolfe separately in 1849. Other cousins came, as well, including Margaret and Elizabeth Maher, daughters of John R. Wolfe's sister Ellen, and Patrick, Dennis, Bridget, and Thomas Sheehan, the children of John R. Wolfe's sister Margaret. Another cousin, John E. Wolfe, and his sisters Ellen J. and Mary Agatha, also immigrated. All of these extended Wolfe family members, except for the Sheehans, settled in LaSalle County, Illinois; a few moved on from there to Clinton County, Iowa.

By 1850, John Wolfe was living in Deer Park Township, LaSalle County, working as a farmer. A decade later he lived in Farm Ridge Township.

Wolfe died on April 7, 1863, in LaSalle County, and is buried at Saint Columba Cemetery in Ottawa, Illinois. His second wife, Bridget, moved to Carroll, Iowa, probably with her daughter Ann, who farmed there with her husband Joseph Collison beginning about 1874. Bridget Foley Wolfe died of dropsy on January 16, 1899. Her obituary appeared in the *Carroll Sentinel* on January 19:

> Grandma Wolfe, as she was called by all her friends, lived a quiet christian life and was loved by all who knew her. Though her span of life extended over nearly the entire century she retained full possession of all her faculties until within a few hours of her death. She was a devout christian woman and of late years especially she lived near the cross. "That life is long which answers life's great end" and in the fullness of time she passed away as quietly as a child lies down to peaceful dreams.

She is buried at Saint Joseph's Cemetery in Carroll.

JOHN WOLFE
(1845–1919)

JOHN WOLFE was born in 1845 in County Kerry, the son of Richard Wolfe, a distiller, and Mary Carney Wolfe. His siblings included Margaret (b. 1841), Richard (b. 1847), Michael (b. ca. 1848), Sarah Elizabeth (b. 1854), Ellen V. "Nellie" (b. ca. 1856), James (b. ca. 1858), and James R. (b. 1863). The first James died sometime before 1862.

Wolfe, his parents, and his siblings immigrated to the United States, arriving in New York City aboard the *Liverpool* on November 10, 1849. They settled in LaSalle County, Illinois, joining other Wolfe relatives there. Richard Wolfe Sr.'s brother John R. Wolfe and his first cousin Maurice Wolfe both immigrated in 1847. (Brothers Richard and John Wolfe shared a grandfather with Maurice Wolfe: James M. "The Barrister" Wolfe.) Wolfe's brother, Thomas R. Wolfe, arrived from Ireland in 1848, while another brother, Maurice R. Wolfe, sailed in 1849, arriving in September. While brother John Wolfe and cousin Maurice Wolfe moved on to Clinton County, Iowa, Richard Wolfe Sr. and his brothers Thomas and Maurice Wolfe remained in Illinois.

John Wolfe married Johanna Dillon, a native of LaSalle County, on June 6, 1876. The couple had three children: Johanna "Jennie" (b. 1880), John (b. 1884), and Richard William (b. 1887).

The federal census of 1880 identifies John Wolfe as a farmer in LaSalle, but by 1900 he worked as the foreman of the buffing department at the Western Clock Company plant in LaSalle. He worked there for twenty-eight years.

Johanna Dillon Wolfe died of a stroke at her home in LaSalle on November 15, 1918, and John Wolfe of pneumonia at Saint Mary's Hospital, LaSalle, on March 27, 1919. On the day John Wolfe Sr. died, John Wolfe Jr. landed in New York from having served overseas during World War I (1914–1918).

John and Johanna Wolfe are buried together at Saint Vincent Cemetery in LaSalle, Illinois.

JOHN B. WOLFE
(1851–1923)

JOHN BUCKLEY WOLFE was born in March 1851, in LaSalle County, Illinois. His parents were John Richard Wolfe, an Irish Catholic farmer, and Honora Buckley Wolfe. He had seven siblings who survived to maturity: James Buckley (b. 1844), Patrick Bernard (b. 1848), Johanna (b. 1849), Maurice Buckley (b. 1855), Margaret I. (b. 1857), Catherine "Kate" (b. 1860), and Richard Boyle (b. 1862). Two sisters, Margaret and Catherine, died in infancy.

In 1847, Wolfe's parents and brother James immigrated to the United States from Listowel, County Kerry, along with John R. Wolfe's first cousin Maurice Wolfe and his family. (John and Maurice Wolfe shared a grandfather, James M. "The Barrister" Wolfe.) The families arrived in New York on August 23, 1847, and from there made their way to Chicago and then to LaSalle County, Illinois, where a number of John R. Wolfe's brothers and cousins settled. John R. Wolfe and his cousin Maurice, with their families, both moved on to Clinton County, Iowa, arriving about 1855.

Wolfe was raised in Liberty Township, Clinton County, and a mention in the *Oxford Mirror* newspaper, dated January 11, 1883, suggests that he farmed near Lost Nation, in Sharon Township.

About 1887 Wolfe married Mary Ann Lyons, of Clinton. They had nine children: John Vincent (b. 1888), Irene Mary (b. 1891), Edward Lyons (b. 1892), Thomas Lyons (b. 1894), Frances Lyons (b. 1896), Richard Lyons (b. 1898), Paul Joseph Lyons (b. 1900), Eugene Maurice (b. 1902), and Cyril Dennis (b. ca. 1906).

The federal census of 1900 identifies Wolfe and his wife as living in the city of Clinton; Wolfe is described as a "capitalist." A notice in the *Oxford Mirror*, dated August 30, 1900, puts him in Lyons, however, just north of the city.

Sometime in the next decade, the couple moved to Jackson Township, in Monroe County, Iowa, where Wolfe farmed. By 1920, Wolfe and family had moved again, this time to Grant Township in Clinton County.

Wolfe died on July 16, 1923, at Mercy Hospital in Clinton after a long illness. He is buried at Saint James Cemetery in Toronto, Iowa. His wife, Mary, died on December 13, 1946.

JOHN C. WOLFE
(1840–1902)

JOHN CAREY WOLFE was baptized on January 16, 1840, in the parish of Listowel, County Kerry. His parents were Maurice Wolfe, a Catholic farmer, and Ellen Catherine Carey. His baptismal sponsors were John Wolfe and Margaret Sullivan.

Wolfe had ten siblings who lived to maturity: James Carey (b. 1831), Ellen (b. 1833), Maurice Carey (b. ca. 1835), Mary (b. 1838), Thomas Carey (b. 1843), Margaret (b. ca. 1845), Johanna (b. 1847), Richard Carey (b. 1848), Catherine "Kate" (b. 1851), and Bridget Veronica (b. 1854).

In 1847, Wolfe, his parents, and several siblings immigrated to the United States, along with Maurice Wolfe's first cousin John R. Wolfe and his family. (Maurice Wolfe and John R. Wolfe shared a grandfather, James M. "The Barrister" Wolfe.) The families arrived in New York on August 23, and after a stop in Chicago made their way to LaSalle County, Illinois.

Many members of the extended Wolfe family made the same journey. John C. Wolfe's uncle John Wolfe immigrated in 1849. John R. Wolfe's brother Thomas R. Wolfe came from Ireland in 1848 and his brothers Maurice R. and Richard Wolfe sailed separately in 1849. Other cousins came, as well, including Margaret and Elizabeth Maher, daughters of John R. Wolfe's sister Ellen, and Patrick, Dennis, Bridget, and Thomas Sheehan, the children of John R. Wolfe's sister Margaret. Another cousin, John E. Wolfe, and his sisters Ellen J. and Mary Agatha, also immigrated. All of these Wolfes, except for the Sheehans, settled in LaSalle County, Illinois. A few moved on to Clinton County, Iowa, including John C. Wolfe's father Maurice Wolfe and Maurice's cousin John R. Wolfe.

In 1858, after attending public schools in Clinton County, Wolfe set out for California. According to the *History of the State of California and Biographical Record of Coast Counties* by James Miller Guinn:

On the Illinois prairies [Wolfe] was reared to habits of thrift and usefulness, and at twenty-one years of age he and six other young men, who had been his boyhood friends, had the opportunity to cross the plains in a band of emigrants, all of whom were home seekers and ambitious of better things.

Wolfe ended up in Grass Valley, Nevada County, California. Established in 1860 and located in the foothills of the Sierra Nevada Mountains, about sixty miles northeast of Sacramento, Grass Valley was the heart of California gold country, the richest and most famous mining district in the state. According to Guinn, in 1863 Wolfe found employment in a drug store owned by a Dr. Tompkins, learning from the man and then going into business for himself:

> From time to time he added to his stock, distinct advantage being found in the fact that he manufactured many of his own medicines, which came to be known for their efficacy in the common disorders. Throughout the length and breadth of the county, and even beyond, Wolfe's liniment, pile cure, worm powder, catarah snuff, and corn cure were household treasures and found their way into thousands of individual medicine chests.

In 1872, Wolfe moved his business to Fourth Street, between B and C streets, in San Rafael, Marin County, just north of San Francisco. On November 27, 1884, Wolfe married Ellen Louise Martin, a native of Chicago, and the couple had one son, Maurice Joseph (b. 1886).

Ellen Martin's father, Peter Martin, was a prominent architect in Chicago, while her uncle, Edward Martin, was a founder of the First National Gold Bank, in San Francisco. This allowed John and Ellen Wolfe access to elite San Francisco social life.

Wolfe bought land at the south end of D Street, in San Rafael, and built a large two-story house there. "I have the prettiest house in California," he told a reporter for the *San Francisco Daily Examiner* on August 14, 1887.

Wolfe admitted to the paper that, "yes, business in my line is pretty dull, I must say. But then that, I should think, is the best thing that can be said in favor of [San Rafael]."

Wolfe died at his home on July 25, 1902, after what his obituary described as "a lingering illness of several weeks." (A portion of D Street was later renamed Wolfe Avenue.) His wife, Ellen, with the help of Wolfe's clerk, Thomas Day, ran the drug store with the hope that the Wolfes' son, Maurice, would take it over. (Maurice Wolfe died in 1918.) The federal census of 1930 identifies Ellen Martin Wolfe as living in Saint Catherine's Home, at 901 Potrero Avenue.

Staffed by the Sisters of Mercy, an order of nuns established in Ireland, the home served both as a shelter and a school and training center for women in need. Wolfe died on December 8, 1930, probably at the home. She, her husband, and their son are buried together at Mount Olivet Cemetery in San Rafael, California.

John C. Wolfe

JOHN E. WOLFE
(1837–1918)

JOHN EDMOND WOLFE was born on November 22, 1837, in Listowel, County Kerry, to an unknown father and a mother with the maiden name O'Sullivan. His paternal grandparents were James Maurice "The Barrister" Wolfe and Johanna McCoy Wolfe. Wolfe's siblings included Ellen J. (b. 1832), Mary Agatha (b. 1834), and Patrick (b. ca. 1844), the latter's relationship remaining unconfirmed.

Wolfe and his known siblings immigrated to the United States, but the circumstances of their travel is unclear. They probably were accompanied by other relatives, and during the 1840s many Wolfes left Ireland and settled first in LaSalle County, Illinois, and then in Clinton County, Iowa. These included John Wolfe's uncle John R. Wolfe and cousin Maurice Wolfe, who sailed together on the *Cornelia* in 1847; Thomas R. Wolfe, who sailed the *James H. Shepherd* in 1848; Richard Wolfe, who took the *Thomas H. Perkins* in 1848; Maurice R. Wolfe, who took the *Senator* in 1849; and Richard Wolfe, who sailed on the *Liverpool* in 1849. All these men shared a descent from Maurice J. Wolfe.

Wolfe's obituary states he came to the United States in 1850 and settled in Clinton County, Iowa, in 1858. Other accounts have him arriving in Iowa a year earlier. Whatever the case, in the federal census of 1860 he is identified as a wagon maker living in Liberty Township in the household of Aurell Grovener, a hotelkeeper. He probably lived briefly in LaSalle County, Illinois, become coming to Iowa, and his sisters remained there.

According to a letter written about 1929 by Timothy Wolfe to one of John E. Wolfe's sons, the Wolfe homestead on the River Feale in Kerry was Garryantanavalla. "The beautiful place which your father and his relatives left vacant when they went to Illinois some seventy years ago has never since been tenanted and has all the time been used as a grazing ranch."

On November 8, 1863, Wolfe married Margaret Mills, a native of County Mayo, in DeWitt, Iowa. The couple had at least nine children:

Edmund Mills (b. 1864), Anthony Mills (b. 1866), Mary Mayme (b. 1868), Maurice Vincent (b. 1874), Patrick Joseph (b. 18714), Cecelia Ellen (b. 1877), Ellen Vita "Nellie" (b. 1879), John (b. 1883), and Arthur Gerald (b. 1885).

In 1870, Wolfe is identified by the census as a farmer living with his wife, children, and his wife's sister, Celia Mills, who worked as a domestic servant. *The History of Clinton County, Iowa*, published in 1879, attributes to him 320 acres of land valued at $30 per acre. By 1900, Wolfe had retired to DeWitt, and he signed his will on August 12, 1917. He died on March 30, 1918, his wife on January 16, 1938. They are buried together at Saint James Cemetery in Toronto, Iowa.

JOHN H. WOLFE
(1807–before May 25, 1856)

JOHN HARNETT WOLFE was born in 1807, probably near Athea, County Limerick. He was the son of Maurice James Wolfe and Hanora Harnett Wolfe. His middle name and his mother's maiden name are sometimes spelled Hartnett. Wolfe's siblings included James Harnett (b. btw. 1780 and 1800), Richard (b. 1802), Edmond, Timothy, Mary, Patrick Maurice, and Catherine.

Family oral history—contained in a letter between Wolfe relatives dated August 1956 from Cratloe, County Limerick, also known as the "Aunt Dollie" letter—relates how John Wolfe and his brother, Richard Wolfe, traveled to the United States in 1836 to inquire after their brother, James. James Wolfe had immigrated in 1819, living first in Virginia and then in Monticello, Lewis County, Missouri. When his regular letters home stopped, his brothers went in search of him.

In letter home dated December 26, 1836, John Wolfe writes that "Brother James Wolfe died in the state of Mississippi the first [of the] year he went to Natchez. The fine learned man. There is nothing grieves Richard [and me] more than to say that we cant see, hear or find our brother alive on his Estate after the bold stroke we made in going to him five thousand miles from home." John Wolfe and Richard Wolfe remained in Missouri, settling next door to one another in Lewis County.

In his letter, John Wolfe vividly describes passage on the Erie Canal and beyond:

> we went on board the steamboat John Jay by the Lake Erie Canal boat towed by a pair of two horses to Buffalo 363 miles, fare 12 cents per mile, to Albany ... We stood great danger in Lake Michigan. The Captain cast anchor several nights. Brother Patrick, we suffered a great deal more than you are aware during the long voyage from Ireland to Monticello. Lake Erie [and the] River Mississippi are the finest I saw in America. Inquired for information in several companies offices where maps of the States were kept but they

could not give me any good information. We were very successful in make out our places of destination thank God. The D[istance] from New York to Monticello are [one] thousand five hundred miles our expenses amounted to about 1001,0 Dollars Breakfast, Dinner, Supper are provided on board at 25 cents per person with every delicacy the season can afford ... Travelling is very expensive in America.

Wolfe described his late brother's Missouri estate as including "first rate land, timber oak and water and trained limestone quarry on it—two eighties 2 forties jambed up with the town."

On July 18, 1838, Wolfe married Louisa Ann Durbin, of Kentucky, in Lewis County. The couple had five children: Mary Ann (b. 1839), Lucretia Ann (b. 1843), Honora L. "Hannah" (b. ca. 1845), Teresa Louisa (b. 1848), and James Maurice (b. 1851).

Wolfe is listed in the federal censuses of 1840 and 1850 as farming in Lewis County. He died sometime before May 25, 1856, in Lewis County. On May 24, 1858, his 160-acre estate—on the southeast quarter of section no. 7, township no. 11, of range 7—was valued at $1.25 per acre, or $200. It was sold to pay his debts.

JOHN J. WOLFE
(1901–1974)

JOHN JOSEPH WOLFE was born on June 13, 1901, in Lost Nation, Iowa. He was the son of Maurice Buckley Wolfe, a farmer in Lost Nation, and Sarah A. McAndrews Wolfe. Wolfe had four brothers: Raymond Bernard (b. 1896), Philip James (b. 1898), Melvin Maurice (b. 1904), and James Emmet (b. 1909).

Wolfe attended public schools in Lost Nation and then Saint Ambrose College in Davenport, Iowa. On November 25, 1936—Thanksgiving day—he married Ida Ann Burke, in DeWitt, Iowa. The Catholic service was officiated by Wolfe's cousin, the Reverend Thomas L. Wolfe. The couple had two children: Marianne and John Joseph "Jack" Jr.

John and Ida Wolfe honeymooned in Chicago, Illinois, before occupying a newly built home just south of Lost Nation, near the homestead of John Wolfe's brother Phil. Wolfe's nephew Thomas Wolfe wrote that he "was an extremely kind man and had the richest brogue of all the Wolfes."

Wolfe farmed his whole life. He died on June 2, 1974, in Davenport, Iowa. Ida Wolfe died November 30, 1979, in Clinton County. They are buried together in Lost Nation.

JOHN L. WOLFE
(1879–1962)

JOHN LOYOLA WOLFE was born on July 31, 1879, in Clinton, Iowa. His parents were Patrick Bernard Wolfe and Margaret G. Connole Wolfe. He had two siblings: a child who was born in 1869 and died the same year, and Mary Zeta "Molly" (b. 1881).

Wolfe graduated from Clinton High School in 1897 and four years later received a bachelor of arts degree from Saint Mary's College, located west of Topeka, Kansas. In 1902, Wolfe earned a master of arts degree from Georgetown University in the District of Columbia and, in 1904, a bachelor of laws from the same university. He was admitted to the bar in October 1904 and, with his father, founded the Wolfe & Wolfe law firm in Clinton.

On March 1, 1906, Wolfe entered the Friedrich-Wilhelms-Universität (later Humboldt University of Berlin) in Berlin, Germany, where he studied municipal laws and political economy. While he lived in Berlin, the Iowa Democratic Party, meeting in Waterloo, Iowa, on August 7, 1906, nominated Wolfe to represent District 45 in the state House of Representatives. He was elected on November 6 and returned from Europe in time to take his seat in January 1907. He was reelected in November 1908 and served until January 8, 1911.

Wolfe married Mary Catherine Kane, a native of Nebraska, in Des Moines, Iowa, on October 16, 1912. The couple had five children: John Patrick (b. 1913), Matthew Kane (b. 1916), Mary Catherine (b. 1918), Robert Francis (b. 1921), and Margaret Ann "Margie." Their daughter, Mary Catherine, died on November 27, 1920. Their son John was commended for his service at Pearl Harbor in 1941, and their son Robert died testing a plane at Quonset, Rhode Island, on March 9, 1943.

Wolfe practiced law in Clinton until his retirement. He died on July 17, 1962, in Clinton. His wife, Margaret, died on April 10, 1976, in Deerfield, Illinois. They are buried together in Saint Ireneaus Cemetery in Clinton.

JOHN M. WOLFE
(1913–1951)

JOHN MAURICE WOLFE was born on June 30, 1913, in San Francisco County, California. He was the son of Maurice Joseph Wolfe, a druggist, and Imogene A. "Jean" Irving Wolfe. He had one sibling: Margaret I. (b. 1915).

Wolfe's father owned a drug store in Oakland and died in a freak accident in 1918. Following his death, John Wolfe went to live in San Francisco with his mother's brother, John M. Irving, and his grandmother, Minna James Irving. By 1930, he was reunited with his mother, living with her, his sister, and grandmother. At some point after 1930, Jean Wolfe married her second husband, E. H. Sage.

The details of Wolfe's education are unknown. He married a woman named Estelle, her maiden name unknown, and the couple had one child, Peter. They lived in Menlo Park, California.

About 1946 Wolfe bought the Peninsula Paper Box Company, of San Carlos, California, and renamed it the Wolfe Paper Box Company. He died in a car accident in Redwood City on July 2, 1951. According to newspaper reports, he fell asleep at the wheel while driving home from San Francisco and struck another vehicle head-on on the Bayshore Highway at 3:32 A.M.

"Wolfe's body was crushed almost beyond recognition by the impact," according to a story on the front page of the *San Mateo Times*, July 12, 1951. "Rescue crews from the fire department here used cutting torches to free the victim from the wreckage. He died before police reached the scene, less than a quarter of a mile inside the north Redwood City limits."

JOHN M. WOLFE
(1922–2009)

JOHN MAURICE WOLFE, who adopted the Irish-language version of his name, Seán Muiris de Bhulbh, was born on September 22, 1922, in Abbeyfeale, County Limerick. His parents were Maurice James Wolfe, a solicitor, and Sarah McCarthy Wolfe. His siblings were Maurice Richard (b. 1925) and Richard (b. 1929).

After attending Springmount School in Abbeyfeale and Saint Gerard's Senior School in Bray, County Wicklow, he studied engineering at Trinity College, Dublin, graduating in 1943. He then worked in London, in Scotland, and, for two years, in Kenya with the Royal Engineers. After returning to Ireland in 1956, he was employed by the Dublin Corporation and the Kerry County Council, being named assistant county engineer on July 16, 1958. In 1968, he began work for the Limerick County Council, retiring from there in 1987.

In 1956, de Bhulbh married Mary Murphy, and the couple had five children: Eibhlin, Sadhbh, Sibéal, Muiris, and Seán C.

De Bhulbh was a fluent Irish speaker and spent much of his life promoting the language. In the 1970s he served as *cathaoirleach*, or presiding officer, of the Limerick branch of Conradh na Gaelige (formerly the Gaelic League), a cultural organization founded in 1893 as a means of ridding, or at least reducing, English influence on Ireland's politics and culture. De Bhulbh's relative, the Reverend Patrick Wolfe, served as president of the league's Limerick branch early in the twentieth century.

By the 1960s and 1970s, the Irish language was taught in Irish national schools and passing the course was required to receive a Leaving Certificate. Nevertheless, there was widespread skepticism of the language and, in some quarters, pessimism about its survival. On March 17, 1962, in the *Kerryman* newspaper, the playwright John B. Keane, in general a supporter of the language, published a column suggesting that other school subjects were more important. He also wondered whether the language was being used for social and political advancement:

> Another sad aspect of the Irish question is the name-changing which has taken place in recent years. People whose names are written in English on Baptismal and Birth Certificates have found it politic and profitable to sign themselves now in Irish. In this category many of the worst type of fanatics are found, fanatics who accuse those who object to compulsory Irish of being West Britons and Shoneens.

Seán de Bhulbh responded in a letter published on March 31. "The question 'what use is Irish,'" he wrote, "really betrays a person, for it means that he has never got beyond thinking in commercial terms." He then addressed the issue of names:

> Finally, I fear I must offend against Mr. Keane's dictum by signing my name in Irish, even though it is in English on my birth certificate. I have been doing this for many years ever since I became convinced, after giving the matter some thought, that Irish was of the utmost importance in our national life. I must confess that so far this procedure has not yielded any profit!

De Bhulbh was particularly interested in names. In 1923, his relative Father Wolfe published *Sloinnte Gaedheal is Gall*, an academic study of naming in Ireland as well as a dictionary of common Irish names. In 1997, after ten years of work, de Bhulbh published his own, updated study, *Sloinnte na hÉireann: Irish Surnames*. Both books, and a new edition that de Bhulbh published in 2002, examined the origins of Irish names and provided a reference for names as they appeared in both Irish and English.

In October 2008, de Bhulbh published *Síth agus Eísíth (Peace and War)*, an Irish-language novella set late in the sixteenth century. He also wrote but never published a survey of West Limerick place names.

Mary Murphy Wolfe died in 2005 and de Bhulbh on February 7, 2009. They are buried in the Wolfe family mausoleum at the Temple Athea graveyard, County Limerick.

Seán de Bhulbh

JOHN P. WOLFE
(1913–1997)

JOHN PATRICK WOLFE was born on September 26, 1913, in Clinton Iowa, the son of John Loyola Wolfe and Mary Catherine Kane and the oldest of five children. His siblings were Matthew Kane (b. 1916), Mary Catherine (b. 1918), Robert Francis (b. 1921), and Margaret Ann "Margie." Mary Catherine died in 1920. Robert Francis died in 1943, testing a plane at Quonset, Rhode Island. Wolfe's father was a lawyer and former member of the state House of Representatives (1908–1911).

Wolfe enlisted in the U.S. Navy Reserve on February 14, 1941, and was commissioned an ensign on May 15 of that year. On December 7, when the Japanese attacked the Pacific fleet at Pearl Harbor, Hawaii, Wolfe was serving as a gunnery officer on the destroyer USS *Blue*. At sea for the previous week, the ship's crew had been given liberty the night of December 6–7, with the top officers still on shore as dawn broke. Japanese planes fired on the ships beginning at 7:55 A.M., and according to later testimony before Congress by Ensign Nathan F. Asher, the ranking officer aboard, approximately 135 men, or about 80 percent of the crew, were on the ship.

"There were several men who, I would say, had been drinking and still had a hangover," Asher told the committee, "but in the morning of the attack they all snapped to and [...] all remarked that they had never sobered—the few that were under the influence of liquor—later said they had never sobered up so fast in their lives."

By 8:05 the *Blue* had opened fire on the Japanese planes with .50-caliber machine guns under Wolfe's charge. The ship eventually made it out of its docking and into the open sea, where it patrolled and eventually joined other survivors of the attack. In the meantime, the crew shot down four planes, with one crashing in Pearl City. "When the crew saw that plane down," Asher recalled, "they stopped shooting and proceeded to pat each other on the back. Then the chief gunner's mate went back there, thinking there was a casualty because he did not hear the firing. Then they went back to their battle stations and continued to fire."

The *Blue* also sank two Japanese submarines. After the first contact, Asher ordered depth charges to be dropped. "I then turned around and observed a large oil slick on the water," he said, "and we observed bubbles coming to the surface along the length of approximately 200 feet."

In both his after-action report and congressional testimony, Asher praised Wolfe's part in the action, which resulted in no casualties or damage to the *Blue*. "Ensign Wolfe, who was assistant gunnery officer [...], performed remarkably well and remained in control during the entire time and solely controlled the battery during the fire."

Wolfe received a letter of commendation for "distinguished service and devotion to duty during the attack." On December 25, 1941, the *Honolulu Advertiser* published a front-page account of the *Blue*, although it was required to keep the crew's names confidential. The *Clinton Herald* later reported that Wolfe wrote his parents on January 3 that "if the credit were to go where the credit is due the story would be all about the men and not so much about the ensigns, but you know how it is: the fellow with the ball always gets the glory."

Wolfe remained in the Navy for the remainder of World War II, serving aboard the USS *Shelton* and USS *Birmingham*. He participated in the attack on the Marshall and Gilbert islands and the assaults on Wake and Marcus islands. At some point during the war he married Olive Cloffie Keuhn, a native of Stillwater, Minnesota. The couple had six children: Mary Catherine (b. 1943), Stephanie Marie (b. 1944), John Patrick Jr. (b. 1947), Sheelah Ann (b. 1949), Francis Kelly (b. 1952), and Bridget (b. 1954).

On October 3, 1945, Wolfe was promoted to the Reserve rank of lieutenant commander. On August 28, 1946, he transferred out of the Reserve and into the Regular Navy, and by 1949 was stationed at the Navy supply depot at Scotia, New York. Later that year, on September 3, the *Los Angeles Times* reported that he had been assigned to be lieutenant commander of the USS *Yosemite*. He was officially promoted to lieutenant commander of the Regular Navy on July 1, 1951, and on September 1, 1961, to captain.

Wolfe retired from the Navy in August 1964 and moved his family from Chevy Chase, Maryland, to San Rafael, in northern

California. He died there on October 12, 1997, and is buried at Mount Olivet Catholic Cemetery. Olive Kuehn Wolfe died on June 11, 2001, and is buried with her husband.

JOHN R. WOLFE
(1809–1883)

JOHN RICHARD WOLFE was born in Listowel, County Kerry, the son of Richard James Wolfe, a Catholic farmer, and Johanna Relihan Wolfe. The birthdate given on his gravestone is November 15, 1809. He was baptized on July 3, 1813, in the parish of Lixnaw. His sponsors were Michael and Bridget Brown. Wolfe's son later published his birth year as 1824.

Wolfe's siblings included James Richard (b. 1800), Maurice Richard (b. 1802), Ellen (b. ca. 1810), Thomas Richard (b. 1811), Johanna (b. 1812), Richard (b. 1815), Margaret Ellen (b. 1818), Edmond (b. 1821), and Patrick (b. 1822).

He married Honora "Nora" Buckley in Listowel on February 25, 1843. The witnesses were Martin Heagarty and Maurice Wolfe, the latter presumably being his brother. The couple had eight children survive to maturity: James Buckley (b. 1843), Patrick Bernard (b. 1848), Johanna (b. 1849), John Buckley (b. 1851), Maurice Buckley (b. 1855), Margaret I. (b. 1857), Catherine "Kate" (b. 1860), and Richard Boyle (b. 1862). Two daughters, Margaret and Catherine, died in infancy.

In *Wolfe's History of Clinton County* (1911), Wolfe's son Patrick wrote that John R. Wolfe "received an excellent education. During his young manhood he helped to organize the 'Young Ireland' party," a nationalist group that staged a failed rebellion in 1848, at the height of the potato famine. John R. Wolfe's great grandson, Thomas A. Wolfe, later wrote that claims of his involvement with Young Ireland are "probably ... incorrect although he may have had something to do with a local branch of it. Had he really been a founder, the chances are good that he would have either been arrested or run out of the country, and there is no evidence of either of those happening."

Whatever the case, Wolfe immigrated in 1847 in the company of his wife, his son James, and other relatives, including his first cousin Maurice Wolfe and his wife Ellen, and several of their children. (John Wolfe and Maurice Wolfe shared a grandfather, James M. "The Barrister" Wolfe.) John Wolfe's brother Thomas immigrated in 1848 and his brothers Maurice and Richard Wolfe in 1849. His cousin Maurice's brother, Richard Wolfe, came from Ireland in 1848.

Records suggest that Wolfe and his family arrived in New York from Liverpool on August 23, 1847, aboard the *Cornelia*, a relatively large ship (1,040 tons) built by Brown and Bell of New York and part of the Black Star Line. Owned by Samuel Thompson, Black Star ran eighteen ships between Liverpool and New York in 1847, sailing every six days. John F. French was the ship's master.

Wolfe traveled from New York to Chicago, where he stayed about seven weeks before moving to Ottawa, LaSalle County, Illinois. By 1856, he was in Clinton County, Iowa. There he quickly purchased 80 acres of government land. He eventually became the largest landholder in Liberty Township, with 1,100 acres. By 1879, when the *History of Clinton County, Iowa* was published, Wolfe owned 840 acres and Maurice Wolfe (presumably his son) 640 acres. According to the *Portrait and Biographical Album of Clinton County, Iowa* (1886), he held 640 acres at the time of his death. The 1860 federal census valued his estate at not much more than $1,000, but a decade later he was worth more than $12,000.

Wolfe became a naturalized United States citizen on May 6, 1857.

In 1870, Wolfe and his family were among the first members of the Saint James Catholic Parish, founded in Toronto by Father James Scallon. A church was erected in 1883 and the first Mass celebrated in December 1885. He did not live to participate.

Wolfe died on August 19, 1883, in Clinton County. His wife died four years later. They are buried at Saint James Cemetery in Toronto.

MARY A. WOLFE
(1834–1897)

MARY AGATHA WOLFE was born in 1834, in Listowel, County Kerry. She was the daughter of an unknown father and a mother with the maiden name O'Sullivan. Her paternal grandparents were James Maurice "The Barrister" Wolfe and Johanna McCoy Wolfe, and her siblings included Ellen J. (b. 1832), John Edmond (b. 1837), and Patrick (b. ca. 1844), the latter's relationship remaining unconfirmed.

Wolfe and all of her known siblings immigrated to the United States, but the circumstances of their travel is unclear. They probably were accompanied by other relatives, and during the 1840s many Wolfes left Ireland and settled first in LaSalle County, Illinois, and then in Clinton County, Iowa. These included Mary Wolfe's uncle John R. Wolfe and cousin Maurice Wolfe, who sailed together on the *Cornelia* in 1847; Thomas R. Wolfe, who sailed the *James H. Shepherd* in 1848; Richard Wolfe, who took the *Thomas H. Perkins* in 1848; Maurice R. Wolfe, who took the *Senator* in 1849; and Richard Wolfe, who sailed the *Liverpool* in 1849. All these men shared a descent from Maurice J. Wolfe.

Census records indicate that by 1860 Wolfe was working as a seamstress in Ottawa, LaSalle County, Illinois. In 1866, she entered Saint Joseph's Convent in Ottawa, run by the Religious Sisters of Mercy, a Catholic order founded in Dublin, in 1831. She joined the order in 1869 and worked as a teacher. In 1870, the federal census indicates that she was the convent's bursar, but by the time of her death she had led the order in both Streator and Lacon, Illinois. She was popularly known as Mother Mary Agatha.

Wolfe died of consumption at Saint Xavier's Academy in Ottawa on June 9, 1897, and is buried at Saint Columba Cemetery in that city.

MAURICE WOLFE
(ca. 1800–1879)

MAURICE WOLFE was born about 1800, possibly at Knockanasig, County Kerry. Some records indicate his name as Maurice Morris. He was the son of Maurice James Wolfe, a Catholic farmer, and Helen (sometimes Ellen) Dore. His siblings included John (b. ca. 1794), Edmund Maurice, Richard (b. 1795), Bartholomew (b. 1809), and Michael (b. 1813).

Little is known of Wolfe's early life. He married Ellen Catherine Carey on February 14, 1830, at Lixnaw, County Kerry. He was living at Tournageehy, Listowel, County Kerry, at the time. Witnesses to the event were Patrick McAuliff and Edmund Carey. (Carey's surname, according to the marriage records, was probably Kearney. Possibly through a transcription error, her name became Carey upon immigration to the United States.) Maurice and Ellen Wolfe had eleven children who lived to maturity: James Carey (b. 1831), Ellen (b. 1833), Maurice Carey (b. ca. 1835), Mary (b. 1838), John Carey (b. 1840), Thomas Carey (b. 1843), Margaret (b. ca. 1845), Johanna (b. 1847), Richard Carey (b. 1848), Catherine "Kate" (b. 1851), and Bridget Veronica (b. 1854).

In 1847, Wolfe immigrated to the United States in the company of his wife, children, and his first cousin John R. Wolfe and his family. (Maurice Wolfe and John R. Wolfe shared a grandfather, James M. "The Barrister" Wolfe.)

Wolfe and his family arrived in New York from Liverpool on August 23, 1847, aboard the *Cornelia*, a relatively large ship (1,040 tons) built by Brown and Bell of New York and part of the Black Star Line. Owned by Samuel Thompson, Black Star ran eighteen ships between Liverpool and New York in 1847, sailing every six days. John F. French was the ship's master.

Wolfe traveled from New York to Chicago, where he stayed long enough for his son Richard to be born in October 1848. He then moved to LaSalle County, Illinois. John Wolfe's brother Thomas R. Wolfe immigrated in 1848 while his brothers Maurice R. and Richard

Wolfe left in 1849. Maurice Wolfe's own brother, Richard, came from Ireland in 1848. They all settled, at least initially, in LaSalle County.

The federal census of 1850 places Maurice Wolfe in Deer Park Township, LaSalle County, and five years later, an Illinois state census has him farming in Richland/Eagle Township. Wolfe's cousin John moved to Liberty Township, Clinton County, Iowa, about 1855. On October 15 of that year, records show Maurice Wolfe purchasing more land in Illinois. In the spring of 1859, however, he, along with his family, joined John Wolfe in Iowa.

Maurice Wolfe spent his remaining years farming in Clinton County. By 1879, when the *History of Clinton County, Iowa* was published, John R. Wolfe owned 840 acres and a Maurice Wolfe (possibly John Wolfe's son Maurice Buckley, but also possibly his cousin) 640 acres.

Ellen Wolfe died on August 14, 1857. Maurice Wolfe signed his will on March 23, 1879, and died on April 1, 1879. They are buried at Saint James Cemetery, Toronto, Iowa.

MAURICE WOLFE
(ca. 1823–1909)

MAURICE WOLFE was born about 1823 in western County Limerick, the son of James Richard Wolfe and an unknown mother. He had at least two brothers, Thomas (b. 1841) and Richard (b. 1842), but likely at least another brother and at least two sisters.

Wolfe's grandfather, Richard James Wolfe, had been a prominent landowner and "the agent having charge of the property of the Knight of Kerry," according to *Wolfe's History of Clinton County* (1911), which likely involved care of Ballinruddery, the residence of Maurice FitzGerald, near Listowel, County Kerry. Wolfe's father inherited land at nearby Dromlought.

Maurice Wolfe farmed at Kiltean, County Kerry, just west of Listowel. He married Mary Cronin and had at least nine children: James M. (b. 1867), Matthew (b. 1869), Richard M. (b. 1870), Mary (b. 1873), Margaret (b. 1874), Elizabeth (b. 1875), John (b. 1879), Timothy M. (b. 1881), and Maurice (b. 1891).

In 1892, the brothers Matthew and Richard Wolfe were accused of murder and eventually indicted for manslaughter in the death of the farmer Michael Dillane at Ballybunion. An early report on the case suggests that boycotted land may have been at the root of the argument, although later the Crown prosecutor contended that it was unclear what started the row. Regardless, a letter to the editor of the *Irish Times*, republished in the *Kerry Evening Post* on August 3, 1893, complained that the Wolfe brothers were never tried and that it was "well known in the county, and evidence would have been produced at the trial to show, that the case was an agrarian murder"—which is to say, violence related to the ongoing Land War between tenants and landlords.

Wolfe sat on the Rural District Council and, for forty years, the Listowel Board of Guardians, one of five such bodies in Kerry empowered by Parliament to aid the poor and help defray the costs of emigration. His son James took his place on both.

Wolfe's obituary in the *Kerry Sentinel* describes him as a man "who cherished his independence" and who "was not of an excitable temperament; on the contrary he was of a most amiable and conciliatory disposition, and even on those contentious days when Tory met Nationalist—sometimes in discussionary mortal affray—his was the voice which essentially induced hands to meet across the table and resume the 'even tenour' of their way—at least temporarily."

Wolfe died in 1909.

MAURICE WOLFE
(1837–after 1915)

MAURICE WOLFE was born in May 1837, in Listowel, County Kerry, the son of John Wolfe and Bridget Foley Wolfe. He had six full siblings: Katherine Marie (b. 1832), Daniel, Johanna (b. ca. 1841), Ann (b. 1845), Bridget (b. ca. 1846), and Julia (b. ca. 1848). From his father's earlier marriage, he also had four half siblings: Margaret (b. ca. 1821), Eleanor (b. ca. 1821), Mary (b. 1826), and Ellen (b. 1827).

In 1849, Wolfe, his parents, and his siblings immigrated to the United States, sailing aboard the *Mary Ann Henry* and arriving in New York on July 9. Numerous members of the Wolfe family immigrated around the same time, nearly all of them settling in LaSalle County, Illinois. A few moved from there to Clinton County, Iowa.

Maurice Wolfe and his parents were living in Deer Park Township, LaSalle County, by 1850. Within a decade, however, Wolfe had moved to Ohio Township, Franklin County, Kansas. By 1870, he had moved to Greenwood Township and was living in the household of Michael and Catherine Fitzgerald, both Irish-immigrant farmers. About 1878 he married Mary Fitzgerald, a native of Illinois and likely the Fitzgeralds' daughter. The couple had three children: Edward (b. 1880), William (b. 1884), and Anna (b. 1898).

Wolfe farmed in Franklin County the rest of his life. His wife, Mary, died sometime between 1898 and 1900. In the federal census of 1910, Wolfe was described as living in the home of Amos Cook in Osage, Kansas. Five years later, a state census identified him as residing in Garden City Township, Finney County, Kansas, with his son Edward.

His death date is unknown.

MAURICE WOLFE
(1912–1989)

MAURICE WOLFE was born on November 21, 1912, in Knockeen, Castleisland, County Kerry. He was the son of Maurice James Wolfe and Johanna Scollard Wolfe. His siblings included Hanora May (b. 1904), Mary (b. 1905), James (b. 1907), David (b. 1909), Richard (b. 1910), and Patrick (b. 1914).

Wolfe's uncle, the Reverend Patrick Wolfe, was a longtime priest in County Limerick and the author of *Sloinnte Gaedheal is Gall*, a study of Irish names and surnames published in 1923. His paternal grandmother, Honora Maher, was herself the daughter of a Wolfe, Ellen Wolfe Maher, much of whose family immigrated to Illinois and Iowa during the mid-nineteenth century.

First educated at the Irish Christian Brothers School in Tralee, Wolfe studied for the priesthood at Saint Brendan Minor Seminary and Saint Patrick Major Seminary, in Thurles, County Tipperary. He was ordained at Saint Mary Cathedral in Thurles on June 13, 1937.

Assigned to the Diocese of Buffalo, New York, Wolfe arrived in New York City aboard the *President Roosevelt* on August 28, 1937. He was naturalized a U.S. citizen on January 25, 1943.

Shortly after his arrival in 1937, Wolfe was reassigned to Saint Mary's Cathedral in Cheyenne, Wyoming, where he served as an assistant pastor until 1939. That year he transferred to Saints Peter and Paul in Jamestown, New York, and the year after to Immaculate Conception, in East Aurora, New York. In 1941 he became associate pastor of Our Lady Help of Christians, in Cheektowaga, New York, near Buffalo, staying for eight years. During that time, he also served as chaplain of the Erie County Council of the Boy Scouts of America (1941–1948) and as an auxiliary chaplain in the U.S. Army (1942–1945).

In 1949, Wolfe was appointed Youth Director of the Diocese of Buffalo, a position he held for thirteen years. In 1963, the national Catholic Youth Organization presented Wolfe its Padre of Youth Award. He also served as administrator of Our Lady of Peace Church, in Clarence, New York, from 1952 to 1955.

In 1946, while a pastor at Our Lady Help of Christians, in Cheektowaga, Wolfe recommended to the bishop that the church purchase property on Cleveland Drive in the town toward the creation of a new parish. The site became the home of Infant of Prague Church, which first opened in 1962. That same year, Wolfe became the parish's second pastor. The thousand-seat church was renovated and rededicated in 1978.

On January 13, 1968, the *Kerryman* newspaper in Ireland reported that Pope Paul VI had appointed Wolfe a Domestic Prelate with the title Right Reverend Monsignor.

Wolfe died in Buffalo on December 16, 1989, and was buried at Mount Olivet Cemetery, in Tonawanda, Erie County.

MAURICE B. WOLFE
(1855–1928)

MAURICE BUCKLEY WOLFE was born in March 1855, in LaSalle County, Illinois. His parents were John Richard Wolfe, an Irish Catholic farmer, and Honora Buckley Wolfe. He had seven siblings who survived to maturity: James Buckley (b. 1843), Patrick Bernard (b. 1848), Johanna (b. 1849), John Buckley (b. 1851), Margaret I. (b. 1857), Catherine "Kate" (b. 1860), and Richard Boyle (b. 1862). Two sisters, Margaret and Catherine, died in infancy.

In 1847, Wolfe's parents and brother James immigrated to the United States from Listowel, County Kerry, along with John R. Wolfe's first cousin Maurice Wolfe and his family. (John and Maurice Wolfe shared a grandfather, James M. "The Barrister" Wolfe.) The families arrived in New York on August 23, 1847, and from there made their way to Chicago and then to LaSalle County, Illinois. John R. Wolfe and his family moved to Clinton County, Iowa, about 1855, likely after Maurice B. Wolfe was born. Wolfe's grandson, Thomas A. Wolfe, wrote, incorrectly, that Maurice was the first Wolfe to be born in Lost Nation, an area of Liberty Township in Clinton County. (A town was established there in 1871.)

John R. Wolfe's brother, Maurice R. Wolfe, who came from Ireland in 1849, stayed in Illinois, while Maurice Wolfe and his family moved to Clinton County in the spring of 1859.

Wolfe married Sarah A. McAndrews, of Lost Nation, on April 3, 1894. Like her husband, McAndrews was the child of Irish immigrants. Her parents, Philip McAndrews and Bridget Caulfield, were from County Mayo. Prior to marriage Sarah McAndrews had worked as a teacher. She and Maurice Wolfe had five sons: Raymond Bernard (b. 1896), Philip James (b. 1898), John Joseph (b. 1901), Melvin Maurice (b. 1904), and James Emmet (b. 1909).

Little is known of Wolfe's life except that he farmed. According to the *History of Clinton County, Iowa* (1879), Wolfe's father was the largest landholder in Liberty Township, with 1,100 acres, before transferring some of his holdings to his sons, including Maurice. In

1879, John R. Wolfe owned 840 acres and a Maurice Wolfe 640 acres. This is probably the same Maurice Wolfe who was his son.

Thomas Wolfe filled in the biographical gaps with humor:

> The writer knows little about [Maurice Wolfe], but it can be assumed he became a Catholic and a Democrat at approximately the same time. It is possible, however, that he inherited some of his father's Marxist revolutionary ideas although there is no record of political insurrection in Lost Nation or Toronto during his lifetime. It is well known in Lost Nation, though, that Grandfather Maurice attended his agrarian pursuits in spurts which he called "five year plans." His favorite tools were the hammer and sickle.

In an email to his niece in 2007, Thomas Wolfe wrote:

> Uncle Dan McGinn always claimed that Grandfather Maurice was once a Texas Ranger, but I don't believe it. He also alleged that he was an excellent shot with a .45 caliber revolver, a gun that is very heavy and difficult to shoot accurately. What he did do was farm, and that's where his five sons were raised.

Mentions of Maurice Wolfe in the press were few and brief. He is probably the same man mentioned in the *Cedar Rapids Evening Gazette*, on May 20, 1898, as having his "place ... swept clear of all except the dwelling" by a tornado. "Mr. McAndrews, near by, lost everything and was severely injured."

A notice in the *Oxford Mirror* on August 30, 1900, mentioned that Wolfe's brother Patrick, a district court judge, was visiting. On December 21, 1905, the same paper reported:

> While Maurice Wolfe had his team in the lumber yard for some lumber the horses became frightened and took a lively gate toward home upsetting the wagon and badly demoralizing it. The horses came out with but little injury.

The *Mirror* reported on March 21, 1907, that Wolfe's father-in-law "accompanied a shipment of cattle to Chicago" for Wolfe.

Sarah McAndrews Wolfe died on October 2, 1922. Maurice Wolfe died at home on January 4, 1928. They are buried at Saint James Cemetery in Toronto, Iowa.

The Wolfe family, ca. 1923. Left to right: James E. Wolfe, Philip J. Wolfe, Maurice B. Wolfe, John J. Wolfe, Sarah McAndrews Wolfe, Raymond B. Wolfe, and Melvin M. Wolfe

MAURICE C. WOLFE
(ca. 1835–1910)

MAURICE CAREY WOLFE was born about 1835, probably in Listowel, County Kerry. His parents were Maurice Wolfe, a Catholic farmer, and Ellen Catherine Carey. Wolfe had ten siblings who lived to maturity: James Carey (b. 1831), Ellen (b. 1833), Mary (b. 1838), John Carey (b. 1840), Thomas Carey (b. 1843), Margaret (b. ca. 1845), Johanna (b. 1847), Richard Carey (b. 1848), Catherine "Kate" (b. 1851), and Bridget Veronica (b. 1854).

In 1847, Wolfe, his parents, and several siblings immigrated to the United States, along with the elder Maurice Wolfe's first cousin John R. Wolfe and his family. (Maurice Wolfe and John R. Wolfe shared a grandfather, James M. "The Barrister" Wolfe.) The families arrived in New York on August 23, and after a stop in Chicago made their way to LaSalle County, Illinois. John R. Wolfe and his family moved to Clinton County, Iowa, around 1855.

Many members of the extended Wolfe family made the same journey. The younger Maurice Wolfe's uncle John Wolfe immigrated in 1849. John R. Wolfe's brother Thomas R. Wolfe came from Ireland in 1848 and his brothers Maurice R. and Richard Wolfe sailed separately in 1849. Other cousins came, as well, including Margaret and Elizabeth Maher, daughters of John R. Wolfe's sister Ellen, and Patrick, Dennis, Bridget, and Thomas Sheehan, the children of John R. Wolfe's sister Margaret. Another cousin, John E. Wolfe, and his sisters Ellen J. and Mary Agatha, also immigrated. All of these Wolfes, except for the Sheehans, settled in LaSalle County, Illinois. A few moved on to Clinton County, Iowa.

Maurice Wolfe never married. The federal census of 1880 identifies him as a farmer living in Liberty Township, Clinton County, living in the same household as his sisters Mary and Bridget, and his nephew Jeremiah "Jerry" Mulvihill, the son of his sister Ellen.

By 1910, he had retired from farming and lived with his brother Richard in the town of DeWitt in Clinton County.

He died on October 28, 1910, and is buried at Saint James Cemetery in Toronto, Iowa.

MAURICE H. WOLFE
(1839–btw. 1910 and 1919)

MAURICE H. WOLFE was born in November 1839 in the townland of Cratloe, parish of Athea, County Limerick, to Philip M. "Old Phil" Wolfe and Elizabeth Herlihy. His siblings included Joseph Philip (b. 1841), Michael (b. 1843), Mary (b. 1849), Elizabeth (b. 1852), John (b. 1853), Philip (b. 1855), Patrick (b. 1857), Cornelius (b. 1858), Richard (b. 1859), Elizabeth (b. 1861), and Patrick (b. 1866). He seems also to have had a brother Bartholomew "Batt."

Nothing is known of Wolfe's early years and education. He likely was the same Maurice who, on August 10, 1863, arrived in New York from Liverpool on the *Hecla*. The manifest lists him as a laborer with a final destination of Canada. However, by September he had moved to Washington, D.C., where he stayed with another Maurice Woulfe and where his uncle Michael Herlihy lived. Herlihy later served on the frontier with Wolfe and was killed by ruffians in 1868.

Wolfe enlisted in the U.S. Army in Washington, D.C., and by May 12 of the following year he was with Company F, 30th U.S. Infantry, stationed at Fort Sedgwick, Colorado Territory. His enlistment papers describe him as a laborer, five feet, nine inches tall, with gray eyes and light hair.

A year later Wolfe had moved with his regiment to Fort D. A. Russell, in the Dakota Territory, and by the end of the year he was in Wyoming Territory, at Fort Fred Steele, on the North Platte River. Both forts had been established to help protect workers on the Union Pacific Railroad from Indians.

On March 31, 1869, the 30th U.S. Infantry Regiment consolidated with the 4th, and Wolfe became a quartermaster sergeant in Company B, 4th Infantry. By March 1870 the regiment had returned to Fort D. A. Russell, and that spring it traveled to the newly established Camp Brown, Wyoming Territory. Wolfe wrote a relative on May 10, 1870, of having crossed the Rockies twice.

In 1871, a small detachment of the 4th, including Wolfe, traveled to the area around Louisville, Kentucky, in order to battle moonshiners. In a letter to a relative, Wolfe wrote disapprovingly of those who drank, citing the unfortunate example of another Wolfe.

Late in 1873, Wolfe was back in Wyoming, at Fort Bridger, and there he got into a fight with an officer who called him a "dirty catholic Irishman," an incident that led to Wolfe's demotion. In a letter Wolfe mentions having written an anonymous report to a Saint Louis newspaper, the *Western Watchmen*, that complained of the treatment of Catholics in Wyoming, admitting that some in the regiment suspected him of being the author. Given the opportunity to apologize in exchange for the restoration of his rank, he refused.

Wolfe was discharged a private on June 23, 1874, at Fort Bridger, and three days later was naturalized an American citizen. He returned to Washington, D.C., and there, on June 9, 1876, he married Mary Carmody, also a native of Ireland. The couple had two children: Philip Maurice (b. 1877) and Mary Ellen (b. ca. 1881).

By 1877, Wolfe was employed on the District of Columbia police force as a clerk at the 4th Precinct Station, but he was fired on May 7, 1879, for striking a prisoner. The next year he took a job as a census enumerator and is listed in the City Directory from 1893 to 1895 as a clerk. In 1906 the directory lists him as a caulker. On December 7, 1907, the *Washington Post* reported he had been appointed a "special policeman" for duty at Kalorama Avenue and Ontario Road NW. The 1910 federal census describes him as a watchman.

Wolfe died sometime between that census and March 9, 1919, when his wife died at their daughter's home. Mary Ellen Wolfe married Joseph F. Krieg, the son of Irish and German immigrants, and the couple had at least three daughters and two sons. Philip, who never married and worked as a plumber, died on March 5, 1921, and is buried at Mount Olivet Cemetery in Washington, D.C.

Maurice Wolfe's letters, dating from 1863 to 1880, are in the private collection of his grandnephew Timothy Wolfe, of Athea, and copies are preserved at the National Archives of Ireland, in Dublin. Transcripts have been made by the U.S. historian Kerby Miller and have been quoted widely by scholars, beginning with the folklorist Kevin Danaher (Caoimhín Ó Danachair), who published excerpts in the military history journal the *Irish Sword* in 1957. In 1994, the filmmakers Ellen and Paul Wagner, of Charlottesville, Virginia, released the documentary *Out of Ireland*, which opens with the actor

Aidan Quinn narrating from one of Wolfe's letters, dated January 26, 1870:

> Michael, I am in first rate health. I was never better in my life. This Rocky Mountain air agrees with me first rate. I have everything that would tend to make life comfortable. But still at night when I lay in bed, my mind wanders off across the continent and over the Atlantic to the hills of Cratloe. In spite of all I can never forget home, as every Irishman in a foreign land can never forget the land he was raised in. But alas! I am far away from them old haunts.

MAURICE J. WOLFE
(ca. 1630–ca. 1700)

MAURICE JAMES WOLFE, a Catholic farmer in County Limerick, is believed to have been born about 1630. He likely married before 1650 (his spouse is unknown) and had at least three children: Maurice, James (b. ca. 1651), and Richard, who never married.

According to family oral history, Wolfe was plowing his fields when a rider whose horse had stumbled informed him that Limerick had fallen. As part of Oliver Cromwell's conquest of Ireland, the city had been under siege from October 1650 until its surrender to Cromwell's son-in-law, Henry Ireton, in October 1651. (The town of Ireton in Sioux County, Iowa, is named for the English commander.)

The Wolfes were already an established family in Limerick city. Several Wolfes had served as mayors, bailiffs, or sheriffs. Two Wolfe brothers were reportedly hanged by the English in 1651: Captain George Wolfe and Father James Wolfe. Some accounts have the captain evading capture, moving to Kent, England, and becoming grandfather to General James Wolfe, the hero of Quebec. Father Wolfe, a Dominican, was presented for beatification as a martyr in 1915 but was not among the seventeen Irish martyrs so honored by Pope John Paul II on September 27, 1992.

In the century before Ireton, Wolfes were also living to the southwest of Limerick city. Gerot (Gerald) Baluff lived in Inis Cuais, near present-day Rathkeale, but lost his land during the Desmond Rebellion (1569–1573 and 1579–1583). Two of his sons may have fled to the hills in the western part of the county.

It is likely that Maurice Wolfe was related in some way to this rural branch of the Wolfe family. He lived in a place called Inchereagh near present-day Athea, on the River Galey, in western Limerick. Athea is about 27 kilometers west of Rathkeale and about 14 kilometers east of Listowel, County Kerry.

Wolfe is believed to have died in Inchereagh about 1700.

MAURICE J. WOLFE
(1690–1792)

MAURICE JAMES WOLFE, known as "Old Maurice," was born in 1690, probably at Inchereagh, near present-day Athea, on the River Galey, in western County Limerick. His father was James M. Wolfe, a Catholic farmer also known as James of Inchereagh. The identity of his mother is unknown. Wolfe had at least seven siblings: six sisters who are said to have immigrated to the United States, and a brother, Richard (b. ca. 1690), who never married.

Family oral history—contained in a letter between Wolfe relatives dated August 1956 from Cratloe, County Limerick, also known as the "Aunt Dollie" letter—suggests that Maurice Wolfe "was strong and energetic, physically and mentally." When his father died in 1704, Maurice took charge of the family. According to the letter, he provided dowries for his six sisters, postponing his own marriage.

In 1730, he married Kathleen Rearden (also Riordan). The couple had five children: Richard Maurice "Short Dick" (b. ca. 1730), James Maurice (b. 1732), Edmond Maurice, Patrick, and Maurice James "Young Maurice" (b. ca. 1763). He bought land at Templeathea, about 2.8 kilometers northeast of Athea. (The letter suggests that Inchereagh was farther than that from Athea.) About 1760, his wife Kathleen died. "The churchyard, Templeathea, where she was buried was in plain sight of his house," according to the letter. "The tradition is that he could not bear to look at it."

As a result, in March 1760 Wolfe leased 2,000 acres of land, which constituted the entire townland of Cratloe, in County Limerick, a few kilometers from Templeathea.

Wolfe died in 1792. According to the Aunt Dollie letter, he died at home on December 24 or 25, at night: "He had eaten his supper, possibly too good a one for his years, and was sitting in a corner of the kitchen beside the fire watching a dance of the young people that was in full swing, when he appeared to fall asleep. It was noticed that he had 31 of his own teeth in his mouth and the 32nd was in his waistcoat pocket when he died that night as he was practically intact."

MAURICE J. WOLFE
(1755–1824)

MAURICE JAMES WOLFE was born in 1755 in the townland of Cratloe, parish of Athea, County Limerick, the son of James Maurice Wolfe and Johanna McCoy Wolfe. He had two and possibly three siblings: Richard James (b. 1763), James, and Edmund, the latter's relationship remaining unconfirmed. James Wolfe died at age twelve.

On February 23, 1784, in the parish of Monagea, County Limerick, he married Helen (sometimes Ellen) Dore. Church records indicate that witnesses to the marriage were Rutlegro Browne and Robert Dore. The couple had six children: John (b. ca. 1794), Richard (b. 1795), Edmund Maurice, Maurice (b. ca. 1800), Bartholomew (b. 1809), and Michael (b. 1813).

Little else is known of Wolfe, except that he farmed at Knockanasig, a townland just south of Listowel, County Kerry, and died in 1824. He is buried at the Temple Athea graveyard, County Limerick.

MAURICE J. WOLFE
(ca. 1763–before 1838)

MAURICE JAMES WOLFE, also known as "Maurice of Dromadda" and "Young Maurice," was born about 1763, probably at Templeathea in western County Limerick. He was the son of Maurice James "Old Maurice" Wolfe, a Catholic farmer, and Kathleen Rearden (also Riordan) Wolfe. His siblings included Richard Maurice "Short Dick" (b. ca. 1730), James Maurice (b. 1732), Edmond Maurice, and Patrick.

Little is known of Wolfe's life except that he married Hanora Harnett (sometimes Hartnett), of County Limerick. The couple had eight children: James Harnett (b. ca. 1780–1800), Richard (b. 1802), John Harnett (b. 1807), Edmond, Timothy, Mary, Patrick Maurice, and Catherine.

Wolfe's son James immigrated to the United States in 1819 and died there in 1836, possibly the victim of murder. His brothers Richard and John Wolfe took up his land claim in Missouri.

Maurice Wolfe and his wife both died sometime before 1838 and are buried at the Temple Athea graveyard.

MAURICE J. WOLFE
(1884–1973)

MAURICE JAMES WOLFE was born on July 21, 1884, in Tickhill Parish, Yorkshire, England. He was the son of Maurice Richard Wolfe, an officer of the Department of Inland Revenue, and Elizabeth Malcolm "Bessie" Cockburn, of Scotland. His siblings included Jane Cooper "Dollie" (b. 1879) and Richard Edmond Maurice (b. 1883).

Before joining Inland Revenue, the elder Maurice Wolfe was raised at the Glen, the family farm in the townland of Cratloe, County Limerick. He was the son of Richard Edmond "Dicky Ned" Wolfe, a celebrated *seanchaí*, or Irish-speaking storyteller and oral historian.

Maurice J. Wolfe attended Robert Gordon's College in Aberdeen, Scotland, and then worked in the London Stock Exchange for several years before deciding to read the law. He apprenticed with the Dublin solicitor Arthur E. Bradley and passed his final examinations in May 1915, after which he opened a practice in Abbeyfeale, County Limerick. In April 1916, during World War I and just weeks prior to the Easter Rising, Wolfe volunteered for the 10th Battalion of the Royal Dublin Fusiliers, an infantry regiment in the British army. By January 1917, he was commissioned a 2nd lieutenant in the 5th (Special Reserve) Battalion of the Royal Munster Fusiliers. He was gassed while fighting at the Battle of the Somme (1916) and was awarded a Silver War Badge in 1918. He was honorably discharged.

Wolfe's cousin, Richard B. Wolfe, ran a pharmacy in Abbeyfeale that became a center of nationalist activity before and during the War of Independence (1919–1921). Dick Wolfe's brother-in-law Con Colbert was one of sixteen men executed by the British after the Easter Rising and Wolfe himself joined the West Limerick Brigade of the Irish Republican Army (IRA).

The veteran Maurice Wolfe, however, did not appear to share his cousin's sympathies. In *Victory and Woe*, his memoir of the West Limerick Brigade, written in the 1940s and published posthumously in 2002, Mossie Harnett recalls a weapons raid he and his comrades undertook early in the war. After taking a Colt revolver and shotgun from the home of a British officer and meeting no resistance, the party arrived at Wolfe's house.

> There we got some shotguns and cartridges after being strongly obstructed in our search. Ned Ryan took strong objection to this behavior, and pointing his gun around, threatened to blow the brains out of anyone not staying quiet. In the confusion created we missed a fine revolver owned by Maurice, later confiscated by the Black and Tans.

Late in the evening of September 18, 1920, an active service unit of the IRA ambushed a six-man patrol of the Royal Irish Constabulary (RIC) outside of Abbeyfeale. A constable was killed and two others wounded. The next day a large number of policemen and soldiers arrived, members of both the RIC and the RIC Special Reserve, or so-called Black and Tans—temporary constables recruited from England and notoriously violent. They fired thousands of rounds of ammunition, bombed several houses, and damaged Dick Wolfe's pharmacy.

The police eventually retreated to their barracks in town, but the violence did not end. On the evening of September 20, a policeman allegedly shot dead two young local men outside town. The victims were Patrick Harnett, a postman, and Jeremiah Healy, a blacksmith's apprentice. According to witnesses, a Black and Tan named Thomas D. Huckerby followed them down a walking path, shots rang out, and then Huckerby returned to the barracks alone. A short time later, Harnett and Healy were found dead in a field, both shot through the head.

On September 22, the British army convened an inquiry, with Maurice Wolfe representing the Harnett and Healy families. On the stand, a policeman testified that Huckerby had confessed to killing the boys, claiming that he had followed them and, when they ran, shot them.

"Further witnesses were then examined and the proceedings adjourned," wrote J. D. H., a pseudonym for the Abbeyfeale journalist J. D. Harnett, who composed an account of the incident that was published in 1948 by the *Kerryman* newspaper and then again in the book *Limerick's Fighting Story, 1916–21* (2009). "That was the last heard of the inquiry. It had been going against the British and almost immediately Mr Woulfe, the solicitor who defended the interests of the next-of-kin, was arrested on a trumped-up charge of possessing firearms without a current permit."

The *Cork Examiner* reported the arrest on October 8, 1920, suggesting that it had "created a sensation in the town." Wolfe was detained upon arriving at his office and relocated to the William Street barracks, in Limerick city. "And amongst his escort," Harnett noted, "was the Black and Tan [Huckerby]." The *Liberator* newspaper, of Tralee, County Kerry, reported Wolfe's release on October 19, and that he had been fined 10s "for having without permit a service revolver and ammunition"—the same weapon he had kept from the IRA in 1919.

On September 14, 1921, Wolfe married Sarah McCarthy, and the couple had three children: John Maurice (b. 1922), Maurice Richard (b. 1925), and Richard (b. 1929). Richard Wolfe eventually joined his father's law practice, which became Maurice J. Wolfe and Son, Solicitors.

In the postwar years, Wolfe joined Fine Gael, the political party that originated with those men and women whose sympathies had been pro-Treaty during the Civil War (1922–1923). (His cousin Dick Wolfe had been anti-Treaty.) On July 18, 1934, the *Irish Independent* reported that Wolfe's Abbeyfeale home "was attacked at night. Mr. Woulfe's bedroom was fired into and the window shattered by gunshot pellets. Several rifle bullets were also fired through the roof of the house." Subsequent police investigations linked the incident to a lawsuit in which Wolfe represented several parties. No charges were ever brought, however.

Wolfe died on May 7, 1973. He is buried with his brother Richard and sister Jane "Dollie" Wolfe in the family mausoleum at the Temple Athea graveyard. His wife is buried in Abbeyfeale.

MAURICE J. WOLFE
(1886–1918)

MAURICE JOSEPH WOLFE was born on April 20, 1886, in San Rafael, California. He was the only son of John Carey Wolfe, an Irish Catholic immigrant who owned a drug store, and Ellen L. Martin Wolfe.

Wolfe was educated in San Rafael and at Saint Ignatius College, a Jesuit-run preparatory school in San Francisco. According to information in the *History of the State of California and Biographical Record of Coast Counties* by James Miller Guinn, Wolfe then enrolled at the School of Pharmacy of the Affiliated Colleges of San Francisco and expected to receive his degree in 1905.

It is not clear whether he did; however, the federal census of 1910 identifies him as living with his mother in San Rafael and working as an electrician for a telephone company.

Aabout 1912, Wolfe married Imogene Ann "Jean" Irving, a native of Canada. She was or at some point became a registered nurse. The couple had two children: John Maurice (b. 1913), and Margaret I. (b. 1915).

Wolfe's children were born in San Francisco County, but at some point he moved to Oakland, where worked as a druggist. He died there on June 20, 1918. According to the notice in an Iowa newspaper, "While going to his store a derrick used on a new building fell and struck him." He is buried with his parents at Mount Olivet Cemetery in San Rafael. His wife, Jean, married a second time, to E. H. Sage, and died on October 7, 1952, in San Rafael.

MAURICE P. WOLFE
(1873–1909)

MAURICE PATRICK WOLFE was born in March 1873, in Missouri. He was the son of Richard Downey Wolfe, a farmer and Irish Catholic immigrant, and his second wife, Margaret Shine Lyons Wolfe, also an Irish immigrant. He had seven full siblings: Johanna (b. 1867), Daniel Maurice (b. 1869), Honoria Euphrasia (b. 1871), Margaret Theresa (b. 1875), Richard (b. 1878), Marie Louise (b. 1881), and Aileen Gregory (b. 1884). He also had a half sibling, Katherine Collins (b. 1863), whose mother was Richard Wolfe's first wife, Margaret O'Kane Wolfe.

Wolfe married Mary Ellen Morrow of Lafayette, Indiana, in 1897, and the couple had six children: Mildred (b. 1897), Richard (b. 1899), Julia (b. 1902), Margaret (b. 1905), Mary (b. 1906), and an unnamed infant born early in 1909. They farmed in Brazoria County, Texas, just west of Galveston, on the Gulf of Mexico.

On July 23, 1909, a hurricane struck the gulf coast of Texas and Louisiana, killing Wolfe, his wife, and all six of their children. According to a contemporary news report, Wolfe was in a boat about four miles from his home when the storm hit; he drowned. He had been returning from Galveston, where he had sold goods from his farm. His body was not recovered until mid-August.

According to the *Angleton Times*:

> Mrs. Woulfe and six children, a negro woman and two children and several white men were at the house. Without warning, a tidal wave swept over them. Every effort was made by the men to save the women and children, but the terrific force of the waves was beyond human power to resist. Mrs. Woulfe and the infant child were found about three miles from the house, in Hoskins' field, within 500 yards of where Morris' boat was found. The lifeless forms of the children were found in the Bayou.

The death toll of the storm reached at least thirty-eight, with damages of more than $2.5 million.

MAURICE R. WOLFE
(1802–1870)

MAURICE RICHARD WOLFE was born in 1802, in the townland of Cratloe, parish of Athea, County Limerick. His parents were Richard James Wolfe, a Catholic farmer, and Johanna Relihan Wolfe.

Wolfe's siblings included James Richard (b. 1800), John Richard (b. 1809), Ellen (b. ca. 1810), Thomas Richard (b. 1811), Johanna (b. 1812), Margaret Ellen (b. 1818), Edmond (b. 1821), and Patrick (b. 1822).

In 1826, he married Johanna Downey in Listowel, County Kerry.

According to a story in the *Kerryman* newspaper (December 10, 1927), Wolfe owned a racehorse called Dimby, bred by King William IV and winner of a hundred-pound wager over Roller at the Ballyeigh races and festival in 1840. Wolfe owned and bred other horses.

Wolfe's brother John R. Wolfe immigrated to the United States in 1847, his brother Thomas R. Wolfe in 1848, and his brother Richard Wolfe in 1849. Two first cousins, Maurice and Richard Wolfe, came from Ireland in 1847 and 1848, respectively.

Maurice Wolfe sailed from Liverpool to New York aboard the *Senator*, a 777-ton ship of the Black Star Line, owned by Samuel Thompson; he arrived on September 22, 1849. Listed on the manifest as a farmer, he brought with him seven children: Margaret (b. 1827), Richard Downey (b. 1829), James Downey (b. 1839), Johanna E. (b. 1840), Catherine "Kate" (b. 1842), and Maurice (b. 1848). His son Stephen (b. 1833) had died. Also accompanying the family was Margaret Maher (sometimes Magher or Meagher), daughter of Wolfe's sister Ellen. He appears to have treated her as his own daughter, and after Wolfe's death, she was considered an heir to his estate. After settling, with his siblings, in LaSalle County, Illinois, Wolfe had two more children: John Francis (b. 1850) and Edmund Dean (b. 1853).

Wolfe applied for U.S. citizenship on August 13, 1852, at the county court in Ottawa, LaSalle County, Illinois; his application was granted on March 20, 1855.

Unlike a number of other members of his extended family, Wolfe did not move to eastern Iowa. According to the federal census of 1860, he remained in Osage Township, LaSalle County, where he owned a farm and lived with several of his children and a thirty-five-year-old Irish-born laborer named Charles Egan. He owned $5,000 in real estate and $1,000 in personal estate. Ten years later, he was still in Osage. He owned $4,200 in real estate and $600 in personal estate. His eldest son farmed the adjacent property.

Wolfe died on October 12, 1870, in Osage Township and is buried in Lost Land Cemetery in Eagle Township, LaSalle County, Illinois. He left no will. The value of his estate was estimated to be $2,500.

MAURICE R. WOLFE
(1853–1928)

MAURICE RICHARD WOLFE was baptized on December 13, 1853, having been born at the Glen, the family farm in the townland of Cratloe, parish of Athea, County Limerick. He was the son of Richard Edmond "Dicky Ned" Wolfe and Catherine White Wolfe, and his siblings included Edward (b. 1852), Honora "Nano" (b. 1855), Mary (b. 1857), Ellen "Nellie" (b. 1858), Catherine (b. 1860), Patrick Richard (b. 1861), John W. (b. 1864), Richard White (b. 1866), Catherine (b. 1868), Mary A. (b. 1870), Michael Richard (b. 1870), and Johanna "Hannah" (b. 1873). Of these, Patrick, Richard, Ellen, John, Mary, and Nano immigrated to the United States. Richard W. Wolfe became commissioner of public works for the city of Chicago. Edward and the first Catherine likely died in infancy.

Little is known of Wolfe's early years and education, although he almost certainly attended classes at a school his father founded at the Glen. As an account from Ireland's National Folklore Project attests, it began as a hedge school but evolved into something slightly more modern. He may then have graduated, like his brother Richard Wolfe, to the Ballagh Townland school and the National School in Athea.

On July 11, 1874, he passed the certification to become a second class assistant of excise in the Department of Inland Revenue. He took the exam in Limerick, but he soon transferred to Scotland, where he met Elizabeth Malcolm "Bessie" Cockburn, a Presbyterian from Glasgow whom he married on December 13, 1878. The couple had three children: Jane Cooper "Dollie" (b. 1879), Richard Edmund Maurice (b. 1883), and Maurice James (b. 1884). Soon after the birth of their first child, they moved south. The English census of 1881 placed them on Sunderland Street, Tickhill Parish, Yorkshire.

Wolfe worked for the Department of Inland Revenue for nearly forty years, and among his duties was gauging, or testing, the alcoholic content of whiskey that had been necessarily watered down when bottled independent of the distiller. For this reason, he became known as the Gauger Wolfe, and his family line took on that nickname as well. He lived the last decade of his life in the Chapelizod neighborhood of Dublin.

Wolfe spoke Irish fluently. His father, Dicky Ned Wolfe, also an Irish speaker, had been celebrated for his knowledge of the history and folklore of West Limerick and North Kerry, and was credited with helping his relative, the Reverend Patrick Wolfe, collect material for *Sloinnte Gaedheal is Gall*, a seminal work on Irish names and surnames first published in 1906. A posthumous notation in the National Folklore Collection identified the elder Wolfe as a *seanchaí*, or storyteller. In 1931, when Richard W. Wolfe was visiting from Chicago, a newspaper report described Dicky Ned's intellectual and cultural position in the community and then noted: "The old man was succeeded by Mr. Maurice R. Woulfe ..."

Wolfe died on April 15, 1928, and his wife in 1943. They are buried at the Temple Athea graveyard.

MAURICE R. WOLFE
(1891–1962)

MAURICE RICHARD WOLFE was born on March 9, 1891, in the townland of Cratloe, parish of Athea, County Limerick, the son of Richard James "Brown Dick" Wolfe, a member of the district council, and Ellen Maher Wolfe. His siblings included Honora "Nora" (b. 1882), John Richard James (b. 1883), Ellen "Ellie" (b. 1885), Patrick (b. 1887), and Catherine (b. 1889).

Wolfe's birth record lists his name as Maurice Patrick; however, all subsequent records, including his gravestone, indicate his name to be Maurice Richard.

Wolfe attended Abbeyfeale National School and Saint Michael's College, in Listowel. He graduated to Saint Patrick's College, a seminary in Thurles, County Tipperary, and then to Oscott College, in the Diocese of Birmingham, in England. Ordained a priest on March 16, 1916, he worked at Saint Peter and Saint Paul Church, in Wolverhampton, West Midlands, from 1916 to 1922, and then at Saint Catherine's, in Birmingham, and Sacred Heart in Hanley, Staffordshire County. From 1924 until his death, Wolfe served as the parish priest in Old Fallings, a suburb of Wolverhampton.

According to an obituary published in the *Limerick Leader*, Father Wolfe in 1924 "bought the property in Old Fallings Lane, now known as St. Chad's College, and invited the Marist Brothers to open a grammar school for boys. He built a primary school—St. Mary's, Cannock Road, in 1928. And in June 1934 he saw the completion of the Church of Our Lady of Perpetual Succour next to the school. In 1938 Father Wolfe was appointed Rural Dean, and a decade later was appointed Canon of the Cathedral Chapter.

The same obituary notes Wolfe's nationalist bona fides.

> Despite his long exile, Canon Woulfe was throughout his life a strong nationalist and at all times maintained a strong love for an allegiance to the old land. In his post-student days he made the acquaintance of many of the men engaged in the independence movement, as his home was a welcome

and ever-open refuge for the officers and men of the West Limerick Old I.R.A. Brigade during the Black and Tan Regime.

Wolfe suffered from Parkinson's disease late in his life, and died at Old Fallings on November 24, 1962. He is buried at Saint Bartholomew's Church in Athea.

MAURICE V. WOLFE
(1882–1927)

MAURICE VINCENT WOLFE was born on May 31, 1882, in Toronto, Clinton County, Iowa, the son of Richard Carey Wolfe and his first wife, Margaret McGonnegle Wolfe. Wolfe had six full siblings: James (b. 1878), Ellen Calista "Nellie" (b. 1880), Edward Anthony (b. 1884), John Gregory (b. 1886), Catherine W. (b. 1889), and Joseph (b. 1892). He also had five half-siblings by his father's second wife, Ellen "Nellie" Murphy: twins Richard Joseph and Leo (b. 1903), Raymond F. (b. 1905), Mary (b. 1907), and Robert (b. 1910).

Wolfe registered for the draft during World War I (1914–1918); his card is dated September 12, 1918. The federal census of 1920 records him as living in Liberty Township, Clinton County, with his sister Ellen, her husband Richard White, and their three children. His younger half-siblings also lived on the White farm: Richard, Raymond, and Mary. The census makes no mention of the youngest, Robert, who may have died.

Wolfe married Gertrude Josephine Scanlan, of Lost Nation, on February 8, 1921, in Lost Nation. The *Oxford Mirror* newspaper, on February 17 of that year, described Maurice Wolfe as "a prosperous farmer near Toronto." Gertrude Wolfe was the daughter of Irish immigrants who had initially settled in LaSalle County, Illinois, before relocating to Iowa. She was born on April 17, 1890, and her mother died while giving birth. Her father died five years later, and she was raised by a brother and an uncle. She and Maurice Wolfe initially made their home in or near Toronto and had a daughter, Mary Virginia, who was born prematurely on December 17, 1921, and died two days later.

About 1923 Wolfe left his farm and moved to Lost Nation. In 1926 or 1927, Wolfe worked for a local railroad and lost the sight of his right eye when, according to a newspaper report, "a piece of chisel struck him." He received a monetary settlement.

By 1927, Wolfe and his wife lived on the north end of Lost Nation. On August 18 of that year the *Oxford Mirror* reported that Wolfe had disappeared ten days earlier. After several days visiting friends in a cabin on the Wapsipinicon River, Gertrude Wolfe returned home to find a note:

> Dear Gertie, I am doing this for the good of both of us. I am going to shoot myself. If there is a God, I hope he is not too hard on me. I still love you, Gertie.

Search efforts did not immediately turn up a body and were abandoned after just one day. At least one sighting of Wolfe was reported, and the paper recalled that Wolfe had disappeared once before, "some years ago." Another publication noted that he "had been accustomed to wandering about the country." "Many are of the opinion," the *Mirror* wrote, "that Mr. Wolfe has merely departed for an extended visit with his brothers who are living someplace in the far south."

After Wolfe's disappearance, Gertrude Wolfe sold their home and personal property and moved to San Diego, California. Then, on November 21, 1927, two high school boys, Russell and Lowell Ellis, discovered Wolfe's body a mile and a half west of Lost Nation. According to the *Davenport Democrat Leader*, "The body was crumpled over a shotgun and part of his skull blown away by the shot which ended his life."

Wolfe is buried in Saint James Cemetery, in Toronto, Iowa. His widow, who returned to Iowa by 1942, is buried next to him.

MELVIN M. WOLFE
(1904–1990)

MELVIN MAURICE WOLFE was born on May 27, 1904, near Lost Nation, Clinton County, Iowa. He was the son of Maurice Buckley Wolfe, a farmer in Lost Nation, and Sarah A. McAndrews Wolfe. Wolfe had four brothers: Raymond Bernard (b. 1896), Philip James (b. 1898), John Joseph (b. 1901), and James Emmet (b. 1909).

In an essay written in 1975, Melvin Wolfe's nephew, Thomas A. Wolfe, wrote:

> The nurse or midwife (or whomever helped deliver [Melvin] in those days near the dawn of creation) reports that thirty minutes after his birth he said to the assembled doctor, nurses, midwives, family, and friends, "Did you ever hear the one about ...?" The story is reported to have lasted sixteen minutes and twelve seconds by actual timing, included three delightful sub-stories, and was told in a marvelous Irish accent which has, unfortunately disappeared among third generation Wolfes.

The 1920 federal census lists the family as farming in Sharon Township, Clinton County, with the help of a thirty-six-year-old domestic servant, Lottie Keyes. Wolfe attended public school in Lost Nation. A newspaper report from 1919 indicated that

> Wolfe met with an unfortunate accident Sunday morning when cranking the car. He hurt his arm severely and was brought to town to Dr. McMeel, who found his arm severely sprained. Melvin considers himself fortunate that no bones were broken.

A report from 1927 notes that he had gone to Chicago with a load of cattle.

On August 26, 1930, Wolfe married Frances M. McLaughlin, the daughter of an Irish immigrant, near her home in Otter Creek Township, Jackson County. (Thomas Wolfe called McLaughlin "the most remarkable and colorful lady this writer has ever known.") The couple had five children: Paul, Robert A. (b. 1935), Patricia, Leo David, and Richard.

Wolfe farmed his whole life, living just north of Lost Nation's Sacred Heart Catholic Church, which he attended. He apparently liked to play cards, winning prizes at a Catholic Ladies Club card party in March 1930; a few months later, the new Mrs. Wolfe also won a card-playing prize from the club. On February 29, 1940, the *Oxford Mirror* wrote that Wolfe had been taken to the Mayo Clinic in Rochester, Minnesota "for observation" for an unnamed ailment.

Frances Wolfe died on February 15, 1967, and Melvin Wolfe on December 29, 1990. They are buried together at Sacred Heart Cemetery in Lost Nation.

MICHAEL J. C. WOLFE
(1922–1995)

MICHAEL JOSEPH COLBERT WOLFE was born on July 14, 1922, on New Street, Abbeyfeale, County Limerick. He was the son of Richard Barrett Wolfe, a pharmacist who lived with his family above the shop, and Catherine Elizabeth Colbert Wolfe. His siblings were Johanna Frances (b. 1914), Hanora Josephine (b. 1915), Cornelius Colbert "Con" (b. 1917), and Richard Michael (b. 1919). All of them became priests or nuns.

Wolfe's parents were active nationalists before and during the War of Independence (1919–1921). Catherine Wolfe's younger brother, Con Colbert, participated in the Easter Rising of 1916 and was one of fifteen men executed at Kilmainham jail, in Dublin. Dick Wolfe's pharmacy became a hub of nationalist activity, and in 1920 it was damaged by the Black and Tans after the Irish Republican Army killed a local constable.

In 1941, Michael Wolfe joined the same Spiritan Congregation, in Kilshane, County Tipperary, as his brothers Con and Richard Wolfe, professing his vows in 1942. He was ordained a priest in 1950 and worked in public relations. From 1959 to 1962 he served in the Archdiocese of Nairobi and then traveled to the United States to raise funds for his order. In 1965, Father Wolfe began work in San Francisco, California, and in 1972 became the chaplain at Laguna Honda Hospital, a city-run facility for the elderly and disabled.

In 1977, Father Mike, as he was known at the hospital, established the Freewheelers program, which arranged for wheelchair-bound patients to take day trips outside the hospital. "When I came here and got to know where I was at," he told the United Press International in 1982, "I realized there was one need that wasn't met. The patients were confined, and it made them angry, bored. I was hearing people wanting to die rather than to live."

Members of the program began regularly traveling to baseball games and wineries. "These people thought the world was something yesterday," the priest said. "They found they could relive it today. People who said goodbye to life found it was there again to enjoy."

The Freewheelers organization incorporated and in 1982 had a budget of $257,000 and a fleet of two specially equipped buses. At the time of his death, it still operated, although separate from the hospital.

In 1992, Father Wolfe was appointed chaplain of the Marian House nursing home in Kimmage, a suburb south of Dublin. He died there suddenly on October 21, 1995.

PATRICK WOLFE
(1872–1933)

PATRICK WOLFE was born in the townland of Cratloe, parish of Athea, County Limerick, on March 9, 1872, the son of James Patrick "Paddy" Wolfe and Honora Maher Wolfe. His siblings included Johanna (Sister Bonaventure) (b. 1871), Richard (b. 1873), Ellen (b. 1876), Maurice James (b. 1877), John J. (b. 1880), James (b. 1882), and Timothy (b. 1885). His mother was herself a Wolfe, the daughter of Ellen Wolfe Maher, while his aunt, Ellen Maher Wolfe, married Richard J. "Brown Dick" Wolfe.

Wolfe was educated at the national school and Saint Ita's College in Newcastle West and Saint Munchin's College in Limerick city. He began his studies for the priesthood at the Irish College in Rome and, after poor health forced a return to Ireland, completed them at Saint Patrick's College in Maynooth, County Kildare. He was ordained there on June 19, 1898.

From 1898 to 1902, Wolfe worked in the town of Wigan in Lancashire County (later Greater Manchester), England, and then, on October 6, 1902, became the curate at Saint Munchin's. He also served as chaplain to the Limerick Workhouse, on Shelbourne Road in the northwest of the city. Workhouses were first established during the Great Famine as "indoor relief," or where the poor could live and work for food. When entering the facility, family members were split up and life there could be harsh and cruel, particularly in the early years. According to the 1901 census, the Limerick Workhouse fed 1,140 inmates. (The workhouse buildings now house Saint Camillus's Hospital.)

Wolfe served as a curate in Kilmallock, County Limerick, from 1905 to 1925, and he became known there as a cultural nationalist. On June 28, 1914, he chaired a large *feis*, or festival, in Kilmallock attended by armed Irish Volunteers, and two years later gave a speech in which he extolled Irish patriotism. On May 28, 1920, during the War of Independence (1919–1921), forces of the Irish Republican Army (IRA) attacked and burned the barracks of the Royal Irish Constabulary (RIC) in Kilmallock, killing anywhere from one to eight policemen. The only IRA man killed was Liam Scully. After being shot, he was taken to a nearby house where, according to a witness, Wolfe administered the last rites. According to Wolfe's obituary in the *Kerryman* newspaper, he celebrated Mass later that day at the workhouse and was forced to pass the barracks in order to get there—"an ordeal few would care to undertake having regard to the temper of the police." The newspaper reports that "from then to the Truce was a very anxious time" for Wolfe, who was not well regarded by the RIC.

Evidence suggests that Wolfe was the subject of official scrutiny even before that. A report in the *Cork Examiner*, dated November 22, 1919, notes that while Wolfe was in London on church business, his residence was searched after Irish prisoners escaped from a Manchester jail. These were almost certainly the six IRA men who broke out of Strangeways on October 25, as reported in the *Manchester Guardian*. (The business that brought Wolfe to London involved the proposed beatification of the so-called Irish martyrs, who included James Wolfe, a Limerick priest hanged by Cromwell's army in 1651.) On September 25, 1920, the *Cork Examiner* again reported that Wolfe was subject to a search. This time, the presbytery at Kilmallock "was surrounded by military [...] and entered by the officers whose presence in the building was not known to the clergymen until their rooms were entered. So far as is known nothing incriminating was found."

On November 25, 1925, Wolfe was transferred to nearby Cappagh, County Limerick, where he served as the parish priest until his death.

While at the Limerick Workhouse, Wolfe began studying Irish names and surnames, a project that resulted in *Sloinnte Gaedheal is Gall*. The book's first part was published in 1906 and then expanded and republished in 1922 and 1923. A seminal work that was widely used in Irish schools during the twentieth century, *Sloinnte Gaedheal is Gall* serves as an academic study of naming in Ireland as well as a dictionary of common Irish names in both English and Irish.

The book arrived at a time when revival of the Irish language was closely aligned with the nationalist cause, a means of ridding, or at least reducing, English influence on the island's politics and culture. The Gaelic League (later Conradh na Gaeilge) was founded in 1893 and Wolfe served as president of the Limerick branch. A 1910 obituary for one of Wolfe's relatives, Richard E. "Dicky Ned" Wolfe, claims that Richard Wolfe "was well versed in folk lore and tradition, spoke Gaelic fluently, and it is to him [...] that the Rev. P. Woulfe, O.C., Kilmallock, was indebted for much of the information on his 'Irish names.'"

In 1932, the Reverend P. J. Carroll, a Limerick priest then living in the United States, wrote in the *Limerick Leader* that Wolfe "believes in the Holy Ghost, the Holy Catholic Church and the Irish language. He uses Irish for thinking, talking, praying, dreaming. He speaks English to you as a concession—because you are a foreigner; but if you can distinguish the difference between *slain leat* and *taim go mait*, he carries you along in Irish."

Wolfe died on May 3, 1933, with a large funeral Mass conducted at Saint John's Cathedral in Limerick. "There were over 100 priests in the choir," one newspaper reported. He was buried in the yard of Saint James Church in Cappagh. Wolfe's estate was settled by a probate court on January 20, 1934, with the Reverend John Moloney and James J. Wolfe—a farmer and likely Wolfe's brother—serving as executors. The value of his effects totaled £923 17s 9d. His large library of books, containing volumes on Irish history, language, literature, and archaeology, was put up for auction.

Father Patrick Wolfe with his sister, Sister Bonaventure (Johanna)

PATRICK B. WOLFE
(1848–1922)

PATRICK BERNARD WOLFE was born on October 7, 1848, in Cook County, Illinois. His parents were John Richard Wolfe, an Irish Catholic farmer, and Honora Buckley Wolfe. He had seven siblings who survived to maturity: James Buckley (b. 1843), Johanna (b. 1849), John Buckley (b. 1851), Maurice Buckley (b. 1855), Margaret I. (b. 1857), Catherine "Kate" (b. 1860), and Richard Boyle (b. 1862). Two sisters, Margaret and Catherine, died in infancy.

In 1847, P. B. Wolfe's parents and brother James immigrated to the United States from Listowel, County Kerry, along with John R. Wolfe's first cousin Maurice Wolfe and his family. (John and Maurice Wolfe shared a grandfather, James M. "The Barrister" Wolfe.) The families arrived in New York on August 23, 1847, and from there made their way to Chicago, where Patrick Wolfe was born. The Wolfes then traveled on to LaSalle County, Illinois, where a number of John R. Wolfe's brothers and cousins settled. John R. Wolfe and his cousin Maurice both moved on to Clinton County, Iowa, arriving about 1855.

Wolfe attended public schools in Liberty Township, Clinton County, and studied one year at the Christian Brothers Academy in LaSalle, Illinois. In 1870, he earned a bachelor of law from the State University of Iowa in Iowa City. In January 1871, he opened a law practice in DeWitt, Clinton County, and six years later partnered with W. A. Cotton, founding the firm Cotton & Wolfe. He remained with the DeWitt firm until 1888.

On May 1, 1878, Wolfe married Margaret G. Connole, the daughter of Irish immigrants, in DeWitt. They had three children: a child who was born in 1869 and died the same year; John Loyola (b. 1879); and Mary Zeta "Molly" (b. 1881).

POLITICAL AND JUDICIAL CAREER

Wolfe was active in public affairs. According to his obituary, he was "for three or four years city solicitor," presumably of DeWitt. He sat on the DeWitt school board for fifteen years and was a member of the public library board of Clinton. On June 5, 1890, he was elected a delegate to the Iowa state convention of the Ancient Order of Hibernians.

In 1885, he was elected to the first of three terms in the Iowa Senate, representing District 22 as a Democrat. He served from January 11, 1886, to January 8, 1888; from January 9, 1888, to January 12, 1890; and from January 13, 1890, to January 10, 1892. Wolfe sat on the Judiciary Committee and the committees on County and Township Organizations and Private Corporations. He appears to have been an active senator, introducing a number of bills in his first session, including File No. 175, "a bill for an act to punish the crime of sodomy or buggary." (The law was passed on March 26, 1892, after Wolfe had left office; it was repealed in 1978.)

On August 6, 1890, the state convention of the Democratic Party, meeting in Cedar Rapids, nominated Wolfe as a candidate for a seat on the state Supreme Court. In November, he narrowly lost to the Republican candidate, J. H. Rothrock, by a vote of 191,394 to 188,248.

In October 1891, Wolfe resigned his Senate seat after being appointed to replace Andrew Howat on the court of the seventh judicial district. Howat had resigned due to ill health. Wolfe sat on the court until September 1, 1904, when he resigned to practice law with his son. He later wrote, "It is a unique fact that Judge Wolfe has resigned from every public office which he has held."

While on the court, Wolfe upheld the provisions of the Mulct Act. Passed by the Iowa Legislature in 1894, it allowed localities to decide for themselves whether saloons could operate, while also providing for petitions and appropriate taxes. (A mulct is a fine or penalty.) In August 1895, Wolfe sentenced four saloonkeepers in Clinton to ninety days in jail each for violating the act. In December 1903, he ordered an investigation into whether blackmail was behind the prosecution of some Clinton liquor dealers.

On March 28, 1903, the *Los Angeles Times* noted that Wolfe had "just rendered an important decision regarding the right of assessors to assess taxes on property in the hands of a trust company as trustee. The court holds such property is liable to assessment both for county and city taxes."

The *DeWitt Observer* newspaper praised the judge in 1903:

Words of praise for Judge P. B. Wolfe can be found in every paper published where he holds court. The *Muscatine News-Tribune* says: "this is said to be the 51st consecutive affirmance of Judge Wolfe in the supreme court, without a single intervening reversal. This is a splendid record for the Judge and probably never been equaled in this state," to which the *Clinton Age* adds: "A most remarkable record sure. We doubt if there are many cases of a like record having been made by any judge in this broad west, or perhaps it might be safe to say in this broad land. Judge Wolfe is to be congratulated by everybody."

On July 27, 1910, the Democratic state convention, meeting in Ottumwa, again nominated Wolfe for the Supreme Court. On November 8, he received the fewest votes of four candidates: Horace E. Deemer, Republican, 208,830; William D. Evans, Republican, 204,561; A. Van Wagenen, Democrat, 155,628; and Wolfe, 153,698.

WOLFE'S HISTORY

In 1911, Wolfe served as editor-in-chief of the mammoth, two-volume *Wolfe's History of Clinton County*, published by B. F. Bowen and Company of Indianapolis. Such publications were in vogue at the time, offering readers a combination of state and local histories and celebratory biographical sketches of the area's leading white citizens, nearly all of them male. The title of the book, no doubt designed to peak interest and sales, suggests something of Wolfe's countywide, and perhaps statewide fame at the time, and among those profiled in *Wolfe's History* were Wolfe's older brother James and the judge himself. The sketch of James Wolfe begins this way:

> The Emerald Isle, far-famed in song and story, has furnished a number of enterprising and high-minded citizens to the United States, and they have ever been most welcome, for we have no better class of citizens. They are, almost with no exceptions, industrious, and they are loyal to our institutions and may always be relied upon to do their full duty as citizens in whatever community they may cast their lot. Among this large class the name of James B. Wolfe, whose long, strenuous and interesting career has resulted in much good to himself, his family and to his friends and

neighbors, for his example has ever been exemplary and his influence salutary.

Such hyperbole probably reflects the tenuous position of Irish and German immigrants at the turn of the century. They were only just beginning to reap the rewards of American citizenship, and such advances could be quickly reversed, as Iowa Germans discovered during World War I (1914–1918).

The sketch of Patrick B. Wolfe contains several curious assertions. It claims that the Wolfe's father was born in 1824 (the more likely date is 1809), that he "helped to organize the 'Young Ireland' party" (so far not corroborated), and that he immigrated in 1848 (it was 1847). He notes that his mother's brother was "the leader of the Belfast bar for many years," suggesting that "it was natural for the American descendants to turn to the bar in choice of a profession."

In spite of its various shortcomings, *Wolfe's History* provides an often fascinating history along with a rich sampling of the attitudes and even, indirectly, the insecurities of the day.

LATER YEARS

Wolfe finished his career with the firm Wolfe & Wolfe in Clinton, founded with his son, John. The younger Wolfe followed his father into the state legislature, serving in the House of Representatives from 1909 until 1911.

P. B. Wolfe signed his will on March 23, 1922, and died at his home in Clinton on June 11 of that year. His wife died on July 28, 1943. They are buried together at Saint Ireaneaus Cemetery in Clinton. On June 14, the *Davenport Democrat and Leader* noted that the federal district court judge Martin J. Wade, a fellow Democrat, had opened his court with a tribute to his former colleague:

> This court ought not to be in session at all today, for today the entire state is paying tribute to Judge P. Wolfe, one of Iowa's most earnest, loyal and sincere jurists. For thirteen years Judge Wolfe was on the bench in this district. He met the arduous duties of his life in a patriotic, earnest and sincere manner. No judge in Iowa had more respect from the public and from his fellow jurists. He realized his obligations deeply, and never failed to fulfill them.

PATRICK R. WOLFE
(1861–1939)

PATRICK RICHARD WOLFE was born in July 1861 at the Glen, the family farm in the townland of Cratloe, parish of Athea, County Limerick. Records indicate he was baptized on March 22, 1862. He was the son of Richard Edmond "Dicky Ned" Wolfe, a Catholic farmer, and Catherine White Wolfe. Wolfe's siblings included Edward (b. 1852), Maurice Richard (b. 1853), Honora "Nano" (b. 1855), Mary (b. 1857), Ellen "Nellie" (b. 1858), Catherine (b. 1860), John W. (b. 1864), Richard White (b. 1866), Catherine (b. 1868), Mary A. (b. 1870), Michael Richard (b. 1870), and Johanna "Hannah" (b. 1873). The first Catherine likely died before reaching maturity.

Patrick Wolfe immigrated to the United States in 1885. Records indicate that his brother Richard Wolfe left Queenstown, County Cork, on May 7, 1885, on a ship owned by the Cunard Steamship Company. The American destination is unclear. It appears that joining Richard were his siblings Patrick, Ellen, John, Mary, and Nano Wolfe. By 1900, Patrick Wolfe had settled in Philadelphia, Pennsylvania, while the other family members lived in Chicago, Illinois.

Patrick Wolfe's uncle, John E. Wolfe, immigrated about 1850, traveling first to LaSalle County, Illinois, and then to Clinton County, Iowa.

The federal census of 1900 identifies Patrick Wolfe as a book agent living in a boarding house in Philadelphia's third ward. In 1901 or 1902, he married a woman named Julia E.; her maiden name is unknown. She was a native of Listowel, County Kerry. They had three children: Catherine (b. ca. 1903), Eileen (b. ca. 1906), and Richard (b. ca. 1908).

By 1910 the family was living in the Bronx, New York, where Wolfe worked for a publishing company. For the next decade he remained in the book business while his wife opened a dress shop. Their daughter Catherine taught school. The 1930 census indicates Wolfe worked as a salesman for a coal company, his daughter Catherine as an officer clerk in a public school, his daughter Eileen and son Richard as school teachers.

Wolfe appears to have moved to Chicago, where he died on June 5, 1939. His wife died there on November 15, 1953, and they are buried together in Holy Sepulchre Cemetery in Alsip, Illinois.

PHILIP M. WOLFE
(1810–1901)

PHILIP MAURICE WOLFE was born in 1810 in County Limerick, to Maurice Richard Wolfe and Mary Danagher. His siblings included Bridget (b. 1795) Bartholomew "Batt" (b. 1809), Michael Maurice (b. 1813), and Mary (b. 1849).

Little is known of Old Phil Wolfe's life. He farmed near Athea, County Limerick. At some point he married Elizabeth Herlihy, and they had a number of children, including Maurice H. (b. 1839), Joseph Philip (b. 1841), Michael (b. 1843), Mary (b. 1849), Elizabeth (b. 1852), John (b. 1853), Philip (b. 1855), Patrick (b. 1857), Cornelius (b. 1858), Richard (b. 1859), Elizabeth (b. 1861), and Patrick (b. 1866). They seem also to have had a son Bartholomew "Batt."

Wolfe's obituary in the *Cork Examiner* notes his descent from James Wolfe (ca. 1651–1704), whose family fled "from the city of Limerick in 1653 under the Cromwellian code, and who settled down at Inchereagh, on the banks of the Gale, which was then but a wild uninhabited moorland." The obituary also describes Philip Wolfe as "a grand type of Irish farmer, straightforward, honourable, industrious, over willing to sympathize and assist those in trouble or difficulty."

Elizabeth Herlihy Wolfe died on September 19, 1897, at the age of seventy-eight, and Philip Wolfe on April 14, 1901. He was ninety-one, and according to his obituary "walked upright as at early manhood, and possessed his faculties fully to the end."

PHILIP J. WOLFE
(1898–1979)

PHILIP JAMES WOLFE was born on July 23, 1898, near Lost Nation, Clinton County, Iowa. He was the son of Maurice Buckley Wolfe, a farmer in Lost Nation, and Sarah A. McAndrews Wolfe. Wolfe had four brothers: Raymond Bernard (b. 1896), John Joseph (b. 1901), Melvin Maurice (b. 1904), and James Emmet (b. 1909).

Wolfe attended three years of public high school, probably in Lost Nation. He registered for the draft on September 12, 1918, and his card describes him as short and of medium build with gray eyes and brown hair.

The 1910 federal census and the census of 1920 both list the family as farming in Sharon Township, Clinton County, with the help of a domestic servant, Charlotte "Lottie" Keyes. The earlier census also indicates that a laborer, Mike Dorty, lived on the farm.

On February 12, 1930, at Saint Joseph's Church in DeWitt, Iowa, Wolfe married Alice Mildred Gribbon, a DeWitt school teacher. (Her mother, Elizabeth Fitzpatrick Gribbon, was a native of County Down.) The couple had no children. They farmed south of Lost Nation.

In an essay written in 1975, Philip Wolfe's nephew, Thomas A. Wolfe, wrote:

> Over the years, Phil has pursued vigorously the task of convincing his nephews of the joys and material benefits he claims to be an integral part of husbandry, the tilling of the soil. Mildred has the distinction, among other things, of being a member of the longest, continual, single bridge club in this part of the world.

The 1940 federal census lists the Wolfes as living in Grant Township, Clinton County, in a home valued at $1,200. They attended Sacred Heart Catholic Church, in Lost Nation.

Phil Wolfe died on August 6, 1979, in Lost Nation, and Mildred Wolfe on August 23, 1990, at the Kahl Home in Davenport, Iowa. They are buried together at Sacred Heart Cemetery in Lost Nation.

RAYMOND B. WOLFE
(1896–1941)

RAYMOND BERNARD WOLFE was born on October 27, 1896, in Lost Nation, Iowa. He was the son of Maurice Buckley Wolfe, a farmer in Lost Nation, and Sarah A. McAndrews Wolfe. Wolfe had four brothers: Philip James (b. 1898), John Joseph (b. 1901), Melvin Maurice (b. 1904), and James Emmet (b. 1909).

Wolfe registered for the draft on June 5, 1918, during World War I (1914–1918). According to Wolfe's son, Thomas A. Wolfe, he entered the United States Navy and served at the Great Lakes Naval Base, in Lake County, Illinois, where he tended animals. He contracted influenza during the pandemic of 1918, but recovered and was discharged early in 1919.

In an essay written in 1975, Thomas Wolfe wrote that his father

> caught no Germans, but he did catch the flu. In 1925 he caught Gladys McGinn of Petersville. (She was only twenty-two at the time, but that didn't stop her from continually telling her own children that no one with a grain of sense married under thirty. To gently remind her of her own age in 1925 only brought about a foot stomping and the response, "That was different.")

In 2007, Wolfe elaborated on how his parents met. Citing a story from Gladys McGinn's brother Peter, he wrote that the two met at a dance in DeWitt. Ray Wolfe regularly rode his horse from Lost Nation to Petersville to meet McGinn, "sometimes taking shortcuts through fields by cutting the fence wires." They married on August 25, 1925, in Delmar, Iowa.

According to Thomas Wolfe, the couple initially farmed in Lost Nation but lost their land and, with help from the McGinn family, bought a stead in Delmar early in the 1930s. The couple had four children: Sara Terese (b. 1926), Mary Kathryn (b. 1929), Margery, and Thomas Anthony (b. 1940).

In addition to farming just under 200 acres, Wolfe was a trustee of Saint Patrick's Church in Delmar, a member of the American Legion, and a member of the Delmar Consolidated school board. Family records include a letter to Wolfe, from 1938, in which a constituent calls into question his decision to send his own children to private school even as he sat on the public schools' board.

Ray Wolfe's son wrote that he had "a very strong personality, was well liked," and loved horses, often traveling to Montana to make purchases. After an extended illness, Wolfe died of cancer on September 9, 1941. He is buried at Saint Patrick's Cemetery in Delmar, where eight members of the Maquoketa post of the American Legion formed a firing squad and one member, Hugh Fletcher, blew taps. Gladys Wolfe died in 1966.

Raymond B. Wolfe, in a staged photograph

RICHARD WOLFE
(1795–1871)

RICHARD WOLFE was born in 1795, possibly at Knockanasig, County Kerry. He was the son of Maurice James Wolfe, a Catholic farmer, and Helen (sometimes Ellen) Dore Wolfe. His siblings included John (b. ca. 1794), Edmund Maurice, Maurice (b. ca. 1800), Bartholomew (b. 1809), and Michael (b. 1813).

He married Mary Foley on an unknown date in County Kerry. The couple had eleven children: Margaret (b. 1826), Mary (b. 1826), Maurice (b. 1828), Mary Ellen (b. 1829), Patrick (b. 1830), Daniel F. (b. ca. 1832), Richard (b. 1836), John Maurice (b. 1838), Bridget (b. 1839), Edmund (b. 1840), and Richard J. (b. 1843). The first Richard died before 1843, and Bridget before 1847.

Wolfe immigrated to the United States in the company of his wife and children, traveling in steerage class aboard the *Thomas H. Perkins*. They arrived in New York from Liverpool on September 29, 1848. The family settled in LaSalle County, Illinois, joining relatives there. Wolfe's brother Maurice had already immigrated in 1847 with their first cousin John R. Wolfe. (Brothers Maurice and Richard Wolfe and shared a grandfather with John R. Wolfe: James M. "The Barrister" Wolfe.) John R. Wolfe's brother Thomas R. Wolfe came from Ireland in 1848 and his brothers Maurice R. and Richard Wolfe sailed separately in 1849. While John R. and Maurice Wolfe, and much later Thomas Wolfe, all moved to Clinton County, Iowa, the rest of the Wolfes remained in Illinois.

Wolfe farmed first in Deer Park Township before, in 1858, purchasing a farm in Waltham Township. His wife, Mary, died there in 1861. Wolfe sold the property and bought a farm in Dimmick Township, where he lived the rest of his life. He died in 1871 and is buried with his wife at Saint Columba Cemetery in Ottawa.

RICHARD WOLFE
(1802–btw. 1850 and 1860)

RICHARD WOLFE was born in 1802, probably at Templeathea, in western County Limerick. He was the son of Maurice James Wolfe and Hanora Harnett Wolfe. Wolfe's siblings included James Harnett (b. between 1780 and 1800), John Harnett (b. 1807), Edmond, Timothy, Mary, Patrick Maurice, and Catherine.

Family oral history—contained in a letter between Wolfe relatives dated August 1956 from Cratloe, County Limerick, also known as the "Aunt Dollie" letter—relates how Richard Wolfe and his brother, John, traveled to the United States in 1836 to inquire after their brother, James. James Wolfe had immigrated in 1819, living first in Virginia and then in Monticello, Lewis County, Missouri. When his regular letters home stopped, his brothers went in search of him.

In a letter home dated December 26, 1836, John Wolfe writes that "Brother James Wolfe died in the state of Mississippi the first [of the] year he went to Natchez. The fine learned man. There is nothing grieves Richard [and me] more than to say that we cant see, hear or find our brother alive on his Estate after the bold stroke we made in going to him five thousand miles from home." John Wolfe and Richard Wolfe remained in Missouri, settling next door to one another in Lewis County.

About 1837 Richard Wolfe married Ellen Hartnett (or possibly Harnett), a native of Ireland. Her name suggests that she may have been a distant relative, one Wolfe knew in Ireland and who joined him soon after he arrived in Missouri. The couple had five children: Honorah A. (b. ca. 1838), Timothy (b. ca. 1840), Richard Maurice (b. 1841), Ellen (b. ca. 1844), and James (b. ca. 1848).

The federal censuses of 1840 and 1850 indicate that Wolfe remained in Lewis County, where he farmed on land that had originally belonged to his brother James. He died sometime before the census of 1860. That year his wife, Ellen, claimed $1,000 in real estate and $970 in personal estate. She eventually moved to Clark County and then, by 1880, Knox County, Missouri. She died there on March 11, 1889. She is buried at Saint Joseph Cemetery in Edina, Knox County.

RICHARD WOLFE
(1815–1906)

RICHARD WOLFE was born in Listowel, County Kerry, and baptized on July 16, 1815, in the Diocese of Kerry, parish of Lixnaw. His parents were Richard James Wolfe and Johanna Relihan Wolfe. His baptismal sponsors were Richard Wolfe and Mary Connel. (Wolfe's gravestone lists his birth year as 1807.)

Wolfe's siblings included James Richard (b. 1800), Maurice Richard (b. 1802), John Richard (b. 1809), Ellen (b. ca. 1810), Thomas Richard (b. 1811), Johanna (b. 1812), Margaret Ellen (b. 1818), Edmond (b. 1821), and Patrick (b. 1822).

On February 26, 1838, he married Mary Carney, of Listowel, in Abbeydorney, a small village just north of Tralee, County Kerry. Witnesses were Richard Wolfe and Maurice Eagan. Carney's surname may originally have been Kearney. The couple had eight children: Margaret (b. 1841), John (b. 1845), Richard "Dick" (b. 1847), Michael (b. ca. 1848), Sarah Elizabeth (b. 1854), Ellen V. "Nellie" (b. ca. 1856), James (b. ca. 1858), and James R. (b. 1863). The first James died sometime before 1862.

Wolfe, his wife, and several of their children immigrated to the United States, arriving in New York City aboard the *Liverpool* on November 10, 1849. Built by Brown and Bell of New York in 1843 and, in 1849, owned by Grinnell, Minturn, and Company, the *Liverpool* was quite large: three decks and more than 1,400 tons. The ship carried between 600 and 700 passengers and completed its run from Liverpool to New York in just over two weeks.

Other Wolfe relatives had already immigrated and settled in LaSalle County, Illinois, including Richard Wolfe's brother John R. Wolfe and his first cousin Maurice Wolfe, who sailed together in 1847. (Brothers Richard and John Wolfe shared a grandfather with Maurice Wolfe: James M. "The Barrister" Wolfe.) Wolfe's brother, Maurice R. Wolfe, immigrated in 1849, arriving in September. While brother John and cousin Maurice Wolfe moved on to Clinton County,

Iowa, Richard Wolfe and his brother Maurice R. Wolfe remained in Illinois.

The 1860 federal census identifies Richard Wolfe as a distiller.

Mary Carney Wolfe died of heart failure on November 21, 1893. The federal census of 1900 finds Richard Wolfe living in the home of his daughter, Margaret Farrell, and describes him as a rectifier of spirits.

Wolfe died on September 12, 1906, and is buried with his wife in Saint Columba Cemetery, in Ottawa, Illinois.

RICHARD WOLFE
(1847–1921)

RICHARD WOLFE was born on March 12, 1847, in County Kerry, the son of Richard Wolfe, a distiller, and Mary Carney Wolfe. His siblings included Margaret (b. 1841), John (b. 1845), Michael (b. ca. 1848), Sarah Elizabeth (b. 1854), Ellen V. "Nellie" (b. ca. 1856), James (b. ca. 1858), and James R. (b. 1863). The first James died sometime before 1862.

Wolfe, his parents, and his siblings immigrated to the United States, arriving in New York City aboard the *Liverpool* on November 10, 1849. They settled in LaSalle County, Illinois, joining other Wolfe relatives there. Richard Wolfe Sr.'s brother John R. Wolfe and his first cousin Maurice Wolfe both immigrated in 1847. (Brothers Richard and John Wolfe shared a grandfather with Maurice Wolfe: James M. "The Barrister" Wolfe.) Wolfe's brother, Thomas R. Wolfe, arrived from Ireland in 1848, while another brother, Maurice R. Wolfe, immigrated in 1849, arriving in September. While brother John and cousin Maurice Wolfe moved on to Clinton County, Iowa, Richard Wolfe Sr. and his brothers Thomas and Maurice Wolfe remained in Illinois.

Popularly known as "Uncle Dick," Richard Wolfe Jr. did not marry. *The Past and Present of La Salle County, Illinois*, published in 1877, identifies him as a "Wholesale and Retail Liquor Dealer" at 36 LaSalle Street in Ottawa. He is described as a Democrat and a Catholic who "keeps a stock of the finest Imported and Domestic Wines, Whiskies and Cigars." He was in business for a time with his cousin, Daniel F. Wolfe.

"From a comparatively poor young man," according to his obituary, "Mr. Wolfe rose to the position of one of the keenest and best known business men of this city, branching out into the real estate field where he became the owner of farms in Illinois, Iowa and Florida." At the time of his death, Wolfe was on the board of directors of the People's Trust and Savings Bank in Ottawa, the Ottawa Building

Homestead and Savings Association, and the United Telephone Company.

His obituary also described Wolfe as "a simple, unassuming man, loving the humbler walks of life, rather than the fleshpots."

Wolfe died on June 13, 1921, in the home of his sister, Margaret Wolfe Farrell. His buried at Saint Columba Cemetery in Ottawa.

RICHARD B. WOLFE
(1862–1940)

RICHARD BOYLE WOLFE, known as R. B. Wolfe, was born on February 16, 1862, in Liberty Township, Clinton County, Iowa. His parents were John Richard Wolfe, an Irish Catholic farmer, and Honora Buckley Wolfe. He was the youngest of seven children who survived to maturity: James Buckley (b. 1844), Patrick Bernard (b. 1848), Johanna (b. 1849), John Buckley (b. 1851), Maurice Buckley (b. 1855), Margaret I. (b. 1857), and Catherine "Kate" (b. 1860). Two sisters, Margaret and Catherine, died in infancy.

In 1847, Wolfe's parents and brother James immigrated to the United States from Listowel, County Kerry, along with John R. Wolfe's first cousin Maurice Wolfe and his family. (John and Maurice Wolfe shared a grandfather, James M. "The Barrister" Wolfe.) The families arrived in New York on August 23, 1847, and from there made their way to Chicago and then to LaSalle County, Illinois, where a number of John R. Wolfe's brothers and cousins settled. John R. Wolfe and his cousin Maurice Wolfe, with their families, both moved on to Clinton County, Iowa, arriving about 1855.

Wolfe was educated in the public schools of Liberty and Grant townships and graduated from DeWitt High School. In 1890, he received a bachelor of laws degree from the State University of Iowa in Iowa City, beginning his law practice in DeWitt, Clinton County, that September. (His brother Patrick Wolfe also practiced law in DeWitt, although at the time he was serving in the Iowa Senate.) R. B. Wolfe was elected mayor of DeWitt in 1892.

On August 5, 1896, Wolfe married Hannah Dunnan, a native of DeWitt, at Saint Joseph's Catholic Church, in DeWitt. They had four children: John Richard (b. 1898); Francis Dunnan (b. 1900), Winifred M. (b. 1903), and Mary Gertrude, whose birthdate is not known but who died as an infant in December 1906.

Wolfe lived his entire adult life in DeWitt working as an attorney. Notices in the *Oxford Mirror* during the winter of 1906–1907 suggest that he owned 140 acres of land three and a half miles southeast of

Lost Nation, Sharon Township, which he sought to rent. On October 7, 1909, the same paper reported that Wolfe's brother John sold him eighty acres from his farm.

Wolfe died at his home in DeWitt on October 17, 1940; his wife died eleven years later. They are buried together at Saint Joseph's Cemetery in DeWitt.

RICHARD B. WOLFE
(1884–1937)

RICHARD BARRETT WOLFE was born on October 26, 1884, in the townland of Cratloe, parish of Athea, County Limerick, the son of Richard Maurice Wolfe and Johanna Barrett Wolfe. His siblings included Johanna (b. 1870), Mary (b. 1872), Maurice (b. 1874), Catherine (b. 1876), John R. M. (b. 1878), Ellen (b. 1880), and Bridget (b. 1882). Maurice Wolfe died in 1891, possibly of tuberculosis.

Little is known of Dick Wolfe's early life except that he studied pharmacy in Dublin, where he met Catherine Elizabeth "Katty" Colbert. The two married on April 16, 1913, in Dublin, and soon after returned to County Limerick, apparently at the urging of Wolfe's father. The couple had five children: Johanna Frances (b. 1914), Hanora Josephine (b. 1915), Cornelius Colbert "Con" (b. 1917), Richard Michael (b. 1919), and Michael Joseph Colbert (b. 1922). All of them became priests or nuns.

EARLY REPUBLICAN ACTIVITIES

Wolfe, known locally as the Chemist, ran a pharmacy on New Street in Abbeyfeale. According to the later testimony of James J. Collins, who apprenticed under and worked for Wolfe and later served in Dáil Éireann (1948–1967), "The Woulfe's were great supporters of the Irish independence movement and their shop and house, from the earliest days of the movement, became a meeting place for men like Con Colbert, Captain Ned Daly and others who later figured prominently in the fight for freedom."

Cornelius Francis "Con" Colbert was Katty Colbert Wolfe's younger brother and participated in the Easter Rising, which began on April 25, 1916. He was executed at Kilmainham jail, in Dublin, on May 8. According to Collins's testimony, given in 1955, Wolfe's pharmacy was a site of rebel activity during this time. In the weeks after the uprising, authorities frantically searched for Robert Monteith, an aide to Roger Casement, a British diplomat who had become an Irish nationalist. The two had landed via German submarine at nearby Banna Strand in County Kerry, but Casement had been captured. "Mr. Woulfe sent me to Fr. O'Flaherty of Brosna, Co. Kerry, to borrow his car for the purpose of bringing Monteith to Co. Limerick," Collins recalled. The mission was accomplished in a Model T Ford.

On June 24, 1916, the *Liberator* newspaper of Tralee, County Kerry, reported Wolfe having attended a meeting in Abbeyfeale of the Irish Aid Association, established to provide support for the families affected by the violence. He made a donation of £2 2s.

WAR OF INDEPENDENCE

During the War of Independence (1919–1921), Wolfe's pharmacy again became a site of nationalist activity. According to Collins, a British spy calling himself Peadar Clancy and claiming to be from the Irish Republican Army's General Headquarters in Dublin attempted to infiltrate the West Limerick Brigade in 1919. He was brought to Wolfe's pharmacy in Abbeyfeale. "I was working in the shop at the time," Collins said. "Mrs. Woulfe called me and told me that she knew the Clancy family of Dublin and that this man was not one of them." Collins explained that "as a result of Mrs. Woulfe's suspicions," the man was arrested, tried, and executed as a spy.

In *Victory and Woe*, his memoir of the West Limerick Brigade, written in the 1940s and published posthumously in 2002, Mossie Harnett does not mention the Wolfes or their role in exposing Peadar Clancy. He notes only that "our intelligence received information that led" to his arrest. Harnett then relates how Clancy was found with hidden money and papers that, once decoded, exposed his guilt. His execution took place in the spring of 1920: "Fully realising now his terrible predicament, and visibly trembling, he clutched his Rosary beads in his hands. Near the place of execution, a priest heard his confession; then he shook hands with his executioners and admitted his crime." The man was eventually identified as Denis Crowley, a former soldier.

A later account by the IRA man Daniel Doody notes that in May 1920 Wolfe accompanied a local doctor on a motorbike with a sidecar to an IRA hideout to treat the wounded. At about 11 P.M. on September 18, 1920, according to a report in the *Kerryman*, an active service unit of the IRA that included Collins and Harnett ambushed a six-man patrol of the Royal Irish Constabulary (RIC) outside of Abbeyfeale. A constable, John Mahony, was killed and two others wounded. The next day a large number of policemen and soldiers arrived, members of both the RIC and the RIC Special Reserve, or so-called Black and Tans—temporary constables recruited from England and notoriously violent. "The Tans remained for a couple of hours while they fired some thousands of rounds of ammunition all round and bombed several houses," Collins recalled. According to the *Kerryman*, "The local Temperance Hall was subsequently burned, [and] Mr. Woulfe's pharmacy was considerably damaged."

The official British report on the incident notes that £1,500 in compensation was sought for damages, that no complaint had been made to the police, and that Wolfe was missing. "It is stated that he and his two assistants are alleged to be members of the Abbeyfeale Company of the I.R.A. and that they were experimenting with some chemical substances and that there was an explosion on the occasion."

In an oral history conducted when she was in her nineties, Wolfe's daughter Hanora, or Sister Íde, recalled how the Black and Tans had attempted to arrest her father. "They were going to shoot him," she said, "and I understand my mother screamed. She was upstairs. They'd locked my mother and one of the babies in [...] They were trying to burn the house and my mother in it." Dick Wolfe, however, was able to free her and escape out the back.

> Now, at the back of our house, our garden opened into the river [Feale], and it seems he got out to the river and walked the river that night. And he walked, the story is told, in such a way that he got to the convent. And the nuns took him in and hid him behind the altar. And the soldiers came to the convent, and the reverend mother met them, but I think she must have told them they couldn't go into the chapel, and they respected that.

On October 5, the *Liberator* reported that one of Wolfe's assistants, Tim Stack, along with Michael Wolfe, who worked at a hardware store in nearby Listowel, County Kerry, were both arrested by the police. Stack may have been connected to the family of Austin Stack, of Tralee, who went on hunger strike during the Civil War (1922–1923). Within a week, Stack had been released, but, as the *Cork Examiner* reported, "Mr. Woulfe, together with his wife and family, have abandoned his pharmacy since the place was raided and partially wrecked. A compensation claim has been lodged."

Wolfe was on the run for the rest of the war, serving as a medical officer with the West Limerick Brigade of the IRA. He sometimes hid out at the nearby home of his sister Catherine Wolfe White, where, with his mustache shaved, he pretended to be "Uncle Jack" to his own children.

CIVIL WAR AND LATER YEARS

Wolfe's actions during the subsequent civil war are not well documented. His sympathies were anti-Treaty, and according to his daughter, the pharmacy was boycotted as a result. She recalled that the mothers, wives, and sisters of irregulars, or anti-Treaty fighters, congregated each night in the Square at Abbeyfeale to say the rosary. One night a group of pro-Treaty locals attacked them, including Katty Wolfe, with rotten eggs.

On April 18, 1923, the same day that the famous anti-Treaty fighter Dan Breen was reported captured, the *Cork Examiner* also noted that "Dick Woulfe, Listowel, a prominent irregular, surrendered to the troops last night with a rifle and ammunition." It's unclear whether this is the same Wolfe.

After the war, Wolfe continued to operate his pharmacy, for a time apprenticing Seán Ó Séadhacháin, who later became a noted folk artist. At some point he brought a younger cousin, David Wolfe, into his business in Abbeyfeale. David Wolfe's brother, Maurice Woulfe, later became pastor of the Infant of Prague Church, near Buffalo, New York.

Dick Wolfe died on April 19, 1937, in Abbeyfeale, after what one obituary described as "a tedious illness, borne with exemplary patience." The *Irish Press* wrote that "many people attributed his death indirectly to the heroic sacrifices which he made in the service of his country," noting that an honor guard from the West Limerick Brigade, which included James Collins, stood vigil over his coffin and that "the funeral procession was more than two miles long." He was buried at the Temple Athea graveyard.

Wolfe's probate was settled on September 7, 1937, and the value of his effects totaled £1,052 15s 4d. The pharmacy remained in the family until its sale in 1950. In 2018, the building and empty storefront were owned by Wolfe's nephew, Richard Wolfe.

RICHARD C. WOLFE
(1848–1919)

RICHARD CAREY WOLFE was born on October 12, 1848, at or near Chicago, Illinois. His parents were Maurice Wolfe, an Irish Catholic farmer, and Ellen Catherine Carey. Wolfe had ten siblings who lived to maturity: James Carey (b. 1831), Ellen (b. 1833), Maurice Carey (b. ca. 1835), Mary (b. 1838), John Carey (b. 1840), Thomas Carey (b. 1843), Margaret (b. ca. 1845), Johanna (b. 1847), Catherine "Kate" (b. 1851), and Bridget Veronica (b. 1854).

The year before Wolfe was born, his parents and several siblings immigrated to the United States from County Kerry, along with Maurice Wolfe's first cousin John R. Wolfe and his family. (Maurice Wolfe and John R. Wolfe shared a grandfather, James M. "The Barrister" Wolfe.) The families arrived in New York on August 23, 1847, and from there made their way to Chicago, where Richard Wolfe was born. The Wolfes then traveled to LaSalle County, Illinois. John R. Wolfe and his family moved to Clinton County, Iowa, about 1855. His brothers Maurice R. and Richard Wolfe, who came separately from Ireland in 1849, stayed in Illinois, as did another brother, Thomas R. Wolfe, who came in 1848. Maurice Wolfe's own brother, Richard, came from Ireland in 1848. Maurice Wolfe and his family, including Richard Wolfe, moved to Clinton County in the spring of 1859.

Richard Wolfe married Margaret McGonnegle, of Jefferson County, Indiana, on April 16, 1877, in Clinton County. The couple had seven children: James (b. 1878), Ellen Calista "Nell" (b. 1880), Maurice Vincent (b. 1882), Edward Anthony (b. 1884), John Gregory (b. 1886), Catherine W. (b. 1889), and Joseph (b. 1892). Margaret Wolfe died on June 8, 1894, in DeWitt, in Clinton County.

Richard Wolfe married Ellen "Nellie" Murphy, of Delaware, in 1900. The couple had five children: twins Richard Joseph and Leo (b. 1903), Raymond F. (b. 1905), Mary (b. 1907), and Robert (b. 1910).

Richard Wolfe farmed in Liberty Township, Clinton County, and served as constable before, in the autumn of 1884, being elected justice of the peace. He remained in the position until his death. In 1895, he retired from farming, renting out his land and moving to DeWitt, in Clinton County. The census of 1910 indicates that his brother Maurice Wolfe lived there with him. In 1916, Wolfe returned to his farm, then presumably run by his children.

Nellie Wolfe died sometime between 1910 and 1919. Richard Wolfe died on May 20, 1919, after a short illness. At the time of his death, he owned 437 acres, between fifty and sixty head of cattle, nine horses, and seventy hogs. He is buried at Saint James Cemetery in Toronto, Iowa.

RICHARD D. WOLFE
(1829–1885)

RICHARD DOWNEY WOLFE was baptized on June 15, 1829, in the parish of Listowel, County Kerry. He is the son of Maurice Richard Wolfe, who bred horses and came from a Catholic farming family, and Johanna Downey Wolfe. (Sponsors to his baptism were Richard Wolfe and Catherine Downey.) His siblings included Margaret (b. 1827), Stephen (b. 1833), James Downey (b. 1839), Johanna E. (b. 1840), Catherine "Kate" (b. 1842), Maurice (b. 1848), John Francis (b. 1850), and Edmund Dean (b. 1853).

Little is known of Wolfe's early life. He, his parents, and his siblings immigrated to the United States in 1849. They sailed from Liverpool to New York aboard the *Senator*, a 777-ton ship of the Black Star Line, owned by Samuel Thompson; they arrived on September 22, 1849. Maurice R. Wolfe's brother John R. Wolfe immigrated to the United States in 1847, his brother Thomas R. Wolfe in 1848, and his brother Richard Wolfe in 1849. They all settled, at least initially, in LaSalle County, Illinois. Richard D. Wolfe and his family bought land there, as well, and stayed.

Wolfe married Margaret O'Kane on February 17, 1863. The couple had one child, Katherine Collins (b. 1863), before O'Kane died in 1865. Richard Wolfe married Margaret Shine Lyons, an Irish immigrant, on November 28, 1866. The couple had eight children: Johanna (b. 1867), Daniel Maurice (b. 1869), Honoria Euphrasia (b. 1871), Maurice Patrick (b. 1873), Margaret Theresa (b. 1875), Richard (b. 1878), Marie Louise (b. 1881), and Aileen Gregory (b. 1884).

In 1870, Wolfe lived in Osage Township, LaSalle County, and owned real estate worth $3,600 and personal goods worth $900. Sometime between April 1871 and March 1873 he and his second wife, along with several of their children, moved to Township 64, Atchison, Missouri. At the time of his death he had returned to Illinois and was living in Ford County.

Wolfe died on April 12, 1885, in Rankin, Illinois, from the effects of being kicked by a horse two weeks earlier. His skull had been fractured. He was buried at Lost Land Cemetery in LaSalle County, Illinois, on April 14.

RICHARD E. WOLFE
(1825–1910)

RICHARD EDMOND WOLFE was born on April 7, 1825, at the Glen, the family farm in the townland of Cratloe, parish of Athea, County Limerick. His parents were Edmond Richard "Old Ned" Wolfe, a Catholic farmer and member of the Board of Guardians, and Ellen "Nellie" Brosnan. His siblings included seven sisters and at least one brother, among them Edmond, Ellen "Nell," Johanna "Joan," Bridget (b. ca. 1829), and Julia (b. ca. 1838).

Dicky Ned Wolfe worked his father's fields in the townland of Cratloe. In *Share the Profits!* (1939), a biography of Wolfe's son Richard W. Wolfe, William H. Stuart writes that Richard E. Wolfe's "farm was one of the largest. He owned at one time fifteen cows, a herd of goats, sheep, pigs, two draft horses, geese, turkeys, chickens and two donkeys. On an extensive acreage he raised oats, rye, flax, and potatoes."

According to church records, he married Catherine White, of Coole, on February 23, 1852, in Athea, with Edmond Woulfe and Maria Mulcahy serving as witnesses. The couple's children included Edward (b. 1852), Maurice Richard (b. 1853), Honora "Nano" (b. 1855), Mary (b. 1857), Ellen "Nellie" (b. 1858), Catherine (b. 1860), Patrick Richard (b. 1861), John W. (b. 1864), Richard White (b. 1866), Catherine (b. 1868), Mary A. (b. 1870), Michael Richard (b. 1870), and Johanna "Hannah" (b. 1873). Of these, Patrick, Honora, Richard, Ellen, John, and Mary immigrated to the United States. The first Catherine likely died before reaching maturity. Michael took over management of the Glen upon his father's retirement.

Stuart's book, which offers a romanticized view of the Limerick Wolfes, describes Richard E. Wolfe as "strict and stern but of great humanity. He was loved by the countryside because of his good heart and his wise leadership, and, when he rescued a little girl from drowning, his popularity grew." According to Stuart, Catherine White Wolfe "spun the wool from her own sheep and made the children's caps, stockings, and sweaters." She also told her children fairy stories—"stories about ghosts, devils, witches, banshees, fairy thorns, devil cats, elves, bewitched butter, horned women, blood-thirsty giants, and weird and startling enchantments."

An account in Ireland's National Folklore Collection describes how Wolfe operated a "hedge school" at the Glen. Such schools dated back to the prohibition on Catholic schools, which lasted from 1723 to 1782, and many survived into the national-school era. Teachers lodged in the homes of the farmers who hosted the schools, the widow Katherine O'Connor told her interviewer. "They were paid by local subscription from the pupils' parents and their meals were provided where they lodged. Irish was not taught but fluently spoken by the teachers and pupils." In his biography, Stuart writes that Wolfe "gave to the children of the community a building for a school and the land upon which it stood. It was far from a modern structure, but a long way ahead of the former hedge-fence school."

Wolfe died on May 24, 1910, at the Glen, of heart disease. His wife had already died. Wolfe's obituary appeared in the *Limerick Leader* on June 1, and describes him as "the 'Grand Old Man' of the Limerick Woulfes," noting that he "was well versed in folk lore and tradition, spoke Gaelic fluently," and provided important background information for the Reverend Patrick Wolfe's *Sloinnte Gaedheal is Gall*, a seminal work on Irish names and surnames, published in part in 1906 and then later expanded. In the book, Father Wolfe credited his relative, "who gave me nearly all the surnames of West Limerick and North Kerry." A translation of a folk story that Father Wolfe published in an Irish language journal also credited Richard Wolfe and even featured a conversation with him, identifying him as a *seanchaí*, or storyteller. A posthumous notation in Ireland's National Folklore Collection identifies him the same way.

The *Limerick Leader* obituary also mentioned Wolfe's love for Daniel O'Connell, the Irish politician known as the Liberator, who won legal rights for Catholics. "He saw the Liberator at three of his monster meetings," the paper wrote, "and it is only a few years ago, while on a visit to Dublin, that [Wolfe] entertained some of the admirers of the great tribune, by narrating some interesting incidents of his life, on beholding his statue in O'Connell street."

The paper then provided a dramatic death scene for Wolfe:

Just after deceased was anointed, and shortly before he died, he said with a brain as clear as a rill, and with all the fortitude that is the priceless heritage of the followers of Christ:—'I am now prepared to meet my God.' His life ebbed peacefully away, almost unnoticeably like the sun stealthily dipping behind the horizon, after the unrelenting hand of death had been for days grappling with his powerful physique.

RICHARD J. WOLFE
(1763–1842)

RICHARD JAMES WOLFE was born in 1763 in the townland of Cratloe, parish of Athea, County Limerick. He was the son of James Maurice "The Barrister" Wolfe and Johanna McCoy Wolfe. He had two and possibly three siblings: James, Maurice James, and Edmund, the latter's relationship remaining unconfirmed.

Wolfe married Johanna Relihan in Cratloe sometime before 1800, and the couple had at least ten children: James Richard (b. 1800), Maurice Richard (b. 1802), John Richard (b. 1809), Ellen (b. ca. 1810), Thomas Richard (b. 1811), Johanna (b. 1812), Richard (b. 1815), Margaret Ellen (b. 1818), Edmond (b. 1821), and Patrick.

Little is known about Wolfe's life, but evidence suggests that his family was relatively wealthy. Wolfe's grandfather was wealthy enough, in March 1760, to lease 2,000 acres of land, which constituted the entire townland of Cratloe. Wolfe's uncle, Richard M. Wolfe, inherited that land. At some point, Wolfe's father moved the family to the area surrounding Athea, County Limerick, which had been the family seat prior to the Cratloe purchase.

In *Wolfe's History of Clinton County* (1911), Wolfe's grandson Judge Patrick B. Wolfe describes Richard J. Wolfe as "the agent having charge of the property of the Knight of Kerry." The eighteenth knight of Kerry was Maurice FitzGerald; his title was hereditary, perhaps dating back as far as the thirteenth century, but not formally recognized by the Crown. He represented Kerry in Parliament from 1801 to 1831, vigorously supporting Catholic emancipation.

From 1812 until 1821, FitzGerald's primary residence was at Ballinruddery, near Listowel, County Kerry, which a visitor in 1823 described as "a mere cottage, but gentlemanlike and comfortable, and ... worthy of its excellent and high spirited owner." The house is believed to date from the sixteenth century and was described, in 1837, as "beautifully situated in a wooded demesne." Although FitzGerald moved his main residence to Glanleam, Valentia Island, it is likely, based on its location, that Richard Wolfe's association was with Ballinruddery. In 1831, FitzGerald informed a government official of his intention to provide employment for local people at Ballinruddery.

The Wolfe family's relative wealth suggests that Patrick Wolfe's claim that Richard Wolfe was the agent in charge of FitzGerald's property may not have been an exaggeration. Whatever the case, FitzGerald's estates were heavily mortgaged at the time of his death in 1849, and it may have been for this reason that the Wolfe family's association with the knight of Kerry likely began and ended with Richard Wolfe.

He died on June 6, 1842, and is buried at the Temple Athea graveyard, County Limerick.

RICHARD J. WOLFE
(1843–1927)

RICHARD JAMES WOLFE was born on May 5, 1843, near Ballybunion, in County Kerry, the son of Richard Wolfe, a Catholic farmer, and Mary Foley Wolfe. He was baptized on October 14, 1843, with the Reverend William Bric and Mary Moloney serving as sponsors. Wolfe's gravestone shows a birth year of 1844.

Wolfe's siblings included Margaret (b. ca. 1826), Mary (b. 1826), Maurice (b. 1828), Mary Ellen (b. 1829), Patrick (b. 1830), Daniel F. (b. ca. 1832), Richard (b. 1836), John Maurice (b. 1838), Bridget (b. 1839), and Edmund (b. 1840). The first Richard died before 1848, and Bridget before 1847.

Wolfe immigrated to the United States in the company of his parents and siblings, traveling in steerage class aboard the *Thomas H. Perkins*. They arrived in New York from Liverpool on September 29, 1848. The family settled in LaSalle County, Illinois, joining relatives there.

In 1871, he married Catherine "Kate" Maher in LaSalle County. Wolfe and Maher were cousins: her paternal grandfather, also Richard James Wolfe, was the brother of her husband's paternal grandfather, Maurice J. Wolfe. The couple had six children: Richard James (b. 1872), Charles A. (b. 1877), Mary (b. 1879), Katie Florence (b. 1884), Bartholomew "Bart" (b. 1886), and Evelyn C. (b. 1891). Katie Florence Wolfe died in 1885.

Wolfe worked as a farmer, at some point purchasing 160 acres on section 33 of Eagle Township and later another 80 acres in section 32. He also bought for his son James a farm belong to the Maher family, bringing the family's total holdings, as of 1906, to about 400 acres.

According to the *History of LaSalle County, Illinois* by U. J. Hoffman (1906) Wolfe worked the land, bred horses, and kept up his home:

> Mr. Wolfe has made all of the improvements upon the home place, has set out all of the trees, which add so much to the attractive appearance as well as value of the farm, has built

a fine, large residence and various outbuildings necessary for the shelter of grain and stock. His success is due to diligent effort and strict attention to business. He has been very prosperous, especially in breeding and handling Percheron horses, and in this connection is widely known, having bred some of the best stock produced in this part of the state.

Percheron horses were a French breed of draft horse originally imported to the United States in 1839 and successfully bred with American draft horse stock.

By 1920, Wolfe lived with his son, Richard, in Dimmick. He died in LaSalle County on May 25, 1927. His wife, Kate, died on February 19, 1932, in Streator. He and his wife are buried at Lost Land Cemetery in LaSalle County.

RICHARD L. WOLFE
(ca. 1837–1904)

RICHARD L. WOLFE was born about 1837 in County Kerry. He was the son of Thomas Richard Wolfe, a Catholic farmer, and Ellen Leahy Wolfe. His siblings included Margaret (b. 1837), John (b. ca. 1839), Thomas L. (b. 1840), Hanora (b. ca. 1843), James (b. ca. 1845), Mary Johanna (b. ca. 1846), Catherine "Kitty" (b. 1847), Ellen "Nellie" (b. 1853), and Maurice (b. ca. 1855). John Wolfe died between 1848 and 1850, and James before 1850.

In 1848, Wolfe immigrated to the United States in the company of his parents and siblings. They sailed from Liverpool to New York, arriving on September 11. From there they traveled to LaSalle County, Illinois, where they joined relatives.

Many members of the extended Wolfe family made the same journey. Wolfe's uncle John R. Wolfe, along with a cousin Maurice Wolfe, immigrated together in 1847. Wolfe's uncles Maurice R. Wolfe and Richard Wolfe sailed separately in 1849. Other cousins came as well, including Margaret and Elizabeth Maher, daughters of John R. Wolfe's sister Ellen; and Patrick, Dennis, Bridget, and Thomas Sheehan, the children of John R. Wolfe's sister Margaret. Another cousin, John E. Wolfe, and his sisters Ellen J. and Mary Agatha, also immigrated. All of these Wolfes, except for the Sheehans, settled in LaSalle County, Illinois. A few moved on to Clinton County, Iowa, John R. Wolfe and his cousin Maurice.

Wolfe and his family initially farmed in Deer Park Township, LaSalle County. By 1870, however, they had moved to Grand Mound in Liberty Township, Clinton County, Iowa. A decade later, he lived 220 miles to the west, in Eden Township, Carroll County, where he boarded in the household of George W. Overmire. (Wolfe's sister Ellen later married Joseph Overmire, perhaps this man's brother.)

In 1889, Wolfe married Mary Fanning, of Ottawa, Illinois, in that city. Her obituary described her "highly educated and refined." They had two children: Richard and Irene (b. 1892). Richard died sometime before 1900.

The family farmed in the town of Templeton, in Carroll County, about fifteen miles south of Carroll, and Wolfe served on the county board of supervisors. By 1900, they lived in Audubon, another fourteen miles south. Soon, however, they returned to Carroll, where they purchased a home on North Main Street.

Wolfe signed his will on May 9, 1901, and died unexpectedly on June 7, 1904, in Carroll. According to his obituary in the *Carroll Sentinel*, he was in downtown Carroll about six o'clock in the evening "and seemed to be in his usual health. After returning home, his wife read to him, as was her usual custom on account of his eyesight. Suddenly Mr. Wolfe became faint and expired before a physician could arrive." Mary Fanning Wolfe died in Carroll in April 7, 1918, and she and her husband are buried together at Saint Columba Cemetery in Ottawa, Illinois.

RICHARD M. WOLFE
(ca. 1730–1824)

RICHARD MAURICE WOLFE was born about 1730, at Templeathea in western County Limerick. He was the son of Maurice James Wolfe, a Catholic farmer, and Kathleen Rearden (also Riordan) Wolfe. His siblings included James Maurice (b. 1732), Edmond Maurice, Patrick, and Maurice James "Young Maurice" (b. ca. 1763).

Wolfe's father was a wealthy farmer who, in March 1760, purchased or leased 2,000 acres of land, which constituted the entire townland of Cratloe, in County Limerick, a few kilometers from Templeathea. Wolfe inherited that property after his father's death in 1792. At some point he married Ellen O'Sullivan. Their children included Maurice Richard (b. 1778), Edmond Richard "Old Ned" (b. 1788), Margaret "Peggy James" (d. 1874), and Patrick "Old Paddy."

Wolfe, whose nickname was "Short Dick," died on October 11, 1824, and is buried at the Temple Athea graveyard.

RICHARD M. WOLFE
(1919–2003)

RICHARD MICHAEL WOLFE was born on December 9, 1919, on New Street, Abbeyfeale, County Limerick. He was the son of Richard Barrett Wolfe, a pharmacist who lived with his family above the shop, and Catherine Elizabeth Colbert Wolfe. His siblings were Johanna Frances (b. 1914), Hanora Josephine (b. 1915), Cornelius Colbert "Con" (b. 1917), and Michael Joseph Colbert (b. 1922). All of them became priests or nuns.

Wolfe's parents were active nationalists before and during the War of Independence (1919–1921). Catherine Wolfe's younger brother, Con Colbert, participated in the Easter Rising of 1916 and was one of fifteen men executed at Kilmainham jail, in Dublin. Dick Wolfe's pharmacy became a hub of nationalist activity, and in 1920 it was damaged by the Black and Tans after the Irish Republican Army killed a local constable.

Richard Wolfe joined the same Spiritan Congregation, in Kilshane, County Tipperary, as his brothers Con and Michael Wolfe, professing his vows on September 10, 1938 He was ordained a priest on July 13, 1947. Founded in 1703, the Spiritans, also known as the Holy Ghost Fathers, began working with former slaves in Haiti in the 1840s and in Africa in the 1860s, opening schools and hospitals.

Father Wolfe worked in The Gambia, in West Africa, for nine years, before transferring to Killmambogo Teachers College, in Kenya, in 1960. He moved to Nairobi in 1969 and lived there for the rest of his life. He died after a short illness on October 11, 2003, and is buried in Saint Austin's Cemetery, Nairobi.

RICHARD W. WOLFE
(1866–1951)

RICHARD WHITE WOLFE was born on August 25, 1866, at the Glen, the family farm in the townland of Cratloe, parish of Athea, County Limerick, the son of Richard Edmond "Dicky Ned" Wolfe, a Catholic farmer, and Catherine White Wolfe. Wolfe's siblings included Edward (b. 1852), Maurice Richard (b. 1853), Honora (b. 1855), Mary (b. 1857), Ellen "Nellie" (b. 1858), Catherine (b. 1860), Patrick Richard (b. 1861), John W. (b. 1864), Catherine (b. 1868), Mary A. (b. 1870), Michael Richard (b. 1870), and Johanna (b. 1873). The first Catherine likely died before reaching maturity. Wolfe's obituary in the *New York Times* mentioned that he "was a descendant of Gen. James Wolfe, conqueror of Quebec," likely referring to stories surrounding Captain George Wolfe.

From about 1873 to 1878 Wolfe attended classes at a school his father founded at the Glen. As an account from Ireland's National Folklore Project attests, it began as a hedge school but evolved into something slightly more modern. Wolfe then graduated to the Ballagh Townland school and the National School in Athea.

Wolfe immigrated to the United States in 1885. A later passport application indicates that he left Queenstown, County Cork, on May 1, 1885, on a ship owned by the Cunard Steamship Company. The American destination is unclear. Wolfe appears to have been joined by several of his siblings. By 1900, Patrick Wolfe had settled in Philadelphia, Pennsylvania, while other family members, including Richard Wolfe, lived in Chicago, Illinois.

Richard Wolfe became a naturalized U.S. citizen in Cook County, Illinois, on April 20, 1891. His passport application, dated May 12, 1902, describes him as a real estate broker, five feet, nine inches tall, with a high forehead, blue eyes, a long and drooping nose, a "rather small" mouth, an average chin, brown hair, and fair complexion.

On September 22, 1897, Wolfe married Helen Lenz, a native of Illinois, in Chicago. The couple had one child, Grace (b. 1902).

EARLY PUBLIC CAREER

Prior to taking public office, Wolfe attended classes at the University of Chicago, lectured on economics at Chicago's Maclean College of Music, Dramatic and Speech Arts, sold fire insurance, and reported for the *Stockyards Daily Sun* newspaper. He ended up in real estate, partnering first with E. B. Roy and then with William F. Friedman. He also served as president of the Real Estate Nonpartisan League, which endorsed William Hale "Big Bill" Thompson, a Republican, in his run for a second term as mayor of Chicago in 1919. Wolfe served as president of the Cook County Real Estate Board and sat on the city's original zoning commission. In 1903, he joined the newly formed William Randolph Hearst League, which supported the newspaper publisher, then a Democratic member of the U.S. House of Representatives, for president. Hearst, who did not run, was known for his anti-British views. Such views were shared by Wolfe, who later in his career publicly decried the king of England's undue influence on Capitol Hill.

Wolfe's antipathy for the king likely was related to his Irish upbringing, and he was active in Irish American affairs in Chicago. He was a member of the Irish Educational Association and, in 1903, was elected treasurer of the Sheridan Club, a fraternal organization of Irish Americans established in 1888 and headquartered in a substantial, three-story building on Michigan Avenue at 41st Street. In 1904, Wolfe was named in a lawsuit against the club initiated by a printing company to which the club owed $310. Wolfe was among a handful of club members in arrears for their dues.

Wolfe also served as secretary of the Irish Freedom Fund, a Chicago organization that advocated for an Irish republic. In 1924, he served as national treasurer of the Progressive Party, a third party formed by Senator Robert M. La Follette, of Wisconsin, as part of his failed bid for president.

During Big Bill Thompson's run for a third term as mayor, Wolfe served as the candidate's "orator and wordsmith," in the words of the historian Gerald Leinwand. Thompson ran in part on an America First, anti-British platform, aided by Wolfe's sometimes inflammatory rhetoric. "Capitol hill is influenced by the king of England," Wolfe wrote in a campaign flyer, "while the plain people are guided by the teachings of Washington, Jefferson, and Lincoln." He vowed that

Thompson would "uphold the Americanism of the fathers." And indeed the mayor later did. Once in office again, he threatened to burn any books in the Chicago Public Library that he perceived to be anti-American, not-100-percent-American, or pro-British.

COMMISSIONER AND CONTROVERSY

After Thompson's election in 1927, the mayor appointed Wolfe commissioner of public works. His tenure was marked by continued efforts to straighten the Chicago River in its course from the North Shore Channel to Belmont Street, the establishment of a water-filtration system, and controversies over the conditions of city streets. Complicating these issues was the air of corruption that surrounded the mayor's office, which many assumed to be on the payroll of the mobster Al Capone.

Wolfe, in particular, was charged by aldermen and taxpayers with paying contractors at "fraudulent prices." When he responded to mounting pressure to repair potholed streets with a plan for property owners to raise private funds and employ city laborers to make repairs, the *Chicago Tribune*, an ideological opponent of the mayor, struck back, on July 26, 1928, with the headline: "Repair Streets Yourself, Wolfe Tells Taxpayers." Calls for Wolfe's resignation were published the next day. A headline on July 28 read, "Critic of Streets Urges Wolfe to a Life of Poesy," quoting an alderman who suggested that Wolfe, author of a published lecture titled *Culture*, ought to "retire and write poetry for a living."

The *New York Times* echoed this caricature in an assessment of the city's government published on May 19, 1929. The story describes Wolfe as "a man of temperament and energy, who is accused of having a greater sympathy for esthetic values than any official in a supposedly hard-boiled administration is entitled to possess."

In April 1930, the *Times* reported of Al Capone's efforts to infiltrate city government. The plumbers' union, controlled by Capone, regularly sent representatives to Wolfe's office. "It has been noticeable to many of the employe[e]s of the office," the *Times* wrote, "that when these men call they brush the secretaries aside and rattle on Wolfe's door until they get in."

A month earlier, a man was murdered under circumstances that seemed especially damning for Wolfe. On March 5, 1930, the Illinois state's attorney announced the resumption of a probe of city hall payroll records. Looking for evidence of graft and payroll padding, he subpoenaed the appropriate records from Wolfe's office and was promised cooperation. When he did not receive it, he informed a judge of his intention to confiscate the records from their storage place in a garage on West Harrison Street. Before he could do so, on March 9, two gunmen entered the garage in a failed attempt to abscond with the records, killing a sixty-two-year-old night watchman.

The next day the records were under the protection of a city police detective when a man dressed as a police officer attempted to obtain the records, mentioning the name of Commissioner Wolfe. He even telephoned a person who claimed to be the commissioner, but he, too, failed to get the records. The state's attorney's office, meanwhile, linked the owner of the garage, Charles E. Patterson, to Wolfe and found that Patterson had been earning about $4,000 a month from the city for minimal services.

In February 1931, Thompson and Wolfe were both investigated for diverting to their own coffers most of the $139,772 raised in a flood-relief campaign. Wolfe, in particular, was fingered as the one to whom the money was entrusted. On February 9, 1931, the *Tribune* published images of canceled checks and a bank statement, signed by Wolfe, all suggesting that relief money had been misappropriated. At the same time, the state's attorney's office opened a separate investigation into allegations of corruption in the finances of the river-straightening project. Not long after that, Wolfe was again accused of mishandling finances, with aldermen charging that he neglected to collect $30,000 in rent owed by a transit company for space leased at Navy Pier.

Thompson failed to win election to a fourth term in April 1931. In May, Wolfe appeared before a grand jury investigating the city's books. He denied receiving illicit money from Capone, but did testify that he and seven others, some of whom were outside of government, had all attended a midnight meeting in which they had each contributed $5,000 toward a $40,000 shortfall in the accounts of an unnamed city employee. The reason for the shortfall was not made clear, and favors paid to those who contributed were assumed.

In June, Wolfe was charged with another misdeed, this time conspiring to commit fraud on a civil service examination in order to fill a city position with a favored employee. None of the accusations against Wolfe led to a criminal conviction, and the taint of unethical behavior that dogged him in office was not mentioned in obituaries that later appeared in the *Chicago Tribune* and the *New York Times*.

LATER YEARS

Wolfe had always supported an isolationist, America First, populist politics that was skeptical, especially, of British imperialism. In 1931, when he had finished his term as commissioner, he began speaking for himself on these issues, focusing on the role of money in international relations. Many of the tropes he employed had long been used to attack Jews. Wolfe directed his ire at what he called the "Tory American." In a 1931 speech he elaborated: "He loves kings, titles and class distinction [...] He is responsible for most of the religious and racial hatreds which curse America. From historical causes he is in control of much of the money and wealth in America, and therefore controls the agencies of publicity and propaganda, as well as dominates our Governmental institutions and our educational life."

On a visit to Ireland in the summer of 1931, he said, "It is the powerful, ruthless hand and brain of big business. It is now practically in control of the money, business and natural resources of America." And after traveling on to Berlin, he complained about how "the international banker and the international profiteer are raising hell with America."

In 1936, Wolfe was named national treasurer of the Union Party, a hastily organized third party that unsuccessfully ran North Dakota congressman William Lemke for president against Franklin D. Roosevelt. The party was organized in part by Father Charles Coughlin, a virulently anti-Semitic, anti–New Deal radio personality who, during the campaign, said that a vote for Roosevelt was a vote for "the Communists, the Socialists, the Russian lovers, the Mexican lovers, the kick-me-downers."

In 1939, the Chicago political reporter William H. Stuart authored a hagiographic biography of Wolfe, *Share the Profits! The Story of Richard W. Wolfe and His Conclusions*. In one chapter, "Manipulation of Money," Wolfe attacks the Jews for their treatment of Jesus Christ, fabricates a Thomas Jefferson quotation on banking, and suggests that Jews conspired to assassinate Abraham Lincoln. Wolfe dismisses Adolf Hitler for his defense of capitalism but urges the United States to steer clear of the war that was imminent in Europe.

Wolfe died on March 29, 1951, at South Chicago Community Hospital. His wife died on January 8, 1961. They are buried together at Holy Sepulchre Cemetery in Alsip, Cook County, Illinois. Wolfe Playground Park, on 108th Street on the city's south side, is named for him.

THOMAS WOLFE
(1841–1915)

THOMAS WOLFE was born in 1841, possibly at Dromlought, in northern County Kerry, the son of James Richard Wolfe and an unknown mother. He had at least two brothers, Maurice (b. ca. 1823) and Richard (b. 1842), but likely at least another brother and at least two sisters.

Wolfe's grandfather, Richard J. Wolfe, had been a prominent landowner and "the agent having charge of the property of the Knight of Kerry," according to *Wolfe's History of Clinton County* (1911), which likely involved care of Ballinruddery, the residence of Maurice FitzGerald, near Listowel, County Kerry. Wolfe's father inherited land at nearby Dromlought.

Wolfe married Catherine "Kate" O'Connor on an unknown date and the couple had nine children: James (b. 1872), Mary "Minnie" (b. 1873), Julia (b. 1874), John "Jack" (b. 1876), Johanna "Hannah" (b. 1881), Margaret "Maggie" (b. 1884), Bridget "Bridie" (b. 1886?), Richard, and Eily. James Wolfe married Maria Stack and died in 1955. Minnie Wolfe married Maurice Stack and died in 1950. Julia Wolfe never married and died in 1911. Jack Wolfe died in 1907. Hannah Wolfe married Patrick Horgan and died in 1954. Margaret Wolfe married Michael Downey, and Bridget Wolfe wed Timothy Griffin, dying in 1963. Richard Wolfe became a priest, moving to Sydney, Australia, and dying there in 1922. Eily Wolfe married Cornelius "Con" Morrissey and died in 1976.

LAND WAR

Thomas Wolfe served for a time as a Poor Law Guardian, helping to distribute aid to the poor. In 1870, or probably right about the time of his marriage, he began renting a little more than 162 acres of land at Beale Hill (sometimes Bale Hill), near Ballybunion, in North Kerry, or about seven miles from his father's land in Dromlought. His absentee landlord was William Hare, third earl of Listowel, a member of the House of Lords.

Wolfe's lease was signed near the start of what historians call the Land War, or a long period of social agitation between landlords and tenants. The latter were led by Charles Stewart Parnell, a member of Parliament whose outspokenness landed him in Kilmainham jail, in Dublin. In March 1882, the landlord Arthur Herbert, reviled by some for having leveled the house of an evicted family, was murdered at Lisheenbaun, County Kerry. Late in April, Richard Roach was murdered in Dromkeen, County Limerick, apparently for having volunteered to work on a farm where the family had been evicted, also known as a "boycotted house."

On April 15, 1882, the establishment *Kerry Evening Post* reported that so-called Moonlighters, or armed, pro-tenant men, had raided the countryside around Ballybunion on April 10 in celebration of the announcement that Parnell would be released from jail. "A farmer named Patrick Quane, Kiloonly, Ballybunion, was taken out of his bed, put on his knee, and a double barrel gun presented at his head by one, and a revolver to his heart by another of the rulers of Ireland," the paper wrote sarcastically, "threatening him with death if he paid his rent—he is a tenant to the Earl of Listowel—or dealt in any 'Boycotted house.'"

The Moonlighters visited Wolfe's house, Beale Hill, and, like other farmers, "he also gave up his gun without a word of refusal or an attempt to defend," according to the *Post*, "though his house is one from which a successful defence could have been made—may it not be said 'You are nice men to have licenses.'"

Whether out of fear, principle, or necessity, Wolfe did not pay his rent during those years, and on April 6, 1885, he was evicted. According to the *Kerry Sentinel*, the sub-sheriff, W. C. Harnett, three bailiffs, Sergeant Thomas Strettan, and three policemen all arrived at Beale Hill to execute the court order issued for non-payment of rent. He owed £528 1s 5d on a yearly rent of £187 0s 8d.

The less sympathetic *Post* described Wolfe's acreage as "prime" and his rent "nominal," at £176 9s 6d, or £1 2s 6d per acre.

The *Sentinel* presented Wolfe's defense at length:

> According to the tenant's statement the rent was a most excessive one, he having taken the farm under a lease for 21 years in the year 1870, when there was an insane competi-

> tion for land, and this particular farm at the time was in a baren irreclaimed condition, and subject to all the disadvantages of land similarly located, it being situated just at the mouth of the Shannon, exposed to all the violence and severity of the Atlantic storms.

Wolfe went on to claim that at least sixty of his acres were unusable, and yet, he said, he had made great strides in improving the farm. "He has built, or rather had been compelled to build, a very fine dwellinghouse, which cost him about £240 towards the erection of which his landlord never allowed him a shilling. He also ran a very good road through the farm which took away a great deal of his time, money and labour."

Wolfe pointed to the gates he had built and the piles of stones, evidence of the toil and industry necessary "to bring even the 80 acres which he only utilise into its present state of less than average quality." In addition, the bog was worthless for turf and the market at Listowel a full twelve miles away, causing him to "thereby [lose] a great deal of the profit of his produce." Worst of all, Wolfe had lost £600 worth of stock since 1877 "owing to the poisonous nature of the grazing."

He took the sick stock into his barn for care so often his neighbors had dubbed the building "Wolfe's Infirmary."

"There was no disturbance or party display," the *Post* wrote, "and the eviction was carried out quietly. Woulfe has nine in family, including himself and his wife. When the Sheriff arrived upon the scene he found but two cows, a few sheep, two horses and a couple of donkeys, all the other stock having been disposed of in Tralee."

Finished with Wolfe, the authorities proceeded to the next eviction. What happened next comes from the *Kerry Weekly Reporter*, about six weeks later:

> Mr. Thomas Woulfe, who was evicted from his holding at Balehill, near Ballybunnion, was allowed the tillage of the farm by his landlord Lord Listowel. When the fact became known in the neighbourhood, some three hundred persons including both sexes came on the farm with horses and carts, accompanied by about twenty musicians, and put

down several acres of potatoes and oats. The greatest merriment prevailed during the day.

Wolfe remained on the land for the rest of his life. In 1892, two of his nephews, brothers Matthew Wolfe and Richard M. Wolfe, were accused of murder and eventually indicted for manslaughter in the death of the farmer Michael Dillane at Ballybunion. An early report on the case suggests that boycotted land may have been at the root of the argument, although later the Crown prosecutor contended that it was unclear what started the row. Regardless, a letter to the editor of the *Irish Times*, republished in the *Kerry Evening Post* on August 3, 1893, complained that the Wolfe brothers were never tried and that it was "well known in the county, and evidence would have been produced at the trial to show, that the case was an agrarian murder"—which is to say, violence related to the Land War.

Over the next few decades such violence subsided and various land acts in Parliament oversaw the transfer of land from landlords to tenants. This 1901 report in the *Kerry Sentinel*, however, makes clear that the terms were often quite complex. A meeting of the Listowel Rural Council featured various members marveling at the law's opaqueness. "It would take a Philadelphia lawyer to understand that letter," the chairman said. "I venture it would take a practiced Old Bailey lawyer to unravel it," the clerk responded. He went on to use Thomas Wolfe's holding as an example of how such land transfers might work.

"You propose to take three roods and twenty-two perches and to give [Wolfe] £32 6s to purchase it out absolutely," he said. "The Land Commission want you to go round, and if their circular means anything it means that you are to find out the value of the different portions of Mr Woulfe's holdings. Supposing he has two hundred acres of land, fifty acres of it might be worth 5s an acre and fifty more £1 an acre, and so on, and when you have found out the proportion required you must add a certain portion for the proximity to the public road and take into account a variety of other circumstances such as the length of time the loan is being paid, etc."

The council adjourned after deciding to seek further guidance.

Later Years

In 1906, Wolfe paid 2s to join the Ballybunion branch of the Irish Land and Labor Association, a successful political advocate for tenants' rights. Four years later he was elected to serve on the Dispensary Committee of the Board of Guardians, charged with distributing medicine to the poor.

Wolfe died on August 29, 1915, at his home, Beale Hill. His funeral was held at the Ballybunion Church and he was buried at the Killehenny Burial Ground. His wife, Kate O'Connor Wolfe, died in 1932 and is buried next to him.

THOMAS A. WOLFE
(1940–2012)

THOMAS ANTHONY WOLFE was born in Maquoketa, Iowa, on December 20, 1940. The youngest child of Raymond Bernard Wolfe and Gladys Elizabeth McGinn Wolfe, he was the great-grandson of Irish immigrants. His sisters were Sara Terese (b. 1926), Mary Kathryn (b. 1929), and Margery. After his father died in 1941, Wolfe found himself set free on not quite 200 acres of farmland just outside Delmar, in Clinton County. He lived inside his imagination, becoming his hero, Jackie Robinson, by throwing balls against the bar and scooping up grounders. He found stacks of freshly mown hay to be occasions for an intense kind of dreaming. "What I remember most about farm life," he later wrote, "was an aching feeling of loneliness."

Wolfe graduated from Delmar High School in 1958 (in a class of nine students) and then, with financial support from an uncle, from Saint Ambrose College, in nearby Davenport, in 1962. He earned a bachelor's degree in history. Later he earned a master's degree in American history from Western Illinois University, in Macomb, Illinois. His thesis examined Father Charles E. Coughlin, an anti-Semitic, anti-Roosevelt propagandist. Wolfe was unaware that his relative, Richard W. Wolfe, of Chicago, had been a prominent supporter of Coughlin.

Soon after finishing his undergraduate work, Wolfe began his teaching career in the farm town of Blue Grass, Iowa. Soon he moved down the road to Walcott, Iowa, another small town where he taught across the hall from Frances Siena Cupp, whom he married on August 1, 1964. The couple—a sometimes uneasy mixture of Irish and French ancestry—raised three children in Davenport: Bridget Colleen (b. 1967), Brendan Martin (b. 1971), and Sara Elizabeth (b. 1973). As the names suggest, Wolfe's Irish side often prevailed, although he lovingly called his wife Françoise. She called him "the old goat," only sometimes lovingly, and they managed until 1993, when they separated. Divorce followed soon after.

Wolfe suffered a heart attack in December 1997, prompting him to retire from full-time teaching. Except for his short stint in Blue

Grass, he spent his entire career at Walcott Junior High School (later middle school), teaching American history and some language arts. His great passion was for teaching, which took him back to the farm he never quite left: it was an exercise in imagination. A colleague remembered his closet full of hats. "He would put on a hat and act out various historical characters," she said, recalling that on one occasion he actually tumbled from a windowsill during a performance.

Wolfe's other great passion was the teachers' union. His wife, he sometimes said, beat him to it, voting to strike on an occasion when he didn't, and her zeal rubbed off on him. He served two terms as president of the Davenport Education Association, and was a near-annual delegate to assemblies of the Iowa State Education Association (ISEA) and the National Education Association (NEA). For at least a decade he served as Midwest regional director of the NEA's Peace and Justice Caucus, and on April 13, 2012, the ISEA presented him with its highest honor, the Charles F. Martin Award for Association Leadership. He accepted with a generous and very funny speech calling for an end to the bitter and unthinking partisanship of American politics.

Wolfe also was an enthusiastic writer: of personal essays, family histories, letters to the editor, and any other form that handily presented itself.

Wolfe died of natural causes probably on August 4, 2012, his body being found in his home several days later.

Thomas A. Wolfe

THOMAS L. WOLFE
(1840–1908)

THOMAS L. WOLFE was born in August 1840 in Listowel, County Kerry. He was the son of Thomas Richard Wolfe, a Catholic farmer, and Ellen Leahy Wolfe. He was baptized on January 5, 1841, with witnesses J. Wolfe and M. McCauliffe.

Wolfe's siblings included Richard L. (b. ca. 1837), Margaret (b. 1837), John (b. ca. 1839), Hanora (b. ca. 1843), James (b. ca. 1845), Mary Johanna (b. ca. 1846), Catherine "Kitty" (b. 1847), Ellen "Nellie" (b. 1853), and Maurice (b. ca. 1855). John Wolfe died between 1848 and 1850, and James before 1850.

In 1848, Wolfe immigrated to the United States in the company of his parents and siblings. They sailed from Liverpool to New York, arriving on September 11. From there they traveled to LaSalle County, Illinois, where they joined relatives.

Many members of the extended Wolfe family made the same journey. Wolfe's uncle John R. Wolfe, along with a cousin Maurice Wolfe, immigrated together in 1847. Wolfe's uncles Maurice R. Wolfe and Richard Wolfe sailed separately in 1849. Other cousins came as well, including Margaret and Elizabeth Maher, daughters of John R. Wolfe's sister Ellen; and Patrick, Dennis, Bridget, and Thomas Sheehan, the children of John R. Wolfe's sister Margaret. Another cousin, John E. Wolfe, and his sisters Ellen J. and Mary Agatha, also immigrated. All of these Wolfes, except for the Sheehans, settled in LaSalle County, Illinois. A few moved on to Clinton County, Iowa, including John R. Wolfe and his cousin Maurice.

Wolfe and his family initially farmed in Deer Park Township, LaSalle County. By 1870, however, they had relocated to Grand Mound in Liberty Township, Clinton County, Iowa.

On May 5, 1875, Wolfe married Katherine Mulvihill, a native of County Kerry. Mulvihill's father's second wife, Margaret, and Thomas Wolfe's father were second cousins. The couple had six children: Thomas Edward (b. 1876), Joseph, Vincent, Nellie (b. 1883), Cornelius (b. 1885), and Francis Leroy "Roy" (b. 1891). Joseph and Vincent both died sometime before 1900.

Described in his obituary as "quiet and industrious," Wolfe farmed for the rest of his life in Liberty Township. He signed his will on May 10, 1908, and died on May 26 of that year, of what his obituary described as "stomach trouble." Katherine Mulvihill Wolfe lived in the household of her son Thomas until her death, at Mercy Hospital in Clinton, on May 19, 1936. She and her husband are buried together at Saint James Cemetery in Toronto, Iowa.

THOMAS L. WOLFE
(1894–1974)

THOMAS LYONS WOLFE was born on December 4, 1894, in Lost Nation, Iowa. His parents were John Buckley Wolfe, an Irish-Catholic farmer, and Mary Lyons Wolfe. His siblings included John Vincent (b. 1888), Irene Mary (b. 1891), Edward Lyons (b. 1892), Frances Lyons (b. 1896), Richard Lyons (b. 1898), Paul Joseph Lyons (b. 1900), Eugene Maurice (b. 1902), and Cyril Dennis (b. ca. 1906).

Wolfe's World War I draft registration card, dated May 31, 1917, lists him as a farm laborer and describes him as being of medium height and slender build, with blue eyes and dark hair.

Little is known about Wolfe's early career in the church. He became a priest about 1923 and served in several parishes, including at Centerville, Appanoose County, and Kinross, Keokuk County, both in Iowa.

In July 1925, the bishop of the Catholic diocese of Davenport appointed him as an assistant at Saint Mary's parish in Fort Madison. A year later he delivered the sermon at the funeral of his first cousin, Sister Mary Scholastica of the Order of Sisters of Mercy.

In May 1939, Wolfe was assigned to Saint Patrick's parish in Burlington. On January 13, 1941, in Des Moines, Wolfe entered military service as a chaplain. He trained at Camp Bowie, in Texas. On February 12, 1944, he left for Europe, where he served as chaplain of the XX Corps, which was part of the Third Army, commanded by General George S. Patton. Wolfe's rank was colonel.

An Associated Press story in August 1944 related that Wolfe and his jeep driver, Sergeant John C. DeWitt, of Freeport, Pennsylvania, were among the first Americans to enter the Chartres cathedral after the arrival of Patton's men. Chartres is about fifty miles southwest of Paris; its Gothic-style cathedral was constructed between 1194 and 1250. According to the report, Wolfe and his driver came under sniper fire on their approach to the church. "I could see no damage [to the cathedral] except [for] a few bullet marks," Wolfe said. The story continued: "During the successful battle to drive out snipers, he related, two middle-aged French women remained alone at devotions before the altar of the Virgin Mary."

Later in the month, Wolfe assisted the Archbishop of New York, Francis J. Spellman, with a Catholic Mass held in the woods at Mars-la-Tour. Spellman was then military vicar to the armed forces; in 1946 he became a cardinal. A memoir by one of Patton's soldiers recalled that the "Mass was held despite the heavy rain and mud, and my Catholic buddies were thrilled to be a part of it, especially since it was celebrated by this well-known cleric [Spellman], who wore his elegant robe during the service, even in the mud."

Wolfe returned to the United States on February 24, 1946, and was honorably discharged. On June 13, 1946, the Most Reverend Ralph L. Hayes, bishop of the Catholic diocese of Davenport, installed Wolfe as the pastor of Saint Mary's parish in Riverside, Washington County. He replaced the Right Reverend Monsignor Bernard Jacobmeier, who had held the position for more than forty years.

In Riverside, Wolfe ran all aspects of the parish, including the Catholic schools. One of his first major acts as pastor was to create a Parent-Teacher Association at Saint Mary's parochial school.

In June 1955, Wolfe was transferred to Saint Boniface parish in Clinton, Iowa. He died on February 19, 1974, in Iowa, and is buried at Saint James Cemetery in Toronto, Clinton County.

THOMAS R. WOLFE
(1811–1876)

THOMAS RICHARD WOLFE was born in Listowel, County Kerry, in 1811. He was the son of Richard James Wolfe and Johanna Relihan Wolfe. His siblings included James Richard (b. 1800), Maurice Richard (b. 1802), John Richard (b. 1809), Ellen (b. ca. 1810), Johanna (b. 1812), Richard (b. 1815), Margaret Ellen (b. 1818), Edmond (b. 1821), and Patrick (b. 1822).

Sometime before 1832 he married Ellen Leahy. The couple had ten children: Richard L. (b. ca. 1837), Margaret (b. 1837), John (b. ca. 1839), Thomas L. (b. 1840), Hanora (b. ca. 1843), James (b. ca. 1845), Mary Johanna (b. ca. 1846), Catherine "Kitty" (b. 1847), Ellen "Nellie" (b. 1853), and Maurice (b. ca. 1855). John Wolfe died between 1848 and 1850, and James before 1850.

In 1848, Wolfe immigrated to the United States in the company of his wife and his children Richard, John, Margaret, Thomas, Hanora, Johanna, and Catherine. They sailed from Liverpool to New York aboard the *James H. Shepherd*, a relatively small, 635-ton ship of the Z Line, owned by Zerega and Company and run by Schmidt and Belchen, out of New York. James Ainsworth was the ship's master. They arrived on September 11, 1848. From New York, they traveled to LaSalle County, Illinois, where they joined relatives.

In 1847, Wolfe's brother John R. Wolfe and their first cousin Maurice Wolfe, had sailed together and settled in Illinois. (Thomas and John Wolfe shared a grandfather with Maurice Wolfe: James M. "The Barrister" Wolfe.) Wolfe's brothers Richard Wolfe and Maurice R. Wolfe both arrived separately in 1849. While brother John Wolfe and cousin Maurice Wolfe moved on to Clinton County, Iowa, Thomas Wolfe and his brothers, at least initially, remained in Illinois.

Thomas Wolfe farmed in Illinois, living in Deer Park Township, LaSalle County, by 1850, and in LaSalle, LaSalle County, by 1860. By 1870, however, he had moved to Clinton County, Iowa, to join his brother and cousin. His wife and children Richard, Margaret, Thomas, Ellen, and Maurice all joined him. They lived in Liberty Township.

Wolfe died on March 23, 1876, and his wife, Ellen, on March 8, 1882. They are buried together at Holy Angels Cemetery in Carroll County, Iowa.

TIMOTHY WOLFE
(1885–1969)

TIMOTHY WOLFE was born in the townland of Cratloe, parish of Athea, County Limerick, on June 12, 1885, the son of James Patrick "Paddy" Wolfe and Honora Maher. His siblings included Johanna (b. 1871), Patrick (b. 1872), Richard (b. 1873), Ellen (b. 1876), Maurice James (b. 1877), John J. (b. 1880), and James (b. 1882). His mother was herself a Wolfe, the daughter of Ellen Wolfe Maher, while his aunt, Ellen Maher Wolfe, married Richard J. "Brown Dick" Wolfe.

Wolfe attended Rockwell College, a private Catholic secondary school near Cashel, County Tipperary, and Holy Cross College, Clonliffe, Dublin. He studied medicine and surgery at the Catholic Medical School of Dublin and in 1911 received his medical degree from University College Dublin. He earned a bachelor of arts from University College Cork in 1920. In October 1911 he was elected medical officer of the Tarbert Dispensary District, in County Kerry, which served the poor under the administration of the Board of Guardians for the Listowel Union. Beginning in 1927 he held the same position in the county's Bruff district.

Wolfe was a nationalist who in 1917 helped to organize a Sinn Féin club in Newtownsandes on the Kerry-Limerick border. According to a biography in a Who's Who publication, he served on Sinn Féin's Ard Chomairle, or Supreme Council, from 1917 to 1918. A report in the *Limerick Leader* on August 8, 1921, during the War of Independence (1919–1921), notes that the British admiralty had "summarily dispensed with [Wolfe's] attendances at Tarbert coastguard station," citing his membership in the nationalist political party. Wolfe's brother, Father Patrick Wolfe, was then a curate in Kilmallock, County Limerick, and suspected by authorities of aiding nationalist rebels.

On December 24, 1930, Wolfe married Mary Malvena Mullaly, daughter of a land commissioner and former chairman of the County Council of South Tipperary. The couple had two children, James Patrick Francis, who was born and died on November 3, 1931, and Malvena, who died in 2010.

Wolfe appeared to have been a difficult person, at least in his youth—"someone who had perhaps an exaggerated view of his own importance," according to a Kerry judge who heard a lawsuit against the doctor. On June 7, 1915, Wolfe's relative, Brown Dick Wolfe, died at the Limerick County Infirmary following an operation, and Timothy Wolfe claimed the body. That afternoon, with the hope of conveying the remains by train to the town of Abbeyfeale, Wolfe went to the station and asked about departure times.

Wolfe became upset by the treatment he claimed to have received at the hands of Jeremiah O'Dwyer, the station's inspector, and, later, of Edward Sheahan, boots, or shoe cleaner, at the Glentworth Hotel in Limerick. He complained to the Great Southern and Western Railway Company, which conducted an inquiry, and published a letter in the *Liberator* newspaper of Tralee, causing both men to sue for libel.

According to O'Dwyer's testimony, Wolfe "came on to the station in an excited state and asked him as to when he could get a mortuary 'hearse'" for his uncle. O'Dwyer responded that "it was usual to give 24 hours notice and asked him by what train he intended taking the remains by and [Wolfe] did not say."

Wolfe claimed that O'Dwyer was reading a newspaper and refused to put it down or look at him. O'Dwyer testified that Wolfe took out a notebook and began writing notes, which Wolfe denied. The doctor eventually reported the inspector to the railroad "for being impertinent, insolent and uncivil towards him," while O'Dwyer claimed that Wolfe had used "objectionable and insulting language." During the investigation, Sheahan, who had been present at the station during the incident, backed up O'Dwyer's account, and Wolfe accused Sheahan of perjuring himself and reported him to his employer.

The *Kerry News* made clear that the judge was sympathetic with O'Dwyer and Sheahan. "He referred to the letters written by defendant to the Railway authorities [...] and expressed hope that [Wolfe's] authorities would deal with him," the paper wrote. "He came to the conclusion that Dr. Woulfe was not justified in the language he used against plaintiff [...] and that the case was a most exaggerated one."

The judge deemed Wolfe's letter of complaint to be libelous but reluctantly ruled that it was not "actuated by malice." He further ruled that the letter to the newspaper was not libelous, and therefore dismissed O'Dwyer's suit. He awarded Sheahan £5 5s 0d.

Wolfe's relationship with his employer, the Listowel Board of Guardians, was also sometimes contentious. In 1917, he sparred with the board over leave time, and in 1920 he took exception to a member's complaint that the Tarbert dispensary was not sufficiently stocked. Wolfe wrote the board a letter, which was read aloud and then denounced by members as personally insulting.

According to a report in the *Kerryman*, "The chairman said it was quite unexplainable how any man should make such a statement in his letter as Dr Woulfe against a highly respected member of their board, and it was still more extraordinary coming from a gold medalist."

A member responded, to laughter, "A little learning is bad but too much is worse."

Wolfe wrote extensively on horse racing, first in letters and then in a regular column for the *Kerryman*, including about the thoroughbred Dimby, bred by his relative Maurice R. Wolfe.

Wolfe died on February 15, 1969, his wife on December 25, 1974. They are buried together at Saint Mary's Cemetery, Abbeyfeale.

WALTER I. WOLFE
(1886–1967)

WALTER IGNATIUS WOLFE was born on September 1, 1886, in Lost Nation, Clinton County, Iowa. His parents were James Buckley Wolfe, an Irish Catholic farmer, and Anne (also Anna) Ignatius O'Connor, the daughter of an Irish immigrant. His siblings included John O. C. (b. 1873), Jeremiah "Jerry" (b. 1876), May R. (b. 1878), Honora L. "Nora" (b. 1880), James Leonard (b. 1881), and Anna (b. 1887).

According to a biographical sketch included in the third volume of *A Narrative History of the People of Iowa*, published in 1931, Wolfe attended public schools in Clinton County and Lost Nation, graduating in 1906. He then briefly attended the Iowa City Academy, after which he matriculated at the State University of Iowa (later the University of Iowa). A yearbook from 1909 includes him among the members of the Philomathian Society, a literary club, although the federal census of 1910 establishes that he was still, at least on a part-time basis, a part of the Wolfe household in Clinton County. After earning a bachelor of arts degree in 1911 (he was class treasurer), Wolfe received a bachelor of laws degree, also from the State University of Iowa, in 1914.

Wolfe practiced law in Dunlap, Harrison County, in western Iowa, until 1917, when he relocated to the town of Logan, in the same county. There he partnered with Sanford H. Cochran.

Wolfe registered for the draft—his card describes him as being of medium height and build with blue eyes—and was called for service in 1917. During much of his brief time in the U.S. Army Wolfe was stationed at Camp Humphreys, Virginia (later Fort Belvoir), about fifteen miles south of Washington, D.C. The training site, named for the Civil War general Andrew Atkinson Humphreys, was constructed beginning in January 1918. By war's end, it served as a demobilization center. Wolfe was a sergeant major in the engineering corps.

Upon his return, Wolfe resumed his law practice until 1927, when he organized the firm Robertson & Wolfe with Harry L. Robertson. The biographical sketch describes the firm as "now one of the strongest legal combinations in the county, both partners being able men, thoroughly versed in the law, and enjoying a fair share of the important litigation of this part of Iowa."

Wolfe married Mary Helen Machemer, of Cedar Rapids, on November 24, 1920, at Saint Ambrose Cathedral in Des Moines. The couple had four children: Thomas W. (b. 1922), Mary Patricia, Dorothy Anne, and Ellen Joan (b. 1932).

Helen Wolfe, as she was known, died on July 20, 1961, in Omaha, Nebraska. Walter Wolfe died on September 8, 1967. They are buried together at Mount Calvary Cemetery in Cedar Rapids.

WILLIAM A. WOLFE
(1889–1967)

WILLIAM ANTHONY WOLFE was born on April 21, 1889, in Peoria, Illinois, the son of Edmund Dean Wolfe and Margaret Estelle Mooney Wolfe. His siblings included Johanna Irene "Generna" (b. 1887), Edward "Don" (b. 1891), Richard (b. 1896), and Maurice Eugene (b. 1897). Richard died as an infant.

Wolfe was the grandson of Irish immigrants who had left County Kerry for LaSalle County, Illinois, in the 1840s. His father owned a hardware and general store in Peoria before moving, in 1891, to Superior, Wisconsin, where he operated Wolfe & Maher Grocers with his nephew, Maurice E. Maher. In 1893 he moved his family to Anaconda, Montana, a copper mining town.

By 1910, Edmund Wolfe and family had moved to Deer Lodge County, Montana, and on or about September 5, 1911, he and his son William purchased about 200 acres there from C. M. and Lottie Hansen with the intention of starting a dairy farm. They soon organized a business they called Big Four Dairy. In 1913, the two bought 1,100 acres of land in Idaho, where Edmund Wolfe and another son operated a stock ranch.

W. A. Wolfe remained in Deer Lodge, and on June 8, 1920, he signed a license to marry Nancy Virginia Cudd, a native of River Falls, Wisconsin, and resident of Great Falls, Montana. According to a subsequent report in the *Montana Standard* newspaper of Butte, friends had been surprised by the wedding, "although those who knew [Wolfe] well were aware of the fact that he made frequent trips to [Great Falls], camouflaged under the name of 'business.'" The couple had two children—William Wellington (b. 1921) and Maurine "Bess" (b. 1928)—before Nan Cudd Wolfe's death on March 24, 1930. W. A. Wolfe married Nellie M. DeKalb in 1942.

In 1922, Wolfe became caught up in the highly publicized trial of the state prison warden on corruption charges brought by the governor. A supplier of milk and swill, or animal feed, to the prison, he was forced to deny on cross-examination that he was in the process of negotiating with the governor for the sale of his dairy farm to the state.

"He admitted, however, he wanted to sell to the state his dairy herd and lease the ranch," the *Anaconda Standard* reported on April 20.

The 1930 census confirms that Wolfe continued to operate his dairy farm, that he had no schooling but was able to read and write, that he owned his own home but not a radio set. On July 17 of that year he won a Republican Party primary election for Deer County sheriff, beating Frank E. Hughes by a vote of 692 to 150. On July 22 he filed a campaign expense report of $46.20. When general election votes were cast on November 4, he lost to the Democrat, L. C. Boedecker, 1,509 to 1,128.

Wolfe died in Tucson, Arizona, on September 4, 1967; his wife died on October 6, 1988. They are buried together in Lewistown Cemetery in Lewistown, Montana.

Edward "Don" Wolfe and William A. Wolfe

William A. Wolfe

ELLEN WOLFE WREN
(1858–1927)

ELLEN WOLFE was baptized on December 7, 1858, having been born at the Glen, the family farm in the townland of Cratloe, parish of Athea, County Limerick. She was the daughter of Richard Edmond "Dicky Ned" Wolfe and Catherine White Wolfe, and her siblings included Edward (b. 1852), Maurice Richard (b. 1853), Honora (b. 1855), Mary (b. 1857), Catherine (b. 1860), Patrick Richard (b. 1861), John W. (b. 1864), Richard White (b. 1866), Catherine (b. 1868), Mary A. (b. 1870), Michael Richard (b. 1870), and Johanna (b. 1873). The first Catherine likely died before reaching maturity.

Nellie Wolfe immigrated to the United States in 1885. Records indicate that her brother Richard Wolfe left Queenstown, County Cork, on May 7, 1885, on a ship owned by the Cunard Steamship Company. The American destination is unclear. It appears that joining Wolfe were his siblings Patrick, Ellen, John, Mary, and Nano. While Patrick Wolfe settled in Philadelphia, Pennsylvania, the rest of the family went on to Chicago, where Richard Wolfe served as the city's commissioner of public works from 1927 until 1931.

Nellie Wolfe married Thomas C. Wren, a Limerick native and Chicago firefighter, and the couple had five children: Maurice (b. 1885), Richard James (b. 1887), Johanna Loretta (b. 1889), Thomas Joseph (b. 1893), and John F. (b. 1896).

On March 29, 1897, Thomas Wren, a driver for Engine Company No. 51, and his captain were injured when their horse-drawn vehicle collided with an electric car on Wentworth Avenue in Chicago. According to the *Chicago Tribune* report, a fire alarm sounded and the engine emerged from its house. "Driver Wren [...] failed to see an electric car approaching from the south," the paper wrote, "and before he was aware of danger the car plunged directly into the horses."

Wren and the captain were both "thrown violently to the street under the wreck." One of the horses was killed instantly. After suffering what likely was a traumatic head injury, Wren was placed briefly in the county insane asylum and died in May 1900. Nellie Wren died on September 26, 1927, and is buried with her husband in Mount Olivet Cemetery, Chicago.

APPENDICES

APPENDIX I:
Letter from Maurice H. Wolfe (1867)

In this letter to his uncle, possibly Bartholomew "Batt" Woulfe (1809–1883), Maurice H. Wolfe reports on army life in America—he was then stationed in Colorado Territory—and asks about his home and family in the townland of Cratloe, County Limerick. Wolfe, who was born in 1839, immigrated to Washington, D.C., in 1863, and enlisted in 1866. He died in Washington between 1910 and 1919.

Camp, 30th U.S. Inf.
(near) Fort Sedgwick. C.T.
Sunday, May 12[h] 1867

Dear Uncle,

I received your very welcome Letter not five minutes ago it being a Sunday & the only day that we have any rest, I thought I would answer your Letter to let you know that I was never in better health in my life, I hope that this Note will find you & family also the Cratloe & Athea people enjoying the Same, Dear Uncle I never felt so happy Since I Come to this Country, as I do at this moment for Receiving your Note, As I thought my neglect in not writing to you before I did would Justify you in not Answering my Letter, But dear Uncle it was not for want of love or respect for you that I did not write oftener, but through Shame. But you must forgive me for its very few Irishmen in this Country that is not Just as bad as me, for a man's mind Changes a good deal in this Country. A man Cant depend upon any friend in this Country, as the whole of them (however near in Kin) would try to get your last Dollar, But I have learned a good deal Since I come here. Dear Uncle I am happy to hear that you and family are getting along well, also that my Grandmother is well, also all the family in Cratloe, I am sorry to hear of the death of Michael Creagan. I know He was a great loss to his family, I had a Letter from Michael from Bantry a few days ago. He gave me all accounts from home. I am Sorry for the foolishness of the Irish people in Commencing a hopeless Rebellion in going to fight trained men, for no matter how brave a Man is, without Military training he Can't have Confidence in himself, and moreover in Such a Country as Ireland where a man would sell the lives of a thousand of his Comrades for one

Pound. I Know all this "damned Fenianism"[1] is generated in this Country where there are a Pack of Scoundrels going around picking the pockets of their foolish Countrymen and then go Sporting & Gambling to Europe & elsewhere laughing in their Sleeves at their dupes. James Stephens is now Sporting around Europe at the expense of his Countrymen. But it's all He or his party ever received off me is a Rotton apple which I threw at his Head in Washington when I heard him getting along with a lot of damned humbug about "The Men in the Gap" as he Calls the fools in Ireland,   There are others in this Country keeping the game up as they find it is a good paying business,   Dear Uncle we have very busy times in this Camp. Drilling and Target practice all day prepareing for an expected Indian Campaign which I am sure will Come off very Soon, As the <u>Red Skins</u> are Showing a very hostile front. They have already attacked Several trains on the Overland Route takeing away Mules & Horses and Slaughtering Men, women & Children in Ranches. I Suppose you heard of the great Massacre at Fort Phil. Kearney, Decotoh Territory, where the Indians to the number of 3000 attacked 93 Men & 3 officers of the 18th U.S. Infantry whom they Cut all to pieces. They lay in a Ravine Close to the Fort. they Sent 90 of their best Riders up to the Fort, and took away all the animals that were there. the aforesaid detachment of men & officers followed them. the Indians were cute enough to draw them into the Ravine. As Soon as the Indians found them in the Ravine They fired a volley of Bullets & Arrows. they killed them all at the first Volley except 17 Privates whom the[y] wounded badly   they fought the Indians ever until they were all killed but one brave Soldier who fought although badly wounded until they Captured him and took him away to their Camp. they then put him to the torture which is very cruel. This account of the Massacre was given by one [of] the Indians who was brought into Camp as none of the Soldiers were left alive to tell the Story---[2]

General Hancock,[3] with 15000 Men is across from here in Arkansas, if he cant make a treaty with the Indian Chiefs He will go to war with them, We expect to go from here to the "Big Horn" in the Rocky Mountains which is 1100 miles from here   The Regiment that James P. Wolfe from the

---

[1] The Fenian uprising, led by James Stephens (1825–1901) and the Irish Republican Brotherhood and funded in large part from America, began on March 5, 1867, and failed in short order.

[2] The battle Wolfe refers to here has come to be known as the Fetterman Fight or the Battle of the Hundred-in-the-Hands. On December 21, 1866, during Red Cloud's War, an alliance of Lakota, Cheyenne, and Arapaho Indians attacked eighty-one U.S. Army soldiers under the command of Captain William J. Fetterman, killing them all.

[3] Major General Winfield Scott Hancock (1824–1886), a hero of the Civil War and future Democratic candidate for president, commanded the Department of the Missouri.

Glen[4] is in is Comeing here from "Omaha"   I expect to see him in a few days,   This is a very wild Country where there is Scarcely any person living. The Prairies look very nice now as the grass is beginning to grow the handsomest flowers that ever I Saw are growing wild here,   I have no more news to Send you at present--but at my next writing I expect to be far away from here and shall have more news. Dear Uncle I must Close this Note, by Sending you wife and family my best love------Grandmother also the Athea family,   Give my love to Mary & Bridget O.Donnell   Tell my father to bind Batt[5] to Some trade Such as Carpenter or Bricklayer for a Man without a trade in this Country can only make poor living as a Soldier in this Country has better pay than a Labouring Man,   Dear Uncle I must Conclude by remaining as usual,

    your affectionate Nephew

    Maurice H. Wolfe
    Co. F. 30 U.S. Infantry
    Fort Sedgwick C.T.

Tell Batt to put all Ideas of Coming to this Country out of his head or he will be sorry

---

[4] The identity of James P. Woulfe is unclear, although the Glen was a farm in the townland of Cratloe first owned by Edmond Richard "Old Ned" Woulfe (1788–1876) and passed down to Richard Edmond "Dicky Ned" Woulfe (1824–1910) [see Appendix III] and, eventually, his granddaughter, Jane C. "Dollie" Woulfe (1880–1964) [see Appendix XIII].

[5] Wolfe's father was Philip Maurice Woulfe (1810–1901) and Batt, or Bartholomew, was Maurice Wolfe's brother.

APPENDIX II:
Letter from Edmond Woulfe White (1906)

In this letter, published in the Kerry People *newspaper on September 29, 1906, Edmond Woulfe White (1854–1922) notes the sale of the Verschoyle-Goold estate to its tenant farmers and tells the history of the Goold family and their sometimes contentious relationship with the people who worked their land. White was the son of Michael White (d. after 1903) and Bridget Woulfe White (ca. 1829–1911) and practiced law in Belfast, a perspective he brings to this letter.*

VERASCHOYLE GOOLD ESTATE, WEST LIMERICK.
TO THE EDITOR.

Ulster Buildings, Waring Street,
Belfast, 5th September, 1906.

Dear Sir,—In the North of Ireland we do not realise the extraordinary revolution that is silently and peacefully taking place in the South under the Land Purchase Acts. Of all the estates in Munster, the history of the Veraschoyle Goold estate in West Limerick the sale of which has just concluded,[6] is probably the most interesting, and I should say the most instructive; and with you[r] indulgence I shall refer to it briefly for a twofold purpose viz:—(a) to refute the charges of bigotry and intolerance levelled time and again against the Catholics of the South, and (b) to exemplify the changes that are passing over the face of that province. The estate was purchased in 1817 by Serjeant Goold, who was a master in Chancery, a cotemporary of O'Connell, and a professional rival not unworthy of that great man.[7] Both were engaged in most of the important cases of the time on opposite sides. One of the oldest surviving tenants on the estate, as venerable in years as he is tenacious of memory, remembers meeting O'Connell and

---

[6] White helped negotiate the sale between about 200 tenants and the landlord, Hamilton Frederick Stuart Goold Verschoyle. Tenants on the estate, which encompassed nearly all of the parish of Athea and the townland of Cratloe, included James Patrick "Paddy" Woulfe (1842–1922), Richard James "Brown Dick" Woulfe (1853–1915), Richard Edmond "Dicky Ned" Woulfe (1824–1910), and Edmond Woulfe White's parents.

[7] Thomas Goold (ca. 1766–1846) was an Irish Protestant lawyer who supported Daniel O'Connell's attempts to repeal the Act of Union (1801), which created the United Kingdom of Great Britain and Ireland.

Goold, and can recall many interesting incidents in their careers.[8] One I shall mention, as it has reference to the estate to which I am referring. In the early thirties O'Connell was engaged in defending prisoners charged with conspiracy and sedition at the Cork Assizes, and Goold, who was prosecuting for the Crown, was having the best of O'Connell, and convictions seemed inevitable. O'Connell, knowing that the serjeant was irascible, frequently interrupted him for the purpose of irritating him and throwing him off the trend of his arguments, and ultimately, after Goold had referred to certain estates with which the prisoners were connected, O'Connell interjected:— "What about that property you purchased in West Limerick from Lord Courtenay, where, if you turn out a two year old in May it comes in a yearling in November with the horns of a four year old?" This inflamed the serjeant, and enabled O'Connell to pull off his prisoners.[9] Both were life-long friends, and I quote the following incident to show how intimate their friendship was. The serjeant was notoriously "near," and on one occasion O'Connell was walking through a dark passage in the serjeant's house when the latter said—"O'Connell, be careful, or you will break your neck." The reply was—"It would be more difficult, Tom, to break the fast here than one's neck." Goold, although a Crown official, boldly avowed to Castlereagh his hostility to the Union, and to the last opposed it. He was a brilliant speaker, and was known as "Goold of the silver tongue." The serjeant was an excellent landlord. When the estate was purchased Europe was held in flames by war and exorbitant prices were paid for farm produce. After Waterloo the prices went down with a bang, and the rents then payable became impossible. The tenants requested the serjeant to have them readjusted, and this he willingly consented to do. He appointed an arbitrator in his behalf and asked the tenants to appoint one to represent them. Both fixed the rents without even the intervention of an umpire, and so moderate were they, the rents remained practically undisturbed until the sale of the estate a few weeks ago. The estate passed in succession to the serjeant's three sons in the order of age, and ultimately to his great-grandson, Mr. Goold Versachoyle, who has just sold, as already explained.[10] The relations between landlord

---

[8] This may have been a reference to Richard E. "Dicky Ned" Woulfe.

[9] A longer version of this story appears in *Folktales from the Irish Countryside* (1998), edited by the folklorist Kevin Danaher, a native of Athea, County Limerick. Its teller was Richard "Old Dick" Denihan, who had been "a parish priest's servant and general factotum."

[10] Thomas Goold died in 1846, and by the early 1850s his son Wyndham Goold, a member of Parliament for Limerick, had inherited the estate. He died in 1854, after which the Very Reverend Frederic-Falkener Goold, archdeacon of Raphoe (1808–1877), became landlord of about 10,966 acres. His wife, Caroline-Newcomen Goold, inherited after him and eventually their grandson, H. F. S. Goold Verschoyle.

and tenant were harmonious and satisfactory until the youngest son, the Archdeacon, came on the scene, and the scene then changed, and the change was swift. Steeped in feudalism, the Archdeacon regarded himself a demigod and his tenants serfs, whose chief duties, in his view, were to earn rents and worship at the shrine of the feudal deity. Shortly after succeeding to the estate he built a dwelling-house at the head of Athea village, which is situated in the heart of the property. He also erected a church within two hundred yards of the house, and simultaneously distributed Bibles among the tenants on the estate, and scattered broadcast among them polemical literature and religious tracts. Up to this no Protestant had settled on the estate, and there was no Protestant church within a radius of eight miles. No person could or ever would take exception to the Archdeacon introducing members of his denomination to the parish and erecting a church for them at which to worship, and no misunderstanding or feeling would follow if he had not tampered with the religious convictions of the Catholics. A few Protestant families came to reside on the estate, and from the time they settled there to the present the relations between them and the Catholics have been of the most exemplary character, as will be seen later on. The archdeacon inaugurated a system, I won't say of proselytism, but akin to it, which led to feuds and demoralisation over the estate. He did not in time realise the harm he was doing, nor did he see until too late that he might as well have attempted to alter against the laws of gravitation the courses of brooks and rivulets that meander over his property as to seduce the Catholics from the fold of their Church. Men were employed at different centres to distribute tracts and take the names of persons who were willing to read them. They were paid in proportion to the numbers enrolled, and once each month those enrolled marched to Listowel, a town eight miles distant, entered the Protestant church, underwent some examination, after which they "drew their pay," and went off smiling, "winking the other eye," to the nearest public-house, and that which they received for "soup" they handed to the publican for a drink. Thus the demoralisation proceeded, and only for the fact the thing would have been ludicrous and laughable in the extreme. The society which the archdeacon induced thus to operate on his Catholic tenantry soon saw they there being humbugged, and the ungodly thing fizzled into the air, where it still dwells, and will until the day of judgment, awaiting its reward. It was inevitable that procedure of that kind would exercise the minds of the spiritual directors of the people and hot controversies followed for years, until they culminated in a number of charges being preferred by the archdeacon against the Reverend Martin Ryan, administrator of the parish, and one of the finest priests Munster ever gave the Church. An ecclesiastical court was duly formed, and a day appointed to hear the charges. The priest accompanied by his parishioners in hundreds proceeded on the day appointed to Newcastle West, where the court was held, prepared to refute the calumnies in which for the moment he was shrouded. But the archdeacon and the "creatures" who were playing and fattening on his fanaticism were non est.[11] Father Ryan was cheered along the road to his home, where he met with a reception unparalleled in the annals of the parish. The archdeacon did a still more extraordinary thing. The Sunday after the court was held he marched into the chapel bearing a wand which was symbolic of his visit to the Holy Land, while celebrating Mass, and forced his way through the congregation to the altar steps. It would be difficult to conceive anything more trying to the patience of a Catholic than an intrusion like this during the celebration of a function so solemn and dear to them. The archdeacon wanted to vindicate before the congregation certain Catholic ladies from trivial aspersions which neither Father Ryan nor the archdeacon should have noticed. Those ladies were altogether too elevated for the tongue of maligner to hurt them. In justice to the archdeacon it must be said he entered the church between the Gospels, and his demeanour was most respectful. He was kindhearted, of imposing presence, a perfect gentleman and the frailties forgotten when his good parts will be remembered. And those frailties I should not now exhume only that I want to point out how much the Catholics endured while the feeling of amity between them and the Protestants remained unbroken. Now, what I want to emphasise is that during all those troublous times the good relations between the Protestant and their Catholics neighbours never waned, as already stated. There are just two Protestant families in that wide estate, and not others with a radius of many miles. I met the head of one of these families (Mr. Gleeson) a few days ago, and he told me that during the fifty years his family have been living in the parish they received nothing but kindness and consideration from their neighbours; that the Catholics always brought home his hay and turf, and that his diffi-

---

[11] In his report on the case, reprinted in the *Evening Freeman* newspaper on January 31, 1867, the Very Reverend Denn O'Brien describes the charges against Father Ryan as "truly grave," but then describes the conduct of the archdeacon as "very singular." "The very rev. gentleman made all the accusations just laid down," O'Brien wrote. "He made them publicly in the newspapers, and to your lordship by private letter. He called very loudly for inquiry, and complained vehemently when inquiry was necessarily delayed. He pledged himself to prove 'everyone of the charges' before an ecclesiastical tribunal, and to 'vindicate his poor tenantry,' who, he said, 'had been victims of Mr. Ryan's abuse.' He 'thanked God' that he did not belong to a church where such things were permitted to disgrace the ministry, and he appealed to the public, over and over again, for sympathy. And after all this, when the inquiry, instituted at his instance, opened the doors and invited him to prove the accusations he had made, Very Rev. Mr. Goold is not there—nor anyone to represent him, or to explain his absence."

culty was to make a selection from those who volunteered to assist him, they came in such numbers. In the parish there are not two families more respected or more popular, and there is no distinction between Protestants and Catholics in the South except where the Protestant ranges himself on the side of the oppressor or attempts to make inroads on people's faith. There they cannot understand why there should be any strife over religious matters, and one very intelligent man said to me—"It would be nearly as good as Home Rule if the Boyne would be blotted out of the map. If it could Derry, apprehending the same fate, would probably fall into line with the people and stop their nonsense." The two Protestant families live adjacent to the districts from which most of the moonlighters radiated, and though these men raided every house in Kerry, Limerick and Cork where they suspected there were firearms, they never interfered with the Protestants, and so secure did Mr. Gleeson's family feel that when retiring for the night they didn't even lock their doors.[12] Not only so, but that gentleman tells me that five men unknown to him spoke to him at a fair in Douagh, and told him he need have on apprehension, and added, "We won't interfere with your sort." Nor did they. Mr. Gleeson also informed me that when moonlighting was rampant he went with a local Protestant landlord to Kerry for a week's shooting. They stayed at a farmhouse in the district over which the moonlighters rambled mightily, but were not interfered with, and what I am writing of Limerick and Kerry holds good over Munster. Gleeson himself said, "We were as safe as if on board a battleship, and we knew it." The worthy clergyman (Canon Vance), who has for upwards of forty years been officiating at the handsome church built by Archdeacon Goold, and who is one of the most popular clergymen in Ireland, experiences as much respect from the Catholics as they extend to their priests. That venerable gentleman's heart is filled with charity and kindness towards Catholics, and what he has done for struggling Catholics from time to time would take more space to describe than I could reasonably demand. I wish now to give an example of the wonderful confidence the Catholics place in Protestants. Mr. Gleeson, to whom I have already referred, has revealed a little secret to me, now for the first time made public. His father, who is long since dead, was a carpenter to trade, and had his workshop in one of the Archdeacon's outhouses in Athea. He was engaged one evening in 1867, when Fenianism was raging through-

---

[12] The Moonlighters were vigilantes engaged in a long-term and often violent social agitation lasting from the 1870s to around the turn of the century that came to be known as the Land War. They collected weapons—including from Thomas Woulfe (1841–1915) of Beale Hill, near Ballybunion, County Kerry—and enforced boycotts, even murdering landlords or those who defied them. The Land War ended with the passage of legislation in Parliament that made the purchase of land such as the Goold estate possible.

out the country, making a coffin, when a man named McMahon, locally known as the "Marshal," and who was the leader of Fenians in the district, came to him and said he intended to camp with this men that night in the Archdeacon's out-offices. The son says when his father heard this daring resolve of MacMahon he stood almost petrified over the unfinished coffin. He was powerless to stop them, and would go into exile before he would betray them. That night the Marshal and his men slept serenely within thirty yards of the room where the Archdeacon slept, and within 200 yards of the nearest police station. Gleeson kept the secret—and he was right—for if the police were warned they would have been overwhelmed by superior numbers, all well armed, trained and fearless.[13] MacMahon was a powerful man, with as little regard for his life as a Japanese soldier once he sniffed the battle breeze. I have just visited the Goold estate, and the changes that have taken place there nobody would have the temerity to tell even twenty years ago. The house erected by the Archdeacon—and which he regarded almost as a sacred temple—has passed into the possession of one of the tenants, having been purchased by him, and the bailiffs, rent warders, understrappers, eavesdroppers, and all the baleful concomitants of feudalism are gone, gone for ever, and their reigns over the estate a feeling of comfort, and confidence and independence such as has not been experienced since feudalism was first forced on a hapless people. It is only fair to add that the last of the Goolds was stripped of all feudal trappings, and left the property after the completion of the sale, leaving behind him memories that will be cherished, and two Protestant families his grandfather brought to the parish half a century ago and whose welfare and happiness every man in that vast estate heartily desires.

With the retirement of Mr. Goold Veraschoyle comes the verification of the prophecy of Father Ryan, to whom I have already alluded. Stung by the encroachment of the Archdeacon on his spiritual domain, he said, pointing to the grove in which stands the church, erected by the Archdeacon—"The thrush will be heard warbling there when the blackbirds are gone"—(i.e., landlords). But fifty years, and with them the faithful priest, passed away before those words were put to the test.—Faithfully yours,

— E. W. White

---

[13] On September 23, 1867, the *Irish Examiner* newspaper reported that Archdeacon Goold held a "splendid banquet" for the Athea station of the Royal Irish Constabulary "in appreciation of their valued services during the late Fenian outbreak." The uprising, led by the Irish Republican Brotherhood and funded in large part from America, began on March 5 and failed in short order.

APPENDIX III:
Richard E. Woulfe Obituary (1910)

In this obituary, which appeared in the Limerick Leader *on June 1, 1910, Richard Edmond "Dicky Ned" Woulfe (1825–1910) is described as "the 'Grand Old Man' of the Limerick Woulfes," an Irish-language speaker who served as an important source of local and family history.*

OBITUARY

DEATH AND FUNERAL OF MR. R. E. WOULFE, CRATLOE, ATHEA.

AN APPRECIATION

On Thursday last, writes our Abbeyfeale correspondent, the remains of the above gentleman were, amid many manifestations of sorrow, grief, and universal mourning, removed to the family burying ground at Templeathea, from his residence, The Glen, where he was born eighty-six years ago, and where he spent his long life, honoured and respected by all. He was looked up to as the "Grand Old Man" of the Limerick Woulfes, and many of the noble and Christian virtues and qualities of his race were in him. A man of fine physique, a clear and level brain, unimpeachable integrity, and indomitable courage—he did not know what fear was, and always did what rectitude prompted without pausing to count the cost or the consequences. His religious fervour and belief in the Divine Inspiration were unbounded, and he never for a moment lost sight of his duties to God, or of the respect due to the Church of God or its ministers. On his death bed he received a letter from his cousin, Sister Teresa Woulfe, Ursuline Convent, New Orleans, sending her felicitations on his 86th birthday, and as evidencing the strength of his religious convictions, we quote the following excerpts from his reply to that letter dictated some days before he died to his nephew, Edmond Woulfe White, solicitor,[14] to whom he was deeply devoted:—"The Woulfes are now, as they always have been, doing much for the Church of God, and the enlightenment of their fellowmen in many lands, and the gifts of intellect with which Providence abundantly endowed them, have been employed by many of them to further the purposes of God and to propagate

---

[14] Edmond Woulfe White (1854–1922) [see Appendix II]

His word. It is this view which brings so much comfort to me, and makes me proud of our race and of our name. Generations ago it was prophesied that there would be Woulfes in Limerick and in Kerry while the Shannon rolled into the Atlantic, and that more than an average number of them would devote their lives to the service of God. When I saw the inscription on your letter (for my vision, thank God, is still clear) I said that is the writing of a Woulfe, and when I read the letter it revived in my mind the memory of the prophecy mentioned, which was related to me in this house nearly eighty years ago by my poor father who survived my present age by three years and to the end retained his faculties undimmed and unclouded." We also quote the following passages from the letter mentioned, as they possess historical value and will be of public interest, and therefore should be placed on the record. They were dictated by the deceased from his memory, which was matchless:—"No information I could transmit to you would probably be more acceptable than a brief sketch of our ancestors, and I am the man, I think, now living that can from personal knowledge and tradition trace them back to the days of Cromwell. During the sanguinary civil war of twenty years which succeeded the rebellion of 1641 in which the five armies belonging to five different parties ravaged the country, numbers of the Woulfes were obliged to leave the rich plains of Limerick, and became scattered and separated never to meet again. Some went to Clare, others settled in the western part of this country, and later on extended their branches into Kerry. Hundreds of them escaped to the Continent of Europe, while many of them perished during the prolonged war, and at the Siege of Limerick in 16[??] some were hanged, others shot in cold blood, for no greater crime than defending their country, and probably the ample possessions they then held in Limerick and Tipperary. But their great crime was their refusal to renounce the Faith as transmitted to mankind through the inspired Channels of Almighty God. Two of the (priests) were condemned to death by Ireton (son-in-law of Cromwell), and perished on the scaffold. The old Woulfes had the incidents of Ireton's career, and his dreadful death as foretold by Bishop Terence O'Brien, whom he cruelly sentenced to death. They were indelibly implanted in their minds, as related by one to the other in each succeeding generation." Deceased was well versed in folk lore and tradition, spoke Gaelic fluently, and it is to him, as referred to in his dedication, that the Rev. P. Woulfe, C.C., Kilmallock, was indebted for much of the information in his "Irish Names."[15] He saw the Liberator[16] at

---

[15] *Sloinnte Gaedheal is Gall*, a seminal work on Irish names and surnames, was published in 1906 and later expanded. In the acknowledgments, Father Patrick Woulfe (1872–1933) credits his relative, "who gave me nearly all the surnames of West Limerick and North Kerry."

three of his monster meetings, and it is only a few years ago, while on a visit to Dublin, that he entertained some of the admirers of the great Tribune by narrating some interesting incidents of his life, on beholding a statue in O'Connell-street. Just after deceased was anointed, and shortly before he died, he said, with a brain as clear as a ril, and with all the fortitude that is the priceless heritage of the followers of Christ, "I am now prepared to meet my God." His life ebbed peacefully away, almost unnoticeably, like the sun stealthily dipping behind the horizon, after the unrelenting hand of Death had been for days grappling with his powerful physique. The vast concourse of people, extending nearly two miles in length, that followed his remains to the graveside, bore striking testimony to his popularity and the esteem in which he was universally held. That genial face, and that voice that is now stilled in death for ever, will long be missed and mourned in Cratloe. May the earth rest lightly over him, and may God extend to him that eternal bliss promised to the faithful and the believers in the resurrection of man. The chief mourners were:—Maurice R. Woulfe, Inland Revenue Dublin;[17] Mrs Murphy, Abbeyfeale; Mrs White, Athea;[18] Mrs Flaherty, Newtownsandes[19] (sisters); Maurice Woulfe, Board of Education, Office, Dublin;[20] Richard Woulfe, stockbroker, do (grandsons); Miss Jeannie Woulfe, do (granddaughter); Mrs Hannah White (daughter);[21] Mrs Maurice Woulfe (daughter-in-law);[22] Edward Woulfe White, solicitor, Athea [...]

---

[16] Daniel O'Connell (1775–1847) was an Irish politician who spent his career campaigning for Catholic rights and an end to the Act of Union (1803), which created the United Kingdom of Great Britain and Ireland.

[17] Maurice Richard Woulfe (1853–1928)

[18] Bridget Woulfe White (d. 1911)

[19] Julia Woulfe Flaherty (ca. 1838–after 1911)

[20] Maurice James Woulfe (1884–1973)

[21] Johanna Woulfe White (1873–1952)

[22] Elizabeth Malcolm "Bessie" Cockburn Woulfe (1856–1943)

APPENDIX IV:
Biographies from *Wolfe's History of Clinton County* (1911)

Published as two volumes in 1911, Wolfe's History of Clinton County *contained information on history, geography, government, transportation, education, and religion, in addition to biographical sketches "of representative citizens of this county whose records deserve preservation because of their worth, effort and accomplishment." These included at least one woman and three Wolfes, one of whom, Judge Patrick B. Wolfe, served as the project's editor-in-chief. County histories such as these became popular in the decades following the centennial of 1876, resulting in about 5,000 books accounting for 80 percent of all American counties.*

JAMES B. WOLFE.

The Emerald Isle, far-famed in song and story, has furnished a large number of enterprising and high-minded citizens to the United States, and they have ever been most welcome, for we have no better class of citizens. They are, almost with no exceptions, industrious, and they are loyal to our institutions and may always be relied upon to do their full duty as citizens in whatever community they may cast their lot. Among this large class the name of James B. Wolfe, whose long, strenuous and interesting career has resulted in much good to himself, his family and to his friends and neighbors, for his example has ever been exemplary and his influence salutary.

Mr. Wolfe was born in Ireland, on April 13, 1843.[23] He is the son of John R. Wolfe, mentioned at length on another page of this work. Most of Mr. Wolfe's life has been spent in the country of his adoption, for he was but a child when his parents crossed the great Atlantic and brought him to Chicago in 1847. Later they moved to Ottawa, Illinois, and in May, 1855, they reached Clinton county, Iowa, and here James B. Wolfe was reared on a farm and educated in the common schools. He was put to work in the fields when old enough, and early in life became acquainted with general farm work. Farming has been his principal occupation and he also engaged in merchandising at Lost Nation for some time. He has been very successful

---

[23] His gravestone gives the year 1844.

as a business man and has laid by a competency for his declining years. He is owner of a valuable and highly improved farm of two hundred and eighty acres, and he has also given his son a fine farm of one hundred and sixty acres. Stock raising has long been one of his hobbies and chief occupations and he has sent out some very fine live stock from his place, being a breeder of Shorthorn cattle. He also feeds cattle and hogs extensively. He is an excellent judge of live stock of all grades, and he has long been regarded as one of the leading general farmers in this township. He has a beautiful home in the midst of forest and fruit trees and he has such substantial outbuildings as his needs require.

Politically, Mr. Wolfe is a Democrat, and while he has never taken a very prominent part in public affairs, he has been more or less active in local matters, and has been school director for twenty years. He and his family are members of the Catholic church and very faithful in their support of the same.

Mr. Wolfe was married in Clinton county, on February 8, 1872, to Anna O'Connor, a native of Jackson county, Iowa, the daughter of Jeremiah O'Connor and wife. Her father was born in Ireland, from which country he came to America in an early day, and here he and his wife spent the rest of their lives, being now deceased. They were highly respected in their community.

To Mr. and Mrs. James B. Wolfe seven children have been born, named as follows: John O. C.; Jerry, a veterinary surgeon of Grand Mound; Mary, Nora, James, Walter and Anna. They are all living and have received good educations and are popular in the social life of their community.[24] There are no more worthy or highly honored people in Clinton county than the Wolfes.

JERRY WOLFE, V. S.

In his chosen field of endeavor Dr. Jerry Wolfe, of Grand Mound, Orange township, Clinton county, has achieved success such as few attain and his present eminent standing among the veterinary surgeons of eastern Iowa is duly recognized and appreciated not only in his own town and township, but throughout the county and in adjoining localities, and as a citizen he easily ranks with the most progressive and influential in his vicinity. His course has ever been above suspicion, and those favored with an intimate acquaintance with him are profuse in their praise of his many virtues and upright character.

---

[24] James Wolfe died on January 27, 1916.

Doctor Wolfe is a native of Liberty township, Clinton county, Iowa, having been born here on August 16, 1875; and he is the son of James B. and Anna (O'Connor) Wolfe, and a nephew of Judge P. B. Wolfe, well known in judicial circles of Clinton county. The father was born in Ireland, and the mother's birth occurred in Jackson county, Iowa.

The Doctor was reared on a farm, where he worked in the fields during the summer months and attended the public schools in the wintertime at Lost Nation. Later he spent three years at the Iowa State Teachers' College, and one year at the State Agricultural College at Ames, Iowa. He applied himself very closely to his text-books and made rapid progress, receiving a high education along general lines. Deciding to turn his attention to veterinary surgery, he took the course at the Chicago Veterinary College, from which he was graduated with honor in 1905. Soon afterwards he returned to Clinton county and located at Grand Mound, where he has since remained, having been very successful from the first, and he has built up a large and ever-growing patronage, his services being in great demand. He has been very successful in his chosen calling and he keeps abreast of the times in all discoveries, research work and whatever pertains to veterinary surgery.

While in college Doctor Wolfe was the champion foot racer of the state of Iowa, and he has thirty-seven gold medals and seventeen silver medals. He became widely known as a foot racer and athlete.

The Doctor is chief of the fire department at Grand Mound, and he has built up a very proficient and reliable force of fire fighters there. Politically, he is a Democrat, and he and his family are members of the Catholic church and faithful in their attendance and support of the same.

On February 11, 1909, the marriage of Doctor Wolfe and Mary Wiley, of Chicago, was solemnized. She is a native of Horton, Kansas, having been born on August 23, 1887. She is a lady of education and culture and the representative of an excellent and highly honored family. To the Doctor and his wife one child, James Wiley, has been born, his birth being recorded as April 7, 1910.[25] Doctor Wolfe is a life member of the Chicago Veterinary Society.

JUDGE PATRICK B. WOLFE.

The present review is concerned with the life of a man whose character and ability are, by reason of his long and honorable connection with the practice of law, well known to the people of Clinton county and of the state

---

[25] The Wolfes had two additional children: Mary I. Wolfe Schulz (1912–1964) and Alice Grace Wolfe Alward (1922–1991). Dr. Jerry Wolfe died at his home in Grand Mound on December 15, 1949.

of Iowa, and whose extensive familiarity with his own county made him especially fitted to serve as editor-in-chief of the history of Clinton county.

Patrick B. Wolfe was born in Chicago, Illinois, on October 7, 1848, the son of John R. and Honora (Buckley) Wolfe. John R. Wolfe was born in county Kerry, Ireland, in 1824,[26] the son of Richard Wolfe, who was the agent having charge of the property of the Knight of Kerry. He received an excellent education. During his young manhood he helped to organize the "Young Ireland" party. He left Ireland in 1848,[27] coming to America, first locating at Ottawa, Illinois. Here he remained on a farm until 1854, when he moved to Clinton county, Iowa, to land near Lost Nation, which he had entered the winter before, and lived there until his death in 1885, becoming one of the largest landholders and most successful farmers of his township. Mr. Wolfe did not take any great interest in politics. He was opposed to slavery. In religion he and his entire family were stanch Catholics, and active workers in the church.

John R. Wolfe was married in Ireland to Honora Buckley. She was member of a family prominent in the church and at the bar, Michael Buckley, her brother, having been the leader of the Belfast bar for many years. The Wolfe family were also prominent in the church and in law, so that it was natural for the American descendants to turn to the bar in choice of a profession. Mrs. Wolfe died in 1888.

Mr. and Mrs. Wolfe were the parents of ten children, two of whom died in infancy, and those who grew to maturity are the following: James, a farmer near Lost Nation; Patrick B.; Johanna, who is now Sister Scholastica of the Order of Sisters of Mercy at Sioux City, Iowa; John, a farmer at Melrose, Monroe county, Iowa; Maurice, a farmer near Lost Nation; Margaret, now the wife of Dr. D. Langan, of Clinton; Katherine, the widow of Judge T. D. Fitzgerald, of Montana, at one time president of the Montana Senate, now living in Clinton; and Richard B., an attorney at De Witt, Clinton county, Iowa.

Patrick B. Wolfe attended the common schools of Liberty township, Clinton county, for a time, then spent one year in the Christian Brothers Academy at La Salle, Illinois. He was a student in the academic department of Iowa State University for two years, then took a full law course from that institution, graduating with the degree of Bachelor of Laws in 1870. In January, 1871, he began the practice of law at De Witt, Clinton county, Iowa,

---

[26] John Richard Wolfe's gravestone in Toronto, Clinton County, records a birthdate of November 15, 1809.

[27] Records indicate that John R. Wolfe and family arrived in New York City from Liverpool on August 23, 1847.

and for a few years suffered the proverbial hardships of the young lawyer, but soon came into an extensive practice. In 1877 he formed a partnership with W. A. Cotton, under the name of Cotton & Wolfe, which continued until 1888. For four years he served as attorney for the town of De Witt, and was a member of the De Witt school board for fifteen years. In 1885 he was elected to the Iowa Senate, and served three sessions, resigning from his position in October, 1891, when he was appointed judge of the district court for the seventh judicial district, holding his first term of court in November of 1891. He served on the bench until September 1, 1904, when he resigned to form a partnership in the law with his son. It is a unique fact that Judge Wolfe has resigned from every public office which he has held. In 1899 he was nominated for judge of the supreme court of the state of Iowa, and was defeated by a close margin. He is again a candidate in 1910. His law office was moved from De Witt to Clinton in May, 1891, and his residence was transferred in 1893. Mr. Wolfe was a member of the public library board of the city of Clinton.

Mr. Wolfe was married on May 1, 1878, to Margaret Connole, the daughter of Thomas and Hannah (Malone) Connole, who came from Ireland and located in De Witt. To this union three children were born. John L. Wolfe was born in 1879; graduated from the Clinton high school; took the classical course at St. Mary's College in Kansas, graduating with the degree of Bachelor of Arts; took a post-graduate course in Georgetown University, Washington, D. C., receiving there his Master of Arts degree, and then took the law course there, and received the degree of Bachelor of Laws. He spent a year in the University of Berlin, Germany, and in 1904 entered into partnership with his father. He is now serving on his second term as a representative in the lower house of the Iowa General Assembly. Mary Wolfe was born on June 27, 1881, and is a graduate of Sinsiniwa College, of Wisconsin, and Trinity College, in Washington, D. C. One child died in infancy.[28]

---

[28] Judge Wolfe died on June 11, 1922.

APPENDIX V:
James B. Wolfe Obituary (1916)

This obituary of James Buckley Wolfe appeared in the Oxford Mirror *newspaper on February 3, 1916. It casts Wolfe in the role of an archetypal pioneer, one who made a Pilgrim's Progress from Ireland to Lost Nation. It's a rhetorical turn that allows the writer to take stock not only of this one individual but of the entire community. The headline is a misnomer, although Wolfe did have a younger brother, John B., who was born in 1851.*

OBITUARY OF JOHN B. WOLFE, PIONEER

James B. Wolfe was born in County Kerry, Ireland, April 13, 1844, and died at his home near Lost Nation, Iowa, January 27, 1916. When an infant he came to this country with his parents.[29] The history of his life is the story of the immigrant and pioneer. They came to Chicago. Where a vast city now stands there were then only swamps and sloughs. Afterwards the family moved to Ottawa, Illinois, and later, in 1854 came to Iowa settling on the same farm, a part of which the deceased owned at the time of his death.

At that time, where there are now prosperous well tilled farms, there was a vast unbroken prairie over which the deer roamed at will and through which surged the all devouring prairie fire sweeping everything before it. Here, the deceased experienced the struggles and privations of pioneer life. Through the sides of the rude hut of a home, the wind and the weather blew. Often did he tell of how he shook the snow from the bed covers on awakening and brushed it aside on the floor to make a bare place upon which to stand while dressing. He lived to see the great evolution and progress of the past almost three quarters of a century. He saw the railroad, the steam engine, and the automobile displace the rail and the ox drawn wagon of the pioneer and the transformation which has made an unbroken, unpeopled prairie the garden spot of the world.

The deceased united in marriage to Annie O'Connor, February 8, 1872, which union was blessed with seven children all of whom with the wife sur-

---

[29] The Wolfe family arrived in New York City from Liverpool on August 23, 1847. They included James; his father, John Richard Wolfe (1809–1883); his mother, Honora Buckley Wolfe (d. 1887); the elder Wolfe's first cousin, Maurice Wolfe (ca. 1800–1879); his wife, Ellen Catherine Carey Wolfe (d. 1857); and several of their children.

vive. They are John O. C., Nora L. and James L., of this place; Mrs. Frank Goodall [May R.], of Toronto; Doctor Jeremiah, of Grand Mound; Mrs. I. S. Ryan [Anna], of Welton; and Attorney Walter I., of Dunlap.[30] Besides, the deceased leaves to mourn his death four brothers and three sisters as follows: Judge P. B. Wolfe, Mrs. T. D. Fitzgerald [Katherine] and Mrs. D. Langan [Margaret I.] of Clinton; Attorney Richard B. of DeWitt; Maurice B. of Lost Nation; and Sister M. Scholastica [Johanna] of St. Joseph's Mercy Hospital, Sioux City.[31]

He was a man of sterling worth and unimpeachable character who counted every man his friend. Always a natural leader of men he held many positions of honor and trust, though never a seeker after public acclaim. At the time of his death, he was president of the Lost Nation Savings Bank.

The funeral services were held at St. James' church, Toronto. Requiem High Mass was celebrated by Father McNamara assisted by Father Regan of Oxford Junction and Father Small of Lost Nation and the choir of the Sacred Heart church, Lost Nation. Father Small paid an eloquent tribute to the faith of the deceased—a life-long Catholic in which faith he so calmly and resignedly passed away.

The remains were borne to their last resting place by sight of his life-long neighbors and friends, namely James Connors, Anthony Early, William Burnett, Thomas Early, Edward O'Donnell, Edward Scanlan, M. P. O'Connor and James Hughes.

Those from a distance who attended were, Judge P. Wolfe and daughter Mollie and Mrs. T. D. Fitzgerald and daughter Margaret of Clinton; R. B. Wolfe and family and Mrs. M. Scanlan of DeWitt, Iowa; John B. Wolfe of Melrose, Iowa; Kate Carroll, Kilkenny, Minnesota; Mrs. B. McBride of Hawarden, Iowa; Hugh Buckley, Chicago; O. S. Gilroy and Jennie McLaughlin of Bettendorf, Iowa; and Mr. and Mrs. T. J. Leahy of Fulton, Illinois.

---

[30] John O. C. Wolfe (1873–1959), Honora L. "Nora" Wolfe (1880–1960), James Leonard Wolfe (1881–1937), May R. Wolfe Goodall (b. 1878) and Frank A. Goodall (1879–1963), Dr. Jeremiah "Jerry" Wolfe (1876–1949) [see Appendix IV], Ann Wolfe Ryan (b. 1887) and Isidore S. Ryan (1887–1958), and Walter Ignatius Wolfe (1886–1967)

[31] Patrick Bernard Wolfe (1848–1922), Catherine "Kate" Fitzgerald (1860–1947) and Thomas D. Fitzgerald (1857–1903), Margaret I. Wolfe Langan (1857–btw. 1930 and 1940) and Dr. Daniel Langan (1836–1914), Richard Boyle Wolfe (1862–1940), Maurice Buckley Wolfe (1855–1928), and Sister Scholastica (1849–1926)

APPENDIX VI:
"Born Near Ballybunion" (1927)

Published in the Kerry News *on December 5, 1927, this short article notes the death in America of Richard J. Wolfe (1843–1927) and connects his family to the once-famous racehorse Dimby.*

BORN NEAR BALLYBUNION
NINETY YEARS AGO.
DEATH OF MR. RICHARD WOULFE IN U.S.A.
OLD TIMES RECALLED.
NOTABLE PERFORMANCE OF RACEHORSE
ON KERRY STRAND.

Mr. Richard Woulfe, born near Ballybunion about ninety years ago, died recently near Streator, Illinois, where he was a very large farmer and breeder of horses. He emigrated eighty years ago amongst a colony of his relatives, who prospered on the land in Illinois and Iowa.[32] His father, Richard Woulfe,[33] and his mother, Mary Foley,[34] emigrated at the same time, and settled at La Salle, Illinois. Deceased and his wife, nee Kate Maher, who survives him,[35] celebrated the golden jubilee of their marriage in 1921. The widow was a second and third cousin of her late husband. She is a daughter of Batt Maher, who emigrated from Trieneragh,[36] and on her mother's side she is a grand-daughter of Maurice Woulfe, who emigrated from Knockanasig after he made a lasting reputation as owner of Dimby, a racehorse whose name is still fresh in the traditions of the once famous Ballyeigh racecourse.[37]

Dimby was bred by William the Fourth, King of England. In the possession of Maurice Woulfe, his most notable performance was the winning

---

[32] Wolfe immigrated in the company of his parents and ten siblings in steerage class aboard the *Thomas H. Perkins*, arriving in New York from Liverpool on September 29, 1848.

[33] Richard Wolfe (1795–1871)

[34] Mary Ellen Foley (1802–1861)

[35] Catherine "Kate" Maher (1853–1932)

[36] Bartholomew "Batt" Maher (1830–1904)

[37] Maurice Richard Wolfe (1802–1870)

of a challenge at the then goodly sum of one hundred pounds aside. The match was decided at Ballyeigh in or about 1840. The defeated horse was Roller, owned by a Mr. Gunn, a connection of the Roches of Athea. Dimby became the sire of The Rambler, also owned by Maurice Woulfe, and a good winner in the forties of last century. But it was, perhaps, the best of Dimby's progeny that met a fatal misadventure and died without being tested on a racecourse. It was from the dam of May Morning, Victory, and Tally-Ho, and was bred by "Johnny Connell, of Rathmorrell," whose memory as a sportsman is still affectionately treasured in Kerry and Limerick.

The colony of relatives who emigrated at or about the same time as deceased, included Maurice Woulfe, owner of Dimby. Maurice's descendants are numerous and wealthy in Illinois. There his son, Richard, once kept a high-class stud of Norman horses.[38] They were a French breed of strong, clean and active horses, famous for all round utility. Later the family moved the stud to Texas with ambitious schemes to improve the breed of horses there; but the enterprise ended in failure and loss. The colony of relatives also included Batt Maher and Richard Woulfe, from Trieneragh, and five families of the Woulfe from Tanavalla.[39] They also have numerous and wealthy descendants in Illinois and Iowa, the majority being still farmers, who held to the land, unlike so many more of the Irish, who sold their land to the Germans and crowded into towns. Amongst the best known members of the family was Judge Patrick B. Woulfe, who died at Clinton, Iowa, not very long ago.[40] He had been a member of the Iowa State Senate. He was first cousin of the late Mr. Batt Maher, of Trieneragh; of the late Mr. "Mike" Nolan, of Moyvane, and of the late Mr. Maurice Woulfe, of Kiltean.[41] The Judge's son, Mr. John Woulfe, is a prominent lawyer at Clinton, Iowa.[42] He was elected as a member of the Iowa State Legislature while he was a student of the University of Berlin, Germany. Another of much prominence is Mr. Edmund Maurice Woulfe, native of Clinton County, Iowa, and practising as a lawyer at Boise, Idaho.[43] His nearest relatives in Kerry would

---

[38] Richard Downey Wolfe (1829–1885)

[39] This is likely a shortened version of Garryantanavalla, a townland near the village of Finuge, County Kerry.

[40] Patrick Bernard Wolfe (1848–1922)

[41] Maurice Woulfe (ca. 1823–1909) of Kiltean was the son of James Richard Woulfe (1800–1875), a brother of Maurice Richard Wolfe (1802–1870) and John Richard Wolfe (1809–1883).

[42] John Loyola Wolfe (1879–1862)

[43] Edmund Mills Wolfe (1864–1952

probably include Mr. O'Sullivan, of Trien, Kilmorna; Mrs. Patk. Mangan, of Bedford, Listowel, etc. Mr. Richard Woulfe, of De Witt, is amongst the best known members of the legal profession in the State of Iowa.[44]

Occasionally some American born members of the colony have come to Listowel to look up their parents' old homes, or their relatives; and they have appreciated the guidance of the late Mr. Gerald McElligott, whose memory extended to the days of Dimby.

---

[44] Richard Boyle Wolfe (1862–1940)

APPENDIX VII:
"The New Ireland" (1931)

In this report, published on August 22, 1931, the Limerick Leader *newspaper describes a visit to Ireland by Richard W. Wolfe (1866–1951). A native of Cratloe, County Limerick, Wolfe served as the commissioner of public works for the city of Chicago from 1927 to 1931. See also Appendix X.*

THE NEW IRELAND
IMPRESSIONS OF CHANGES
VIEWS OF EX-COMMISSIONER WOULFE

Our Killmallock correspondent writes:—
Mr. Richard Woulfe, one of the most prominent of the Irish race in America, and late Commissioner of Public Works, Chicago, who has spent an extended holiday in Ireland, while making a short stay at the Dunraven Arms Hotel, Adare, has, accompanied by his wife, called on Dr. and Mrs. Woulfe, Grove House, Bruff;[45] also on Mr. Maurice Woulfe, Manager National Bank, Bruff,[46] and on Father Woulfe, P.P., Cappagh,[47] who introduced him to Very Rev. Canon Begley, P.P., V.F., Kilmallock,[48] and Senator Bennett,[49] at Summerville.

IMPRESSIONS.
In conversation with Dr. and Mrs. Woulfe, and Dr. and Mrs. Clery, Hospital, Mr. Woulfe referred to the remarkable intellectual prowess of Canon Begley and observed that his writings, as well as those of Father Woulfe, are very widely read in America and added that their works are doing much to make known to the outside world the importance of Irish history and civil and ecclesiastical, and Irishmen like them and Senator

---

[45] Dr. Timothy Woulfe (1885–1969) and Mary Malvena Mullaly Woulfe (d. 1974)

[46] Maurice Woulfe (ca. 1881–1949)

[47] Patrick Woulfe (1872–1933) [see Appendix VIII]

[48] John Canon Begley (1861–1941), author of a three-volume history of the Diocese of Limerick published in 1906, 1927, and 1938

[49] Thomas Westropp Bennett (1867–1962), *Cathaoirleach*, or chairman, of the Irish Senate

Bennett are viewed by Mr. Woulfe as bringing Ireland to a point of great stability, politically and industrially compelling England for the first time in her connection with this country to take serious notice of Irish progress. That progress has most happily impressed Mr. Woulfe himself, who was last in Ireland 23 years ago, in 1908. He referred particularly to the now bright and prosperous appearance of rural Ireland.

CESSATION OF BRITISH HOLD.

The cessation of the British hold, he says, has benefited the Irish people in material things, but much more so because that grip has ceased to hamper our manly self-respect, in which connection one of the happiest things he observed was the almost universal temperance of our population.

ENGLISH PROPAGANDA.

Visitors to Ireland, said Mr. Woulfe, could see for themselves the utter falsehood of English propaganda and added that it was the same class who attributed lawlessness to America, and particularly to Chicago, who so discredited this country for which he anticipates so great a future.

In reply to Dr. Woulfe, he explained that in the matter of organised relief of the poor we are ahead of America, which has nothing to correspond exactly with our Medical Charities, County Hospitals, County Homes, Home Assistance and Old Age Pensions.

TIME OF O'CONNELL RECALLED.

The ex-Commissioner learned with pride and interest the details of an incident in the life of his grandfather, Mr. Edmund Richard Woulfe, a well-known personality in West Limerick from the early days of O'Connell to those of the pre-eminence of Butt.[50]

Dr. Woulfe explained the conditions which prevailed in Ireland 90 years ago, three or four decades before the Land Agitation had become an organisation. The franchise was so limited that the great majority of Parliamentary and Poor Law electors were tenant farmers who were unprotected by any security of tenure, and on the other hand the voting was without ballot or secrecy and Parliamentary elections were often decided by one very extensive landlord, who frequently drove his tenantry like cattle to the station where they were left with practically no option but to vote for their landlord or the candidate of his party. In Poor Law elections where the area

---

[50] Edmond R. Woulfe (1788–1876); Isaac Butt (1813–1879), a member of Parliament from 1871 to 1879 and, like Daniel O'Connell, a proponent of Home Rule for Ireland

was comparatively small nobody outside of the landlord and his nominee could dare to seek election. Under those circumstances the "Castle" at Newcastle West was as autocratic as its namesake at Dublin. It was the headquarters of the vast estate of the Earl of Devon, whose agent, as a matter of course, was annually elected unopposed to represent Monegay on the local Board of Guardians. However, in 1842 the grandfather of ex-Commissioner Woulfe went forward as a candidate in opposition to the estate agent, and all who have any idea of the conditions of the time will understand the magnitude of that venture and the task that he accomplished in being about the first farmer in Ireland to defeat, which he did, his landlord's nominee, for a seat on a public board.

Mr. Woulfe has just left Ireland for Germany and will shortly return to America to resume the duties of his present offices. He is Secretary to the Commission dealing with the gigantic proposal to make the Mississippi and other rivers navigable the entire way from the Gulf of Mexico to Lake Michigan.

APPENDIX VIII:
Father Patrick Woulfe Obituary (1933)

In this obituary, published on May 13, 1933, in the Kerryman *newspaper, the life of Father Patrick Woulfe (1872–1933) is remembered.*

LATE REV. P. WOLFE.
REGRET IN KILMALLOCK AT CAPPA P.P.'S DEATH.

The death of Rev. P. Woulfe, P.P., Cappa, evoked deep regret in Kilmallock. As a mark of respect to his memory houses were shuttered and a number of residents attended the obsequies.

Father Woulfe ministered for 22 years in Kilmallock parish. He was an exemplary priest who took the greatest interest in the spiritual welfare of the faithful, which he exercised with the utmost diligence and when ever he found one remiss in attention to religious duties he brought him along by gentle persuasion and inspired a spirit of devotion in him. Father Woulfe was also very solicitous for the temporal well-being of the people, and his advice was always available and willingly given. He encouraged the co-operative movement in the district and was associated with the local show. He supported the candidature of Mr. T. W. W. Bennett, now Chairman of the Senate, in the Parliamentary election for Co. Limerick about 1900;[51] but perhaps what appealed to him most was the movement to revive the Irish language. He was very active in connection with the progress of the Gaelic League, gave a number of lectures, displaying much research, and in other ways did much to inculcate in the people a love for the native tongue. Following the insurrection of 1916 he was one of the committee who organised the Dependents' Fund in the parish, and afterwards, when the menace of conscription had been defeated[52] he supported the proposal—which was adopted—that the money collected for that purpose, and no longer required—about £400—be sent to Dail Eireann.[53]

---

[51] Thomas William Westropp Bennett (1867–1962)

[52] An April 1918 policy to conscript Irishmen into the British army to fight in France during World War I was fiercely opposed by Irish nationalists, Catholic clergy, and labor unions and never enforced.

[53] Dáil Éireann was established in 1919 as a single-chamber parliament for the Irish Republic; the 1922 Anglo-Irish Treaty made it the lower chamber of a bicameral legislature.

On the 28th May, 1920, Father Woulfe administered to Liam Scully, who was fatally wounded in the attack on Kilmallock barrack.[54] He afterwards had to celebrate Mass in the workhouse and to get there had to pass the barrack, which was an ordeal few would care to undertake, having regard to the temper of the police, but Fr. Woulfe did not hesitate; he went and discharged his sacred duty. That evening, possibly coming from a sick call at the workhouse, he passed a lorry of police at the cross at the hotel; as he did so, one of their number descended, joined Fr. Woulfe proceeded down the street with him for some distance, and then returned to the lorry. It was believed the action of the constable—who it appears was a stranger—was due to something he heard taking place among the other occupants, which impelled him to accompany Fr. Woulfe to safety. There was no doubt that from then to the Truce was a very anxious time for Fr. Woulfe, who had to be abroad day or night, as duty called. The Crown forces were regarded as having anything but a friendly feeling for him and many people entertained a sense of apprehension as to what might be the outcome. There was reason to know that Fr. Woulfe was not unaware of this, but he never wavered in attending to his duties.

Possibly the largest meeting ever held in Kilmallock—a Feis which was attended by Thomas Ashe and Count Plunkett—was presided over by Father Woulfe.[55]

Father Woulfe was author of such well known works as "Irish Names and Surnames," and "Irish Names for Children."—"Cork Examiner."

---

[54] The attack by members of the Irish Republican Army on the barracks of the Royal Irish Constabulary killed several policemen

[55] The *feis*, or festival, was held on June 18, 1914. Thomas Ashe (1885–1917) was a founding member of the Irish Volunteers, a nationalist paramilitary organization. Count George Noble Plunkett (1851–1948) was an Irish nationalist whose son Joseph was executed after the Easter Rising of 1916.

APPENDIX IX:
"Last of the Limerick Hedge Schools" (1935)

In this article, which appeared in the Limerick Leader *newspaper on April 27, 1935, "J. D. H." writes about a "hedge school" located in an outbuilding at the Glen, a farm near Athea, County Limerick, owned by Richard Edmond "Dicky Ned" Woulfe (1825–1910). Such schools dated back to the prohibition on Catholic schools, which lasted from 1723 to 1782, and many survived even into the national-school era. "J. D. H." was the journalist J. D. Harnett. For more on the school, see Appendix X. For more on Woulfe, see Appendix III.*

LAST OF THE LIMERICK HEDGE SCHOOLS
THE ACADEMY IN THE GLEN
QUAINT SYSTEM OF TIMEKEEPING

(By J. D. H.)

In an interesting description of the times in which he lived, William Carleton, the novelist, found a place for his youthful experiences of an Irish Hedge School, and over a more extensive area, Mr. P. J. Dowling, has, in recent times, collected much that might be written on the subject in his "Hedge Schools of Ireland." There were still, however, some places off the beaten track, like South-West Limerick, where the last of the southern hedge masters brought their honourable labours close to our modern times.

It may be in the nature of coincidence, but the lot of the last of West Limerick's hedge masters was cast amongst the descendants of that Richard Woulfe, of Corbally, Limerick, whose lands were forfeited after the 1641 Rebellion.[56]

While time and opportunity offer, and living witnesses survive to attest the fact, it may be helpful to recall a period, not so many years back, which marks the severance of the last link which brought the Irish Hedge School along from the dark days of the confiscation to the hills of West Limerick, on the Kerry border, and to the doors of the National Schools which severed it.[57]

---

[56] See Jane C. "Dollie" Woulfe's letter in Appendix XIII.

[57] The British government established the National School system in Ireland in 1831.

He was an old man when I first saw him, and it was with rather unquiet feelings that curiosity prompted me, while visiting some relatives, who lived halfway between Abbeyfeale and Athea, that I made the acquaintance of Master Michael Sheahan,[58] at what came to be ironically known amongst his pupils as "Sheahan's Academy." Although the National School had penetrated the surrounding districts for many years previously, the Academy was still struggling on, but was seriously on the wane when I dropped in there one day amongst its mixed attendance.

No Longer Held in the Open.

The classes were no longer held in the open under hedges, or in secluded valleys, and the fear had long before departed, when an informer might have easily changed the head of the master for a five pound note. However uncomfortable it might have been for the master, or his pupils, it was a vast improvement on the cross-roads, or the bleak mountain side, to find a thatched roof over their heads. The rough stones of the walls might be unsightly in the old out-house which was placed at their service by the late Mr. Richard E. Woulfe, the father of a very distinguished Commissioner of Public Works in one of America's largest cities,[59] but its situation was ideally chosen amidst picturesque old world surroundings. The donor, who has long since past away, was a sound Gaelic scholar, a man of rare intellectual gifts, whose memory was stored with a fund of interesting traditions which some well-known Irish historians found helpful in their researches.[60]

I have forgotten many faces since that winter morning long ago, when I set out for that famous Academy at "The Glen," Cratloe, but I can distinctly recall the kindly face of the old master.

He was of medium height, with a placid face, clean shaven, except for a little grey stubbed beard at the sides. He spoke without affectation, and with an assured command of language, in a voice generally low. Sometimes it was raised, but in the heat of argument, such as when I once afterwards heard him maintaining some thesis of his against an enlightened past pupil. As a master he never seemed to look for any more deference because of his position than that which one of the more well to do farmers, amongst whom he spent his life, might naturally be entitled to expect. Prior to his advent to the Glen, he took over temporarily the charge of an earlier Hedge School, which had been held, time out of mind, at a place called Harnett's Cross,

---

[58] Michael Sheahan (ca. 1832–1902)

[59] Richard White Wolfe (1866–1951) [see appendices VII and X]

[60] The Irish-language scholar Father Patrick Woulfe (1872–1933), in particular, credited Richard E. "Dicky Ned" Woulfe for his help.

now Healy's Forge, at Knockbrack, about two miles from Abbeyfeale. This school appears to have been conducted by another popular teacher, Master Foley, until his death, probably about the middle fifties of the last century. There was also a master Denny Wrenn teaching elsewhere at that time in an adjoining parish.

SAINT AND SCHOLAR.

From about 1860 to 1880, Michael Sheahan taught on an average 80 or 90 pupils. When burdened by approaching old age and debility, his attendance of scholars had fallen to five, in the year 1900. He apparently made no provision for the rain day (if he had ever been enabled to do so), and with a pension, consisting only of "the slings and arrows of outrageous fortune," he went into the workhouse at Newcastle West, where he died on the 5th of May, 1902—no doubt, another saint and scholar of the old country. Those who knew him would never have permitted his last days to be spent at the expense of the rates, but in his private affairs his innate principles permitted no sympathetic interference.

Amongst the better off farmers he was treated as a respected member of the family, and at stated times voluntary contributions of very small dimensions were accepted to meet the master's pressing needs; modest, but hardly remunerative. In return he taught their children entrusted to him, and according to a Mrs. John O'Connor, of Cratloe, a past pupil who still survives at the age of 98, he trained them well.

There were no maps on the rough walls of this humble school, and barely the furniture required to carry on without headaches. Interstices in the walls marked where mischievous pupils dug the mortar away to make pigeon holes for their inks and pencils. The seats consisted of plain or wooden planks, and the slates, which were worked for mathematics, on the scholars' knees, belonged to the common family of the roof tree variety. These had been laboriously polished, with a kind of sandstone, to a writing surface, at the Glen stream, which flowed beneath a one arch bridge, and sang through its pretty course, cheered by the rustling trees that overhung it. There also it lent its services to lick into shape the pencils in use in the school, supplied in rough form from its gravelled bed.

THE NEIGHBOURING CLOCK.

The school boasted no clock, but in a farm dwelling thirty yards away there was one, by which master and pupil alike might measure the flight of Omar's "Hunter of the East." The striking of the hours of this old friend brought more joy to the trained ears of some of those pupils than did the melody of Cathedral chimes in distant cities in after years. It is still associated with pleasant memories by the few who survive, because of its joyous signals of release when the days were warm and long, and the flower laden fields outside were teeming with the gaiety of summer.

In winter, when the days were short and sharp, and the clock was a tardy monitor, the limit of the school's hours was determined by the life of the sods of turf, which the attendants brought with them in the morning under their arms. There, in the big open hearth, at the end of the old house, they were piled to make the interior inhabitable, and send the blue and scented smoke through a "sauganed" opening above, and out among the centuries old trees that lined the slopes of the Glen. The old man's blood was no longer hot, and when the fire itself turned cold towards the winter evening, it was usually a suggestion for dispersing the classes. The crisis was often precipitated by an unscrupulous pupil, whose communal duty it was, if sitting next to the fire, to hasten the departure of any lingering coals on the hearth by burying them beneath the ashes of their deceased companions, whenever the old man turned his back.

A Cry That Brought Mercy.

He had not the reputation of a harsh master, but there are times in a school-boy's life when he must be punished in some form (an axiom admitted by ex-pupils, who are assured that the school door was closed definitely behind themselves). Whenever occasion arose for any severe punishment the preparatory cry of the victim would ring loud and long enough in the school to bring Mrs. Woulfe[61] hastening over the intervening yard from her kitchen, some yards off, scattering the farmyard fowl in her eagerness to make her appeal for mercy timely and effective.

As the days grew older, the ripened scholars divined that the master allowed the music of the condemned scholar to rise high enough, and suspended punishment long enough, through his homilies, to make certain that Mrs. Woulfe would be in full time to curtail the impending penalty.

His old pupils always took pride in repeating that Master Sheahan's boys always carried off the honours for Catechism before the Bishop on parish holidays, because of the assistance they derived from their knowledge of Latin, which their old tutor imparted to them. They also realised the idea that his equipment was a cause for surprise, and even a little jealousy too, amongst the more important national teachers, against whose excellent training they competed towards the end of the Academy's days. In justice, however, it must be added, that their training must have been of a very high order to enable them to compete successfully with the late Master Martin

---

[61] Catherine White Woulfe (1828–1900) [see Appendix X]

O'Sullivan, N.T.,[62] who was one of the most intellectual members of the profession then in West Limerick.

Sheahan was also an expert in handwriting, and had his head lines charged with usual moral lessons, which left quotations floating through every day life in the district for a subsequent generation.

The Master and a Past Pupil.

It was customary for a past pupil, particularly if a matrimonial candidate for Shrove, to visit, with a free and easy assurance, his old alma mater, to have another go at his calligraphy for practice sake. This, usually on a day unfit for plough or scythe. One day the son of an old patron called the way, and sitting down amongst the students set about copying the current head line of the school. On this occasion Master Sheahan addressed a question to the visitor, while he was engaged, as much with the movements of his mouth as with the quill pen he was driving at some word or other, and was so intent on the process that he adjourned his answer until he had placed the customary flourish to the end of his labour. Irritated at the delay, the master charged him with ill-manners. The important student retorted by reversing the accusation, because he was disturbed, he said, with a question while struggling with a long word when the inspiration to execute it correctly lasted. The master reminded him that he had lost that respect for his elders, which he had tried to impress on him formerly, and the ex-pupil pleaded the deformity of his art that might have been risked by the courtesy of suspending his operation. And so to the delight of the scholars the interchange went on above their heads for almost half an hour, ending in an exchange of apologies.

The old man never forgot to devote one hour each day to religious instruction, which included the recital of the Rosary.

Only the Old-Time Setting Remains.

The Glen, with its old time setting, is still as charming as of old. The old school teacher—last of his patriotic profession—is gone, and left to his later pupils the distinction of having graduated in the last of Limerick's Hedge Schools. Gone, too, is the kindly donor of the school. The centuries old trees, which sheltered the old school from the winter blast, and the summer heat, have strewn their leaves full forty times over the paths the old teacher and his pupils trod. And still the little stream turns on below. It still runs on to join the Oulagh farther down the valley. Past the old culm and

---

[62] N.T. stands for National School teacher.

coal pits, which mark an industrial enterprise of a former landlord[63] but not his perseverance. That innocent little stream did not always flow so gently though. Once upon a time a certain widow, who still survives in a happy home at Keale, had cause to remember its mood when it was angry some sixty years ago. One evening, hurrying home from the school in the Glen, she attempted to cross the stream at Reacock, which was in flood, and was carried a hundred yards along its course before being rescued, more dead than alive by the same man who had given the school to her master.[64]

BORN IN PARISH OF ATHEA.

Master Michael Sheahan, I learned, was born in Knocknagorna, in the parish of Athea, and sprang from a respectable family of the farming class, one of whom, a young doctor, graduated with some distinction. Had he been at his kinsman's school he would not have been the only member of the profession indebted to him for his rule of three.

The future master himself spent his early years in Causeway, Co. Kerry, from which his mother, of the Lyons family, came. He had been intended for the priesthood, but some trivial indiscretion, while at college, together with the intervention of the "bad times," sent him adrift on the world to fend for himself, like many another genius of his time.[65]

---

[63] The Goold family owned the land from 1817 until 1906 [see Appendix II].

[64] The same story appears in *Share the Profits! The Story of Richard W. Wolfe and His Conclusions* (1939) by William H. Stuart [see Appendix X].

[65] Sheahan died of bronchitis on May 5, 1902, at the Newcastle West Workhouse.

APPENDIX X:
"The Home Land" (1939)

"The Home Land" is chapter 1 of Share the Profits! The Story of Richard W. Wolfe and His Conclusions, *by William H. Stuart and published in 1939. Ostensibly a biography of Wolfe (1866–1951), who served as commissioner of public works in Chicago from 1927 to 1931, the book was likely co-written by Wolfe and does not consider any of the various controversies of his term in office. Instead, it serves as an opportunity to mythologize his native Ireland and pronounce on the "manipulation of money" by "international bankers." See also Appendix VII.*

RICHARD W. WOLFE WAS born on a farm in the Townland of Cratloe, four miles from Athea, County Limerick, Ireland, on August 21, 1869. His family have lived on that farm, at first as tenants and later as owners, for 150 years. The place is known as "The Glen."

Richard and many others of his kin who came to this country never have been far away in the thought from the historic countryside of the home land. The past always lives with the Irish, active though they may be in the present.

Dollie Wolfe, born in Glasgow, now owns and lives in "The Glen." She is the niece of the subject of this biography.[66] A recent letter from her, written to her Chicago uncle, showed that in heart and appearance the old neighborhood was much the same. She wrote of a recently issued book telling the history of the countryside, including, of course, much about the Wolfe family, always outstanding. It told of the kindness of her great grandfather, Richard Wolfe's grandfather, who was known as "Ned of The Glen"[67]—how he had befriended a poor woman and her three children as they were on the way to the poorhouse—how he had lifted the whole family up beside him on his horse and ridden with them to the Board of Guardians of Newcastle West, of which he was a member. He saved them from the almshouse. Memories are long over there, in recalling good deeds, or in holding resentment against injuries inflicted.

---

[66] Jane C. "Dollie" Woulfe (1879–1964) was the daughter of Maurice Richard Woulfe (185e–1928), an older brother of Richard W. Wolfe [see Appendix VII].

[67] Edmond Richard "Old Ned" Woulfe (1788–1876)

Dollie Wolfe wrote also of witnessing the northern lights and of the superstitions connected with the brilliant beams rising up out of the Arctic vastness. She told too of seeing, from the top of the cutting near James Paddy's place,[68] strange lights at night coming across the fields, sometimes with incredible speed, and always AGAINST the wind. Dick's niece may have trembled as much as the other onlookers but bravely she wrote to the Chicago folks:

"It is just marsh gas, jack-o'-lantern, will-o'-the-wisp, or 'Friar Rush.'"

"Some people are very afraid of it, but fortunately the Woulfes generally are not superstitious."

Oh, not a bit superstitious!

And the niece then proceeds in her letter to ask:

"Did you know that Spirit na Barbagh was a real woman?"

"She was one Margaret O'Shanessy, hanged at Reens Pike in 1801 for the murder of a child.

"Many the honest man went up Gowndraugh top speed years after she was in dust on account of her. I expect their wives were thankful and didn't let the yarn die."

The Gael back in his home land has not changed much. He still sees strange shapes in the mist, fairy lights in the gloaming; and every glen and brook is brimful of sentiment. Throughout all the land, the legends of the past are held in memory and not challenged, not even the tales of the prodigious feats of vehement, valorous Cuchulain of early medieval times about whom the snow melted when his anger rose to the boiling point.

Thirty miles from Athea is the City of Limerick—"City of the Violated Treaty"—fine old city through which the River Shannon runs on its way to the sea.

Dick Wolfe's family goes back to four brothers whose names are indelibly written into the history of battles against the English to save Limerick. In that period the Wolfes, or Woulfes, owned extensive lands in the richest section of the county, known as "The Golden Vale." The Cromwell invasion changed radically and tragically the fortunes of the family. Of the four Wolfe brothers, who fought at Limerick, two were executed, one escaped to England, and the fourth fled into the Irish hills, there, in the less desirable part of the county, to establish a new home. The line of "The Glen" comes directly from this fourth brother.

Dollie Wolfe, writing to her uncle, tells in inimitable style:

"We don't belong here, really—on the spur of the Mullaghareirk Mountains, not we.

---

[68] James Patrick "Paddy" Woulfe (1842–1922).

"We were rich and powerful once, to the east, entirely of Limerick, in the good land, not in the hills as now.

"So rich and proud were we, we took a crack at 'the Great Queen' (Elizabeth) and, faith, she cracked back. Signs on, there was more to her powers and venom than ours. She blasted us clean out of Corbally, and scattered us here and there over the plain of Limerick—a few of us without heads, to be talking about mistake.

"Well, we got together again after a while, being careful and prudent in everything but politics. Along comes Cromwell and again we stuck our heads in, through the wrong door of course, and, by herrings, there was a job made of us this time. Some he hanged on the Walls on the Limerick. Some got away to England—I remember one of us saved the life of a big fellow there, Walpole was his name.

"The cripples and the ones who couldn't get away took every short cut to here—and here we stayed. Not but what we have done well in a way. There are millionaires of our name in America, and judges and doctors and professors, but we don't fight any more, and we don't know the glory of being murdered for a lost cause."

Dick Wolfe's father, Richard Edmund Wolfe,[69] was strict and stern but of great humanity. He was loved by the countryside because of his good heart and his wise leadership, and, when he rescued a little girl from drowning, his popularity grew.

Richard Edmund Wolfe's farm was one of the largest. He owned at one time fifteen cows, a herd of goats, sheep, pigs, two draft horses, geese, turnkeys, chickens and two donkeys. On an extensive acreage he raised oats, rye, flax, and potatoes. Of course, near the house was a vegetable garden, and all about the house flowers. Always the Irish, rich or poor, loved flowers—cultivated them in profusion.

The father was civic-minded. He gave to the children of the community a building for a school and the land upon which it stood. It was far from a modern structure, but a long way ahead of the former hedge-fence school.[70]

Catherine Wolfe, the mother, was born in the Townland of Coole, parish of Athea.[71] Her maiden name was White—of an old, widely known and respected family. Born to her were ten children, all of whom grew to maturity. She was noted for her comely appearance, gentle, religious ways, and her success in maintaining her home and family up to the best traditions of Irish life.

---

[69] Richard Edmond "Dicky Ned" Woulfe (1824–1910)

[70] See Appendix IX.

[71] Catherine White Woulfe (1828–1900)

Dick's mother worked hard, and put joy into her work, and color into everything about her. She spun the wool from her own sheep and made the children's caps, stockings, and sweaters, and into the clothes and blankets went the colors of the flowers of her garden.

She was inclined to believe that in her youth she had seen fairies, and innumerable were the tales she told the children—fascinating stories about ghosts, devils, witches, banshees, fairy thorns, devil cats, elves, bewitched butter, horned women, blood-thirsty giants, and weird and startling enchantments. How much of it all she really believed Dick never knew, but this he does know, as did all the countryside—that she was a deeply religious woman whose trust in God was implicit.

From his seventh to twelfth year Richard went to the school his father had given the community. There he and the other children learned the three R's, the Catechism, and prayers from Mr. Wren and Mr. Sheahan.[72] When he had absorbed the rudimentary wisdom of the country school, he went to the Ballagh Townland school, later to the Athea school, National Government institution. At both schools there was a woman teacher always for the girls, and at Ballagh a Mr. McAuliff was head master for the boys, a Mr. Sullivan serving in like capacity at Athea.[73] The boys and girls were kept separate.

Young Richard's education was not confined to school courses. Much he secured at home from his father's library—particularly from the writings of Henry Grattan, John Stuart Mill, Oliver Goldsmith, and Shakespeare The "Sesame and Lilies" of Ruskin and Edmund Burke's essays on the sublime and the beautiful were boyhood treasures destined for life-long companionship.

But in school-time and in vacation periods always there was work for the youth on the farm. The cows were his particular charge, and so great a herd—great for those days—created an important obligation. Dick was assigned to watch the cattle as they grazed and roamed through the low hills. As he tended herd, he looked at the clouds sailing toward the sea, and he dreamed of the land of promised freedom and wealth far away in the western world. On the hills he found time to read a bit, and he searched for flowers and hazel nuts, and explored the mysteries of life beneath the slippery stones of the brook—always searching, exploring, thinking.

The distant, mist-covered, green Kerry Mountains intrigued and coaxed him. Beyond them was the ocean which carried ships to the wonder land, the United States of America, where men could own land, say what they

---

[72] Denny Wren (or Wrenn) and Michael Sheahan

[73] This likely was the national school teacher Martin O'Sullivan [see Appendix IX].

pleased, and worship as their hearts dictated. It was his belief that some day he would go there. What a country that must be! He and other Irish lads had been told that the first man actually to step upon New World soil was an Irish sailor whom Columbus recruited in Galway. He had been told too that two brothers from his own Limerick—Michael and Nicholas MacDonald—were the first white men to explore upper New York.

The tide to America was running as strong as ever. During the "unendurable fifties," 914,000 person had emigrated from Ireland to America, and the movement showed no sign of abatement in young Wolfe's time. Everywhere were the placards and folders of the steamship companies proclaiming the glories of the land of opportunity.

But young Richard could not hope to go until he had finished his schooling, if then. There were years of preparation ahead, and much for him to do on the farm.

The boy used the brain back of his eyes and sought the meaning of things. The brook in which he waded so often had in it a horse-shoe curve in a corner of the pasture. Young Dick reflected. Why should there be that detour, lost motion, delay, in the flow to the sea? He brought a spade next day and laboriously dug out a channel making a straight line that eliminated and made unnecessary the laggard curve. Dick had straightened his first water course. He got more of a thrill in that than he did in his great achievement, straightening the Chicago River, years after.

Close to the soil the boy lived as did all those around him. Together they fought against all the hazards of nature—storm, drought, late frost, blight, and all the diseases that plant and animal are heir to. It was a rough, never-ending battle to win a living out of the earth, but a wholesome one, with feet always on the ground. However, many were the pleasures these soil people found. There were social gatherings with music. Gaelic flutes, concertina, and violin brought smiles and laughter and quickened the feet of youth never too tired to dance. Strict was the surveillance over the boys and girls, but love found trysting places, and from marriage vows came new ties, new paths between homes, to bind the community closer together.

Great was the joy in the harvesting of the crops—the pleasure that comes out of achievement. The swish of the scythes, swung by a lines of men and boys advancing into waving acres of grain, was a music that thrilled.

The boys dug and sacked potatoes, and raked the hay. The girls churned butter, weeded the garden, and helped in the house-work. They took the butter and eggs to Athea to trade for flour and sugar. Dick and his father went to the bog a mile away, cut out the peat, loaded it on a donkey cart, and brought it home to be stacked and dried behind the house.

Richard Wolfe never forgot those scenes. Fifty years afterwards in Chicago he wrote for the New World the poem, "We Cling to Thee Erin." In part it follows:

> "Oh, Erin, acushla, tho' I ne'er see thee again,
> I roam in my dreams by they streams and thy glen,
> Sadly sweet are the moments tinged with delight,
> Away from the throng in the silence of night,
> When on fancy's wing backwards swiftly I fly
> To the land of my youth where folks laugh while they cry,
> Where smiles through the darkness of sorrow doth gleam,
> Where the sun through the mists shoots its radiant beam.
> 'Twas the song of the maiden, the smile of the lad,
> The warble of birds that made the place glad;
> 'Twas the lark in the sky, the thrush in the glade,
> Not the whistle or noise or bustle of trade;
> 'Twas the swish of the mowers in the meadow 'beyant'
> And the flash of the scythes as they swung them aslant—
> A memory as sweet as the scent of the hay,
> As soothing and soft as the troubadour's lay."

The blight of alien landlordism could not take all the joy out of Ireland. Although there was poverty all around Richard Wolfe declares that he never saw poverty as pitiful as he witnessed in the period of depression, right here in Chicago, when, before the dole came, men in instances were forced to go to garbage heaps in search of food.[74]

It was the time of the Land Wars. Long before the yoke of England had been pressed down. What the Irish had done in enlightening the world in medieval times we have told in the preface. The softening, refining influence of Gaelic education had worked a miracle in Europe, but at heavy expense to Ireland. It was still a world of force, and the priests, professors, philosophers, and bards of Eire had not built up home defenses sufficient to stand against the hosts of war which swept down upon Ireland from England, the land the Gael had led out of darkness. Moral influence may count upon ultimate victory, despite many defeats, but that lessens but little the

---

[74] The population of County Limerick in 1841, a few years before the Great Famine, was 330,029. By 1911 that number had dropped to 143,069, due in large part to starvation, emigration, and general poverty. "The long held view," according to the historian Gerard Curtin, "was 'that Limerick escaped the worst rigours of the famine.' Nothing could be further from the truth." "No pen has recorded the numbers of forlorn and starving who perished by the wayside or in the ditches," an Irish census worker wrote in 1851; "whole families lay down and died."

suffering when the power of might crushes down upon a land. Might had triumphed over right as it does so often that Napoleon came to the belief that heaven is on the side of the heavier guns. The world is not yet safe for philosophers, and there are not so many protected groves for those who would court the muses.

The English had overrun Ireland, created huge bonfires out of tomes of precious Irish literature, and made once dominant Eire a political chattel of England.

The English landlords—hereditary holders of huge estates—were oppressing Ireland in the time of young Dick Wolfe, as they had for centuries before.[75] They rented patches of their acreage to the soil people. The tenant farmers knew that, even if by a life of toil and sacrifice they could save up enough to buy the land they worked, they would not be permitted to acquire title to their farms. So they worked as tenants, with little or no hope ever of being anything but tenants. The English landlords, most of them of royal titles, demanded the last farthing. They kept spies in Ireland of the type of the shoneen, servitors of the absentee landlords. These spies watched the renters. If one showed evidence of prosperity, even as much as the purchase of new clothes or the installation of a new chimney, that fact was at once reported. Invariably the rent was then raised.[76]

Game-keepers watched over the land and there was medieval punishment for all who poached or otherwise violated the hunting and trapping laws and rules, but the tenant farmers had no appeal or redress when English hunting parties rode over their lands and ruined the crops the tenants had planted.

Evictions were of almost everyday occurrence, and, to make certain the evicted did not creep back into their former homes for shelter, crowbar brigades came from London and burned and razed the cottages. The evicted had no place to go.

Young Dick saw such fires. At first he and his brothers thought they were "fairy fires" but his parents told them the truth. Men who had never been harmed were burning down houses occupied by poor people. "Why?" asked Richard. He asked that question less often through the years for with maturity came the realization that in many other ways "man is a wolf to man."

---

[75] The family that owned the estate on which Wolfe was raised, the Goolds, were Irish Protestants from Cork [see Appendix II].

[76] In Appendix II, Edmond Woulfe White tells a very different story, insisting that the Goold family negotiated with tenant representatives when rents became difficult to pay, with the adjusted rate remaining "practically undisturbed" for at least six decades.

Later the boy learned of an affair that made a deep impression upon him. Captain Charles Cunningham Boycott, agent for the Mayo estates of the Earl of Erne, by continued cruelties had created bitter resentment. For him a day of reckoning came. No man would work for him. No one spoke to him. His servants fled, and his mail was intercepted. His crops were fired, his fences demolished, and he had difficulty in getting food supplies.

Finally it took 900 English soldiers to protect the Ulster Orangemen who were imported from the north of Ireland to care for the Boycott land and crops.

"Boycott."—the subject of this biography heard that word often afterwards in America.

Came a parish drama in which Dick's father was the hero. It centered about a sad scene, typical of many in those days. Nearby "The Glen" in a shack lived a man, his wife, his children, and his cow. The crops had failed; the rent was long overdue; the landlord's agent came to take the cow away. He put a rope around the cow's neck and led her down the road. Behind walked the wife, the oldest boy and lastly the youngest child, howling. It was a mournful procession. As it proceeded other farmers and their wives and children swung into line, following in single file. Dick saw the parade of poverty. He summoned his father.

"I'll not be allowing that," said Richard Edmund Wolfe. He hastened to the side of the landlord's agent and after a little dickering paid the rent that was due. The cow was saved.

The procession turned back in the road, now a parade of joy. The man and his wife could hardly believe their good fortune. The children gleefully patted the cow. Saved for them was their nourishment.

Richard was growing up. He understood many things now. His father realized that, so one day he took his son with him to the railroad station of a near-by town. An excited, earnest crowd had gathered about the depot. Soon a train pulled in. The crowd, mostly farmers, pressed about the last car. There was no cheering, no brass band. Everyone was tense.

A tall, bearded man came out on the platform and began to speak. What a speech! Dick remembers it to this day. He listened to campaign slogans never heard before in those parts, but later to be written on banners and unfurled throughout Ireland. Among the words indelibly impressing themselves on the mind of the youth were:

"Irish Unity—Home Rule—the Manchester Martyrs—Abolition of the Gat—and the three F's: Fair Rent, Fixed Hold, and Free Sale."

Charles Stewart Parnell had spoken. The train pulled out. Young Dick stood in silence and bewilderment for some minutes. He wondered if ever he could make such a speech, phrase such stirring words. He began to think about "the money Kings of England." He began to think about the power of money—and who controlled it—and why what meant so much to all was in the hands of the few.

That was a revealing day for Richard Wolfe. It opened for him a new line of thought, one that led far from fields of grain, but always came back to where it started, the land.

He paid more attention thereafter when at night neighbors gathered in the Wolfe home to talk on all sorts of subjects. Those were wholesome gatherings, home meetings of neighbors exchanging ideas. Such gatherings were usual too in America when the country was young, and it is not good that there are less of them today.

Nor did all the talk in and about the chimney corner concern affairs of the present. There were tales of ancient Ireland, and of the supremacy of the Gael in medieval times. The stories that the boy liked best of all were those told by his father.

Father James Cregan, parish priest and good friend, called Richard Edmund Wolfe, "the book of Athea," for Dick's father knew all about the immediate community and he knew Irish history through the long centuries as few other men did.

The father, "The Book," quoted pages of authentic record when he told of his ancestors—all the Wolfes or Woulfes who had gone before.

There was Nic Wolfe who in 1345 was guardian of the peace for the County of Limerick and Maurice Wolfe who in the fourteenth century was Canon of Emly. Thrilling was the story of Philip Wolfe, an officer in Sarsfield's Munster regiment who fought so gallantly against William of Orange in defence of "The City of the Violated Treaty."

Yet more stirring was the life of David Wolfe, born in Limerick, a member of the Jesuit Order. Trained by Loyola himself he became rector of the College at Modena. In him though was the blood of the soldier, as well as the heart of the spiritual adviser. He invited danger. In 1560 he came back to Ireland with St. Francis Borgia, carrying the Pope's authority of apostolic legate. Times were indeed dangerous, for Elizabeth was on the throne in England and persecution was general. Father Wolfe's task was to maintain discipline, safeguard Catholic worship, and keep open the line of communication with dignitaries of his church abroad. How boldly and well he carried out his mission is evidenced by the fact that he incurred the displeasure of Queen Elizabeth. The English queen, because of him, refused to send representatives to the Council of Trent complaining in a letter to the Pope that "Woulfe had been sent from Rome to excite disaffection against the Crown." Father Wolfe became a hunted man. For six years he eluded his pursuers, being the hero of many sensational episodes, but finally he was arrested and lodged in Dublin Castle. He made a dramatic escape and took refuge in Spain. Within a year, however, the fearless priest was back in Ireland. Again he was heard of in Spain, with the English no doubt in hot pursuit. Mystery shrouded the end of the life of this heroic priest of the Wolfe line. One risked life for the faith in those days.

"The Book" too told of his ancestors who forfeited near Rathkeal in 1586 for their part in the Desmond rebellion. Yet with greater fervor he recited the story of Captain George Wolfe who assisted his Brother Francis, Superior of the Dominicans, in the endeavor to hold Limerick "for faith and country against both Cromwell and parliament." They were charged with conducting a rebellion of their own. After Limerick surrendered they were listed with twenty-four who were specifically exempted from quarter. Francis was put to death, probably after tortures.

The siege of Limerick immortalized another Wolfe—James—Superior of the Dominicans. A plague had fallen upon the city. James was safe outside the walls but when he learned that all the clergy within had died, he entered the town to minister to the plague-stricken patients in the pesthouse. The Cromwellians discovered him and he was hanged without ceremony. Not so long ago, in Richard Wolfe's lifetime, the cause of his heroic ancestor, James of the Dominicans, was presented to Rome for canonization.

Captain George Wolfe succeeded in escaping to England. His grandson was General Edward Wolfe who, commanding troops in London mobilized against rioters, saved the life of Walpole. For that act he was offered a peerage—but the proud Gael refused it.

The same Captain George Wolfe was the great-great-grand-father of General James Wolfe, the hero of Quebec. The soldiers who under his leadership triumphed for England against Montcalm on the Plains of Abraham were mostly Irish and Catholic.

But impressing Richard Wolfe as much as any story he heard in his boyhood was the fairy tale concerning "the geasa." A youth there who, because of his stepmother's cruelty, was launched upon a career of amazing, weird adventures. He began by fighting with the three giants, Slat Mor, Slat Marr, and Slat Beag Beag. As it should be in a fairy tale, the boy killed all three—then he killed the cailliach, the old hag whose magic could restore them to life. However, just before dying, the cailliach put the lad under geasa. Now that was something mighty grave, as the narrators would explain as the children crowded closer.

Geasa was an unshirkable obligation to do a certain thing, or refrain from a certain action. There was no escape from the obligation. It just had to be fulfilled.

The brave youth fulfilled the geasa the old hag had put upon him: He buried the Bull of the Iron Horn, but not before that creature had put him under another geasa—to fight the Black Goat of the Hill of Fire. The gallant lad did that, too, and triumphed, but, as the Black Goat was passing out, he put upon the boy a geasa to tie up the Jester of the Prince of Darkness. That also the youth did, only to have another geasa put upon him. There seemed to be no end to this geasa business. But there is no limit to valor and endurance as presented in fairy tales.

The lad, with stout heart, proceeded to fulfill the new obligation—to destroy the Seven Cats of the Blue Vale. Just think of what an undertaking that was, considering each of the seven cats was supposed to have nine lives. Nine times seven is sixty-three, young Dick had learned at school.

However, the troubles of the lad of the fairy tale were nearer to an end than he realized. One of the cats suddenly changed into a beautiful princess. She had been bewitched and transformed into a cat, doomed to stay forever in that shape unless released by a youth of super valor.

Well, of course the end is, the brave boy married the lovely princess who was no longer a cat, and, in a castle overlooking the sea, they lived happily ever after.

That story could not be told too often for the children of "The Glen." It never seemed to lose anything in the telling. For young Richard in particular it had a fascination. He thought of it often, and made changes in it, as he turned it over in his imaginative mind.

He wondered, when child fancy winged him into day dreams, whether he had been put under geasa when he was born, If so what was the task put upon him? What monster, or monsters, must he slay? He would brandish a stick and clip the top off a road-side bush. He would pretend for a moment at least that he was swinging his sword against a giant, a Slat Mor or a Slat Marr. He was of serious mind and whatever came, geasa or no geasa, he would meet his obligations, fight for the right, as his ancestors, heroic priests and soldiers, had done.

Yes, we are part of all that has gone before, and of no race is that truer than of the Gael, sentimental, spiritual, and often superstitious.

Richard Wolfe's character was moulded as much by past centuries as by the years in which he has lived. So with most people.

APPENDIX XI:
"Written Over a Century Ago" (1939)

In this article, published in the Limerick Leader *newspaper on May 13, 1939, the tragic story of James Harnett Woulfe (btw. 1780 and 1800–ca. 1838) is told using a letter from Woulfe's brother John Harnett Woulfe (1807–1856). "J. D. H." was the journalist J. D. Harnett.*

WRITTEN OVER A CENTURY AGO
INTERESTING LETTER FROM WEST LIMERICK EXILE
DESCENDANT OF A CROMWELLIAN VICTIM
DIFFICULTIES OF EARLY DAYS IN U.S.A.

(By J. D. H.)

The underquoted letter, not previously published, and in possession of the Woulfe family of Cratloe, Abbeyfeale, gives an interesting account of some of the life incidents of the writer, John Woulfe, and was written over a century ago, on St. Stephen's Day, 1836. This John Woulfe, it is interesting to note, was a descendant of Richard Woulfe, of Corbally, Limerick, whose property, consisting of 776 acres (I.P.M.) was confiscated by Ireton, under the Cromwellian confiscations. Richard, the great-grandfather, had been banished to the moorlands of West Limerick, and appears to have been a nephew of the Rev. James Woulfe, Dominican Friar, who, with the Rev. Francis Woulfe, was executed by Ireton. Captain George Woulfe, who had fought with the Royal Army, had been exempted from pardon, but escaped to England.

THE HERO OF QUEBEC.

He had been reputed to be the ancestor of General James Woulfe, who captured Quebec a little over a century later. Most of the General biographers, Irish and non-Irish, hold he was of Limerick origin, and had a married aunt living there in his lifetime.

Borlace, writing on the Cromwellian period, in a marginal note to "Wolf's Insurrection at Limerick," says:—"The brothers, Francis and George, and likely Richard, the nephew, headed a party to keep out the troops of the King under Ormond, and also of the Commonwealth."[77] From records copied in the Four Courts, prior to their destruction, Richard Woulfe's possessions at Ballybricken, Corbally, Caheroe, Cooleenishamroge, Ballyphillip, etc., consisted of 776 acres (I.P.M.).

James Woulfe, the missing brother mentioned in the letter below, went to America in 1824, and was subsequently drowned in the Mississippi. He had been intended for the Priesthood, but being scrupulous that he had not a proper vocation, decided on going to America.

THE LETTER.

The letter is interesting from the point of view of the conditions prevailing in America prior to the exodus from Ireland following the Famine:—

December 26th, 1836.

Dear Brother,

New York, October 1st, we went on board the steamboat, John Jay, by the Lake of Erie; canal boat towed by a pair of team horses to Buffalo, 360 miles (fair)? Twelve cents per mile to Albany, 400 wooden bridges on it; very dangerous coast, Erie River, Mississippi, until we land in Tully convenient to Canton; safe, thank God, on November 7th. We stood great danger in Lake Michigan. The captain cast anchor several nights. Brother Patrick, we suffered a great deal more than you are aware of during the long voyage from Ireland to Monticello. Lake Erie, River Mississippi, are the finest I see in America. I enquire for information in several exchange offices where maps of the States are kept, but they would not give me any good information and we were very successful in making out our place of destination, thank God. The distance from New York to Monticello is one thousand five hundred miles. Our expenses amounted to 1,001 dollars; breakfast, dinner and supper are provided on board at 25 cents per meal, with every delicacy the season can afford; you please yourself about taking them. In America a man may go on board the steamboat, at any hour, for any distance he may have to go. Shore travelling is very expensive in America. Brother Patrick,[78] our brother, James Woulfe, lived in Virginia 12 years. He kept an establishment instructing all the nobility till he made a power of money. He left it and came to Louis (sic.), County Missouri; distance 12 hundred miles. He bought this estate in the Land Office, Palmyra, distance 28 miles, three years ago, off the Government of the U.S., at dollar quarter per acre. It is first-rate land; timber (oak), water stream, and lime-stone

---

[77] Edmund Borlase (1620–1682), *The History of the Execrable Irish Rebellion* (1680)

[78] Patrick Maurice Woulfe (d. 1849)

quarry on it—two eighty's, two forty's jambed up with the town. I expect the county seat built on one of these 40 which would make it most valuable.

BROTHER'S ASSIGNMENT.

The county road passed through these 240 acres from town by my house, and then 100 miles long, no repairs. I got a lawyer's opinion on my brother's assignment, and he gave it as his opinion that James Woulfe's brother was equally entitled to his estate, provided he made a will or testament. But the assignment he made holds it for us both; he advised me to settle on that at once, so I did. I contracted with a joiner to build a wooden house for me, and that I would pay him what a respectable man in the neighbourhood would award him for his work; so he complied with … but for the agreement made he would cheat me 35 dollars. I built in section 7— the south half of section, the 7th, containing 240 acres. It lies distant two miles from Monticello. 50 acres cleared of wood by my house fit for cultivation. Two yoke of oxen would plough it. It is very rich. There is no other timber on than what is necessary. I intend to till this much at once: per acre would produce 25 bushels of wheat—80 pounds weight to the bushel; corn, 40 bushels to the acre—70 pounds weight to the bushel, and of potatoes, 300 bushes, 15 cwts. A long square corn, 6 feet high; second year's stick it produces thousand grains; large. The people feed the stock with it.

I bought a suit of clothes in Liverpool, on count of the best £3, sterling.

Our brother, James, board Ruce house for 3 months; distant, one mile from this farm, where I built; he intended to build on it. For fourteen months he chopped some timber; his hands blistered; he looked for men on the hire, but he could not find any man to board them, and he had to give up his building after this.

TRUNK BROKEN AND RIFLED.

Ruce's wife found [f]ault with him, without much reason. Ruce gave him great abuse; he left the house and went to board with one Smith, Monticello. The same day after going he discovered his trunk broken, and was robbed of the sum of 70 dollars, by a black domestic in Ruce's house. He threatened Ruce by law, but in a short time he got him his money. My brother meeting these disappointments caused him to leave his estate and go to Natchez. There he was well known four years ago. The County seat was located Monticello; 40 houses at present; courthouse; five rich shops; goods of every description; three publichouses; bottles full of all sorts of liquors; 2 law offices, post office, 2 medical doctors, 2 joiners (Smith). There is a bank expected. The respectable people of Monticello are kind to me. They ask me how I like the County Seat situation of the State. I told them I liked it good, considering the short time it has been located. It will be improved, and the State are settling people every year. It is a new State, very productive.

A Vow of Temperance.

Brother Pat, I have made a vow not to drink in Monticello, except a little in my own house. I would feel very glad that you would do the same. It is the ruin of man to get drunk. Take care of your health; you know how much your brothers and sisters need you. That God may spare you to them a long time. Use good diet. We have left you our father's property. I would expect that you could live respectably. I count you happy as living amongst your friends (Tim). Keep your son, young Maurice, at school regular: his good mother's child.[79] I would be glad to hear from my brother Maurice. We feel lonesome here. Ellen Harnett[80] would be glad to hear from her mother, brothers, sisters, child. We enjoy good health at present, thank God—except what you know, but I am much better. I wrote to you from New York. Margaret stopped at New York, thinking that her uncle James would send for her. I would wish to know whether you have built your new house and whether you have made good sale of the cullum, whether you have kept the contract. You have the interest if you avail yourself of it, and if you live to any age (line and a half here illegible).

The Home Longing.

Dear uncle, brother Pat, Reverend Tim Harnett, John Forde, I have a great grievance to let you know that our brother, James Woulfe, died in the State of Mississippi, the first year he went to Natchez, the fine learned man. There is nothing that grieves Richard and me more than to say that we can't see, hear, or find our brother alive on his estate, after the bold stroke we made in going to him five thousand miles from home. If God would spare him to us we would live happy. If I live I will not forget James Richardson.

Dear Uncle, Brother Pat, I never felt your advice so much wanting as at present. I would wish to know form you whether I would sell the estate and go home. Happy is the man that can live at home amongst his friends. As this estate is considered to be worth nine thousand dollars at present, I intend to sell 40 acres to improve my farm; to buy some cows, yoke, oxen, pair of horses, some pigs; they feed and fatten in the woods at the time of

---

[79] Maurice Woulfe, life dates unknown, was the son of Patrick M. Woulfe and his first wife, Hannah McAuliffe.

[80] Possibly the wife of Richard Woulfe and sister-in-law of John and the late James Woulfe

the ... I don't know but that I should go home to Ireland to get myself qualified to take this estate. Mr. Richardson told me that his opinion was that Richard's and Ellen's evidence would do to ascertain that I was James Woulfe's brother, and that he himself would prove his handwriting.

When we arrived at Monticello we boarded in two or three weeks. Our bill amounted to twenty dollars. I enquired of the inn-keeper, Mr. Griggsby, who was James Woulfe's agent to this estate, and he mentioned to me who Mr. James Richardson was. I went to his house immediately and asked him where my brother, James Woulfe, was, or how long ago since he had heard from him. He told me he did not hear from him since he sent him the Power of Attorney from the Western County two years ago to take charge of his estate. "It is surprising to me," said he, "if your brother would be alive but that he would have written to me in so long a time. I advertised him in the papers. The Power of Attorney was not sufficient we thought, the Chief Magistrate having signed it. The people of Monticello chopped to the value of 100 of his timber. They came to me and owned to the trespass they had done. I told them they had broken the law and that I would bring them to account. The reason they gave me was that it was suspected that James Woulfe was dead, and that he had no one to the estate, and that it would be sold out.

DOCTOR'S STATEMENT.

Mr. Richardson told me that Dr. Sloan, who lives 26 miles below Monticello, brought the account of his death to Monticello. I went at once to Dr. Sloan's house. I asked him did he know anything for me concerning my brother's death "I do," said he to me. "I travel though different States in the Western country. Last spring in my travelling through the State of Mississippi I was told that James Woulfe died. That he had land—(obliterated)—in his trunk of estate, that he had bought near Monticello. I make no doubt of this," said he. This gentleman was well acquainted with my brother. I would go at once to the State of Mississippi to make enquiry after my brother, but the river Mississippi freezes in the winter. I wrote three letters to the house at Palmyra, to different people in the State of Mississippi, requesting them to make an enquiry after my brother, to advertise him in the papers, and that I would make them compensation for their trouble. Dr. Sloan told me that he would go to the Western country in the spring and that he would give me every assistance in his power to make out my brother; his effects or his money if we get it, or if he made any property. It was supposed that he had from one thousand to two thousand dollars. Mr. Richardson bought 7 cwt. of pork for me, 6 dollars per cwt. If Michael Neville and John Hartnett would come to me I would give them a living during their lives, and very good. If I go home I will employ Michael Sheehy and some young laboring men and women, and pay their fare to Monticello if they will have the courage to come with me. This is a good place for labouring men. Dollar quarter a day and board. Hands are very scarce here.

A KNOWING AND WELL-SPOKEN PEOPLE.

The Americans are knowing and well-spoken people. They sit to a comfortable breakfast, dinner and supper, bread, tea, meat, vegetables regularly. They are all marksmen; keep arms regularly. They have as good houses and furniture as ever I saw. They are in numbers in Monticello every day. James Richardson and his wife are my chief friends here. He is acting the same as agent for me. He has pledged himse[l]f to do justice; is considered respectable and a man of good experience. He is surprised that I did not change my condition before I left Ireland. He knows what Daniel O'Connell is doing for Ireland.[81] The black people are very numerous in the States. The most of them are slaves, cooks for table. They are employed in all vessels on sea and are civilised. There are numbers of men and women emigrating to America every year from Ireland, England and Scotland. There is no priest nearer than St. Louis, 200 miles to the west of Monticello, on the brink of the Mississippi. This hurts our feelings very much. The people of Monticello buy their goods in [?], twelve miles distant. American prairies are twenty miles long, 20 miles broad; no human being, no wood, price dollar quarter an acre; Monticello corn mill 2 miles. This is considered good climate, but extremely cold in winter. Frost and snow continue up to 1st of April. No rain except the month of April. May some days are fine. The people are subject to many complaints here. No man works with the spade here; throughout America oxen are worked; six in number tackled in ploughing the prairies. A man has great difficulty in setting up here in the beginning. No less than 400 dollars would do, but if a man gets settled once he is a gentleman for life. I don't know what trouble I may be put to yet. Let no man attempt to come here until you receive another letter from me. I will administer on this estate with James Richardson—the law requires it. Direct your letter to me—Louis County, Missouri, Monticello, the County seat of Lewis County.

JOHN WOULFE.

---

[81] Daniel O'Connell (1775–1847) was a longtime member of Parliament who fought for the rights of Irish Catholics and against the Act of Union (1803) that created the United Kingdom of Great Britain and Ireland.

APPENDIX XII:
Testimony of James J. Collins (1955)

This is an excerpt of a statement given by James J. Collins in 1955 about his time in the Irish Republican Army during War of Independence (1919–1921). A total of 1,773 witness statements were taken between 1947 and 1957 about the war and collected in Ireland's Bureau of Military History archive. Collins (1900–1967) represented West Limerick in Dáil Éireann, or the lower house of the Irish parliament, from 1948 until his death. When the war began, he was working in a pharmacy operated by Richard B. Woulfe (1884–1937).

I WAS BORN IN the parish of Abbeyfeale on the 31st October, 1900, and was one of a family of three boys and three girls. My parents, who were farmers, sent me to the local national school until I was fourteen years of age, after which I attended a private school run by a man named Mr. Danaher. While attending the private school, I became an apprentice to a chemist in the town of Abbeyfeale whose name was Richard B. Woulfe. After completing my apprenticeship, I was retained in his employment for some years until I was forced to go on the run during the Black and Tan terror.

Mr. Woulfe's wife was Miss Cathie Colbert,[82] sister of Con Colbert (executed after Easter Week 1916) and James Colbert, and cousin of Michael Colbert who later became Brigade Vice O/C, West Limerick Brigade.[83] The Woulfe's were great supporters of the Irish independence movement and their shop and house, from the earliest days of the movement, became a meeting place for men like Con Colbert, Captain Ned Daly and others who later figured prominently in the fight for freedom.

A Company of the Irish Volunteers[84] was formed in Abbeyfeale in May, 1914. I did not become a member at the time. The strength of the

---

[82] Catherine Elizabeth "Katty" Colbert (1878–1951).

[83] The West Limerick Brigade was one of three brigades of the Irish Republican Army operating in Limerick during the war.

[84] The Irish Volunteers were a nationalist paramilitary group that split, in September 1914, over the Irish member of Parliament John Redmond's support of the British war effort. A small minority, still calling themselves the Volunteers, supported a republic, by force if necessary, while the rest, calling themselves the National Volunteers, supported the moderate

Company was about three hundred. A Dr. Hartnett was the chief organiser, and an ex British soldier, named James Wall, was one of the drill instructors. They did not hold together for long and ceased to exist early in the year 1915, after John Redmond's speech in the House of Commons in which he offered the semi-trained Volunteers of Ireland to fight for the freedom of small nationalities.

Some time later in the year 1915, Ernest Blythe visited Abbeyfeale and reorganised the Company. I was one of nine members who joined the Company at its inception. I was only fifteen years of age at the time. A man named Thomas Fitzgerald of the Railway Bar, Abbeyfeale, was our first Company Captain.

A short time previous to Easter Week, 1916, Captain Ned Daly and Con Colbert visited Woulfe's where I was employed. They were in uniform. On Thursday of the Holy Week previous to Easter Week, the late Batt O'Connor, who later became T.D.[85] for a Dublin constituency, visited Woulfe's on his way from Dublin to Tralee with dispatches. He was on a bicycle which he asked me to take past the R.I.C.[86] barracks for him, in case the R.I.C. became suspicious. On Easter Sunday morning, the late Pierce McCann arrived at Woulfe's in a Wolseley motor car on his way to Tralee. He enquired for the best road to take there and was advised to take the Castleisland road. I got into the car and acted as his pilot for part of the way. Just as we left Woulfe's, four R.I.C. men put up their hands to stop the car in the town. McCann slowed down but, just as he got abreast of the R.I.C., he shot off again on his way. When we arrived at Feale's bridge, we saw a couple more R.I.C. men on duty at the bridge and avoided them by taking a bog road via Knocknagoshel to Tralee.

Immediately after Easter Week, the local R.I.C. were on the look-out for Monteith who had landed with Roger Casement at Banna strand.[87] My employer had got word that he was in the Ballymacelligott area of Co. Kerry. Mr. Woulfe sent me to Fr. O'Flaherty of Brosna, Co. Kerry, to borrow his car for the purpose of bringing Monteith to Co. Limerick. Fr. O'Flaherty agreed to lend the car which was a model T-Ford. Soon after, Peter Byrne, Junior, of Abbeyfeale, who was usually employed by Fr. O'Flaherty to drive

---

Redmond. By the end of the war the groups had largely reunited, and with the start of the War of Independence, the Volunteers morphed into the IRA.

[85] *Teachtaí Dála*, or member of Dáil Éireann

[86] Royal Irish Constabulary

[87] Robert Monteith (1879–1956) was an aide to Roger Casement (1864–1916), a British diplomat who had become an Irish nationalist. The two landed via German submarine at Banna Strand in County Kerry; Casement was captured and later executed.

the car, collected it and later brought Monteith from Ballymacelligott to Batt Laffan's of Killowan. From this to early spring of 1917, there was no activity.

In the spring of 1917 the same nine or ten men, who had previously formed the Company before Easter Week of 1916, met once again. Captain Fitzgerald again became O/C. We held routine meetings and drilled up to the end of the year. A short time after the general release, Abbeyfeale Company, with Athea, Tournafulla, Mountcollins and Templeglantine Companies, were formed into a Battalion. Dr. E. Hartnett of Abbeyfeale became Battalion Commandant.

During the conscription scare of 1918,[88] our Company strength increased to forty-seven men. We collected some shotguns and intensified drilling at the time. After the scare, a number of the Volunteers, including some of our officers, left the Company. A re-election of officers then took place. I became Company Captain, the late P.J. O'Neill, 1st Lieutenant, and Laurence Hartnett, 2nd Lieutenant. About the end of June of this year, a dispatch from G.H.Q., Dublin, arrived at Woulfe's for delivery to P.J. Cahill, Brigade O/C, Kerry No. I Brigade. I took the dispatch to Listowel where members of the local Company refused to accept it or have it transmitted to Cahill. I then proceeded to Tralee where I contacted some members of the Tralee Volunteers in a railway signal Cabin near the town. They also refused to accept the dispatch but directed me to where Cahill resided. After some abuse by Cahill's relatives, the dispatch was accepted. The reason for the refusal of the Listowel and Tralee Volunteers to accept responsibility for the delivery was that curfew was in operation at the time following the shooting of two R.I.C. men in the town of Tralee on the 14th June, 1918, by Tom MacEllistrim and another Volunteer for their part in the shooting of two Volunteers some time previously. At the latter end of the year, with other Volunteers of West Limerick, I assisted in the election campaign in East Limerick where Dr. Hayes was the Sinn Féin candidate.[89] Con Collins, the Sinn Féin candidate in West Limerick, was returned unopposed.

Routine drilling continued during the year 1919. Following the rescue of Seán Hogan at Knocklong railway station in May of this year, Seamus Robinson, Dan Breen and Sean Treacy, with Seán Hogan, arrived in the West Limerick Brigade area where they stayed in various farm houses for

---

[88] An April 1918 policy to conscript Irishmen into the British army to fight in France during World War I was fiercely opposed by Irish nationalists, Catholic clergy, and labor unions, and never enforced.

[89] Sinn Féin was an Irish nationalist political party founded in 1905. In 1918, the party won 73 of Ireland's 105 seats in the British Parliament, but rather than go to London they formed Dáil Éireann in Dublin.

some time. They had been in the area for some time when a man, who gave his name as Peadar Clancy of G.H.Q., Dublin also arrived in the area and was taken to Mrs. Kennedy's of Castlemahon where Dan Breen and the other three men had stayed for a while. After a while, 'Clancy' disappeared for a few weeks but returned again. This time he arrived at Woulfe's of Abbeyfeale in a pony and trap, driven by a Volunteer named Mick Sheehan of Templeglantine. At Woulfe's he announced his name as 'Clancy' of G.H.Q., Dublin, and produced identity papers which seemed to be in order. I was working in the shop at the time. Mrs. Woulfe called me and told me that she knew the Clancy family of Dublin and that this man was not one of them. She was very suspicious of him and warned me to be careful. 'Clancy' had said he wanted to go to Co. Kerry on very important business and asked to be taken part of the way there. I procured a pony and trap and called on another Volunteer, named Michael Downey, and sent him to Hickey's of Ballinatrin to warn them that I was taking 'Clancy' there. Breen and his companions had stayed at Hickey's for a while. I brought 'Clancy' to Hickey's and handed him over to a Volunteer, named John Carmody, to proceed on his journey.

As a result of Mrs. Woulfe's suspicions, 'Clancy' was eventually arrested and tried as a spy specially employed by the British to track down Seán Hogan and his three friends. Seán Hogan, who was in Dublin at the time of the arrest, came down for the court martial and identified 'Clancy' as a man named Crowley of Fermoy. Crowley was subsequently executed and labelled "spy".

Earlier in the year 1919, agrarian trouble started in the parish which lasted for nearly two years. It appears to have been started by a creamery manager, named O'Mahony, who dismissed a number of labourers and employed some farmers' sons in their place. It was a common practice for one or other of the two parties to come out at night and fire a few shots through the windows of their opponents' houses. Eventually, the farmers formed themselves into what they called a vigilance committee and, in company with members of the R.I.C., patrolled the parish. No members of the I.R.A. were involved on either side. This was the position that existed when an order was received at the latter end of the year 1919 from the Brigade O/C, Seán Finn, to collect all shotguns in the area. We managed to collect a few guns but these farmers refused to co-operate and held on to their guns.

The position continued up to May, 1920, when the 'London Daily Mail', in an item of news one day referring to this and other incidents in Ireland, said that Abbeyfeale was the one bright spot in the Empire", or words to that effect. An evening or two later, I again saw a group of armed farmers in the town. They were joined by a number of R.I.C. men and, in a body, they proceeded to patrol the town and parish. I reported the matter to the Brigade O/C. In the meantime, our 1st and 2nd Lieutenants, Laurence Hartnett and P.J. O'Neill, respectively, raided the home of the Chairman of the vigilance committee and seized his shotgun and revolver. Seán Finn later contacted me and, after a short discussion, we decided to raid every farmer connected with the Committee and seize their arms in daylight.

Accompanied by Seán Finn, P.J. O'Neill, Slope Reidy and Con Creegan, I seized a motor car, the property of O'Mahony, the creamery manager who had started the trouble, and went from one farm to another and collected a total of seventeen shotguns and a number of revolvers which had been issued by the R.I.C. As we drove into the farmyard of James Lane, who was a Justice of the Peace, his son, Dan, opened fire with a revolver on us and wounded Reidy in the arm. As he discharged the shot, I jumped out of the car. He recognised me and approached with his hands up and apologised for firing. He, it appears, had taken us for the labour agitators. He handed over his revolver and a shotgun, afterwards bringing us into the kitchen and treating us to our dinner.

We returned to Abbeyfeale with our car loaded with rifles and revolvers, and proceeded to the residence of William Creagh-Hartnett, another J.P., and seized a rifle and shotgun. We then went to the residence of a man named Woulfe, also a J.P., of The Glen, Cratloe, Abbeyfeale, where we got another rifle.[90] By the 1st June, every farmer in the area, including those attached to the vigilance committee, had joined the I.R.A. I swore them in and administered the oath. Our membership went up to one hundred and twenty men.

About the first week of June, 1920, Humphrey Murphy, Battalion O/C of Kerry No. 2 Brigade, with the help of Duagh Company, Kerry No. 1 Brigade, and members of the West Limerick Brigade, decided to attack an R.I.C. barracks at Brosna in Co. Kerry. I mobilised Abbeyfeale Company for the occasion. Other Companies in the West Limerick Brigade were also mobilised for the same night. We blocked all main roads and placed armed men at each road block. Unfortunately, the R.I.C. got word of the impending attack and had a party of military stationed on and around Feale's bridge. An advance party of the Duagh Company, who were in a motor car, drove right into the military at the bridge. Six I.R.A. men in the car were arrested. I got word of the arrests in a short time and sent a dispatch rider—P.J. O'Neill—to Mountcollins where Humphrey Murphy and the attacking party had mobilized at a creamery there. Murphy decided to call off the attack.

---

[90] The Glen, a farm near Athea, County Limerick, had been owned by Richard Edmond "Dicky Ned" Woulfe (1824–1910). This may have been Maurice J. Woulfe (1884–1973).

About 14th June, I received a despatch from G.H.Q., Dublin, signed by Gearoid O'Sullivan, through Seán Finn, Brigade O/C, to seize R.I.C. correspondence from Co. Kerry to the Castle, Dublin. I contacted P.J. O'Neill and Michael Collins (nicknamed Bird) from Abbeyfeale Company, James Roche and two others from Templegantine Company. We proceeded to Barna railway station on the 15th. The Mail train was just steaming into the station. As it came to a standstill, Bird jumped on to the footplate of the engine and ordered the driver and fireman on to the platform. The driver, seeing me, pointed to a coach where a number of military officers were chatting to a local solicitor named Lavin. I opened the door of the coach and, pointing my revolver, ordered, "Hands up". To my surprise, they obeyed. They were all unarmed. In the meantime, the rest of my party were busy throwing the mail bags, further along in another compartment, out on to the platform. While this was happening, the officers kept their hands up. The train was held until the mail bags were carried to the roadside. We then let it proceed.

We had just carried the last of the mail bags on our backs to a dip in the first bye-road west of Barna station when two lorry loads of R.I.C. and Black and Tans flashed by the end of the bye-road. The stationmaster had 'phoned the R.I.C. in Newcastlewest and reported the raid while it was in progress. Later, we took the mails to Sugar Hill bog where we got in between some turf banks and sorted them out. We found the R.I.C. bag enclosed in a larger one. Among the parcels we found one which, for some reason or other, we thought suspicious. It was a pie addressed to an R.I.C. man. We opened it and inside found a letter from a Miss Collins of Abbeyfeale. Unknown to her friends and neighbours, she had married the R.I.C. man some time previously. He was apparently fond of pie. The letter informed her husband, among other things, that if James Collins (myself) P.J. O'Neill and Mahony were arrested, opposition to the R.I.C. would collapse in Abbeyfeale. We returned the letter to Miss Collins with our compliments and a warning that she would be held responsible if any of the three men were arrested. She immediately reported the matter to the local parish priest. We sent the police bag to Seán Finn who had it sent to G.H.Q., Dublin. It contained a complete report of the I.R.A. Organisation in Co. Kerry. […]

APPENDIX XIII:
Letter from Jane C. "Dollie" Woulfe (1956)

In a letter to her American cousin Sister Mary Caelan, the former Helen Wolfe, dated August 1956, Jane C. "Dollie" Woulfe (1879–1964) provides a long and detailed version of the family's history. Sister Mary Caelan taught art at the College of Saint Teresa in Winona, Minnesota, and was studying for a year in Italy on a scholarship from her own Order of Saint Francis.

The Glen, Abbeyfeale,
County Limerick.

August, 1956.

Dear Cousin Helen,
(or Sister M. Caelan—a dual personality?).

Well, I promised most surely, with your eyes fixed earnestly on me, that I would write this letter outlining the history of our common family. You know what I mean by the over-worked adjective "common". I am referring to those several parties called generically the Woulfes or, as you would say, the Wolfes. If you notice any mistakes in spelling or punctuation kindly put it down to my eye-sight—it sounds nicer. Moreover, they spell some words differently in America having developed a most inexplicable dislike to the letter "u", so allow for that. What follows may sound somewhat vainglorious, and in the end generally futile, but it is as near as I can get to the facts.

Making a long cast I start as far back as a Hugh Lupus of Avranches in Normandy in the time of that Duke William who invaded England, won at Hastings in October, 1066, and became William the First of England. This Hugh Lupus was made Constable of Chester and lived at a place now called Church Laughton in that county. It is odd that the present English Dukes of Westminster whose family name is "Grosvenor" and have their country house near the same place on the Cheshire border have a custom of inserting the words "Hugh Lupus" amongst their numerous christian names. What their connection with the man from Avranches may be I do not know but presumably they claim some. A daughter of the last Duke of Westminster runs a racing stable in this county. A descendant of this Hugh Lupus came to Ireland, landing at Bannow, County Wexford, with the first band of Norman invaders in 1169. They moved west and north grabbing such land as the owners were too weak to defend, after the custom of all such pioneers or bandits, whichever you like to call them, and finally infiltrated into the County Limerick. Now gradually we get on to firm ground in the matter of family history. In course of time the Norman-French of the invaders under the pressure of trade interests gave way to the ruder English tongue in the seaport towns and to the Irish language everywhere else. The "Lupus" presumably translated into "Woulfe" or "Wolfe" and, in Irish, to De Bulb, (for the Irish have no "W" in their alphabet and express the sound by a "B" aspirate). So our family name appears in English guise phonetically as Woulfe or De Wuluff or even De Baluff—this last being the form given in Canon Begley's "History of the Diocese of Limerick"[91] and taken by him from an official "Inquisition" made by the English towards the end of the 16th century setting out, inter alia, the list of landholders, adherents of Garrett, the last Earl of Desmond, whose properties had been confiscated as rebels. However, we first appear in the records of Limerick City in the person of a Nicholas Woulfe who is named as a Bailiff of the City in 1383. The next appearance is a Garrett Woulfe who is listed as a holder of the same office in 1470. Six years after this last date we have a Thomas Woulfe who was Sheriff of the City, a person of importance in those days. After that there is silence for many years. The next high light is the Reverend David Woulfe of Limerick City, a secular priest in the reign of the English king, Edward VI (1552–58). While on a visit to Rome David Woulfe met Ignatius Loyola and joined the latter's newly formed Society of Jesus. Elizabeth had then succeeded to the English throne and in the confused conditions of the time was moving or rather drifting into the Protestant camp. Father Woulfe was sent back to Ireland and landed in Cork in the beginning of 1561. More lucky than many of his contemporaries, especially his personal friends, Richard Creagh and Edmond O'Donnell, both priests and both martyred by the English invaders, Father David, after many years of strenuous support of the Earl of Desmond and the Earl's fighting cousin, James Fitzmaurice,[92] died a natural death in the northern part of the County Clare about 1580.

Leaving the Limerick City branch of the family alone for the moment we will turn to the Limerick County branch with whom, I believe, we are

---

[91] Archdeacon John Begley (1861–1941) wrote a three-volume history of the Diocese of Limerick: *The Diocese of Limerick, Ancient and Medieval* (1906), *The Diocese of Limerick in the Sixteenth and Seventeenth Centuries* (1927), and *The Diocese of Limerick from 1691 to the Present Time* (1938). He preceded his friend and fellow historian Father Patrick Woulfe (1872–1933) as the parish priest of Kilmallock.

[92] James FitzMaurice FitzGerald (d. August 18, 1579) helped arrange for the papal troops that would later be defeated by Sir Walter Raleigh at Smerwick (see note below).

more immediately connected. A certain Gerald, (spelt "Gerot" in the above-mentioned "Inquisition"), Baluff, otherwise "Woulfe" held land on a tenure called "knight's fee" from Gerald, the Earl referred to above, when Desmond's resistance began.[93] It became clear afterwards that there was an agreed division of the plunder amongst the invaders. In pursuance of the scheme Queen Elizabeth had authorised the despatch of numerous and well equipped bands of thieves into Ireland. The programme was simple. Owners of land were attacked, murdered, if possible, and the land seized by the Crown was granted back to the immediate assassins subject to a rent payable to Elizabeth and her successors. If the proposed victims took arms in their own defence they were called "rebels". One of the main attacks on the Earl of Desmond was led by two adventurers, Malby and Raleigh—the latter being the Sir Walter Raleigh whose character, since white-washed by certain historians and other fiction writers, finally brought him to the scaffold in the following reign.[94] Gerald Woulfe or "Gerot De Baluff", if you like, lived at a place called in Irish Inis Cuais, (Inish Coosh is the English pronunciation), near the present town of Rathkeale in the County Limerick. He with many other landholders, Gaelic and Norman, lost his life and his land in the ensuing war and of his family, two sons, as I believe, fled to the hills in the western and largely uninhabited part of the county, settled there and became the progenitors of all the Cratloe and other Woulfes. I should have mentioned that according to the English "Inquisition" the name of this Gerald's father was Philip, a name that did not come back into the family until modern times. My opinion that the flight to the West Limerick hills took place during the Geraldine war and before the death of James Fitzmaurice is based on a curious story told by my grandfather[95] which I shall relate to you some other time. Whatever the details the main fact remains that the County Limerick Woulfes from being people of established position in the rich plain of central Limerick became fugitives in the western hills and woods. In the

---

[93] The Desmond Rebellion (1569–1573, 1579–1583) represented armed resistance to English control in the southern Irish province of Munster, which included the counties Limerick and Kerry. It was led by Gerald FitzGerald, fifteenth earl of Desmond (ca. 1533–1583), and his followers, known as the Geraldines.

[94] Sir Nicholas Malby (ca. 1530–1584) served as Lord President of Connaught. Sir Walter Raleigh (ca. 1552–1618) landed in Ireland during the Second Desmond Rebellion, which was led by the FitzGerald family and supported by papal troops from Spain and Italy. In November 1580, Raleigh joined English troops in a three-day siege of the Catholic fort at Smerwick, County Kerry. When the papal troops surrendered, the fort's women were hanged, its priests gruesomely executed, and its soldiers put to the sword, much of the work being done by men under Raleigh's command. Raleigh was later executed by Elizabeth's successor, King James I.

[95] Richard Edmond "Dicky Ned" Woulfe (1824–1910) [see Appendix III]

turmoil that prevailed all over Ireland the result of continuous attacks from overseas for more than a hundred years after the murder of the Earl of Desmond in 1586 the personalities of our family, or rather of the County branch of them, are lost to sight until towards the end of the 17th century. They were too busy trying to keep alive to keep records. The curtain rises again on two brothers bearing the now recognised family names of Maurice and James who were living at a place called Inchareagh on the bank of the river Gale west of the village of Athea. One of them James,[96] died in 1704 leaving six daughters and two sons. His eldest son, Maurice, had been born in 1690. Although he was only 14 years of age when his father died he was strong and energetic, physically and mentally, and he soon took charge of the family affairs. His younger brother, Richard, died a young man. The story is that he got chilled while on a visit eastward down the plain of Limerick and was buried in Monagay churchyard. It was winter and the snow lay so deep that the body could not be brought home. Maurice meantime at Inchareagh made headway as far as the political and economic conditions of his time would permit. He gave dowries to his six sisters and that task postponed his marriage until he was 40 years old, a very unusual circumstance for those days. His wife was a Kathleen Rearden. He then left Inchareagh and took better land at Beenmore nearer Athea. After many years, (thirty apparently), his wife, Kathleen, died. The churchyard, Templeathea, where she was buried was in plain sight of his house. The tradition is that he could not bear to look at it. He left Beenmore and took the entire Townland of Cratloe, some 2,000 acres, in March 1760. That also had once been Desmond land. He lived at the house you photographed, below ours, here at the Glen and died there on Christmas night, 1792, being then, you will notice, 102 years of age. He had eaten his supper, possibly too good a one for his years, and was sitting in a corner of the kitchen beside the fire watching a dance of the young people that was in full swing, when he appeared to fall asleep. It was noticed that he had 31 of his own teeth in his mouth and the 32nd was in his waistcoat pocket when he died that night so that he was practically intact. That man was your great-great-great-great grandfather as appears below. He had five sons. One, Edmond, was married before 1760.[97] One of the other four, called "Short Dick" succeeded his father in the old house.[98] Short Dick died in 1824, his son, Edmond, died in 1876,[99] and Edmond's son, Richard, died

---

[96] James Woulfe (ca. 1651–1704).

[97] Edmond Maurice Woulfe (d. ca. 1798).

[98] Richard Maurice "Short Dick" Woulfe (ca. 1730–1824).

[99] Edmond Richard "Old Ned" Woulfe (1788–1876).

in 1910,[100] leaving amongst his children, your grandmother, Mary Woulfe,[101] and my father, Maurice Richard.[102] The house we occupy at the Glen was built in 1815 by your grandmother's grandfather, the above Edmond Woulfe. The latter was a rather prominent man in the district in his day. Amongst other things he was what was called a "warden" in Daniel O'Connell's Repeal organisation in the thirties and forties of the last century. The house you photographed, the older one, was occupied before 1760 by a certain James Lacy. He was of a family that had lost still more than we had in the Tudor wars as can be seen from the size of the ruins of their castle at Glenogra not far from Limerick. Some of these De Lacys had escaped to the Continent and one, County Peter Lacy, acquired the somewhat risky job of being a field-marshal in the service of the Czar, Peter the Great. Another of them was Bishop of Limerick in the first half of the 18th century. He had, of course, to keep under cover as the Anti-Irish penal laws were then in full swing. Now, if you are not too bored we will return to the Limerick City branch of the tribe. I had mentioned Thomas Woulfe, the Sheriff of Limerick in 1476. He is described as of "Bally Philip", evidently the name of his house. Now recollect that there is no doubt about him; the contemporary record is there to be read yet. There is a big jump to the next mention of the family in the civic life of Limerick in 1585 when they had the Sheriff's job again. He was James Woulfe of Corbally, (just outside Limerick on the Clare bank of the Shannon). We know something of this James. He had six sons:—(1).—Patrick, whose son, Richard, took part in the defence of Limerick when the city was besieged by Cromwell's army under Ireton in 1651. He escaped after the surrender and got away to France. His descendants settled in Paris and as far as I know all connection with them was lost. (2). Richard, who had descendants in Limerick a hundred years afterwards. (3). Stephen, whose descendants still live in County Clare. (4). James, a Dominican friar. (5). Francis, Superior of the Franciscan Order in Ireland, who was appointed Papal Legate to this country. (6). George, a soldier, about whom there is some confusion. Apparently he had a son of the same name who took part in the defence of the City in Cromwell's war. These last two had very different fates. Francis Woulfe, the Legate, was captured by Ireton's forces and promptly hanged on the double fatal charge of being a "rebel" and a "papist priest". George evaded capture and, of all places, took refuge

---

[100] Richard Edmond "Dicky Ned" Woulfe (1824–1910), i.e., Dollie Woulfe's grandfather

[101] Mary A. Wolfe (1870–1916) married Michael C. Wolfe (1867–1928) and immigrated to Chicago, Illinois.

[102] Maurice Richard Woulfe (1853–1928)

in the north of England then mainly royalist and anti-Cromwellian in sympathy. He, George, had a son, Edmond, and this Edmond who settled in Kent was the grandfather of the General James Woulfe, (or "Wolfe" as he spelt it), who took Quebec for the English in 1759. There is no doubt about the General's descent from the Limerick Woulfes—so much is known from purely English sources—but in fact most of the family are not inclined to boast about it. They consider that he was on the wrong side. The general's father was a lieutenant-colonel in the English army and a Protestant, but that, in the circumstances of the time, was almost inevitable. On that point it should be mentioned that there are Protestant Wolfes living at Forenaughts in the County Kildare and it has been said that they are descended from the General's grandfather, Edmond. Of that I know nothing but they, the Kildare family, have a good record politically, always steadily Irish in sentiment, and the "Wolfe" in Wolfe Tone's name derives from them. The patriot's father was a neighbour and a friend at Forenaughts.

I hope sometime to find out the particulars of the personalities who link the present County Clare Woulfes with the old Limerick city worthies—only a few miles away in a straight line—but so far I have not got round to it. Now I am approaching the end of this instalment of the story but I should like to add the little I know about the first of our emigrants from Cratloe to America. The first to turn his face westward, apart from the Man of Quebec was a James Woulfe,[103] a grandson of the old Maurice above. This James Woulfe had intended to go into the Church and had acquired a good knowledge of the classics. He changed his mind, however, and left for the United States in 1824. Virginia was, apparently, the most promising territory for his purpose and he established there a school which his abilities and qualifications turned into a distinct success. He appears to have been a restless character. Like many who came after him "the noise of the road was in his ears" and after some years he left Virginia and pushed far to the north west to a place now called Monticello in Iowa.[104] He took land there and worked it as efficiently as he had in his classic studies. He had, throughout, kept in communication with his kinfolk in Cratloe and one, at least, of his letters is extant. Then the letters suddenly stopped. After a considerable interval two of his brothers, John and Richard Woulfe,[105] set out in 1836 to find him. They went first to his former Virginian address and by chance met a travelling dentist who had not only known James Woulfe but who also told

---

[103] James Harnett Woulfe (btw. 1780 and 1800–ca. 1836), the son of Maurice James Woulfe (ca. 1763–before 1838) [see Appendix XI]

[104] There is a Monticello, Iowa, but this should be Monticello, Missouri.

[105] John Harnett Woulfe (1807–1856) and Richard Woulfe (1802–btw. 1850 and 1860)

them that he had died at Natchez on the Mississippi the year before, (1835). He had been drowned in the river and there had been a suspicion of foul play. In any event the exact circumstances of James Woulfe's death were never ascertained. The brothers, John and Richard, continued on to Iowa; claimed and established title to James' land and became the ancestors, as far as my information goes, of the Wolfe colony in Iowa and the rural parts of Illinois.[106] It was nearly thirty years afterwards that the real exodus began and has continued until there are almost as many of the family in the United States as there are in the County Limerick. Now I must really put the brake on. With the exception of the reference to the ancient Hugh Lupus, admittedly guess-work but quite probably not far off the mark, the rest of this letter is very close to the actual facts and in the matter of long, honourable and at times even distinguished, descent you can hold up your head in any company you may be in in Europe or America. To finish in a lighter vein and if you had been able to make a longer stay I could have told you stories of local legends, of odd events, ghosts, witches and the like that would have made you draw closer to the light. We had some of the last-named hereabouts in the old days. There was Joan Grogan of Athea who, one night at the Glen, called on the dead of previous generations naming each individually as they came in, one after another, out of the dark in response to her call until my grandfather, then a young man, was driven into a fire-place corner by the press of the weird, if friendly, visitors. There was Biddy Airly, the Limerick witch and Moll Anthony, the Clare witch. Biddy Airly was seen on both sides of a fence at the same moment which, you will admit, demands a considerable degree of technical skill in her trade even for a boss-witch. Then there is a stretch of ground in Cratloe called the "Second Hill" whereon no man or woman in their senses will be found after nightfall. However, that can wait and moreover it does not do to become involved too deeply in certain matters. When you get the chance, tar aris, i.e., come again.

Yours ever,
Jane Woulfe,
(alias "Dollie").

Sister M. Caelan, (alias Helen Woulfe),
Villa Schifanoia,
Via Boccaccio, 123
Firenze, Italia.

---

[106] The first Wolfes to immigrate to Illinois came in 1847 and then moved on to Iowa by the mid-1850s [see appendices IV and V]. It's not clear whether they knew of the Wolfes in Missouri.

APPENDIX XIV:
"Origin of the Species; or, Whatever Happened to Good Old What's-His-Name" (1975)

In this humorous essay, dated August 10, 1975, and written on the occasion of a biannual family reunion in Clinton County, Iowa, Thomas A. Wolfe (1940–2012), of Davenport, Iowa, details the history of his paternal line.

THIS SKETCH IS MERELY an attempt to outline the descendants of Maurice and Sarah Wolfe and is not an attempt to trace the entire Wolfe or McAndrew lineage. If the writer digresses here or there and the reader should happen to learn something, he should savor this knowledge like a fine wine, lobster, or, at today's prices, hamburger. The writer leaves to others the task of tracing the lineage of Grandfather Maurice Wolfe's nine brothers and sisters. The early information on the Wolfes was found in *Wolfe's History of Clinton County*, edited by Patrick B. Wolfe (1911),[107] which can be found in the Davenport Public Library. Most quotations used here will be from that work. The writer refuses to claim the responsibility for any errors of commission or omission. It's always easier that way. He does insist, however, that the reader not take anything written below too seriously. Certainly, no attempt has been made to embarrass anyone. The intent has been merely to put some life into something that might otherwise be about as exciting as outlining a declarative sentence for an English grammar class.

The writer's great grandfather, John R. Wolfe, was born in County Kerry, Ireland in 1824,[108] the son of Richard Wolfe.[109] He received an "excellent education," which no doubt gave him pinko ideas because he helped organize the "Young Ireland" Party, an obviously leftist group, while supposedly studying. He left Ireland in 1846 or 1848 (no doubt chased out for advocating political radicalism but barely possibly because the potato famine was in full swing that year). His ship took him to Ottawa, Illinois (which is impres-

---

[107] See Appendix IV.

[108] The inscription on his tombstone suggests that John Richard Wolfe was born in 1809.

[109] Richard James Woulfe (1763–1842)

sive since the nearest ocean is about 1500 miles away).[110] He farmed in Ottawa until 1854 when the irresistible lure of little Lost Nation forced him to once again pack his bags. (One can only speculate as to whether he was active in radical Illinois politics and was forced to skedaddle again.)

At any rate, move to Lost Nation he did, where he farmed successfully until his death in 1885. He was a Catholic, an "active worker in the Church," an opponent of that peculiar institution known as slavery, and a man who was not interested in politics. (At least that's what he said, but he probably knew the police were watching, having been run out of two different areas already.)

About John's wife we have little information beyond the fact that her family was apparently given to drink. Her name was Honora Buckley, a member of a family "prominent in the church and at the bar." Her brother Michael was either active in the Belfast bar or hung around one a great deal. Honora Buckley Wolfe died three years after her husband, in 1888.

John and Honora had ten children. They were James, a farmer near Lost Nation; Patrick, a DeWitt and Clinton lawyer and judge; Johanna, who became Sister Scholastica of the Order of Sisters of Mercy at Sioux City; John, a Melrose farmer; Maurice, a Lost Nation farmer (and grandfather of the writer); Margaret, the wife of Dr. D. Langan (Lanigan? Lanagan?) of Clinton; Katherine, wife of Judge T.D. Fitzgerald of Montana and Clinton (he was once a Montana politician who doubtlessly was chased from that state for advocating seditious extremism like his father-in-law); Richard, a DeWitt lawyer; and two children who died in infancy.[111]

It should be noted here that a Horse Thief Protection Society was formed in the Delmar area in 1859–60. The motivation for the Society is unknown to the writer, but in a land heavily populated with English and Germans, as well as with the Irish, it must have been distressing indeed to see so much evidence of what Sir Walter Raleigh unflatteringly called the "Wilde Irish" so dangerously near them. Prudence alone would have dictated such a move.

---

[110] Wolfe immigrated to the United States in 1847, arriving in New York from Liverpool on August 23 aboard the *Cornelia*. From there he traveled to Chicago, where he stayed several weeks before moving to Ottawa, LaSalle County, Illinois. He traveled in the company of his wife, Honora Buckley Wolfe (d. 1887), their son, James Buckley Wolfe (1844–1916), John Wolfe's first cousin Maurice Wolfe (ca. 1800–1879), his wife, Ellen Catherine Carey Wolfe, and several of their children. John R. Wolfe died in 1883.

[111] Patrick Bernard Wolfe (1848–1922), Sister Scholastica (1849–1926), John Buckley Wolfe (1851–1923), Maurice Buckley Wolfe (1855–1928), Margaret I. Wolfe Langan (1857–btw. 1930 and 1940) and Dr. Daniel Langan (1836–1914), Catherine "Kate" Fitzgerald (1860–1947) and Thomas D. Fitzgerald (1857–1903), and Richard Boyle Wolfe (1862–1940).

The attitude of Delmar's English and Germans was not unique. William Thomas was an Englishman who wrote in 1552 that "the wild Irish, as unreasonable beasts, lived without any knowledge of God or good manners...."[112] Fifteen years later, another Englishman[113] wrote the queen:

> I cannot find that they make any Conscience of sin, and I doubt whether they christen their children or no; for neither find I place where it should be done, nor any person able to instruct them in the rules of a Christian; or if they were taught I see no grace in them to follow it; and when they die I cannot see they make any account of the world to come.

(These quotations did *not* come from *Wolfe's History*.)

Patrick Wolfe, second son of John and Honora, adopts a slightly different attitude towards the "Wild Irishe." Picture a choir of angels with trumpets blaring as he makes the following introduction of his older brother.

> The Emerald Isle, far famed in song and story, has furnished a large number of enterprising and high-minded citizens to the U.S., and they have even been most welcome, for we have no better class of citizens. They are, almost without exception, industrious, and they are loyal to do their full duty as citizens in whatever community they cast their lot. Among this large class the name of James B. Wolfe, whose long, strenuous, and interesting career has resulted in much good to himself, his family, and to his friends and neighbors, for his example has ever been exemplary and his influence salutary.

James B. Wolfe was born in Ireland in 1843, arriving in Chicago in 1847 or '48. He was a farmer and a businessman, "and he laid by a competence for his declining years." (How's that for phrasing?) He was a Democrat but not active in public affairs except at the local level, having been school director for twenty years. We are assured that he and Anna O'Connor Wolfe, daughter of Jeremiah O'Connor, were faithful members of the Catholic Church.

James and Anna Wolfe had seven children. They were John O.C.; Jerry, a veterinary surgeon in Grand Mound; Mary; Nora; James; Walter; and

---

[112] From *The Pilgrim* (1552) by William Thomas (d. 1554), a Welsh historian and clerk of the Privy Council who was executed for treason by Queen Mary

[113] Henry Sidney (1529–1586), Lord Deputy of Ireland, to Queen Elizabeth I, April 20, 1567

Anna.[114] We are assured that "there are no more worthy or highly honored people in Clinton County than the Wolfes."

One of James' children, Jerry, was born in 1875. He became a Catholic at birth, a Democrat shortly after, the champion foot racer in the state of Iowa for a time, a veterinarian and Grand Mound fire chief. He married Mary Wiley of Chicago in 1909. As of 1911, they had only one child.[115]

Judge Patrick B. Wolfe, second eldest of John and Honora's clan was born in 1848 and married Margaret Connole in 1878. They had three children: John L., a lawyer (eventually in partnership with the judge); Mary; and a third child who died in infancy.[116]

That brings us to the end of our digressions into various other lines of the John R. Wolfe clan. Were the writer at all knowledgeable on the subject, he might have continued, but perhaps someone else can do this. There apparently exists somewhere some written material along this line, although it would need updating.

We must now rein sharply inward and direct our attention to the immediate Wolfe line, that of MAURICE and SARAH WOLFE. Maurice, fifth living child of John and Honora Wolfe, was the first of that family born in Lost Nation.[117] The writer knows little about him, but it can be assumed he became a Catholic and a Democrat at approximately the same time. It is possible, however, that he inherited some of his father's Marxist revolutionary ideas although there is no record of political insurrection in Lost Nation or Toronto during his lifetime. It is well known in Lost Nation, though, that Grandfather Maurice attended his agrarian pursuits in spurts which he called "five year plans." His favorite tools were the hammer and sickle.

Sometime in the 1890s, Maurice met Sarah McAndrew, probably at a party rally, found her to be a twin soul, ideologically speaking, and married her.

Sarah McAndrew, daughter of Phil McAndrew of Toronto (or Lost Nation?), was born about 1866. Whether Sarah supported the Bolsheviks as ardently as did her husband during the revolution of 1917 is not a matter of public record. What is known is that she bore five children, all boys. They

---

[114] John O. C. Wolfe (1873–1959), Jeremiah "Jerry" Wolfe (1876–1949), Mary R. Wolfe Goodall (b. 1878), Honora L. "Nora" Wolfe (1880–1960), James Leonard Wolfe (1881–1937), Walter Ignatius Wolfe (1886–1967), and Anna Wolfe Ryan (b. 1887).

[115] Their children were James Wiley Wolfe (b. 1910), Mary I. Wolfe Schulz (1912–1964), and Alice Grace Wolfe Alward (1922–1991).

[116] John Loyola Wolfe (1879–1962) and Mary Zeta "Molly" Wolfe (b. 1881).

[117] Maurice Wolfe was born in March 1855 in LaSalle County, Illinois, before the family had moved to Iowa.

were Raymond, Phillip, John, Melvin, and James. Sarah died at the age of 56 in 1922, followed five years later by her husband, the "Old Comrade."

RAYMOND WOLFE, the eldest son of Maurice and Sarah and the writer's father, was born in 1896. He joined the Navy in World War I. He caught no Germans, but he did catch the flu. In 1925 he caught Gladys McGinn of Petersville. (She was only twenty-two at the time, but that didn't stop her from continually telling her own children that no one with a grain of sense married under thirty. To gently remind her of her own age in 1925 only brought about a foot stomping and the response, "That was different.")

Ray and Gladys farmed in Lost Nation and later in Delmar, where they were that town's only Irishmen (almost) and were proclaimed honorary members of the Horse Thief Protection Society. They had four children: Sara, Mary, Margery, and Thomas.[118] Ray died in 1941, one month short of his 45th birthday. Gladys lived on until 1966, dying at the age of 63.

Sara, the eldest child of Ray and Gladys, sets high standards for herself and usually accomplished her goals. Sara has inherited the very liberal communist ideas of Grandfather Maurice and Great Grandfather John R. When vexed, she will even accuse her little brother, the only begotten son of Ray and Gladys, of being a Republican or a fascist, terms she considers synonymous and uses interchangeably. Besides raising a family, she presently works at Marycrest College coordinating a group of radical leftists whose theme songs are "I Am Woman" and "the Internationale." She is married to G.R. (Dick) Wissing, a Davenport lawyer with a dry wit and an inordinate interest in Clinton County happenings. (Maybe he wishes he were Irish.) They have four children: Matthew Richard, Mary Elizabeth (Beth), Katherine Constance (Kate), and John Martin.

Mary K. is best remembered for having once put a pair of children's tennis shoes inside her oven and for remembering vividly the details of her elder sister Sara's birth. Actually, Mary K.'s birth was unique enough by itself in that almost immediately after her birth was announced in the paper the nation plunged into the Great Depression. She married John Welsh, a salesman and arch conservative somewhat to the right of Louis XIV, and live in Davenport surrounded by the smell of burning rubber and old copies of the *National Review,* as well as copies of the taped telecasts of William F. Buckley. Compared with John, Pope Paul is a Protestant. John and Mary have four children: Michael Joseph, Anne Marie, Thomas James, and Mary Kathryn.

---

[118] Sara Terese Wolfe Wissing (1926–1998), Mary Kathryn Wolfe Welsh (1929–2004), Margery Wolfe Butler, Thomas Anthony Wolfe (1940–2012).

Margery Wolfe married Edmund Butler of the law firm of Butler, Butler, and Butler, Philadelphia. Ed is the one between "and" and "Philadelphia," so he can't get too cocky. Marge is best remembered for having allowed once that the crops were not doing very well. It was Christmas and there were three feet of snow on the ground at the time. Their children are named Edmund Jr., Patricia, and Thomas Brendan. (Middle names are included only when known.)

Tom married Frannie Cupp of Moline, teaches, and lives in Davenport. They have three children: Bridget Colleen, Brendan Martin, and Sara Elizabeth.

The second of Maurice and Sarah was PHIL,[119] born in 1898. He married Mildred Gribbon of DeWitt forty-five years ago, in 1930. Phil and Mildred live on a farm south of Lost Nation. Over the years, Phil has pursued vigorously the task of convincing his nephews of the joys and material benefits he claims to be an integral part of husbandry, the tilling of the soil. Mildred has the distinction, among other things, of being a member of the longest, continual, single bridge club in this part of the world.

JOHN WOLFE,[120] the third son, was born in 1901, marrying Ida Burke of DeWitt on Thanksgiving Day, 1936. John was an extremely kind man and had the richest brogue of all the Wolfes. Their farm is south of Lost Nation, near Phil's. They had two children, Marianne and Jack. John died in 1974.

Marianne Wolfe, John and Ida's first born, married Leon McGarry, and they farm near DeWitt. They have seven children: John L., Maureen, Ann Marie, Sheila, Lisa, Coleen, and Leo Patrick.

Jack Wolfe (John III) married Pierrette Duirioux,[121] an Irish girl from Brooklyn, and they now live in Des Moines. Years ago this couple always struck this writer as being the nearest thing to real live intellectuals the Wolfe clan had recently produced. However, they have eight children, and one assumes that somewhere around the third or fourth child abstractions were tossed aside in favor of such basics as food, clothing, shelter, nerve pills, and lunch money for the kids. Their offspring are named Mary Lynne, John Joseph, Kevin, Katherine, Christine, Susan, Jennifer, and Sara Elizabeth.

MELVIN WOLFE,[122] the fourth son of Maurice and Sarah, was born in 1904. The nurse or midwife (or whomever helped deliver him in those days

---

[119] Philip James Wolfe (1898–1979)

[120] John Joseph Wolfe (1901–1974)

[121] Pierrette Duriaux

[122] Melvin Maurice Wolfe (1904–1990)

near the dawn of creation) reports that thirty minutes after his birth he said to the assembled doctor, nurses, midwives, family, and friends, "Did you hear the one about …?" The story is reported to have lasted sixteen minutes and twelve seconds by actual timing, included three delightful sub-stories, and was told in a marvelous Irish accent which has, unfortunately disappeared among third generation Wolfes.

In 1929, Melvin met and married Frances McLaughlin of Otter Creek, the most remarkable and colorful lady this writer has ever known. She gave birth to five children: Paul, Robert, Patricia, Leo (David), and Richard. Their farm is located a very short distance north of the church. Frances died in 1967, and Melvin moved into town about then and son David took over.

Paul, the eldest child of Melvin and Frances, married Patricia Kurtz and lives in Lawrence, Kansas. (The writer vaguely remembers, from those misty days of antiquity, a large Polish wedding in Detroit.) The two eldest of the Melvin Wolfe clan have taken the benediction, "May your tribe increase," even more seriously than the issue of John Wolfe, and that is indeed hard to do. The children of Paul and Pat are as follows: Michael, Timothy, Steven Philip, Mary, Kathleen, Margaret, Thomas, John, and Maureen (also Therese, who belongs somewhere in the middle).

Robert Wolfe, Melvin's second son, married Kathy McGuire of Streator, Illinois, lives in Davenport, has varied business pursuits, including the management of Happy Joe's Pizza places, and had at the latest roll call, nine children. They are Anne Marie, Sheila Eileen, Mary Elizabeth, Kathleen Mary, Patricia Frances, Steven Joseph, Christopher Philip, Thomas Peter, and Matthew Robert.

Patricia Wolfe, the third-born, married Eugene Higuera and lives in Simsbury, Connecticut. They have two children: Michael and Mary.

David, the fourth-born, is best known for his huge brown eyes and a voice with volume and vibrancy sufficient to rattle a raging rhinoceros. David and his wife Thora (Tori) Walshe (of Pasadena) run the family farm and teach. David has no leisure time whatsoever, and that's the way he likes it, while Tori has made a remarkable adjustment from the southern California environment to that of a Midwestern farm. Their children are Shaun Patrick, Mary Erin, and Kevin Walshe.

Richard, the youngest of the Melvin Wolfe family, lives in Bettendorf and is reputed to have once made a comfortable living by recharging the lightning rods of Midwestern farmers. He now strives mightily to ensure that collegians are sweet looking and sweet smelling, a task which has grown more challenging in recent years. His vehicle for this is his own creation, a company called Superbox. He is married to Mary Schepker of

Davenport. Their two children are Richard Joseph, Jr. (Duke), and Tucker Duffy.

The youngest of Maurice and Sarah was JAMES.[123] He was born in 1909 and promptly began enjoying himself. Life was seldom dull when he was around. In 1937, he married Alice Heath of Waterloo. Their farm was located southeast of Lost Nation. Jimmy died in 1965, and Alice soon moved into town. Their five children are Celine, James (Patrick), Sarah, Alice (Maureen), and Raymond.

Celine, the eldest, is employed by Illinois Bell in Chicago's Loop and works feverishly at the task of uniting the extended family through modern, instantaneous communication and simultaneously gouging Ma Bell. As we write our monthly telephone checks, which do so much to enrich AT&T, let us silently thank brave Celine for striving so selflessly in her efforts *to get us back some of our own!* Celine is married to Daniel Wicks, a fellow employee, and they live in Lake Villa, Illinois.

Pat, the second born, married La Donne Henry from the Kansas City area. They now live near Denver (Lakewood) where Pat is doing construction work. They have two girls: Colleen La Donne and Kathleen La Dawn.

Sarah married Roger McNeil of rural Calamus, and they presently are farming in that area. Their home is an active place nowadays, and one could almost gather the impression that Roger and Sarah are just a bit busy. Their children are Michael James, Kathleen Marie, Patricia Ann, and Christopher Roger.

Maureen married Henry Olsen from Council Bluffs, and they now live in Iowa City. Henry works for MRC and Maureen for ACT. (The writer has no idea what either of these sets of initials represents.) They have one child, Henry R. Olsen, II.

Ray, the youngest child of James and Alice, is now living in Denver and married a native of that city, Annette Nelson. She works for the VA, and Ray is presently doing welding work on pipelines.

In the manner just described, we find the Wolfe line extending from John R. and Honora through Maurice and Sarah brought to date. Certainly, we third generation Wolfes and McAndrews have been blessed, and we presumably don't wish to see our own children faced with any unnecessary ordeals. Let us all thank our Irish God that the youngest generations will be half so lucky as we have been.

---

[123] James Emmet Wolfe (1909–1965)

APPENDIX XV:
"Looking Back: Our Irish Legacy" (2007)

In this essay, dated August 9, 1981, and revised in November 2007, Thomas A. Wolfe (1940–2012), of Davenport, Iowa, investigates the origins of the Wolfe family in Ireland. It was originally written for a biannual family reunion in Clinton County, Iowa.

BECAUSE THE WOLFES HAVE always claimed to be Irish, it seems fitting that we look back today to both the history of the Wolfes and that of Ireland itself. The past is everything to the Irish, and that past is shrouded in mysticism, which has always been considered more important than reality. Thus, dedicated Irish mystics like Wolfe Tone, Lord Edward Fitzgerald, Robert Emmet, Smith O'Brien, Patrick Pearse, and today's IRA hunger strikers have all gone to their deaths for a cause supported at first by few and approved by little more; yet, the public eventually rallied to their support because there have always been poets and balladeers around to create demigods out of confused and desperate mortals. From the grim slaughter resulting from Wolfe Tone's Rising of 1798, for example, there arose the stirring ballad known to all would-be Irish revolutionaries, "The Rising of the Moon":

> Down along yon singing river, that dark mass of men was seen;
> High about their shining weapons floats their own beloved green;
> Death to every foe and traitor! Forward strike the marching tune.
> And hurrah, my boys, for Freedom! 'Tis the Rising of the Moon.

"In Ireland, states one writer, "the past is the present and the present won't be important until the future has arrived and the present becomes the past."

Ireland's problem with the English all began, of course, because of a woman. Had Tiernan O'Ruairc, a truly unfortunate Celt, been single rather than married, there might never have been an English invasion, and nearly eight hundred years of British rule might have been avoided. It seems that O'Ruairc was angry with Dermot MacMurrough because the latter had borrowed the former's wife, Dervogilla, a matter not to be taken lightly even today—either wife-stealing or naming her Dervogilla. O'Ruairc raised an army and invaded MacMurrough's lands. The latter promptly fled to England with his pretty daughter Eva. Finding King Henry II, he asked him to invade Ireland and smite O'Ruairc in the process. Now, the king had a large family to find kingdoms for, so the idea appealed to him. He gave MacMurrough permission to recruit a force of Norman-English. (The Normans, from the northwestern province of Normandy in today's France, had successfully invaded England a hundred years earlier, in 1066.) As a pretext for invasion, Henry persuaded the Pope, an Englishman named Adrian IV, to grant him permission to invade, the excuse being some obscure ecclesiastical irregularity dating back four hundred years, to a Papal conference in the 8th century.

Richard Fitz-Gilbert, Strongbow to the Irish, invaded Ireland in 1170 with a small band of well-armed Normans and received MacMurrough's Eva as a prize. Strongbow's Normans established a few beachheads in eastern Ireland and added some names to Irish and American history like Fitzpatrick, Fitzgerald, Butler, Burke, and, dear reader, even Wolfe. These Norman Wolfes, like their friends the Burkes and Fitzgeralds, were an avaricious lot, carving huge chunks of previously Celtic lands for themselves, mostly in counties Kildare and Limerick, the Kildare land being known as Wolfe Country. Their attitude seems to have been, "What is mine is mine, and what is thine is mine also."

The writer is unaware if the Norman family is the one from which we've descended. There are at least three other possibilities. There is an old Celtic name called Mactyre or O'Mactyre which becomes Wolfe in English. There was a pre-Norman Wulf who arrived with the Vikings in the 10th and 11th centuries, and there may have been a Prussian family (Prussia was the largest kingdom in what later became Germany) by that name who came to Ireland in the 16th century seeking religious freedom after Martin Luther's beliefs were accepted by the Prussian king. (During the Reformation, one embraced the King's religion if one valued one's skin.) It is this Prussian family whom the writer's Uncle Melvin[124] believes to be our direct ancestors. If so, the writer has no evidence.

It is the Norman Wolfes who are the most well-known in early Irish history though. The Wolfe name appeared again in Irish history during the Penal days of the 18th century. They clearly had land and money. It is not clear if we are related to them or another family, nor is it clear whether this is the Celtic, Viking, Norman, or Prussian branch. It is probably, though, that this is our family line, if for no other reason than that they had money. We know that John R. who emigrated in 1846,[125] had money, and because

---

[124] Melvin Maurice Wolfe (1904–1990)

[125] John Richard Wolfe (1809–1883) immigrated to the United States in 1847, arriving in New York from Liverpool on August 23 aboard the *Cornelia*.

this was highly unusual among Irish Catholics, it seems reasonable to believe that this pro-English family is our line of ancestry.

The struggle for Irish freedom from England grew more complicated when the Protestant Reformation spread to England and sectarian as well as economic differences manifested themselves in Ireland. There had always been hostility between the haves and have nots in Ireland; now, many of the haves were Protestants as well, making religion even more of a division within the country.

Two years after the first English colony was planted in Jamestown, Virginia, the English established another one in northeastern Ulster. In 1609 and later, the English settled thousands of Scottish Presbyterians (first cousins of the righteous Puritans). From that time until the present, Protestants rather than the native Catholics have had the advantage in employment. When Ulster, minus the three counties of Donegal, Fermanagh, and Cavan obtained home rule after World War I, these "Orangemen" set about systematically denying Catholics of Northern Ireland their basic civil rights, reducing them to the status of America's Southern blacks before the 1960s. Catholics could not own land or homes (with a few token exceptions), they could not vote or hold public office, and most of all, they were usually the last hired and the first fired. The British parliament dissolved Ulster's parliament in 1972 and restored many of the Catholics' rights, but guerrilla war now rages between terrorists of the IRA and the Ulster Defense League, with Britain pledged to keep Northern Ireland within the United Kingdom. Once again, Irishmen are killing Irishmen. All of the because of a decision made in 1609!

Religious warfare became especially serious throughout the 17th century. In 1641, there began a huge rebellion against Protestant landowners in Ulster. The Wolfes apparently lost all or most of their land as a result. Oliver Cromwell crushed the rebellion in 1652. One-third of Ireland's Catholics died during the eleven-year struggle. In 1690, the former Catholic king, James II, led an Irish army against the new Protestant king, William of Orange. James' defeat at the River Boyne, north of Dublin, is celebrated every July 12th by Orangemen. These wars have had a lasting effect on Irish mythology.

After the defeat at the Boyne, Parliament determined to punish all our ancestors through the Catholic Penal Laws, hoping to make them a permanently impoverished race of serfs.

1. No Papal-approved priests were allowed.
2. No Catholic could hold a public office.
3. No Catholic could vote.

4. No Catholic could teach children about Catholicism.
5. No Catholic could enter any professions and most trades.
6. No Catholic could hold land.

Irish humor was not totally obliterated during this period, though. Over the gates of Bandon in County Cork allegedly appeared these words:

> Enter here Turk, Jew, Or Atheist,
> Any man except a Papist.

To which were added the following words one night:

> The man who wrote this wrote it well,
> For the same is writ on the gates of Hell.

A delightful but probably apocryphal story going around during that period was that the Anglican archbishop of Dublin was so delighted that a Catholic named Myers had joined the Church of England that he held a dinner honoring this man and his most singular act. In front of many Protestant notables, Myers was asked on what grounds he had decided to reject Catholicism. "The grounds!" he growled. "Why, twenty-five hundred acres of the best agricultural grounds on the county of Roscommon!"

The Penal Laws, which were mostly repealed by 1782, effectively removed Catholics from public life. Thus, nearly all the great patriots and political leaders of the 18th and 19th centuries were Protestants, usually descendants of Cromwell's soldiers. Nearly all the leaders of the Rising of 1798, for example, were Protestants, including the most famous patriot of them all, Theobald Wolfe Tone. Therein lies a tale well told.

William Tone, Wolfe Tone's grandfather, lived on the Wolfe estate beginning in 1706, as did his descendants throughout the century, including Tone's mother, a servant in the home of Theobald Wolfe. The reader doubtless awaits with baited breath details regarding the Tone Connection, but the writer's Cousin Jack has deliberately confused him on this matter. The gist of it all seems to be that the great patriot, Wolfe Tone, is unrelated genetically to the Wolfes; however, he may have been the illegitimate son of one of the Wolfes.

Credence is lent to this theory in that Tone never once mentioned the Wolfes in his memoirs although they had played such a large part in his life, and by the curious actions of Lieutenant Governor Arthur Wolfe in 1794 and 1798. In 1794, Tone was implicated in a treason trial involving a fellow member of the Society of United Irishmen, which was devoted to independence and republicanism. Using his position in the British government to advantage, Wolfe helped persuade army prosecutors to spare Tone. Why did he do this? One historian phrased it this way: "Making use of his aristocratic friends' influence with the government ...," he agreed to various governmental demands, including emigration. It somehow pains the writer to think of his ancestors as pro-English aristocrats, but that is one of the risks one must accept when looking too far up the family tree.

In 1796, Tone accompanied a powerful French invasion fleet to Bantry Bay in County Kerry where a "Protestant wind" kept the ships from landing the troops. For the week or so while the fleet was thrown about the bay, Irishmen in Kerry busied themselves feeding British soldiers rather than French ones! The writer's great, great grandfather, Richard Wolfe from Listowel, Kerry,[126] may have been one of them. Digging deeply into family history can be a melancholy task sometimes.

This brings up two points often overlooked in Irish history. Seldom have Irishmen actually fought to replace British rule in Ireland, usually fighting instead to redress land grievances. Secondly, those government troops used to subdue the "Wilde Irish" were usually Irishmen themselves. The British used much the same technique in India and Africa; thus, when Tone's rebellion in 1798 was brutally crushed, the soldiers doing most of the slaughtering were poor Irish farm boys serving in the Royal Irish Constabulary and in the regular army.

Tone did not escape attention either. He was captured, convicted of treason, sentenced to be hanged, beheaded, disemboweled, and quartered. In his memoirs, he allowed that so long as the hanging occurred first he didn't care a flip about the rest, although he later panicked, attempted suicide, and succeeded after a week of agony. Right before the suicide, Lieutenant Governor Arthur Wolfe once again tried to help Tone (did he think he owed the arch-traitor something?), but this time the army would not consider releasing him.

The Kunta Kinte of our Wolfe family was John R. Wolfe of Listowel, County Kerry, born in 1824.[127] His father was Richard Wolfe (possibly spelled *Woulfe*).[128] Since the family was wealthy at a time when nearly everyone was quite poor, he received what great uncle P.B. Wolfe[129] called an "excellent education." This probably meant a college education or at least *some* college education. P.B. Wolfe further states that his father, John R.,

---

[126] Richard James Woulfe (1763–1842)

[127] The birthdate on his gravestone in Toronto, Clinton County, Iowa, is November 15, 1809.

[128] Richard James Woulfe (1763–1842)

[129] Patrick Bernard Wolfe (1848–1922)

helped organize the "Young Ireland" Party. This probably is incorrect although he may have had something to do with a local branch of it. Had he really been a founder, the chances are good that he would have either been arrested or run out of the country, and there is no evidence of either of those happening.

Young Ireland was begun in the late 1830s by a group of largely Protestant intellectuals who wanted to rebuild Irish nationalism. Their leaders were, among others, Thomas Davis and Smith O'Brien. Through their newspaper, they generally supported Daniel O'Connell's efforts to gain political freedom for Catholics and some sort of home rule within the empire. All went smoothly until the potato famine struck.

There had been many potato famines before in Irish history but nothing like this one. When the blight began in 1845, it affected about half the farms in Ireland, with the potatoes actually turning black in people's hands. It was worse a year later, and in 1847, the last year the crop failed, perhaps a million people had actually died from starvation! The poor croppies couldn't count on a decent meal until the next harvest, September, 1848. Starvation, disease, and emigration reduced the population of Ireland from around eight million in 1800 to about four million in 1860 and to two million by 1920. The Famine had reduced Ireland to a mere shell of its former self.

When the Famine began, Daniel O'Connell set aside his efforts to gain home rule for Ireland and concentrated upon persuading Parliament to give practical aid and comfort to Ireland's starving population. In this, he met with some limited success, possibly saving a few lives. This angered the young lions who comprised Young Ireland, and they began to openly criticize him for not being sufficiently nationalistic. By this time, John R. Wolfe was probably one of O'Connell's critics. In early 1848, the leaders of Young Ireland resolved to lead another rising. Perhaps that is what prompted Wolfe to emigrate. The plans were hardly a secret since the British knew all about them and crushed the handful of rebels immediately. It is possible that John R., with a lovely Belfast bride named Honora Buckley and several young children, decided that discretion was the better part of valor and headed west. This may be just wild speculation, but this is not a doctoral dissertation and a little fanciful conjecture adds a little spice to the narrative. It *is* true, however, that members of Young Ireland were in a lot of trouble by the time of Smith O'Brien's rising. Besides, since John and Honora Wolfe were relatively wealthy, why wouldn't they have wanted to stay instead of risking their futures in a strange land three thousand miles away? This is interesting and somewhat gratifying, at least to the writer, because John R. seems to have been the first Wolfe to possibly antagonize the British. All the others seemed to have supported them and were often even in their pay! Maybe

John R. wasn't a horse thief after all, as was alleged by the writer's father, Ray Wolfe,[130] but it's nice to know he may have had a spark of rebellion in him.

Like so many Irish American immigrants, John and Honora soon became totally engrossed in the struggle to tame their new land, first in Ottawa, Illinois and then in Lost Nation, raising ten children as Americans. It has been 161 years since John and Honora crossed the water with their growing family to begin their American experience, and as of this writing, a sixth generation of Wolfes graces this troubled planet. Let us hope their efforts are better than ours.

May their days be filled with blessings
Like the sun that lights the sky,
And may they always have the courage
To spread their wings and fly!

---

[130] Raymond Bernard Wolfe (1896–1941)

FAMILY TREES

KEY:

IN THE DICTIONARY

Emigrant

Expanded Below

MAURICE JAMES WOLFE (ca. 1630–ca. 1700)

(Farmed at Inchreagh, near Athea, County Limerick, and was likely related to a branch of the family sent west from Limerick city by the English after the Desmond Rebellion of the mid-sixteenth century)

Richard (never married)

Maurice

JAMES MAURICE (ca. 1651–1704), of Inchreagh

   (six daughters)

   Richard (b. ca. 1690)

   MAURICE JAMES "OLD MAURICE" (1690–Dec. 24, 1792) [m. Kathleen Riordan]

      JAMES MAURICE "THE BARRISTER" (1732–1817) [m. Kathleen Riordan]

         (A family line that includes the Iowa and Illinois Wolfes, Father Patrick Wolfe, and Thomas Wolfe of Beale Hill)

      Edmond Maurice

         (Little is known about this line except that some were transported to Australia; however, other fragments of family trees included below may connect through this brother)

      RICHARD MAURICE "SHORT DICK" (1730?/1752–Oct. 11, 1824) [m. Ellen O'Sullivan of Direen (d. 1830)]

         (A family line that includes Old Phil Wolfe, the soldier Maurice H. Wolfe, Richard E. "Dicky Ned" Wolfe, Richard W. Wolfe, and Seán de Bhulbh)

      Patrick "Wiggie"

         (Nothing yet is known about this brother)

      MAURICE JAMES "YOUNG MAURICE" (ca. 1763–bef. 1838) [m. Hanora "Norrie" Harnett (d. 1830)] "Maurice of Dromadda"

(A family line that includes the immigrant James H. Wolfe, Father Patrick Wolfe, Dr. Timothy Wolfe, and the teacher Caitlín de Bhulbh)

***

JAMES MAURICE "THE BARRISTER" (1732–1817) [m. Johanna McCoy (d. 1811)] of Garryantanavalla, near Listowel; buried Templeathea

James (d. 1817/1822?) twelve years old; buried Templeathea

RICHARD JAMES (1763–1842) [m. Johanna Relihan] of Dromlought

    JAMES RICHARD (1800–May 16, 1875) took over father's land at Dromlought in 1837; buried Templeathea

        MAURICE (ca. 1823–1909) of Kiltean [m. Mary Cronin]

            James M. (Dec. 11, 1867–Feb. 12, 1934), of Ballyouneen, Liselton, farmer [m. Mary (d. after husband)]

            Matthew (b. May 1, 1869) accused of murder in 1892, never tried

            Richard M. (b. May 24, 1870) accused of murder in 1892, never tried; vice chairman of the Listowel Rural Council

            Mary (b. Jan. 21, 1873)

            Margaret (b. March 29, 1874)

            Elizabeth (b. Aug. 5, 1875)

            John (b. Dec. 12, 1879)

            Timothy M. (July 29, 1881–1919), rep. of the Ballyegan Electoral District of the Listowel Union

            Maurice (b. July 2, 1891)

    [Daughter?]

        [John Dalton, of Ashgrove, Newcastle West]

    Richard (1842–1932) [m. Margaret Mulcahey]; buried Templeathea

> Richard

> John

Margaret (d. 1910) [m. Patrick T. O'Connor (d. after 1910)]

> Mary Agnes "Minnie" O'Connor (b. ca. 1870) [m. Timothy Devane (b. ca. 1872), April 24, 1900]

>> Daniel Joseph (b. March 16, 1901)

>> Charles Gerard (b. June 9, 1902)

>> Eileen Mary (b. Dec. 16, 1903)

>> Mary Josephine (b. April 22, 1905)

> Margaret O'Connor (b. Sept. 21, 1874) [m. Denis Harnett (b. ca. 1880) June 16, 1908]

> Julia O'Connor (b. ca. 1875) [m. John Lambe (b. ca. 1867), Feb. 2, 1897]

> Terence O'Connor (b. Dec. 31, 1877)

THOMAS WOULFE, of Beale Hill (1841–Aug. 29, 1915); given land in 1870, evicted 1885 [m. Catherine "Kate" O'Connor, 1852–April 19, 1932]

> James (Feb. 8, 1872–Feb. 19, 1955?) [m. Maria Stack (1880–1934) Feb. 24, 1906)]

>> Kathleen (1909–ca. 2006) [m. Thomas Mulvihill]

>>> Philomena "Phil" [m. Tim Buckley]

>> Edmond "Ned" (1910–1985) bachelor

>> John "Johnny" (1911–1992) [m. Bridget O'Connor (1912–1981)]

>>> Séamus [m. Philomena "Mina" Denihan] four daughters

>>> Marie [m. Gerry Quane] three daughters, one son

>> Sheila (b. 1913) [m. Pat O'Carroll] three sons, three daughters

>> Thomas (Sept. 20, 1915–May 7, 2015) [m. Cáit Purcell Kilkenny (d. 1972)]

>>> Siobhán (d. thirteen months)

> > Eithne (nun)
> >
> > Gemma [m. Hensey] twin
> >
> > Thomas [twin] banker
> >
> > Úna [m. Nolan]
> >
> > Muiris
> >
> > Richard (1916–1922)
> >
> > Mary B. (1920–2003)
>
> Mary "Minnie" (May 5, 1873–1950) [m. Maurice Stack]
>
> Julia (Jan. 1, 1875–1911)
>
> John "Jack" (Feb. 20, 1876–April 30, 1907)
>
> Richard (ord. All Hallows, Dublin, 1902; d. Feb. 1, 1922)
>
> Johanna "Hannah" (July 3, 1881–1954) [m. Pat Horgan]
>
> Margaret "Maggie" (b. Jan. 24, 1884) [m. Michael Downey]
>
> Bridget Mary "Bridie" (b. March 24, 1886) [m. Timothy Griffin, d. 1972] d. March 28, 1963
>
> > Sheila Griffin (d. 1983)
> >
> > Sean Griffin (d. 1990)
>
> Eily (d. Oct. 20, 1976) [m. Cornelius "Con" Morrissey, d. June 30, 1950; six children; Brosna, Co. Kerry, Eily taught at National School, Con ran a pub]
>
> > Margaret Mary "Peggy" (1921–April 30, 2008) Convent of Mercy, Abbeyfeale; entered convent in 1950; one report says youngest daughter?]
> >
> > <u>Mary</u> (July 26, 1927–2013) [m. Laurence "Larry" O'Dowd, July 31, 1963]
> >
> > Rachel (1931–March 13, 2003) took over pub; never married
> >
> > Sheila [m. Lyons] two sons, three daughters
> >
> > Kitty [m. McLoughlin]
> >
> > Edward "Eddie" Morrissey (Nov. 15, 1932–Jan. 30, 2014; born in Brosna, Kerry [ordained June 13, 1959] former, PP Saint Edward's, Rush-

olme, Manchester, died at Saint Ita's Community Hospital, Newcastle West

MAURICE RICHARD (1802–1870) DIMBY [m. Johanna Downey, 1826] of Knockanasig

> **MARGARET** (Aug. 1827–Oct. 12, 1906) [m. Bartholomew "Batt" Maher (1830–1904), May 2, 1852]
>
>> Catherine "Kate" (March 8, 1852–Feb. 19, 1932) [m. **RICHARD J. WOLFE** (May 5, 1843–May 25, 1927, 1871)]
>>
>>> Richard James (April 1872–1927)
>>>
>>> Charles A. (Feb. 1, 1877–Oct. 26, 1925) [m. Mabel Snyder (1883–1981), 1908]
>>>
>>>> Angeline E. (Feb. 11, 1915–Sept. 27, 1984)
>>>>
>>>> Charles R. (March 2, 1919–Feb. 20, 1999) [m. Lorraine Lillian (Sept. 26, 1922–Nov. 28, 1998)]
>>>
>>> Mary (b. 1879)
>>>
>>> Katie Florence (1884–1885)
>>>
>>> Bartholomew "Bart" (b. 1886)
>>>
>>> Evelyn C. (1891/1892–1968)
>>
>> **JOHN WALLACE** (Dec. 18, 1856–July 30, 1936) [m. Sarah Cecilia "Sadie" Coleman (b. 1868), May 29, 1884]
>>
>>> Mary (b. 1885)
>>>
>>> Josephine (b. 1886)
>>>
>>> Kathleen S. (b. 1889)
>>>
>>> Charles Howard (b. 1891)
>>>
>>> John Wallace Jr. (b. 1893)
>>>
>>> Evangeline G. (b. 1897)
>>
>> Johanna (b. 1857)
>>
>> Jerry (1860–1862)
>>
>> Jeremiah Leonard (July 19, 1867–April 23, 1966) [m. Emma Helena Mooney (March 6, 1865–April 30, 1943)]
>>
>> Bartholomew "Bartie" (1865/68–April 2, 1880)

> **MAURICE EDWARD** (April 24, 1869–Nov. 20, 1964) [m. Julie L. Casey (1873–1936), May 10, 1892]
>
>> Edward N. (b. ca. 1893)
>>
>> Jeremiah Leonard (b. ca. 1896)
>>
>> Julia (b. ca. 1899)
>
> James Francis (1870–Aug. 10, 1880)

RICHARD DOWNEY (bap. June 15, 1829–April 12, 1885) [m. Margaret O'Kane (1836–1865), Feb. 17, 1863] [m. Margaret Shine Lyons (1845–1908), Nov. 28, 1866]

> Katherine Collins (1863–1954, mother O'Kane)
>
> Johanna (1867–1899)
>
> Daniel Maurice (1869–1919)
>
> **HONORIA EUPHRASIA "HONOR"** (1871–1951)
>
> **MAURICE PATRICK** (1873–1909)
>
> Margaret Theresa (1875–1951)
>
> Richard (1878–1907)
>
> Marie Louise (May 31, 1881–March 6, 1965)
>
> **AILEEN GREGORY** (Feb. 20, 1884–March 17, 1956) [m. Hawley Sweet McCall (1883–Feb. 18, 1939), Feb. 21, 1914]
>
>> Richard Hawley (Feb. 15, 1917–Sept. 17, 1988) Capt. US Army, WWII
>>
>> Maurice Woulfe (May 19, 1920–Aug. 5, 2009) [m. Kathryan Jodelle Gaines (1923–1999), 1943] bomber pilot WWII
>>
>>> David Gaines (May 22, 1948–Jan. 21, 1975) died of cancer
>>>
>>> Joseph Hawley "Joe" (b. 1951)
>>>
>>> Marilyn Ruth (b. 1953) [m. Puffer]
>>
>> Margaret Frances (b. June 11, 1925)

Stephen (1833–before 1849)

JAMES DOWNEY (March 1, 1839–Feb. 19, 1923) [m. Mary Matilda Curtin (1851–Dec. 21, 1911), May 27, 1890]

Margaret (March 14, 1893–Aug. 15, 1976) [m. Luke Neary Finnerty (July 9, 1891–Jan. 4, 1971)

Johanna Josephine M. "Josie" (May 14, 1895–Dec. 17, 1985) [m. Frank J. Corrigan (July 9, 1896–July 27, 1961)] three sons

James

Johanna E. (1840–Aug. 22, 1862)

CATHERINE "KATE" (bap. Dec. 7, 1842–Nov. 6, 1922) [m. Joseph G. Hepler, Jan. 16, 1890] no children

Maurice (b. 1848)

John Francis (b. 1850)

EDMUND DEAN (bap. Oct. 19, 1853–July 14, 1921) [m. Margaret Estelle Mooney (July 26, 1859–July 22, 1946)], Dec. 29, 1886]

Johanna Irene "Gerena" (Oct. 24, 1887–Feb. 16, 1983) [m. John Mathias Briggeman (Oct. 7, 1875–Jan. 8, 1949)]

WILLIAM ANTHONY (April 22, 1889–Sept. 4, 1967) [m. Nan Virginia Cudd (1898–March 24, 1930), 1920] [m. Nellie M. DeKalb (July 18, 1912–Oct. 6, 1988), 1942]

William Wellington (April 24, 1921–Dec. 31, 2008) [Dorothy Grace (Oct. 5, 1928–Nov. 16, 2007)]

Edward "Don" (April 26, 1891–Feb. 4, 1977) [m. Dorothy Velma Green (1912–2003)]

Donna [m. Parsons]

Richard (b/d 1896)

Maurice Eugene (Sept. 19, 1897–Aug. 19, 1974) [m. Lucile Firth Anderson (Sept. 20, 1912–Sept. 21, 1997)]

Margaret Ann (May 31, 1938–July 9, 2010) [m. Gough]

James Harve (June 2, 1954–Nov. 11, 2010) Dentist [m. Jean Brewer, June 28, 1983]

Alex (b. 1990)

JOHN RICHARD (1809–1883) [m. Honora Buckley]

JAMES BUCKLEY (b. 1844–1916) [m. Anne Ignatius O'Connor, Feb. 8, 1872]

    John O. C. (Aug. 1873–1959) [m. Rose L. McAndrew (1872–1952)]

    Jeremiah "Jerry" (1876–1949) [m. Mary Wiley, Aug. 23, 1887]

        James Wiley (b. April 7, 1910)

        Mary I. (1912–1964) [m. Schulz]

        Alice Grace (1922–1991) [m. Alward]

    May R. (b. 1878) [m. Frank Goodall]

    Honora L. "Nora" (1880–1960)

    James Leonard (Sept. 7, 1881–July 27, 1937)

    WALTER IGNATIUS (1886–1965) [m. Mary Helen Machemer (Oct. 1892–1961), Nov. 24, 1920]

        Thomas W. (b. 1922) Capt. USCG

        Mary Patricia

        Dorothy Anne

        Ellen "Joan" (Sept. 12, 1932–Nov. 19, 2011) [m. Nathaniel "Nat" Kutzman (Aug. 18, 1938–July 9, 2017), Aug. 18, 1964]

            John

            Lise [m. Jeff Pinkham]

    Anna (b. 1887) [m. Isidore S. Ryan (1887–1958)]

PATRICK BERNARD (1848–1922) [m. Margaret G. Connole, May 1, 1878]

    JOHN LOYOLA (July 31, 1879–July 17, 1962) [m. Mary Catherine Kane (Feb. 3, 1890–April 10, 1976), Oct. 16, 1912)

        JOHN PATRICK (Sept. 26, 1913–Oct. 12, 1997) [m. Olive Cloffie Keuhn (May 19, 1917–June 11, 2001)]

            Mary Catherine (b. 1943)

            Stephanie Marie (b. 1944)

            John Patrick Jr. (b. 1947)

Sheelah Ann (b. 1949)

Francis Kelly (b. 1952)

Bridget (b. 1954)

Matthew Kane (June 1, 1916–Sept. 10, 1999) [m. Marilyn L. Corson (1920–1985)]

Mary Catherine (1918–1920))

Robert Francis (Oct. 25, 1921–March 9, 1943) died WWII

Margaret Ann "Margie"

Mary Zeta "Molly" (b. 1881)

JOHANNA (1849–1926) Sister Scholastica, Order of Sister of Mercy

JOHN BUCKLEY (March 10, 1851–July 16, 1923) [m. Mary Ann Lyons (Dec. 1861–1946]

    John Vincent (b. 1888)

    Irene Mary (March 2, 1891–Jan. 26, 1968) [m. Timothy James Lahey (March 7, 1876–June 12, 1946)]

        Cyril Timothy (July 30, 1924–Jan. 30, 1928)

    Edward Lyons (b. 1892)

    THOMAS LYONS (Dec. 4, 1894–Feb. 19, 1974) priest

    Frances Lyons (b. 1896)

    Paul Joseph Lyons (May 29, 1900–Feb. 18, 1960) [m. Rosalie Anna Burnett (Dec. 15, 1900–July 18, 1992)]

    Eugene Maurice (b. 1902)

    Cyril Dennis (b. ca. 1906)

MAURICE BUCKLEY (1855–Jan. 4, 1928) [m. Sarah McAndrews, April 3, 1894]

    RAYMOND BERNARD (1896–1941) [m. Gladys Elizabeth McGinn, Aug. 25, 1925)

        SARA TERESE (1926–1998) [m. George Richard Wissing]

        MARY KATHRYN (1929–2004) [m. John Welsh]

        Margery [m. Edmund Butler]

THOMAS ANTHONY (Dec. 20, 1940–Aug. 4, 2012) [m. Frances Siena Cupp (b. Nov. 17, 1942), Aug. 1, 1964]

    Bridget Colleen (b. April 2, 1967)

    Brendan Martin (b. Aug. 31, 1971) [m. Kate J. Grossman, 2003] [m. Mary Wharton "Molly" Minturn, 2008]

        Beatrix Minturn (b. Oct. 22, 2009)

    Sara Elizabeth (b. Dec. 16, 1973) [m. Albert S. Womble III, Aug. 15, 1993]

        Sienna N.

        Indigo A.

PHILIP JAMES (July 23, 1898–Aug. 6, 1979) [m. Alice Mildred Gribbon (1906–Aug. 23, 19990), Feb. 12, 1930] no children

JOHN JOSEPH (June 13, 1901–June 2, 1974) [m. Ida Ann Burke, Nov. 25, 1936]

    Marianne

    John Joseph "Jack" Jr.

MELVIN MAURICE (May 27, 1904–Dec. 29, 1990) [m. Frances M. McLaughlin (1900–Feb. 15, 1967), Aug. 26, 1930]

    Paul

    Robert A. (b. 1935)

    Patricia

    Leo David

    Richard

JAMES EMMET (Sept. 11, 1909–April 28, 1965) [m. Alice Marie Heath (1911–Feb. 1, 2000), July 27, 1937]

    Celine (b. 1938)

    James Patrick "Pat"

    Sarah

    Alice Maureen

Raymond

MARGARET I. (1857–btw. 1930 and 1940) [m. Dr. Daniel Langan (1836–1914), Nov. 28, 1894]; no children; Dr. Langan widower with seven children

CATHERINE "KATE" (March 1860–1947) [m. Thomas D. Fitzgerald, Nov. 28, 1894]

    Margaret M. (b. 1897)

RICHARD BOYLE (Feb. 16, 1862–Oct. 17, 1940) [m. Hannah Dunnan, Aug. 5, 1896]

    John Richard (b. 1898)

    Francis Dunnan (b. 1900)

    Winifred M. (b. 1903)

    Mary Gertrude (d. Dec. 1906)

ELLEN (ca. 1810–1886) [m. Patrick Maher, ca. 1828]

    MARGARET MAHER (1829–1872) [m. James Twohey, June 26, 1854]

        Jeremiah (b. 1855)

        Mary A. "Mollie" (b. 1857)

        Ellen Honora (b. 1858)

        John Joseph (b. 1860)

        Jeremiah Lawrence (b. 1861)

        James William "Will" (b. 1864)

        Thomas Francis "Frank" (b. 1867)

        Clara Elizabeth (b. 1869)

        Margaret I. (b. 1872)

    Patrick Maher (b. ca. 1831)

    ELIZABETH MAHER (1836–1900) [m. Richard McCormick, Feb. 1860]

        Elizabeth "Lyda" (b. 1860)

        John Patrick (b. 1862)

        Andrew J. (b. 1864)

        Richard "Dick" (b. 1866)

Mary Ellen (b. 1867)

MARGARET MARY (July 18, 1877–March 15, 1910) [m. John Kuhn (1867–1970), Feb. 19, 1901]

    Margaret Elizabeth "Bessie" (b. 1902)

    Mary K. (b. 1905)

    Arthur (b. 1909)

Johanna Maher (b. 1838)

HONORA "NANNO" MAHER (1844–April 22, 1927) [m. **JAMES P. "PADDY" WOULFE** (1842–April 26, 1927), Feb. 26, 1870]

    Johanna (Sr. Bonaventure) (1871–1929)

    PATRICK (1872–1933) priest

    Richard (b. Aug. 25, 1873)

    Ellen (b. April 2, 1876)

    Maurice James (April 10, 1877—June 7, 1970) of Knockeen House [m. Johanna "Jo" Scollard, of Castleisland (1878–1941)]

        Hanora May (b. Jan. 6, 1904)

        Mary (b. Sept. 13, 1905)

        James (b. May 8, 1907)

        David Woulfe, MPSI (b. May 15, 1909)

        Richard (b. Dec. 19, 1910)

        MAURICE (Nov. 21, 1912–Dec. 18, 1989)

        Patrick Austin "Paddy" (Nov. 19, 1914–July 23, 1977) senator

    Unknown (b/d. July 10, 1879) male, lived 1 hour

    John J. (b. June 13, 1880) [m. Ellen Reidy (d. Dec. 17, 1945?) Feb. 11, 1902]

        James (b. Oct. 26, 1904)

        John (b. Oct. 26, 1905)

        Elizabeth (b. Feb. 7, 1908)

        Patrick (b. July 26, 1911)

    James (b. June 29, 1882)

TIMOTHY (June 12, 1885–1969) [m. Mary Malvena Mullaly, Dec. 24, 1930)]

    Malvena (d. 2010)

Bartholomew Maher (b. 1846)

Mary Maher (b. 1848)

ELLEN MAHER (b. ca. 1849–Sept. 29, 1943) [m. Richard James "Brown Dick" Woulfe (April 6, 1853–June 7, 1915) Feb. 26, 1881]

    <u>Honora "Nora" Woulfe</u> (Feb. 15/23, 1882–Aug. 1927) [m. James Joseph Roche (1875–1928)] Imm. 1897, d. Brewster, New York

        Margaret V. Roche (1903–1985)

        James J. Roche (1908–1983)

        John Patrick Roche (1910–1955)

        Thomas F. Roche (1912–1943)

        Lawrence Stephen Roche (1913–1993)

        Anne Theresa Walsh (1915–2007)

        Raymond J. Roche (1919–1971)

    John R. J. Woulfe (Aug. 21, 1883–March 7, 1960) [m. Nora Woulfe (d. Aug. 3, 1973)] farmer, chairman of Cratloe branch of Irish Creamery Milk Suppliers' Association

        Richard

        Helen

        Kathleen

        Nora

        Ann

        May [m. Kenneth Juffkins]

    Ellen "Ellie" (Aug. 31, 1885–Oct. 11, 1894) died of meningitis

    Patrick (May 15, 1887–March 1963) [m. M. Courtney] managed Creamery

    Catherine (b. March 4, 1889)

MAURICE RICHARD (March 9, 1891–Nov. 24, 1962) Ordained March 16, 1916

THOMAS RICHARD (1811–March 23, 1876) [m. Ellen Leahy]

    RICHARD L. (ca. 1837–June 7, 1904) [m. Mary Fanning (d. April 7, 1918), 1889]

        Richard (d. before 1900)

        Irene (b. 1892)

    Margaret (b. 1837)

    John (ca. 1839–btw. 1848 and 1850)

    THOMAS L. (Aug. 1840–May 26, 1908) [m. Katherine Mulvihill, May 5, 1875; her father's second wife was MARGARET WOLFE MULVIHILL (ca. 1845–1888), daughter of MAURICE WOLFE (ca. 1800–1879)]

        Thomas Edward (b. 1876)

        Joseph (d. before 1900)

        Vincent (d. before 1900)

        Nellie (b. 1883)

        Cornelius (b. 1885)

        Francis Leroy "Roy (b. 1891)

    Hanora (b. ca. 1843)

    James (ca. 1845–before 1850)

    Mary Johanna (b. ca. 1846)

    Catherine "Kitty" (b. 1847)

    Ellen "Nellie" (b. 1853)

    Maurice (b. ca. 1855)

Johanna (b. 1812)

RICHARD (bap. July 16, 1815–Sept. 12, 1906) [m. Mary Carney, Feb. 26, 1838]

    Margaret (b. 1841)

    JOHN (1845–March 27, 1919) [m. Johanna Dillon (d. Nov. 15, 1918), June 6, 1876]

        Johanna "Jennie" (b. 1880)

Wolfe's History

John (b. 1884)

Richard William (b. 1887)

RICHARD "UNCLE DICK" JR. (March 12, 1847–June 13, 1921) never married

Michael (b. ca. 1848)

Sara Elizabeth (b. 1854)

Ellen V. "Nellie" (b. ca. 1856)

James (b. ca. 1858)

JAMES RICHARD (April 19, 1863–Oct. 25, 1941) [m. Johanna Josephine Wolfe (d. June 24, 1903), Oct. 27, 1890; her parents, Patrick and Catherine, were from Co. Kerry] [m. Mary Cull (d. Nov. 18, 1905), 1904]

    Mary Josephine (1891–1906)

    Catherine (b. 1893)

    Edna (b. 1895)

    Richard (b. 1897)

    Arthur (ca. 1900–1903)

    Margaret Cull (b. ca. 1905) (mother Mary Cull)

MARGARET ELLEN (b. Sept. 27, 1818) [m. Dennis Sheehan]

Mary (b. 1841)

PATRICK W. SHEEHAN (Nov. 13, 1843–Oct. 19, 1894) did not marry

Margaret Ellen (b. 1847)

DENNIS WOLFE SHEEHAN (June 15, 1852–Aug. 25, 1907) [m. Julia Ann Halpin (d. 1946), Sept. 12, 1882]

    Pauline Ellen Genevieve (b. 1884)

    Theresa Clarissa (b. 1886)

    May A. (b. 1889)

    Dorothy E. (b. 1892)

    Natalie D. (b. 1892)

    Marguerite M. (b. 1896)

> **BRIDGET ELLEN** (June 28, 1853–Oct. 28, 1910) [m. John Nixon (d. Feb. 10, 1912), Nov. 27, 1900]
>
>> James Joseph Nixon (b. 1889)
>
> Thomas (b. 1860)

EDMOND (b. 1821; bap. Feb. 2, 1822) began to work father's land in 1844; moved to Ashgrove, near Newcastle in 1851 [m. Mary Liston, at least six children]

> **EDMOND EDWARD** (ca. 1842–March 25, 1889) [m. Nancy Hartnet (d. Jan. 19, 1905), June 29, 1867] immigrated to Illinois
>
>> Maurice M. (b. 1869)
>>
>> Catherine (b. 1872)
>>
>> Mary (b. ca. 1874)
>>
>> Richard J. (b. 1876)
>
> James (b. 1848)
>
> Margaret (b. 1849)
>
> Maurice
>
> John E. (1852–1897) d. in Chicago

Patrick (Oct. 27, 1822–June 14, 1878) [m. Catherine O'Connell (d. after 1878)] Irramore; Patrick died of dysentery

> Ellen
>
> Mary (b. 1842) nun
>
> Edmond (b. July 21, 1853) [m. Honora Stack (d. May 14, 1889); m. Johanna Hannon, Nov. 9, 1889] farmer, Finuge
>
>> Maurice (b. Sept. 14, 1877) [mother Stack]
>>
>> Catherine "Katie" (b. June 29, 1879) [m. James McDonnell, 1909] [mother Stack]
>>
>> Mary Teresa "Minnie" (b. July 24, 1881) [m. James O'Sullivan, 1921] [mother Stack]
>>
>> John (b. Nov. 16, 1883) [mother Stack]
>>
>> Richard (b. July 18, 1892)
>>
>> Michael (b. Aug. 23, 1893)
>>
>> Ellen Aloysius (Aug. 4, 1895)

Edmond (b. Dec. 13, 1897) served time as IRA in Maidstone Prison

Johanna (b. May 28, 1900)

Margaret (b. Aug. 7, 1901)

Thomas (b. 1854) Jesuit

John (b. 1858) Jesuit

Patrick (b. 1860) Jesuit

Michael Joseph (b. Sept. 29, 1864)

Catherine Teresa (b. 1866) nun

Margaret [m. Ginell]

Richard [moved to Australia, disappeared]

[Unknown Son] [m. O'Sullivan]

ELLEN J. (April 1832–Feb. 21, 1902) [m. Eugene P. Redmond (b. 1825), April 23, 1854]

Jane (b. ca. 1855)

Arthur (b. ca. 1859)

Margaret (b. ca. 1859)

Edward J. (b. ca. 1861)

Richard (b. 1868)

MARY AGATHA (1834–1897) nun

JOHN EDMOND (Nov. 22, 1837–March 30, 1918) [m. Margaret C. Mills (May 21, 1844–Jan. 16, 1938), ca. 1929]

Edmund Mills (Aug. 26, 1864–Feb. 1, 1952) [m. Alice Margaret Lahey (1865–1941), Aug. 17, 1893, Bankston, Iowa] Northern Ill. College, Fulton, Ill., Ph.B., 1886; LL.B. State U of Iowa, 1888; bar, 1887

Margaret Ailene (1895–1897)

Marie Lucille (Feb. 4, 1897–May 26, 1975) never married

Alice Colette (Dec. 11, 1898–Dec. 17, 1982) [m. Harry W. Farrar (June 25, 1878–Aug. 8, 1936)]

Helen M. (Nov. 9, 1904–Dec. 4, 1985)

John James (April 19, 1907–Dec. 4, 1983)

Anthony Mills (April 16, 1866–Sept. 5, 1958) [m. Maude Alice Thompson (1873–1960)]

John Edmund (1902–1921)

Norbert Anthony (1904–1998)

Mathew Vincent (1906–1939)

Margaret Cecile (1909–1921)

Bessie Marie (1912–1990) [m. Oliver]

Mary Mayme (b. 1868)

Maurice Vincent (Jan. 14, 1874–Aug. 11, 1945) [m. Anna Marie Hart (1884–1979)]

Vincent Joseph (1915–1958)

Mary Ann Marie (1919–1993)

Patrick Joseph (b. 1874)

Cecelia Ellen (b. March 1875/1877–Oct. 7, 1966)

Ellen Vita "Nellie" (b. 1879/80–Dec. 12, 1950) [m. Edward Alphonsus Hart (b. 1871), April 25, 1916]

John (b. 1883)

Arthur Gerald (Dec. 6, 1885–June 4, 1972) [m. Dorothy E. McGarry (1889–1950)]

MAURICE JAMES (1755–1824) [m. Ellen Dore (also O'Dower) (1770–1827), Feb. 23, 1784] of Knockanasig, buried Templeathea

JOHN (ca. 1794–1863) [m. Julia Stack, March 6, 1821] [m. Bridget Ann Foley, ca. 1831]

Margaret (b. ca. 1821) [mother Stack]

Eleanor (b. ca. 1821) [mother Stack]

Mary (b. 1826) [mother Stack]

Ellen (b. 1827) [mother Stack]

Katherine Marie (b. 1832)

MAURICE (1837–after 1915) [m. Mary (d. btw. 1898 and 1900)]

Daniel

Johanna (b. ca. 1841)

ANN (1845–1912) [m. Joseph Collison, Feb. 1874]
    William (b. 1875)
    John R. (b. 1877)
    Joseph B. (b. 1878)
    Daniel A. (b. 1880)
    Frederick Paul (b. 1882)
    Mary (b. 1885)
    MAURICE L. "MORT" (Oct. 19, 1887–Feb. 5, 1981, twin) [m. Florence Ryant, June 12, 1923]
        Margaret Mary
        Marilyn
        Carol
        Art
        Pheanis
    Frank L. (b. Oct. 19, 1887, twin)
    ARTHUR (April 1890–Nov. 1, 1903)
Bridget (b. ca. 1846)
Julia (b. ca. 1848)

RICHARD (1795–1871) [m. Mary Foley (1802–1861)]
    Margaret (1826–April 9, 1883) [m. Patrick Fanning (1816–1862)]
    Mary (March 1826–March 23, 1912) [m. Edmund O'Donnell, 1849]
        Edmund
        James
        [Daughter] [m. John F. McDonald]
    Maurice (1828–1887)
    Mary Ellen (1829/1820?–March 30, 1900) [m. Michael Flahaven (April 19, 1824–before 1860)] [m. John Kennedy (1821–1909), Jan. 25, 1860]
        Mary (1845–1910) [father Flahaven]
        Thomas Richard (1849–1923) [father Flahaven]

> > Margaret Rachael (1852–before 1900) [father Flahaven]
> >
> > Daniel (1860–1932)
> >
> > John (1862–1938)
> >
> > Ellen "Nellie" Brennan (1864–1924)
> >
> > Anna Barron (1866–1945)
>
> Patrick (March 17, 1830–June 20, 1915) blacksmith, did not marry
>
> **DANIEL F.** (ca. 1832–Nov. 16, 1882) did not marry
>
> Richard (1836–before 1843)
>
> John Maurice (b. 1838)
>
> Bridget (b. 1839)
>
> Edward (July 14, 1840–Dec. 12, 1911) [m. Catherine O'Donnell (1847–1914)]
>
> > Richard (1869–1883)
>
> **RICHARD J.** (May 5, 1843–May 25, 1927) [m. Catherine "Kate" Maher (March 8, 1852–Feb. 19, 1932), 1871]
>
> > Richard James (April 1872–1927)
> >
> > Charles A. (Feb. 1, 1877–Oct. 26, 1925) [m. Mabel Snyder (1883–1981), 1908]
> >
> > > Angeline E. (Feb. 11, 1915–Sept. 27, 1984)
> > >
> > > Charles R. (March 2, 1919–Feb. 20, 1999) [m. Lorraine Lillian (Sept. 26, 1922–Nov. 28, 1998)]
> >
> > Mary (b. 1879)
> >
> > Katie Florence (1884–1885)
> >
> > Bartholomew "Bart" (b. 1886)
> >
> > Evelyn C. (1891/1892–1968)
>
> Edmund Maurice (d. 1832)
>
> > Maurice Edmund (d. 1864) of Dromala, Co. Kerry, buried Templeathea
> >
> > James (d. 1870), ofr, buried Templeathea

MAURICE (ca. 1800–April 1, 1879) [m. Ellen Catherine Carey (1811–1857), Feb. 14, 1830] 12 children, 11 survived to maturity

James Carey (b. 1831)

ELLEN (Nov. 17, 1833–April 20, 1908) [m. Edmund George Mulvihill, Sept. 28, 1854]

> Jeremiah (March 3, 1858–Jan. 11, 1916) [m. Johanna Mulvihill (1868–1963)]
>
> Mary Agnes "Minnie" (b. ca. 1860)
>
> Maurice (b. 1860)
>
> Ellen "Nellie" (b. 1862)
>
> Edward (b. 1864)
>
> John Ambrose (b. 1866)
>
> Catherine "Katie" (b. 1867)
>
> James (b/d 1870)
>
> Thomas S. (1872–1899)
>
> William Henry (b. 1875)

MAURICE CAREY (ca. 1835–Oct. 28, 1910) never married

Mary (1838–Aug. 9, 1909) [m. Thomas W. Welch (1839–1918)]

JOHN CAREY (bap. Jan. 16, 1840–July 25, 1902) [m. Ellen Louise Martin, Nov. 27, 1884]

> **MAURICE JOSEPH** (April 20, 1886–June 20, 1918) [m. Imogene Ann "Jean" Irving, ca. 1912]
>
>> **JOHN MAURICE** (June 30, 1913–July 2, 1951) [m. Estelle]
>>
>> Peter
>>
>> Margaret I (b. 1915)

Thomas Carey (1843/1845–March 18, 1932) [m. Mary Ann James (b. Feb. 15, 1874)] nine children

> Cecilia (May 1875–1910) [m. Joseph Henry Meyers (1871–1959), Aug. 16, 1899]
>
>> Rita Marie (July 7, 1900–Jan. 9, 1988) [m. Ivo H. Baumhover, Aug. 23, 1920]
>
> Anna (Aug. 20, 1877–Aug. 1956) did not marry
>
> Maurice Vincent (April 4, 1879–April 24, 1965) [m. Adelaide C. Meyers (1882–1968)]

> Helen M. (1908–1951) [m. Paul L. Rudy (1905–1944)]
>
> Maxine Adeline (Aug. 12, 1910–Feb. 20, 1999) [m. Leroy E. Stroder (1903–1961), 1938]
>
> Raymond Lewis (May 10, 1914–March 13, 1978) [m. Marion Irene Blackmer (1920–1992)]
>
> Maurice James (April 30, 1926–April 29, 1970)

Florence R. (1881–1968)

Joseph James (1883–1971)

Thomas Arthur (1885–1977)

Edmund Bernard (1888–1970)

John P. (1891–1974)

MARGARET (ca. 1845–Jan. 5, 1888) [m. Cornelius Mulvihill (1833–1887), 1871]

> Honoria (b. ca. 1874)
>
> Elizabeth "Bessie" (1876–1898)
>
> Thomas Edward (b. 1878)
>
> Cornelius (March 1880–Jan. 18, 1910)

Johanna (Jan. 1847–Dec. 8, 1908) [m. Frederick A. Collison (1848–1937), April 15, 1880]

> Ann J. (March 1881–Aug. 11, 1961) did not marry
>
> Elnora "Nell" Clara (Dec. 25, 1882–Dec. 19, 1974) did not marry
>
> Frederick F. (March 10, 1884–March 16, 1988) [m. Mary Hoeft, April 2, 1913]
>
>> Richard
>>
>> Dorothy
>>
>> Cathleen
>>
>> Ned
>>
>> Mary Joan
>
> Mary Veronica (April 29, 1887–March 26, 1971) nurse, did not marry

RICHARD CAREY (Oct. 12, 1848–May 20, 1919) [m. Margaret McGonnegle (d. June 8, 1894), April 16, 1877]

    James (March 1878–Feb. 13, 1921) mining engineer

    Ellen Calista "Nell" (May 24, 1880–April 11, 1960) [m. Richard Joseph White (1885–1952), 1913]

        Richard Martin (April 22, 1924–Dec. 2, 2010)

    MAURICE VINCENT (May 31, 1882–1927) [m. Gertrude Josephine Scanlan (b. April 17, 1890), Feb. 8, 1921]

        Mary Virginia (b. Dec. 17–19, 1921)

    Edward Anthony (Aug. 3, 1884–Feb. 4, 1950) [m. Anna Luetta Murphy (March 11, 1894–Dec. 6, 1966]

        James Edward (March 30, 1921–Oct. 14, 2012) [m. Dorothy Mae Bonds (1923–2005)]

            Margaret Rose "Peggy" (Jan. 30, 1953–Oct. 15, 2014) [m. Moore] fourth of seven children

        Julianna A. "Julie" (Feb. 9, 1923–Aug. 3, 2012) [m. Clancy Mulvaney (d. 2000)]

            Ana

            Barbara

            John

        Margaret Sue (1925–Sept. 26, 2003) [m. Mark E. Darrough (1922–1976) m. James Phalen]

            Susan Darrough

            Patricia Darrough [m. Holm]

            Joseph Darrough

            Katie Phalen

            Molly Phalen

            Martha Raaka

            James Phalen

            Patrick Phalen

        EDWARD ANTHONY "ED" (Jan. 2, 1929–March 8, 2009) pitched for Pittsburg Pirates, 1952

> > Jack Frankhobart (Aug. 2, 1931–Aug. 8, 1990) [m. Docia Frances Duncan (1920–2008), Aug. 8, 1971, Carson City, Nevada]
>
> John Gregory (Nov. 28, 1886–Oct. 15, 1963)
>
> Catherine W. (April 2, 1889–April 4, 1979) [m. John George Verkamp (1877–1944)]
>
> > Margaret Mary "Peggy" (Feb. 24, 1913–Sept. 1, 1989) did not marry
> >
> > Mary Janet (March 25, 1915–Aug. 8, 1971) [m. Richard Max Trisler (1918–1974)]
> >
> > > Richard Max (Aug. 21, 1947–Nov. 18, 2016) [m. Martha Brooks Alexander]
> > >
> > > > Richard Thomas
> > > >
> > > > Daniel Max
> > > >
> > > > Meaghan "Kate" [m. Jensen]
> > > >
> > > > Rosemary [m. Wegmann]
> > > >
> > > > Christine
> > >
> > > Catherine Irene "Cat" (May 21, 1953–June 6, 2010)
> >
> > John George (June 13, 1916–March 18, 2001) [m. Mary Elizabeth O'Leary (1917–1957), 1939] [m. Betty Eileen Cannon (1924–2001), 1960]
> >
> > Catherine (Oct. 25, 1919–Jan. 19, 1971) [m. Tom Allen Martin (1914–1974)]
>
> Joseph (b/d 1892)
>
> Catherine "Kate" (June 1, 1851–Aug. 24, 1938) [m. Frank Staak (d. April 29, 1912)]
>
> > [Son] died in infancy
>
> Bridget Veronica (Nov. 4, 1854–Dec. 8, 1902) did not marry

Edmond [per obit of Richard Maurice Woulfe of Kiltean, d. 1915, this could be son who lived at Cratloe and did not have sons of his own]

> (Daughter) [m. Sheehy]
>
> > Edmond Sheehy, of Cratloe, first county councilor (1899) for Monegay Division of Co. Limerick

***

Edmond Maurice (d. ca. 1798) [m. before 1760? d. 1824?; buried Templeathea]

    Maurice Edmond (d. 1826), buried Templeathea

    Catherine "Kate" (d. 1818) [m. Colbert], buried Templeathea

    Edmond (d. 1824?/1840?), farmed Bennaline; buried Templeathea

        Richard (d. 1910) [m. Mary]

            Maurice Richard

    Richard (b. 1765) [m. ?]

        Maurice (ca. 1795–after 1849) Dromadda

            Mary [m. Edmond Dillane, 1834] [in conflict with Wolfe family, transported to Australia]

                Bridget (b. Jan. 24, 1835), Athea

                Edmond (b. Feb. 3, 1837), Athea

                John (b. Feb. 5, 1842), Athea

                Johanna (b. ca. 1843)

                [Unknown child]

***

RICHARD M. "SHORT DICK" (1730?/ca. 1752–Oct. 11, 1824) [m. Ellen O'Sullivan of Direen (d. 1830)] took over father's 2,000 acres; lived at the Glen; buried Templeathea

    Maurice Richard (1778–Nov. 17, 1841) of Gragure [m. Mary Danagher, daughter of Philip Danagher of Glenagower or Gleanagore, Athea, d. 1882], buried Templeathea

        Bridget (1795–April 8, 1860) [m. Patrick Arthur O'Keeffe (ca. 1790–Oct. 31, 1857, in Urbana, Ohio, at house of his daughter, Mrs. Nelligan; he had been exiled, Bridget stayed in Ireland] [m. Hartnett]

Bridget O'Keeffe (b. 1817), Ballaghbehy, Abbeyfeale Parish

Mary O'Keeffe (b. 1819)

Johanna O'Keeffe (b. 1821)

Maurice O'Keeffe (b. 1823)

Arthur Patrick O'Keeffe (1825–Jan. 7, 1906) Mason City, Iowa [m. Ellen O'Keeffe (1828–1915)]

    Cornelius (1858–1919)

Michael O'Keeffe (Oct. 1822–April 22, 1905) Quiver Township, Mason County, Illinois

Hanora O'Keeffe (1833–May 12, 1870) Urbana, Ohio

Bartholomew "Batt" (1809–Jan. 16, 1883), buried Templeathea

PHILIP MAURICE "OLD PHIL" (1810–1901) [m. Elizabeth Herlihy]

    MAURICE H. (1839–btw. 1910 and 1919) [m. Mary Carmody]

        Philip Maurice (1877–March 5, 1921) plumber

        Mary Ellen (b. ca. 1881) [m. Joseph F. Krieg]

    Joseph Philip (bap. Oct. 2, 1841–1918) [m. Johanna Roche (1854–Dec. 7, 1893) March 2, 1881]

        Philip Joseph (b. Jan. 21, 1882) could not speak

        Michael (May 23, 1883–1916) died at the Somme

        Elizabeth (b. April 7, 1885)

        Mary (b. Nov. 15, 1886)

        Margaret (b. Oct. 6, 1888)

        Annie (b. March 17, 1892)

    Michael (bap. Oct. 12, 1843)

    Mary (bap. Dec. 22, 1849) [m. John Breen, Feb. 23, 1878)]

    Elizabeth/Judith? (bap. June 16, 1852)

    John (bap. May 15, 1853)

Philip "Old Phil" (bap. July 7, 1855–Feb. 5, 1933) [m. Mary Breen (ca. 1851–May 28, 1931), Feb. 6, 1883]

    Philip (b. July 13, 1884)

    Michael P. "Mick" (March 28, 1886–March 20, 1968) [m. Ellie Roche (d. Jan. 26, 1925) on April 28, 1921] [m. Mary "Molly" O'Connor (1892–Sept. 4, 1959), March 4, 1930]

        Mary "May" (mother Roche)

        Timothy (b. June 1, 1934) [m. Nancy O'Donnell]

            Mary (b. Dec. 17, 1961) principal

            Michael (b. Nov. 29, 1963) civil engineer Tipperary county council

            Liam (b. June 10, 1965) principal

            Bernadette (b. Nov. 11, 1969) physiotherapy Camilla's Limerick, Saint Ite's Newcastle West

            Margaret Noelle (b. Dec. 21, 1971) environmental scientist

        Phillip (b. April 2, 1931) [m. Eileen Broderick]

            Michael

            Dona

            Phillip [m. Mary O'Connor]

        Margaret Christina (1935–1937)

        Hanora "Nora" (b. 1936) [m. Sean Broderick]

    Maurice (b. April 4, 1888)

    John P. "Jack" (May 5, 1890–June 23, 1979), buried Templeathea

Patrick (bap. March 6, 1857)

> Cornelius (bap. Sept. 23, 1858)
>
> Richard (bap. Sept. 7, 1859)
>
> Elizabeth (bap. April 16, 1861)
>
> Bartholomew "Batt"
>
> Patrick (b. Jan. 19, 1866)

Michael Maurice (1814–Feb. 23, 1889), Gragure, buried Templeathea

> Maurice "Maurice Mickey" (1854–May 1, 1946) of Gragure [m. Annie Marie Foley (1860–Aug. 22, 1898), Aug. 26, 1879] buried Templeathea, Inland Revenue; Customs and Excise; Clonmel

Mary (d. ca. 1880)

EDMOND RICHARD "OLD NED" (June 15, 1788–May 13, 1876) [m. Nellie Brosnan of Islandanny (1795–1869) on June 15, 1812] (7 daughters, at least 2 sons) died in Clash

> Edmond (d. after 2.27.00) [m. Ellen Flaherty?]
>
>> Richard (bap. April 3, 1859), Clash
>>
>> Edmond (b. April 1868, Clash North)???
>>
>> James (bap. March 16, 1862)
>>
>> Mariana (bap. May 31, 1864)
>>
>> James Edmond (ca. 1872–Aug. 20, 1924) [m. Margaret Quill (ca. 1876–March 18, 1963), Feb. 27, 1900]
>>
>>> Edmond [also Edward] Michael "Ned" (Aug. 24, 1901–Dec. 20, 1980) [m. Katharine]
>>>
>>>> Michael
>>>>
>>>> James
>>>>
>>>> Tony
>>>>
>>>> Margot [m. McHugh]
>>>>
>>>> Joan [m. Threadwell]
>>>>
>>>> Bernadette [m. Gerry Galvin]
>>>
>>> Ellen (b. Nov. 11, 1902)
>>>
>>> Denis (Jan. 16, 1904–April 20, 1964)
>>>
>>> Richard (April 1, 1905–Sept. 19, 1975)

Timothy (b. April 8, 1906)

Mary (b. June 10, 1907)

Margaret (b. June 14, 1908–April 20, 1963)

Patrick (b. Aug. 30, 1909)

James (b. May 14, 1911)

Unknown (b/d. April 11, 1913) son, lived five minutes

RICHARD EDMOND "DICKY NED" (1824–1910) [m. Catherine White (1828–May 2, 1900)]

Ellen "Nell Óg" [m. Daniel McAuliffe, Feb. 7, 1844, Monagea] Daniel McAuliffe related to Mary McAuliffe of Crioch Woulfes

    Cornelius (bap. Feb. 21, 1845, Monagea)

    Margaret (bap. Dec. 9, 1846, Monagea)

    Ellen (bap. Jan. 26, 1849, Monagea)

    Mary (bap. April 7, 1851, Monagea)

    Johanna (bap. May 4, 1853, Monagea)

    Catherine (bap. Jan. 16, 1855, Monagea)

    Bridget (bap. April 26, 1857, Monagea)

    Edmond (bap. Jan. 28, 1860, Monagea)

Johanna "Joan" [m. Harnett of Tournafulla] [m. William Harnett, Feb. 16, 1846, Monagea?]

(Daughter) [m. Murphy]

Bridget (ca. 1829–June 1911) [m. Michael White (d. after 1903)] Athea

    John Michael White (bap. Nov. 24, 1852–Feb. 6, 1930) of Clash [m. Johanna Leahy (ca. 1854–Oct. 2, 1924)]

        Michael (b. Dec. 16, 1884)

        Mary "Molly" (April 30, 1888–July 23, 1921) [m. O'Kelly]

        Bridget (b. May 15, 1890)

        James (b. May 12, 1894)

    Edmond Woulfe White (bap. Jan. 21, 1854–April 10, 1922) [m. Susan McAteer, Belfast, June 10, 1887]

> > Gerald Woulfe White (b. Nov. 3, 1887, St. Patrick's Belfast)
> >
> > Edmond Stuart White (b. April 29, 1889, St. Patrick's, Belfast) Lt. Royal Navy
> >
> > John Wyndham White (b. March 10, 1891, St. Patrick's Belfast)
>
> Thomas Michael (bap. April 21, 1855)
>
> Patrick (bap. Dec. 10, 1856)
>
> Honorah "Nano" (bap. April 20, 1858–Dec. 27, 1927) [m. Michael Dalton (ca. 1854–April 23, 1933), Feb. 12, 1882] Coole
>
> > James (b. Dec. 22, 1882)
> >
> > Thomas (April 18, 1890–1963)
> >
> > Johanna (b. March 7, 1893)
> >
> > Bridget (b. June 1, 1894)
> >
> > **PATRICK** (Feb. 23, 1896–May 12, 1921)
> >
> > Richard (May 13, 1897–1971)
> >
> > Mary "Mollie" (b. July 9, 1901)

Julia (ca. 1838–after 1911) [m. Denis Flaherty (ca. 1818–Feb. 7, 1887)] Newtowndillon

> Denis Flaherty
>
> Ellen Flaherty (b. July 12, 1864)
>
> Edmond Flaherty (b. May 25, 1865) [m. Catherine McEneiry (b. Jan. 24, 1881) April 19, 1902] Toberatoreen, Listowel
>
> > Denis (b. May 21, 1902)
> >
> > John (b. Dec. 26, 1903)
> >
> > Michael (b. July 31, 1905)
> >
> > James (b. March 3, 1907)
> >
> > Julia (b. June 13, 1908)
> >
> > Mary (b. Oct. 14, 1909)
> >
> > Ellen (b. Feb. 18, 1911)
>
> Joanna Flaherty (b. Nov. 18, 1867)

Michael Flaherty (b. Feb. 28, 1870) Toberatoreen, Listowel

Margaret "Peggy James" (d. 1874) [m. Edmond Sheehy]; buried Templeathea

    John (bap. April 4, 1849)

    Margaret (bap. Aug. 8, 1851)

    Catherine (bap. March 8, 1853)

    Bridget (bap. June 20, 1854)

    James (bap. July 7, 1855)

    Edmond (bap. Sept. 9, 1856)

    Mary

Patrick "Old Paddy" [m. Anna "Nance" Hartnett]

    Patrick (bap. March 11, 1831)

    Johanna (bap. March 7, 1833)

    Timothy (bap. March 9, 1835)

    James (bap. March 3, 1838)

    Edmund (bap. Feb. 8, 1842)

    Maurice [m. Bridget ?]

        Thomas (b. Dec. 26, 1870) [m. Elizabeth McCarthy]

            James "The Doctor" (b. Oct. 28, 1892)

                Thaddeus "Thady" (b. ca. 1934)

***

RICHARD EDMOND "DICKY NED" (1824–1910) [m. Catherine White (1828–May 2, 1900), Feb. 23, 1852]

Edward (bap. Sept. 5, 1852)

MAURICE RICHARD (bap. Dec. 13, 1853–April 15, 1928) – Elizabeth Malcolm "Bessie" Cockburn (1856–1943) m. Dec. 13, 1878, Milton Glasgow Lanarkshire

    JANE C. "DOLLIE" (1880–Aug. 8, 1964) [born in Glasgow, buried Templeathea]

Richard Edmund Maurice (1883–May 5, 1963) The Glen

MAURICE JAMES (1884–May 7, 1973) [m. Sarah McCarthy, Sept. 14, 1921] solicitor

    JOHN MAURICE (SEÁN DE BHULBH) (Sept. 22, 1922–Feb. 7, 2009) [m. Máire Ní Mhurchú, or Mary Murphy, 1956; d. 2005]

        Eibhlín

        Sadhbh

        Sibéal

        Muiris

        Seán C.

    Maurice Richard (1925–2018) [m. Mary Kemp, 1954] veterinary surgeon

        Deirdre

        Cayley

    Richard (1929–June 28, 2012) [m. Elaine Murphy, 1960], Solicitor

        Richard

        Carol Ann

        Lorraine

Honora "Nano" (bap. June 14, 1855) [m. Roney]

    Charles

    John

Mary (bap. April 3, 1857)

ELLEN "NELLIE" (bap. Dec. 7, 1858–Sept. 26, 1927) [m. Thomas C. Wren (1859–1900) also Limerick native, Chicago fireman] 1897, horse cart and electric car collide, Insane Asylum

    Richard James (Aug. 10, 1887–1939) [m. Theresa L.]

        Thomas J. Wren (April 29, 1922–Oct. 7, 2010) U.S. Army Air Corps, Chicago Metropolitan Sanitary District

        Mary Margaret [m. William Dillon]

        Richard J. Wren Jr. [m. Mary Letitia Birge d. 2006]

        Sr. Mary Richard Therese, BVM (1926–1988)

Maurice (b. Sept. 1885)

Johanna Loretta (b. June 1889) [m. Fred Belton]

Thomas Joseph Wren (Aug. 17, 1893–Nov. 4, 1955) [m. Marie W.] a Thomas Wren, who had since immigrated to USA, is listed as having served in H Company, 2nd Battalion, of the West Limerick Brigade, IRA

    Marie [m. Graver]

    Ellen L.

    Damien T.

John F. (b. July 2, 1896)

Catherine (bap. June 14, 1860) presumably died as infant

PATRICK RICHARD (July 1861 [bap. March 22, 1862]–June 5, 1939) [m. Julia E. (1879–1953)]

    Richard (1908–July 28, 1952) b. Bronx, NY, d. Chicago [m. Frances T.]

<u>John W.</u> (May 21, 1864 [bap. May 25]–Dec. 12, 1920) (d. Chicago), city engineer; imm. 1885 [m. Mary O'Connor (1873–1932)]

    Kathleen Isabelle (1896–May 8, 1930) [Kindergarten teacher, leader Chicago Federation of Teachers]

    Margaret E. (1897–1977) [m. Ralph Lewis "Jake" Lanum (1896–1968)

    Richard

    Marie [m. Kinnally]

    John (d. 1953?)

    Charles (1907–1961), Chicago city water department employee

    Anastasia H. "Ann" (1909–April 12, 1993) [m. Joseph McCabe (d. 1977)]

RICHARD WHITE (Aug. 25, 1866–1951) [m. Helen Lenz (1873–Jan. 8, 1961) Sept. 22, 1897]

    Grace C. (March 18, 1902–Oct. 26, 1983) [m. Ned Hume McCormack (1900–Oct. 7, 1995)] died at her home in Chicago Athletic Club

        Mark H. McCormack (Nov. 6, 1930–May 16, 2003) [m. Nancy Breckenridge, 1954–1984); m. Betsy Nagelsen] Godfather was the poet Carl Sandburg

            Scott Breckenridge "Breck" McCormack (b. 1957) [Hawken School, '76; Stanford, '81; UCLA School of Law, '84]

            Todd Hume McCormack (Sr. Corporate VP, IMG)

        Mary Leslie McCormack (b. March 1966) [m. Gathy]

        Maggie [daughter from second marriage]

Catherine (b. Aug. 25, 1868) [died Sept. 2, 1934, unmarried?]

Mary A. (Jan. 1870–Oct. 21, 1916, Cook Co., Ill.) [m. Michael C. Wolfe (Sept. 18, 1867–July 11, 1928)] (USA) [Father Patrick Wolfe, mother O'Connor]

    Edgar Richard Wolfe (Jan. 22, 1888–Sept. 28, 1969) [m. Nellie H. Hoever (ca. 1894–1980)]

        Helen (Sister Mary Caelan), O.S.F. (b. 1918 to 1920)

        Mary Elizabeth (Jan. 10, 1925–Oct. 26, 2013) Dominican nun

        Edgar R. Jr.

        Jean [m. Dangillo]

    Helen (Feb. 1886–May 13, 1962) [m. William P. Carroll (1872–1951)] b. New Hampshire, d. Cook Co.

        Richard J. (1914–Jan. 14, 1943), 2nd Lt., Army Air Forces, O-724703; died prisoner on sinking enemy sub, Med. Sea, 48th Fighter Squadron, 14th Group

    John Edward (March 20, 1892–Jan. 20, 1962) [m. Lillian R.]

        John P.

        Patricia E. [m. Troeger]

        Father Michael C., O.M.

    Marion V. (1895–1954) [m. Joseph P. Lavin (d. 1959)]

        Joseph P. Jr.

        Helen McKay

        Therese Collentine

Michael Richard (Nov. 26, 1870–March 24, 1903) [m. Ellen White, Feb. 11, 1902]

Johanna "Hannah" (Dec. 10, 1873–March 23, 1952) [m. Edward/Edmond J. "Ned" White (ca. 1870–Sept. 18, 1950), Feb. 11, 1902] Coole

    Margaret Mary (b. Dec. 21, 1902)

    James (b. Dec. 9, 1903)

    Catherine Mary (March 21, 1905–March 19, 1978)

    Thomas (b. Aug. 7, 1906)

    Bartholomew (b. Aug. 25, 1907)

Patrick Joseph (b. March 13, 1909)

Bridget (b. July 16, 1910)

Mary (b. March 2, 1913)

Johanna (b. July 14, 1914)

***

MAURICE JAMES "YOUNG MAURICE" (ca. 1763–bef. 1838) [m. Hanora "Norrie" Harnett, of Abbeyfeale, d. 1830] "Maurice of Dromadda"

JAMES HARNETT (btw. 1780 and 1800–ca. 1836)

RICHARD (1802–btw. 1850 and 1860) [m. Ellen]

    James (1843–1869)

    Ellen (b. 1844)

JOHN HARNETT (1807–1856) [m. Louisa Durbin]

    Mary A. (b. 1840)

    Lucretia (b. 1842) [m. Musgrove]

    Honora (b. 1845)

    Teresa Louisa (b. 1845) [m. Black]

    JAMES MAURICE (1851–1921))

Edmond

Timothy

Mary (d. before 1838) [m. Cain]

    Mary Cain

Maurice

Patrick Maurice (d. 1849) [m. Johanna "Hannah" McAuliffe, Feb. 25, 1807; m. Johanna Walsh of Knocknagoshel (d. 1870)] Hannah McAuliffe related to Mary McAuliffe of Crioch Woulfes

    Maurice [mother McAuliffe]

        Thomas (b. May 1, 1865, son of Maurice/Mary Sullivan of Abbeydorney; birth in Tralee workhouse?)

Honora (bap. Jan. 20, 1834)

Bridget (bap. Jan. 25, 1836) [mother Walsh]

Ellen (bap. June 4 1840) [Walsh] [m. J. D. Harnett, auctioneer]

JAMES PATRICK "PADDY" (bap. Dec. 27, 1842–April 26, 1922) [m. **HONORA "NANNO" MAHER** (1844–April 22, 1927) Feb. 26, 1870; sister Ellen Maher m. Richard James "Brown Dick"]

    Johanna (Sr. Bonaventure) (1871–1929)

    PATRICK (March 9, 1872–1933) priest

    Richard (b. Aug. 25, 1873) [d. March 25, 1893, pneumonia, a medical student?]

    Ellen (b. April 2, 1876)

    Maurice James (b. April 10, 1877—after 1954) of Knockeen House [m. Johanna Scollard, of Castleisland]

        Hanora May (b. Jan. 6, 1904)

        Mary (b. Sept. 13, 1905) civil service

        James (b. May 8, 1907)

        David Woulfe, MPSI (b. May 15, 1909)

        Richard (b. Dec. 19, 1910)

        MAURICE (Nov. 21, 1912–1989) priest

        Patrick (b. Nov. 19, 1914)

    Unknown (b/d. July 10, 1879) male, lived 1 hour

    John J. (June 13, 1880–May 6, 1976) [m. Ellen Reidy (d. Dec. 17, 1945?) Feb. 11, 1902]

        James (b. Oct. 26, 1904)

        John (b. Oct. 26, 1905)

        Elizabeth (b. Feb. 7, 1908)

        Patrick (b. July 26, 1911)

    James (b. June 29, 1882)

    TIMOTHY (June 12, 1885–Feb. 15, 1969) [m. Mary Malvena "Vena" Mullaly (d. Dec. 25, 1974) Dec. 24, 1930]

        James Patrick Francis (b/d Nov. 3, 1931), Bruff, premature, died at birth

Malvena Gerardine (Oct. 27, 1938–March 14, 2010)

John (bap. July 22, 1844)

Mary (bap. Aug. 4, 1848–July 1940) [m. Edmond C. "Minor" Leahy (d. July 25, 1978)]

Cornelius E. "Connie" (d. Oct. 1931)

Katherine (d. Sept. 1956)

Edmond C. (ca. 1881–July 25, 1978)

Patrick J. (ca. 1922–Sept. 22, 2003)

Catherine (d. before 1838) [m. Nevel]

Bridget

Patrick

Michael

Hannah

***

John Maurice (1830–May 8, 1876) [m. Hanora Barry (b. 1831), Feb. 2, 1845] died of typhoid fever?

Catherine (bap. Sept. 3, 1848)

Patrick (bap. April 3, 1850), of Athea

Maurice (bap. April 19, 1851), of Wicklow

Richard James "Brown Dick" Woulfe (bap. April 6, 1853–June 7, 1915) [m. **ELLEN MAHER** (ca. 1849–Sept. 29, 1943); sister **HONORA "NANNO" MAHER** m. **JAMES P. "PADDY" WOLFE**]

John (bap. July 26, 1854), of Tournafulla (born in Cratloe)

Johanna (bap. March 26, 1856–ca. 1911) [m. David Egan (ca. 1838–1910), Feb. 14, 1874]

Michael (bap. March 5, 1875)

John (bap. June 5, 1876)

John (bap. July 13, 1877)

Hanora (bap. Dec. 28, 1878)

Hanora (bap. April 17, 1880)

Catherine (bap. Jan. 22, 1882)

Richard (bap. Dec. 30, 1883)

Patrick (bap. Feb. 18, 1890)

David Joseph (bap. July 30, 1893–1973) d. in Brooklyn, New York

Daniel (bap. Oct. 13, 1895)

Maurice (bap. March 12, 1898)

***

Maurice James (d. after 1873) [m. Johanna Frawley?]

Mary (b. ca. 1849) [m. John Fitzgerald, Feb. 1, 1871]

Ellen (b. ca. 1850) [m. James Corridan, widower, Jan. 21, 1873]

James Woulfe (d. after 1913)

RICHARD MAURICE (ca. 1843–Nov. 13, 1913) [m. Johanna Barrett (bap. 1844–ca. 1901), Feb. 12, 1870]

 Johanna "Hannah" (Dec. 25, 1870–March 29, 1949) [Luke F. O'Keeffe, (ca. 1866–March 1943)] farmer, Meenscovane, Abbeyfeale

  Francis (b. Feb. 20, 1902), Gárda Síochána, Limerick

  Johanna (b. Sept. 8, 1903)

  Richard (b. Dec. 10, 1904), Meenscovane

  Luke (b. Dec. 6, 1905)

  John (b. Feb. 1, 1907), Meenscovane

  Patrick (b. March 20, 1908)

  Margaret (b. May 20, 1909)

  Mary Bridget (b. July 4, 1912)

  Mrs. M. Horan [not sure which daughter this is]

 Mary (ca. 1872–March 23, 1948) [m. Michael Denis Murphy (ca. 1872–1941); poor rate collector, Feb. 24, 1903] Ballaugh, Abbeyfeale

  Denis (Jan. 5, 1904–before 1967)

Richard (June 17, 1905–after 1967)

Rev. Michael (Sept. 20, 1906–May 30, 1967, in British Cameroons, West Africa) b. Ballaugh; Springmount N. S., Mill Hill Fathers, Kilkenny (ord. 1937) spent thirty years in West Africa; built Holy Family Church in Tabenken

Edmond, MPSI, Kilkee (June 14, 1908–after 1967)

Patrick (Nov. 7, 1910–after 1967)

Maurice (May 5, 1912–after 1967)

Maurice (Feb. 4, 1874–May 6, 1891)

Catherine (b. June 1, 1876), [m. Patrick White, Feb. 25, 1911] Clonehard, Co. Kerry

Mary (b. Feb. 13, 1913)

John (b. April 3, 1915)

John Richard Maurice (b. July 1, 1878) (married to Bridget [Hayes, 1904?] by 1913)

Richard J. (d. Nov. 1923)

Joan

Ellen (b. July 10, 1880)

Bridget (Dec. 25, 1882–Jan. 10, 1960) [m. James Joy] publican, St. Mary's Cemetery, Abbeyfeale

John Joseph

RICHARD BARRETT "DICK" (Oct. 26, 1884–April 19, 1937) [m. Catherine Elizabeth Colbert (1878–1951), April 16, 1913, in Dublin]

JOHANNA FRANCES (Jan. 17, 1914–Dec. 5, 1997)

HANORA JOSEPHINE (Dec. 3, 1915–July 4, 2015)

CORNELIUS COLBERT "CON" (June 11, 1917–2006)

RICHARD MICHAEL (Dec. 9, 1919–Oct. 11, 2003)

MICHAEL JOSEPH COLBERT (July 14, 1922–Oct. 21, 1995)

***

Patrick Michael (ca. 1815–ca. 1899) of Athea [m. Margaret Barry (b. ca. 1831)], only son of John, lived in The Corner House, Keale, on Abbeyfeale Road

John P. Woulfe (bap. Oct. 5. 1855–March 27, 1923; Gravestone at Athea) [m. Mary Anne (also Maryanne) O'Connor (ca. 1872–June 13, 1941), April 3, 1894] draper, farmer

    Margaret (b. March 12, 1895)

    Maryanne (b. March 13, 1896)

    Patrick (b. July 11, 1897), never married

    JAMES JOSEPH "JIM" (June 9, 1899–Sept. 5, 1937) died at Belchite in Spanish Civil War

    Bridget (b. Aug. 21, 1902)

    Louise (b. March 16, 1904)

    John (b. Dec. 19, 1905)

***

Patrick (d. after 1886) [m. Catherine]

    Maurice (bap. Feb. 22, 1848)

    Johanna (bap. April 3, 1849)

    Thomas (bap. Sept. 3, 1852), Dromadda

    Cornelius "Con" (bap. Oct. 26, 1854), Dromadda

    Patrick (bap. Dec. 24, 1859), Keale, Athea

    Richard (bap. May 10, 1857–1945) [m. Johanna Shine, in Keale, Athea, Feb. 27, 1886]

        Maurice (March 1, 1888–Nov. 5, 1930), b. Knocknagorna, d. Marrickville, Sydney, NSW [m. Bridget Herbert, 1921] immigrated to Australia, 1930, died shortly after arriving? Buried in Woronora Cemetery

            Richard Maurice [m. Lorna Grace Maycock]

            John Christopher

            Mary [m. John Joseph McGovern]

> Johanna [m. David Malcolm Keith Rae]
>
> Sheila (b/d 1930) Marrickville, Sydney

Catherine (b. March 15, 1891), Knocknagorna, d. Sydney [m. Patrick "Jimeen" Woulfe]

> James Jameen "Dummy," shoemaker in Dublin
>
> Michael, went to New Zealand
>
> Nora (Sr. Dympna)
>
> Josie (Sr. Monica)
>
> Maryanne (Sr. Philomena)

Michael "Old Mick" (b. Oct. 1, 1894–1979), b/d Knocknagorna, buried Templeathea [m. Nora Shine, Jan. 15, 1924] 2nd Battalion, West Limerick Brigade, IRA

Patrick "Paddy" (March 15, 1896–June 20, 1980), b. Knocknagorna, d. Sydney [m. Johanna Windle, 1918] IRA

> Patrick "Pateen" (b. 1919), immigrated to Australia in 1931; left Dublin on Nov. 11, 1931, on *Hobson's Bay*. Stayed with Dick in house on Centennial St., Marrickville, now site of high school

Mary (b. May 18, 1897), b/d Knocknagorna

John Joseph "Jack" (June 6, 1898–March 2, 1972), b. Knocknagorna, d. Kogarah, Sydney [m. Catherine "Kit" Barrett, 1932, in Marrickville], immigrated to Australia, 1922

Hanora (b. June 24, 1900), Knocknagorna

Margaret Mary "Peg" (Aug. 13, 1901–Oct. 25, 1989), Knocknagorna, d. Sydney, immigrated to Australia, 1928 [m. Edward Clarence "Ted" Murphy]

Richard (March 22, 1903–Aug. 22, 1903), Knocknagorna

Richard Patrick "Dick" (b. May 1, 1905), b. Knocknagorna, d. Sydney [m. Mary Ann "Molly" Sheridan, 1928], immigrated to Australia, 1925

> Mary Ann (d. 1937)

Cornelius Michael "Con" (July 20, 1906–Dec. 14, 1986), b. Knocknagorna, d. Sydney [m. Kathleen Fuer, also Fewer], immigrated to Australia, 1925

Ellen (b. Aug. 5, 1908–Sept. 8, 1925), Knocknagorna, died of TB

Bridget (b. Nov. 30, 1909), Knocknagorna

***

CHAPTER WOLFES

Michael Woulfe (b. 1760) [m. Johanna ? (1769–Jan. 21, 1871)] moved from Athea in 1795 with nephew John and together leased 170-acre farm at Meenoline

    Richard (b. ca. 1790) [m. Hanora Hayes]

        Michael (bap. Sept. 19, 1830, Monagea) [m. Ellen Harnett, March 3, 1859]

            Bridget (bap. Jan. 5, 1860)

            Patrick (bap. Aug. 25, 1862)

            John (b. April 17, 1864)

            Johanna (bap. March 22, 1866)

        Bridget (bap. Sept. 11, 1831–1880) [m. William Colbert, Feb. 11, 1858]

            Johanna (bap. April 26, 1857)

            Elizabeth (bap. Jan. 4, 1859)

            <u>Richard</u> (bap. Jan. 21, 1860–1940) [m. Johanna Woulfe, of Crioch Woulfes] immigrated to Minnesota

                Mary Anne "Maime" (1886–1951)

                Bridget Loretta (1888–1969)

                Johanna M. (1891–1929)

                William Richard "Bill" (1892–1965)

                John James "Jack" (1894–1961)

                Catherine Margaret (1899–1988)

                [Baby] (b/d 1900)

        John (bap. Jan. 11, 1862–1864)

        Catherine (bap. Jan. 9, 1863)

        Edmond (bap. Aug. 19, 1864–1911)

Edward "Ed" (1866–1944) [m. Mary Ward] immigrated to Minnesota

    William H.

    Edward S.

    Joseph

    John

    Monsignor Paul

    Mary T.

John William (bap. April 8, 1867–1932) [m. Margaret O'Keeffe]

Catherine (b. 1869)

William (bap. Feb. 1, 1872–1948)

Patrick (1874–1951)

John (bap. June 15, 1835) [m. Ellen Dunworth, Feb. 21, 1860]

    Richard (bap. Feb. 17, 1861)

    Michael (b. 1862)

    James (bap. July 31, 1864)

    Patrick (bap. Feb. 26, 1866)

    John (bap. May 23, 1868)

    Timothy (bap. July 31, 1870)

    Mary (bap. July 12, 1872)

    Honora (bap. June 12, 1875)

    William (b. 1878)

    Catherine (bap. Oct. 5, 1881)

Patrick (bap. May 15, 1837–before 1886) [m. Mary O'Donnell, April 6, 1861]

    Catherine (May 1865–May 29, 1934) [m. John Joseph Harnett (b. 1855)] This John Harnett present at death of Johanna Woulfe in 1871

        Maurice Joseph (bap. June 23, 1886–1977)

        Patrick (1887–1957)

        Timothy J. (bap. April 27, 1890–1974)

    James (1891–1973)

    Daniel Joseph (1891–1966)

    William (bap. Feb. 27, 1893)

    Michael J. (1895–1950)

    Mary (1896–1981)

    Richard Joseph (bap. Jan. 3, 1898–1982)

    James (bap. Feb. 14, 1899)

    Thomas (bap. May 11, 1900–1904)

    William (bap. May 11, 1900)

    Catherine (bap. Oct. 19, 1901–1995)

    Honora (bap. Aug. 21, 1903)

    Thomas (bap. Oct. 24, 1904–1990)

    John M. (1913–1967) ??

Richard (1866–1908)

John P. (b. 1867)

Hanora (1868–1915)

Maurice Patrick (Feb. 2, 1871–Nov. 28, 1930) [m. Bridget Johanna O'Donnell (1872–1949)]

    Anthony Patrick (May 19, 1896–Aug. 2, 1955)

    Cornelius J. (1898–1976)

    Mary Catherine (1900–1982)

    Thomas J. (1902–1933)

    Richard (1906–1946)

    Maurice J. (1908–1955)

    Timothy (1911–1978)

<u>James Patrick</u> (Nov. 16, 1877–June 11, 1915) [m. Mary Boucher (1800–1966)] d. in St. Paul, Minnesota

    Mary (1906–1986)

    Patrick J. (May 1, 1908–Aug. 29, 1956) [m. Helen Myrtle Schwope (1907–1996)] d. in St. Paul, Minnesota

James (1937–1999)

Thomas J. (1909–1976)

Johanna (b. 1912)

Richard (bap. March 18, 1840)

***

CRIOCH WOLFES

Richard Woulfe (b. ca. 1790) Templeathea West [m. Johanna Woulfe (b. ca. 1794), 1820] husband and wife cousins

    Richard Woulfe (1821–1910) servant, Direen [m. Mary McAuliffe (1834–1912), July 18, 1857, Monagea] inherits family farm, Crioch, in 1831, eventually lost it to his brother-in-law Lawrence McAuliffe; buried Templeathea

        Patrick (bap. April 29, 1858, Athea)

        Patrick (bap. March 19, 1859–1945) [r. Johanna Howard] [m. Bridget F. Howe (b. 1867)] immigrated to Minnesota 1884

            Patrick William "Paddy" (March 5, 1877–April 11, 1959) Howard (ill.) served in British Army (Boer War, WWI, taken prisoner by Germans) [m. Gertrude Payne (1892–Nov. 26, 1970, Camberly, Surrey, England), 1910, London] buried Preston cemetery, Heidelberg

                Mabel (1911–2000) [m. Wallace "Wally" Matthews (ca. 1910–June 11, 1996), April 16, 2938, Our Lady of Visitation Church, Greenford] immigrated to Australia, 1956

                Molly (b. 1920) [m. Harold Mathews, younger brother of Wally] immigrated to Australia 1952

                Raymond

                Eileen (1922–June 17, 1991) d. in London [m. Albert Barker] immigrated to Australia in 1955

                Brian

                Besme

                Michael

> > Janet
> >
> > John Patrick (b. April 11, 1930) immigrated to Australia in 1953 (his mother had already gone in 1952) [m. Margery McIntyre, April 30, 1954, Saint John's Church, Heidelberg] no children
> >
> > John (March 1880–1912) Howard (ill.) died in trolley accident in England
> >
> > Mary "May" (b. 1895)
> >
> > Richard Patrick (1896–1985)
> >
> > Catherine T. (1899–1996)
> >
> > William "Bill" (b. 1901)
>
> Thomas (bap. Jan. 20, 1861–1927)
>
> <u>Johanna</u> (bap. Sept. 14, 1863–1937) [m. Richard Colbert (May 21, 1860–March 18, 1940), Nov. 10, 1884, St. Paul, Minnesota] immigrated in 1882 (Richard Colbert himself son of William J. Colbert and Bridget Woulfe)
>
> > Mary Anne "Maime" (1886–1951)
> >
> > Bridget Loretta (1888–1969)
> >
> > Johanna M. (1891–1929)
> >
> > William Richard "Bill" (1892–1965) [m. Gertrude Rose Fleissner (1891–1975)]
> >
> > > Jerome Francis (1921–2001)
> > >
> > > Gertrude Lorraine (1923–2007)
> > >
> > > Rosemary E. (1928–1965)
> >
> > John James "Jack" (1894–1961) [m. Ann Wolf (1894–1937)] [m. Marie Eugenie Colbert (1903–1962) native of Quebec]
> >
> > > John James Colbert (1931–1989)
> >
> > Catherine Margaret (1899–1988)
> >
> > [Baby] (b/d 1900)
>
> William (bap. July 3, 1865–1937)
>
> <u>Catherine "Kate"</u> (July 8, 1867–Aug. 26, 1963) [m. Thomas Hennessy (1865–1951), 1895] immigrated to Minnesota, arr. NYC May 9, 1885

George Thomas (1894–1951) [m. Marie L. Maloney]

William (b. 1898)

Mary (1900–1927)

Edward (b. 1903)

Frank P. (1905–1964)

John P. (1907–1991)

Louise (b. 1911)

Mary (bap. March 15, 1869–Aug. 26, 1963)

Cornelius

Maurice (bap. March 21, 1871–March 1927) [m. Catherine "Black Kate" O'Sullivan (1872–1920, d. of peritonitis), Dec. 9, 1891, Athea] buried at Templeathea

Patrick Francis (bap. June 10, 1893, Athea)

Richard Joseph (bap. June 27, 1894–1950) immigrated to USA ca. 1916–1919 [m. Nellie Marie Kearney (1898–1964), of Moyvane, Kerry] d. Kansas City

Mary Catherine (1919–2002)

Richard Joseph (Nov. 29, 1921–March 7, 1997) Kansas City, seven children

Eileen "Nellie" Marie (1923–2008)

Kathleen Theresa (1925–1988)

Maurice

Francis "Frank" Patrick (1896–?) immigrated to USA ca. 1916–1919, settled in San Francisco [m. Rita ?] no children

Thomas (bap. Nov. 14, 1897–April 28, 1974) [m. Catherine Ryan, dressmaker, Nov. 29, 1921, at Saint Mary's Church, Moyhill, Glasgow, Scotland] immigrated to Scotland, joined brother William; returned to Athea in 1926; worked on roads in same job as father; eventually inherited uncle Con Sullivan's house and shop in Athea village. Died at "Bridge House," Athea. Buried New Cemetery.

Mary "Masie" (b. May 1922, Glasgow) [m. John McGee (d. 1995), ca. 1947]

       Mary

       John

       Catherine

       George

       Theresa

William (b. 1923, Glasgow) d. in infancy

<u>Maurice</u> (April 15, 1924–Feb. 11, 1993) b. Glasgow, returned to Ireland with parents in 1926; immigrated to England in late 1940s, never married; buried Holy Cross, Athea

Thomas "Tommy" (1925–1984) b. Glasgow [m. Nora Costello] buried Glasgow

       Thomas

       Nora

       William

       James

       Philip

Catherine "Kitty" (b. 1927, Lower Athea)

Josephine "Josie" (b. 1930, Lower Athea) [m. Patrick Golding, in USA] returned to Newcastle West

       Joseph Golding (b. USA) civil engineer, Brighton, England

       Gerald, cabbie, Brighton

       Patrick, engineer, UN

       Mary

Bridget (b. 1932, Lower Athea)

<u>Anna "Nancy"</u> (b. Aug. 15, 1934 Lower Athea) immigrated to England in 1954 [m. Raymond Brouder, of Shanagolden, at St. Augustine Catholic Church, Datohet, June 19, 1954]

       Margaret

Patrick (b. in Lower Athea)

Richard "Dick" (b. July 2, 1935, Lower Athea) [m. Peg Woulfe, Clash]

    Kattie

    Thomas

    Ellish

Ellen Ann (b. March 6, 1937, Lower Athea) immigrated to USA age 19, Chicago [m. Christy Roche, of Athea, Jan. 2, 1965]

    Marietta

    Christina

    Karen

    Edward

Cornelius (b. April 5, 1941)

Agatha (b. Feb. 5, 1945)

William (bap. May 30, 1900–1968) immigrated to Scotland ca. 1920 [m. Ires ?] nine children, buried in Scotland

Mary Ellen (1903–1963) joined Frank P. in 1923 [m. John Mullins]

    Beverly

    June

    Shirley

Ellen Mary "Nellie" (1905–Feb. 11, 1974) joined Frank P. in 1923; d. in Chicago [m. Thomas Culhane]

    Mary Lou (Sister Marietta, Midland, Maryland)

    Maurice

    Tommy

Bridget Ita (1907–1985) [m. Frank Creegan, Phoenix, Arizona]

    Frank "Frankie" Jr.

    Mary Catherine

Maurice Francis (Dec. 18, 1909–May 15, 1951) d. in Kansas City [m. Eleanor Brassfield (1908–1974)]

> > Eleanor
> >
> > <u>Catherine Marie "Kitty"</u> (1911–Aug. 30, 1991) [m. William Stack] husband and wife died in traffic accident, buried in Kansas
> >
> > Mary
> >
> > Virginia
> >
> > Tommy
>
> <u>Bridget</u> (b. 1872)
>
> Michael (bap. Jan. 30, 1875–1937)

William (bap. March 24, 1831) twin

Hanora (bap. March 24, 1831) twin

Maurice (bap. Aug. 7, 1835)

INDEX

Abbeyfeale, Co. Limerick, location of, *41*, 41, 57, IRA ambush near, 67, 72–73, 99 (n.), 252, 293–294, Black and Tans attack on, 68, 73, 169, 252, 294, "one bright spot in the Empire," 398

Agatha, Mother Mary. *See* Wolfe, Mary A. (1834–1897).

Agatha, Sister Mary. *See* Wolfe, Johanna F. (1914–1997).

Ahern, Catherine Ita "Kat" (1915–2007), Irish politician, 146–147

Anderson, Benedict (1936–2015), political scientist, 22, 89 (n.)

Anglo-Irish War. *See* War of Independence, Irish.

Athea, Co. Limerick, *43*, location, pronunciation, and etymology of, *41*, 41, 62, Protestants and Catholics in, 46–48, symbolic meaning of, 50–51, 57

Aunt Dollie Letter (1956), 39–40, 53–54, 57, 82, 160, 186–187, 191, 193, 199–200, 218, 248, 285, text of, 401–407

Ballinruddery, home of knight of Kerry, 137, 157, 196, 234, 304–305, 318

Ballybunion, Co. Kerry, 43, 79, 306, 314, 318, 364, Moonlighters strike near, 43–44, 321, murder at, 45, 49, 234, 321, 352 (n.)

Barry, Sebastian (1955–), novelist, 71–72

Béaslaí, Piaras (1881–1965), playwright and politician, 145. *See also* Na hAisteoiri (The Players).

Begley, John (1861–1941), priest, historian, 26–27, 30, 367, 402

Behan, Brendan (1923–1964), writer, 76, 78, 102 (n.)

Belchite, Battle of (1937), 189, *190*

Bennett, Thomas William Westropp (1867–1962), politician, 367–368, 370

Bhulbh, Caitlín de. *See* Wolfe, Catherine (1890–1989).

Bhulbh, Seán de. *See* Wolfe, John M. (1922–2009).

Black and Tans, 35, 110, 148, 206, 266, 311, attack on Abbeyfeale, 68, 73, 169, 252, 294

Blue, USS, American destroyer, 226–227

Boland, Eavan (1944–), poet, 60

Bonaventure, Sister. *See* Wolfe, Johanna (1838–1929).

Caelan, Sister Mary. *See* Wolfe, Helen.

Capone, Al (1899–1947), gangster, 23, 32–33, 314–315

Carson, Ciaran (1948–), writer, 41.

Casement, Roger (1864–1916), Irish rebel, 64, 292–293, 396

Chapter Wolfes, 466–469

Chartres cathedral, liberation of during World War II, 59, 328

Civil War, Irish (1922–1923), 29, 69, 76, 188, 253, 294–295
Clancy, Peadar (*also* Denis Crowley), British spy, 67, 293, 398
Clancy Brothers, singing group, 76–77
"Cliffs of Dooneen," Irish ballad, 80–81, 82
Coláiste Mhuire, Abbeyfeale school, 146–147
Colbert, Cornelius "Con" (1888–1916), Irish rebel, 65, 71, 108, 148, 169, 188, 206, 251, 266, 292, 311, 395–396, letter by, 65, poem by, 71, 74
Collins, James J. "Jimmy" (1900–1967), IRA member, politician, 67–68, 73, 292–295, testimony of, 395–400
Collison, Ann Wolfe (1845–1912), farmer, 13, 87 (n.), 105, 106, 107, 208, 443
Collison, Arthur (1890–1903), 105, 106, 107, 443, premature death of, 13, 106
Collison, Maurice L. (1887–1981), farmer, hog-buyer, 106, 107, 443
Conradh na Gaeilge. *See* Gaelic League.
Coughlin, Father Charles E. (1891–1971), American political leader, 36–37, 316, 323
Coughlin, Thomas, security guard, murder of, 34–35
Cratloe, Co. Limerick, location of, 41, family banished to, 147, 403, leased land in, 192, 201, 248, 304, 404, memories of, 246

Crioch Wolfes, 453, 459, 466, 469–474
Cromwell, Oliver (1599–1658), English politician and military leader, 30, 53–54, 56, 167, 179–180, 247, 269, 278, 355, 379–380, 387, 389, 405–406, 418–419
Crowley, Denis. *See* Clancy, Peadar.
Curran, Charles Courtney (1861–1942), painter, 177

Dalton, Patrick (1896–1921), IRA member, ix, 108–111, ballad about death, 110–111, 454
Daly, Edward "Ned" (1891–1916), Irish rebel, 292, 395–396
Danaher, Kevin (1913–2003) (*also* Caoimhín Ó Danachair), folklorist, 93–94 (n.), 245, 349 (n.)
Davis, Thomas (1814–1845), Irish writer, 58, 60, 421
Death, its importance in genealogy, 13–14, suspected murder on riverboat, 11–12, 187, 407, stroke on beach, 12–13, 135–136, run over by wagon, 13, 106, set ablaze on prairie, 13–14, 150–151, swept away by hurricane, 13, 16, 174, 255, at sea, 14, 121, by falling derrick, 16, 254, by car crash, 16, 222, hanged by English, 29–30, 39, 180–181, while watching young people dance, 40, 57, 201, 248, 404, executed on side of road, 110, struck by lightning, 163, in

Spanish Civil War, 189, by suicide, 263, by torture, 387, by freezing, 404
Dee, Cornelius "Con," IRA member, 109–110
Desmond Rebellion (1569–1573, 1579–1583), 53–54, 65, 74, 155, 247, 387, 402–404, 425
Dillane, Michael, Wolfes indicted in manslaughter of, 45, 234, 321
Dimby, racehorse, 256, 334, 364–366
Doody, Daniel, IRA member, 99 (n.), 293

Easter Rising (1916), 56, 64, 71, 108, 148, 169, 188, 206, 251, 266, 292, 311, 373 (n.), 395–397

Fenian Uprising (1867), 47, 65, 74, 346, 352–353
Fetterman Fight (1866) (*also* Battle of the Hundred-in-the-Hands), 346 (n.)
Fitzgerald, Catherine Wolfe (1860–1947), judge's wife, 112–113, 117, 163, 360, 363, 409, 435
FitzGerald, James FitzMaurice (d. 1579), Irish rebel, 155–156, 402–403
FitzGerald, Maurice (1774–1849), eighteenth knight of Kerry, 20, 53, 137, 157, 196, 234, 304–305, 318
Friel, Brian (1929–2015), playwright, 62

Gaelic, language. *See* Irish, language.
Gaelic League (*also* Conradh na Gaeilge), 29, 63, 145–146, 223, 269, 370
Glen, Wolfe family farm in Cratloe, Co. Limerick, *52*, building of house at, 37, 161, 199, hedge school at, 38, 51, 199, 258, 302, 312, 372–377, 380, IRA visits, 72, 251–252
Goold, Frederic-Falkener (1808–1877), archdeacon of Raphoe and landlord, 45–47, 350–353
Goold, Thomas (ca. 1766–1846), landlord, 42, 348–349
Great Famine (1845–1849 (*also* an Gorta Mór), 1, 7, 12, 229, 268, 383 (n.), 390, 408, 421, in Listowel, 20

Hancock, Winfield Scott (1824–1886), general, 346
Harnett, J. D. (*also* J. D. H.), journalist, 93 (n.), 101 (n.), 252–253, 376, article on hedge schools by, 372–377, article on lost letter by, 389–394
Harnett, Maurice "Mossie," IRA member, author, 65, 67, 72–73, 99 (n.), 251–252, 293
Harnett, Patrick, killed by Thomas Huckerby, 73, 251
Healy, Jeremiah "Jerry," killed by Thomas Huckerby, 73, 251
Hedge school, at Glen, 38, 51, 199, 258, 302, 312, 372–377, 380
Hepler, Catherine Wolfe (1842–1922), farmer, 114, 431

Huckerby, Thomas D. (1901–1921), Black and Tan, 73–74, 101 (n.), 252–253
Hyde, Douglas (1860–1949), first president of Ireland, 145

Íde, Sister. *See* Wolfe, Hanora J. (1915–2015).
Ireton, Henry (1611–1651), English general, 30–31, 167–168, 179–180, 247, 355, 389, 405
Irish, language, xi, 27, 29, 51, 53, 54, 57–64, 74, 81, 145–147, 152, 170, 172, 194, 199, 223–224, 259, 269–270, 302, 354–355, 370, 373, 402
Irish Republican Army (Old), xi, 28–29, 35, 69, 76, 148, 169, 206, 253, 266, 269, 293–294, 311, attack in Kilmallock, barracks attacked in Kilmallock, 29, 268–269, 371, ambush near Abbeyfeale, 67, 72–73, 99 (n.), 252, 293–294, West Limerick Brigade, 67, 72, 108, 188, 251, 261, 293, 295, 395–400, North Kerry Brigade, 108, activity in Listowel, 108–110, 294–295

Keane, John B. (1928–2002), playwright, 47–48, views on Irish language, 63–64
Kerry, Knight of. *See* FitzGerald, Maurice (1774–1849).
Kuhn, Margaret M. McCormick (1877–1910), farmer, 115, 436

Land War, Irish (1878–1909), 43, 45, 47, 72, 234, 318–319, 321, 352 (n.), 383
Langan, Margaret I. Wolfe (1857–btw. 1930 and 1940), school superintendent, 112–113, 116–118, 360, 363, 409, 435
Lemke, William (1878–1950), American politician, 36, 316
Limerick city, siege of (1650–1651), 30, 54, 167–168, 179–180, 247, 355, 387, 405, family banished from, 54, 147, 247, David Wolfe's description of, 152
Listowel, Co. Kerry, during Famine, 20, location of, 40–41, *41*, symbolic meaning of, 57, IRA activity in, 108–110, 294–295
Lost Nation, Iowa town, *18*, *48*, *63*, origin of name, 17, symbolic meaning of, 17–18, 49–50, 62

Maher, Ellen Wolfe (ca. 1810–1886), 119, 128, 140, 166, 194, 212, 237, 242, 256, 260, 268, 308, 326, 332, 435
Maher, John W. (1856–1936), lawyer and journalist, 120–121, 122, 124, 429, shot by client, 14, 120–121
Maher, Margaret Wolfe (1827–1906), farmer, 120, 122–123, 124, 429
Maher, Maurice E. (1869–1964), grocer and real estate broker, 120, 122, 124, *125*, 430

Mahony, John, constable, killing of, 67–68, 72–73, 294
McCall, Aileen G. Wolfe (1884–1956), suffragette and Shakespeare enthusiast, 126–127, 174, 255, 299, 430
McCormick, Elizabeth Maher (1836–1900), farmer, 115, 128, 435
Menabochta, quasi-religious order for "fallen" women, 153
Miller, Kerby, historian, ix, 86 (n.), 245
Momaday, N. Scott (1934–), writer, 61
Monteith, Robert (1870–1956), aide to Roger Casement, 292–293, 396–397
Moonlighters, vigilante group, 43–44, 72, 81, 319, 352
Moore, George (1852–1933), novelist, 175–176
Mulvihill, Ellen Wolfe (1833–1908), farmer, 129–130, 131, 242, 445
Mulvihill, Margaret Wolfe (ca. 1845–1888), farmer, 129, 131–132, 326, 438

Na hAisteoiri (The Players), Irish-language theater troupe, 145–146
Nixon, Bridget E. Sheehan (1853–1910), 87 (n.), 129, 131, 133, 135, 137, 138, 207, 212, 242, 308, 440

Ó Séadhacháin, Seán, folk artist, 295

O'Connell, Daniel (1775–1847), politician, 42, 160, 302, 348–349, 356, 368, 394, 405, 421
O'Donnell, Hugh (d. ca. 1600), chieftain, 155
O'Neill, Hugh Dubh (1611–1660), soldier, 180
O'Neill, Shane (ca. 1530–1567), chieftain, 155

Patton, George C. (1885–1945), American general, 59, 328–329
Pearl Harbor, bombing of, 221, 226–227
Pearse, Patrick (1879–1916), poet, educator, revolutionary, 65, 71, 416
Pirates, Pittsburgh, baseball team, 164–165, 447

Raleigh, Sir Walter (ca. 1552–1618), 402 (n.), 403, 409
Redmond, Ellen J. Wolfe (1832–1902), 134, 441
Royal Dublin Fusiliers, 69, 251, during Easter Rising, 69
Royal Irish Constabulary (RIC), 47, 109, 353 (n.), 396–400, 420, barracks attacked in Kilmallock, 29, 268–269, 371, ambush of in Abbeyfeale, 68, 72, 252, 293
Royal Munster Fusiliers, 72, 100 (n.), 251

Scholastica, Sister Mary. *See* Wolfe, Johanna (1849–1926).
Shammas, Anton (1950–), writer, poet, translator, 50

Share the Profits! The Story of Richard W. Wolfe and His Conclusions (1939), by William H. Stuart, 37, 38–39, 301, 316–317, 377 (n.), excerpt from, 378–388
Sheahan, Michael (ca. 1832–1902), teacher, 38–39, 93 (n.), 373–377, 381
Sheehan, Dennis W. (1852–1907), grocer, 12, 87 (n.), 129, 131, 133, 135–136, 138–139, 207, 210, 212, 242, 308, 326, 439, death of, 12–13, 135–136
Sheehan, Margaret E. Wolfe (b. 1818), 87 (n.), 129, 131, 133, 135, 137, 138, 207, 210, 212, 242, 308, 326, 439
Sheehan, Patrick W. (1843–1894), 87 (n.), 129, 131, 133, 135, 137, 138–139, 207, 210, 212, 242, 308, 326, 439, will of, 138–139
Sidney, Henry (1529–1586), English official, 155, 410 (n.)
Sloinnte Gaedheal is Gall (1923), book of Irish names and surnames, 57, 224, 237, 259, 269, 302, 355 (n.). *See also* Wolfe, Patrick (1872–1933).
Sloinnte na hÉireann: Irish Surnames (1997), 64, 224. *See also* Wolfe, John M. (1922–2009).
Somme, Battle of the (1916), 72, 251, 450
Spenser, Edmund (1553–1599), poet, 29, 58
Stuart, William H. *See Share the Profits! The Story of Richard W. Wolfe and his Conclusions* (1939).

Thompson, William Hale "Big Bill" (1869–1944), Chicago mayor, 23, 26, 32–33, 313–315
Tone, Theobald Wolfe (1763–1798), Irish rebel, 71, 100 (n.), 406, 416, 419
Twohey, Margaret Maher (1829–1872), farmer, 140–141, 435

"Valley of Knockanure, The," ballad, 110–111. *See also* Dalton, Patrick (1896–1921).

Wagner, Ellen and Paul, filmmakers, 245–246
War of Independence, Irish (1919–1921) (*also* Anglo-Irish War), 29, 66–69, 72–74, 108–110, 148, 169, 188, 206, 251–252, 266, 268–269, 293–295, 311, 332, 395–400
Welsh, Mary K. Wolfe (1929–2004), nurse, 142–143, 144, 281, 323, 412, 433
White, Edmond Wolfe (ca. 1854–1922), solicitor, 42, 46–47, 51, 94 (n.), 354, 356, 453, letter of regarding land sale, 348–353
Wissing, Sara T. Wolfe (1926–1998), social worker, 142, 144, 281, 323, 412, 433
Wolfe, Bartholomew "Batt" (1809–1883), 450, letter from nephew Maurice H. Wolfe, 345–347

Wolfe, Catherine (1890–1989) (*also* Caitlín de Bhulbh), teacher, 143–145

Wolfe, Cornelius C. (1917–2006), priest, 65, 148–149, 169, 206, 266, 292, 311, 463

Wolfe, Daniel F. (ca. 1832–1882), liquor retailer and bartender, 150–151, 284, 288, 306, 444, murdered on the prairie, 13–14, 150–151

Wolfe, David (1528–after July 23, 1579), Jesuit, 56, 96–97 (n.), 152–156, 386–387, 402

Wolfe, Edmond (b. 1821), farmer, 119, 137, 157, 196, 229, 256, 286, 304, 330, 440

Wolfe, Edmond E. (ca. 1842–1889), 157, 158, 440

Wolfe, Edmond R. "Old Ned" (1788–1876), farmer and political organizer, 33–34, 37, 42, 92 (n.), 93 (n.), 160–161, 199, 301, 310, 347 (n.), 378, 405, 452

Wolfe, Edmund D. (1853–1921), hardware store owner, miner, and dairy farmer, 112, 114, 116, 122, 124, 162–163, 184, 204, 256, 299, 337, 431

Wolfe, Edward A. Jr. (1929–2009), baseball player, 164–165, 447

Wolfe, Ellen Maher (ca. 1849–1943), farmer, 96 (n.), 97 (n.), 119, 128, 140, 166, 172, 260, 268, 332, 437

Wolfe, George (fl. 1643–1651), merchant, 30, 167–168, 178, 179, 247, 312, 387, 389, 405–406

Wolfe, Hanora J. (1915–2015) (*also* Sister Íde), nun, 65, 68–69, 148, 169–171, 206, 266, 292, 311, 463

Wolfe, Helen (*also* Sister Mary Caelan), nun and educator, 374, letter to, 39–40, 53–54, 57, 82, 160, 186–187, 191, 193, 199–200, 218, 248, 285, text of, 401–407

Wolfe, Honora Maher (1844–1927), farmer, 92 (n.), 96 (n.), 119, 166, 172, *173*, 194, 436

Wolfe, Honoria E. (1881–1951), 126, 174–176, *177*, 255, 299, 430

Wolfe, James (d. before 1638), merchant, 167, 178, 405

Wolfe, James (d. 1651), priest, 179–181, 247, 355, 389, 405, execution of, 29–30, 39, 180–181, debate over beatification, 31, 181

Wolfe, James (1727–1759), hero of Quebec, 30, 167–168, 247, 312, 387, 389–390, 406

Wolfe, James B. (1844–1916), farmer, cattle breeder, and bank president, 9, 10, 112, 116, 182–183, 202, 210, 229, 239, 272, 290, 335, 409, 410–411 432, obituary of, 9, 182, 362–363, 410, in *Wolfe's History*, 357–358

Wolfe, James D. (1839–1923), farmer, 114, 122, 162, 184, 204, 256, 299, 430

Wolfe, James E. (1909–1965), farmer, 185, 220, 239, *241*, 264, 279, 281, 412, 415, 434

Wolfe, James H. (btw. 1780 and 1800–ca. 1836), teacher and farmer, 11–12, 186–187, 218, 250, 285, 389–394, 406–407, 459, thought to have been murdered, 11–12, 187, 407

Wolfe, James J. (1899–1937), IRA member and communist organizer, 188–189, *190*, 464, death during Spanish Civil War, 189

Wolfe, James M. (ca. 1651–1704), farmer, 97 (n.), 191, 425, hears about fall of Limerick, 57

Wolfe, James M. "The Barrister" (1732–1817), 37, 48, 82, 93 (n.), 112, 116, 129, 131, 134, 192, 199, 202, 207, 209, 210, 212, 216, 229, 231, 232, 239, 242, 272, 284, 286, 288, 290, 297, 304, 330, 425, 426, source of nickname, 37, 192

Wolfe, James M. (1851–1921), laborer, 193, 219, 459

Wolfe, James P. "Paddy" (1842–1922), 50, 92 (n.), 96 (n.), 119, 166, 172, 194, *195*, 268, 332, 379, 436, 460, 461, purchase of land, 50, 348 (n.)

Wolfe, James R. (1800–1875), 119, 137, 157, 196, 229, 256, 286, 304, 330, 365 (n.), 426

Wolfe, James R. (1863–1941), grocer and laborer, 197–198, 209, 286, 288, 439

Wolfe, Jane C. "Dollie" (1879–1964), 39, 42, 53, *55*, 69, 82, 99 (n.), 199–201, 251, 253, 258, 347 (n), 373 (n.), 378–379, 455, letter to Helen Wolfe, 39–40, 53–54, 57, 82, 160, 186–187, 191, 193, 199–200, 218, 248, 285, text of, 401–407. *See also* Aunt Dollie Letter.

Wolfe, Johanna (1838–1929) (*also* Sister Bonaventure), 58, 172, 194, 268, *271*, 332, 436

Wolfe, Johanna (1849–1926) (*also* Sister Mary Scholastica), nun, 112, 116, 182, 202–203, 210, 229, 239, 272, 290, 360, 363, 409, 433, funeral of, 328

Wolfe, Johanna Downey (ca. 1810–1886), 114, 122, 162, 184, 204–205, 256, 299, 429, court petition of, 204–205

Wolfe, Johanna F. (1914–1997) (*also* Sister Mary Agatha), nun, 65, 148, 169, 206, 266, 292, 311, 463

Wolfe, John (ca. 1794–1863), farmer, 207–208, 232, 249, 284, 442

Wolfe, John (1845–1919), farmer and laborer, 197, 209, 286, 288, 438

Wolfe, John B. (1851–1923), farmer, 86 (n.), 97 (n.), 112, 116, 182, 202–203, 210–211, 229, 239, 272, 290, 328, 360, 362–363, 409, 412, 413, 414, 433

Wolfe, John C. (1840–1902), pharmacist, 15–16, *15*, 129, 131, 212–214, *215*, 232, 242, 254, 297, 445, manufactured own medicines, 15, 213, street named for, 16, 214

Wolfe, John E. (1837–1918), farmer, 87 (n.), 119, 128, 129,

131, 140, 157, 158, 166, 172, 196, 207, 212, 216–217, 242, 276, 308, 441
Wolfe, John H. (1807–before May 25, 1856), farmer, 11, 87 (n.), 186–187, 193, 218–219, 250, 285, 406, 459, letter of, 11, 186–187, 218–219, 389–394
Wolfe, John J. (1901–1974), farmer, 185, 220, 239, *241*, 264, 279, 281, 413, 434
Wolfe, John L. (1879–1962), lawyer, 221, 226, 365, 272, 411, 432
Wolfe, John M. (1913–1951), business owner, 222, 254, 445
Wolfe, John M. (1922–2009), engineer and scholar, ix, 62–64, 74, 76, 82, 98 (n.), 223–224, *225*, 253, 425, 456, work with names, 64, 224, dispute with John B. Keane, 63–64, 223–224. *See also Sloinnte na hÉireann: Irish Surnames* (1997).
Wolfe, John P. (1913–1997), U.S. Navy officer, 221, 226–228, 432, at Pearl Harbor, 226–227
Wolfe, John R. (1809–1883), farmer, 1–4, 6–21, 23, 37, 43, 45, 48, 79, 82, 85–87 (n.), 112, 116, 119, 137, 157, 182, 196, 202, 210, 229–230, 239, 256, 260, 272, 286, 290, 304, 330, 408, 411–412, 415, 417, 420–422, 431, and Young Ireland, 6–8, 16, 58, 229, 275, 360, 408, 421, inscription on tombstone, 6, historical problems regarding, 6–8, immigration of, 10–13, 229–230, move to Iowa, 17–18, 230, in Ireland, 20–21, as possible speaker of Irish, 58, 60, in *Wolfe's History*, 357, 360

Wolfe, Mary A. (1834–1897), seamstress and nun, 129, 131, 134, 207, 212, 216, 231, 242, 308, 326, 441
Wolfe, Maurice (ca. 1800–1879), farmer, 10, 15, 86 (n.), 112, 116, 119, 157, 158, 196, 202, 207, 209, 210, 229, 239, 249, 272, 284, 286, 288, 290, 330, 409 (n.), 444
Wolfe, Maurice (ca. 1823–1909), farmer, 94 (n.), 196, 234–235, 318, 365, 426, sons accused of murder, 45, 234
Wolfe, Maurice (1837–after 1915), farmer, 105, 207, 236, 442
Wolfe, Maurice (1912–1989), priest, 237–238, 460
Wolfe, Maurice B. (1855–1928), farmer, 2, 4, 8–9, 17, 48, 112, 116, 182, 185, 202, 210, 220, 229, 233, 239–241, *241*, 264, 272, 279, 281, 290, 360, 363, 408–409, 411–413, 415, 433
Wolfe, Maurice C. (ca. 1835–1910), farmer, 86 (n.), 129, 131, 212, 232, 242–243, 297, 445
Wolfe, Maurice H. (1839–btw. 1910 and 1919), soldier and laborer, ix, 9–10, 49, 82, 86 (n.), 94 (n.), 244–246, 278, 425, 450, letter to uncle (1867), 345–347

Wolfe, Maurice J. (ca. 1630–ca. 1700), farmer, 57, 247, 404, 425
Wolfe, Maurice J. "Old Maurice" (1690–1792), farmer, 37, 40, 42, 47–49, 57, 82, 93 (n.), 191, 200–201, 248, 406, 425
Wolfe, Maurice J. (1755–1824), farmer, 192, 249, 442
Wolfe, Maurice J. "Young Maurice" (ca. 1763–before 1838), 82, 86 (n.), 192, 248, 250, 310, 425, 459
Wolfe, Maurice J. (1884–1973) (*also* the Solicitor), lawyer, 69–76, *70*, 82, 199, 251–253, 258, 356, during World War I, 69, 71, 456, during Easter Rising, 71–72, during Irish War of Independence, 72–74, 251–253, 399 (n.), attack on home, 74–76, 253
Wolfe, Maurice J. (1886–1918), pharmacist, 213, 222, 254, 445, death of, 16, 254
Wolfe, Maurice P. (1873–1909), farmer, 87 (n.), 126, 174, 255, 299, 430, killed with family in gulf coast hurricane, 13, 174, 255
Wolfe, Maurice R. (1802–1870), farmer and horse breeder, 119, 137, 157, 196, 229, 256–257, 286, 304, 330, 334, 364–365, 429. *See also* Dimby, racehorse.
Wolfe, Maurice R. (1853–1928) (*also* the Gauger), Department of Inland Revenue, 69, 82, 258–259, 276, 301, 312, 340, 356, 378, 405, 455
Wolfe, Maurice R. (1891–1962), priest, 260–261, 438
Wolfe, Maurice V. (1882–1927), farmer and laborer, 262–263, 297, 447, disappearance and suicide, 263
Wolfe, Melvin M. (1904–1990), farmer, 17–18, 82, 88 (n.), 185, 220, 239, *241*, 264–265, 279, 281, 412–414, 417, 434, storytelling, 17, 264, 414
Wolfe, Michael J. C. (1922–1995), priest, 65, 148, 169, 206, 266–267, 292, 311, 463
Wolfe, Patrick (1872–1933), priest and scholar, 26–29, *28*, 31, 50, 52, 57–58, 63, 82, 90 (n.), 92 (n.), 96 (n.), 172, 194, 268–270, *271*, 332, 425, 436, 460, during Irish War of Independence, 29, 268–269, obituary of, 370–371. *See also Sloinnte Gaedheal is Gall* (1923).
Wolfe, Patrick B. (1848–1922) (*also* the Judge), lawyer and judge, 4–6, *5*, 9, 11, 17, 20, 82, 112, 116, 130, 137, 157, 182, 192, 202, 210, 221, 229, 239, 272–275, 290, 304, 357, 363, 365, 408–409, 411, 429, 432, *Wolfe's History*, 359–361. *See also Wolfe's History of Clinton County* (1911).
Wolfe, Patrick R. (1861–1939), book agent, 23, 89 (n.), 258, 276–277, 301, 312, 340, 457
Wolfe, Philip J. (1898–1979), farmer, *ii*, 185, 220, 239, *241*, 264, 279–280, 281, 412–413, 434

Wolfe, Philip M. "Old Phil"
(1810–1901), farmer, 244,
278, 347 (n), 425, 450
Wolfe, Raymond B. (1896–1941),
farmer, *ii*, *2*, 2–3, 82, 142,
144, 185, 220, 239, *241*, 264,
279, 281–282, *283*, 323, 412,
422, 433
Wolfe, Richard (1795–1871),
farmer, 86 (n.), 207, 232, 249,
284, 364, 443
Wolfe, Richard (1802–btw. 1850
and 1860), farmer, 186, 218,
250, 285, 375, 406, 459
Wolfe, Richard (1815–1906), distiller, 119, 137, 157, 196,
229, 286–287, 304, 330, 438
Wolfe, Richard "Uncle Dick"
(1847–1921), liquor retailer,
150, 197, 209, 288–289, 439
Wolfe, Richard B. (1862–1940),
lawyer, 112, 116, 182, 202,
210, 229, 239, 272, 290–291,
363, 366, 409, 435
Wolfe, Richard B. (1884–1937)
(*also* the Chemist), pharmacist and IRA member, 64–69,
72–74, 76, 82, 98 (n.), 100
(n.), 148, 169, 206, 266, 292–
296, 311, 395–399, 463, during the War of Independence,
65–68, *66*, 293–295, 398–
399, during civil war, 68,
295, death of, 27–29, 295
Wolfe, Richard C. (1848–1919),
farmer and justice of peace,
129, 131, 164, 212, 232, 242,
262, 297–298, 447
Wolfe, Richard D. (1829–1885),
87 (n.), 114, 122, 126, 162,
174, 184, 204, 255, 256, 299–
300, 365, 430
Wolfe, Richard E. "Dicky Ned"
(1825–1910), farmer, 1, 37–
42, 46, 51–54, *52*, 56–59, 62,
69, 81, 94 (n.), 108, 160, 251,
258, 276, 301–303, 312, 340,
347 (n), 349 (n.), 373 (n.),
380, 385, 399 (n.), 403 (n.),
404–405, 407, 425, 453, 455,
obituary of, 51, 265–266,
298–299, 354–356 (text), as
seanchaí and storyteller, 52,
199, 302, prophecy of, 51, 74,
nickname Book of Athea, 51,
386, purchase of land, 348
(n.), hedge school at Glen,
302, 372–377
Wolfe, Richard J. (1763–1842),
farmer, land agent, 6, 20, 119,
137, 157, 196, 234, 249, 256,
304–305, 318, 360, 408, 420,
426
Wolfe, Richard J. (1843–1927),
farmer and horse breeder,
150, 284, 306–307, 429, remembrance of, 364–366
Wolfe, Richard J. "Brown Dick"
(1853–1915), farmer, 50–51,
82, 96 (n.), 97 (n.), 166, 172,
194, 260, 268, 332–333, 437,
460–461, purchase of land,
50–51, 348 (n.)
Wolfe, Richard L. (ca. 1837–
1904), farmer, 308–309, 326,
328, 330, 438
Wolfe, Richard M. "Short Dick"
(ca. 1730–1824), farmer, 37,
82, 93 (n.), 192, 248, 250,
310, 404, 425, 449

Wolfe, Richard M. (1919–2003), priest and educator, 65, 148, 169, 206, 266, 292, 311, 463

Wolfe, Richard W. (1866–1951) (*also* the Commissioner), city official, 23–26, *24*, 31–39, 42–43, 45, 51–53, 82, 89 (n.), 258, 276, 301, 312–317, 340, 373, 457, ridiculed for poetry, 26, 314, corruption of, 31–35, 314–316, anti-Semitism of, 36–37, 49, 316–317, confusion over age, 89 (n.), visit to Ireland, 367–369, excerpt from biography of, 378–388. See also *Share the Profits! The Story of Richard W. Wolfe and His Conclusions* (1939) by William H. Stuart.

Wolfe, Thomas (1841–1915), farmer, 43, 81, 94 (n.), 196, 234, 318–322, 352 (n.), 427, evicted from land, 43–44, 81, 319–321

Wolfe, Thomas (1915–2015), civil servant, 427, oral history of, 80–81

Wolfe, Thomas A. (1940–2012), teacher, ix, *2*, 82, 142, 144, 281, 323–324, *325*, 412, 434, as genealogist, 1–3, 6–8, 17, drinking of, 1, 76, 78, his son resembling him, 16–17, returning to farm, 18, childhood memories, 19, trip to Ireland, 19–21, 50, 78, on Father Coughlin, 37, on not farming, 48–49, leaving Catholicism, 59, 78, fearing Irish, 60–61, adoption of daughters, 78–79, essays by, 408–415, 416–422

Wolfe, Thomas L. (1840–1908), farmer, 308, 326–327, 330, 438

Wolfe, Thomas L. (1894–1974), priest, 97 (n.), 210, 328–329, 433, liberation of Chartres cathedral, 59, 328

Wolfe, Thomas R. (1811–1876), farmer, 86 (n.), 114, 119, 122, 128, 129, 131, 134, 137, 140, 157, 158, 166, 172, 184, 196, 207, 209, 212, 216, 229, 231, 232, 242, 256, 284, 286, 288, 297, 299, 304, 308, 326, 330–331, 438

Wolfe, Timothy (1885–1969), doctor, 50, 92 (n.), 96 (n.), 160, 172, 194, 216, 268, 332–334, 426, 437, 460, meets with Commissioner Wolfe, 26, 31, 33, 35, 367–369

Wolfe, Walter I. (1886–1967), lawyer, 183, 335–336, 363, 411, 432

Wolfe, William A. (1889–1967), dairy farmer, 162, 337–338, *338*, *339*, 431

Wolfe's History of Clinton County (1911), 4, 6–7, 17, 112, 130, 137, 157, 182, 192, 196, 202, 229, 234, 304, 318, creation of, 274–275, excerpt from, 357–361. See also Wolfe, Patrick B. (1848–1922).

Woulfe & Co., bookstore, 174

Wren, Ellen Wolfe (1858–1927), 258, 276, 301, 312, 340–341, 456

Young Ireland, 6–8, 16, 58, 65, 229, 275, 360, 408, 421

www.ingramcontent.com/pod-product-compliance
Lightning Source LLC
Chambersburg PA
CBHW032013230426
43671CB00005B/64